CUNARD AND THE NORTH ATLANTIC 1840–1973

By the same author

MR. GLADSTONE AT THE BOARD OF TRADE
BLUE FUNNEL: A HISTORY OF ALFRED HOLT & COMPANY 1865–1914
SHIPPING ENTERPRISE AND MANAGEMENT
LIVERPOOL AND THE MERSEY: AN ECONOMIC HISTORY OF A PORT
FAR EASTERN TRADE 1860–1914 (*with others*)
A NEW PROSPECT OF ECONOMICS
THE SENIOR: JOHN SAMUEL SWIRE 1824–1898 (*with S. Marriner*)

CUNARD
AND THE
NORTH ATLANTIC
1840-1973

*A History of Shipping
and Financial Management*

by

FRANCIS E. HYDE

*Chaddock Professor of Economic History
in the University of Liverpool*

© Francis E. Hyde 1975

Softcover reprint of the hardcover 1st edition 1975

All rights reserved. No part of this publication may be
reproduced or transmitted, in any form or by any means,
without permission.

First published 1975 by
THE MACMILLAN PRESS LTD
London and Basingstoke
Associated companies in New York
Dublin Melbourne Johannesburg and Madras

ISBN 978-1-349-02392-9   ISBN 978-1-349-02390-5 (eBook)
DOI 10.1007/978-1-349-02390-5

To
my wife
ANN ELIZABETH

To
my wife
ANN ELIZABETH

Contents

List of Plates		xii
Preface		xiii
Acknowledgements		xvii
CHAPTER 1	Foundation, Capital Structure and Control of the Company 1840–80	1
	I Samuel Cunard: early business enterprise: securing the mail and shipbuilding contracts	
	II The foundation of the British and North American Royal Mail Steam Packet Company: the Burns and MacIver brothers: the original partners and the new co-partnership contract	
	III Burns and MacIver family backgrounds: the Mediterranean and Levant trades: control and the division of capital in the Atlantic and Mediterranean companies	
	IV Incorporation and the Agreement of 1880: role of the managing agents and reorganisation of capital	
CHAPTER 2	Men, Ships and Mails 1840–80	27
	I The inauguration of the Atlantic service: improvement in design, power and size of ships	
	II Mail contracts and competition	
	III The Collins line and intensification of competition	

- IV Secret agreement between Cunard and the Collins line: the fixing of rates and pooling of earnings
- V Charles MacIver's management of the ships
- VI John Burns and the new mail contract
- VII Financial progress and growth 1840–80: the assumption of control in new hands

CHAPTER 3 *Cunard and the Emigrant Trade 1860–1900*   58
- I Liverpool as focal point for the emigrant trade: competition between Liverpool based shipping companies: fluctuations in the trade
- II Cunard's participation in the emigrant trade and government involvement in the maintenance of services
- III Changes in the direction of the trade: efficiency and goodwill of agents
- IV Relative profitability of the trade

CHAPTER 4 *Cunard and North Atlantic Conferences 1860–1914*   90
- I The growth of competition and the need for agreement
- II The Liverpool Steamship Conference: controversy on rates for slow and fast ships: the depression 1874–8: growing strength of German lines
- III The use of the Conference system by the German lines: Conference agreements and rate wars: Cunard leaves the Conference: the Atlantic Pool
- IV Alliance of Morgan Combine and German shipping companies: the impact of this alliance on Cunard: the Frankfurt Conference and the Continental Pool: the 1908 Agreement: attempt by United States to break Conference agreements

CHAPTER 5   *Costs, Revenue and Returns 1880–1914*   119
    I The new shipbuilding policy: resignation of MacIver brothers
   II The building programme and trade fluctuations: Admiralty agreements: fluctuations in costs and receipts: the problem of large ships at Liverpool
  III Cunard's earning capacity and allocation of resources: purchase of Thomson line
  IV The Morgan Combine and the 1903 Agreement
   V The return on capital

CHAPTER 6   *War, Peace and Depression 1914–34*   159
    I Cunard's contribution to the war effort
   II Post-war difficulties: amalgamation and expansion
  III United States immigration policy and post-war shipbuilding programme
  IV Fluctuations in receipts and costs
   V Cunard's attempts to increase revenue and reduce costs
  VI Assessment of managerial efficiency

CHAPTER 7   *No. 534 and the Formation of Cunard White Star Limited*   191
    I Events leading to merger
   II White Star negotiations
  III No. 534 and the Government: hopes of a two-ship express service
  IV Growing competition and the need for action: the Government and the tripartite agreement
   V The launching of Cunard White Star Ltd: *Queen Mary* in service: final analysis

CHAPTER 8   *North Atlantic Conferences 1921–39*   219
  I   Agreements F.1., S.1., T.1.: fluctuations in membership: maintenance of security in home ports
  II   Disagreements on rates: rebuilding of rate schedules: conversion of ships' classes
  III   Introduction of tourist class and disagreements arising
  IV   Share of traffic to each line
  V   The operation of the Freight Conference
  VI   Advantage of conference membership: value of cabin class schedule: cooperation between Cunard and White Star

CHAPTER 9   *Advent of War and Survival 1935–45*   247
  I   Changes in capital structure
  II   Efforts to increase revenue and reduce costs: the new *Mauretania* and *Queen Elizabeth*: the meeting of financial obligations: the problem of replacing war losses
  III   Requisition and war service: *Queen Mary* and *Curaçoa*
  IV   Cunard's growing awareness of competition from air travel
  V   The death of Sir Percy Bates and the effectiveness of management in peace and war

CHAPTER 10   *Cunard and the North Atlantic 1946–73*   282
  I   The change-over from war to peace
  II   The phasing out of Cunard White Star Ltd: increase in Cunard Company's capital
  III   Effects of penal fiscal legislation: plans for new Queen
  IV   Cunard's participation in transatlantic air travel

x

V Rationalisation and entry into container services: the financing of the new Queen: passenger shipping and the leisure industry

VI Cunard and Trafalgar House Investments Ltd

VII Conclusion

Appendix	326
Notes	336
Index of Persons	377

List of Plates

between pages 172 and 173

1, 2 Samuel Cunard
3 Charles MacIver (*by permission of the Walker Art Gallery, Liverpool*)
4 George Burns
5 *Britannia*
6 *Persia*
7 John Burns
8 Cunard advertisement
9 Sir Alfred Booth
10 The first *Mauretania*
11 Sir Thomas Royden
12 *Queen Mary*
13 Sir Percy Bates
14 *Queen Elizabeth* as a troopship
15 *Queen Elizabeth 2*
16 *Queen Elizabeth* on fire (*by permission of Keystone Press Agency Ltd*)

Preface

Students of maritime history have always been exercised by the fact that no definitive full-scale history of The Cunard Steam Ship Company has been published. In order to obtain information about the activities of this Company one has had to glean from a wide range of sources concerned generally with the history of British shipping. Though some of these sources have been, and still are, most valuable in providing perspectives, they do not give a continuous account of Cunard's widespread interests nor an appraisal of the forceful characters of the successive generations of men who built up and directed the use of the Company's resources. Furthermore, very little of the information about the Company had been drawn from an overall examination of the Cunard archives. It was, therefore, as an endeavour to fill in the many gaps in Cunard's long history that the author of this volume was given permission by the Cunard Board (and subsequently by Trafalgar House Investments Ltd) to make free use of the Cunard archives and to publish a business history of the Company.

Of the published works referred to in the previous paragraph the most important references to Cunard are to be found in Volume 4 of W. S. Lindsay, *History of Merchant Shipping and Ancient Commerce* (1876); A. J. Maginnis, *The Atlantic Ferry* (1892); Sir William Forwood, *Reminiscences of a Liverpool Shipowner* (1920); F. C. Bowen, *A Century of Atlantic Travel* (1930); F. L. Babcock, *Spanning the Atlantic* (1931); Sir Westcott Abell, *The Safe Sea* (1932); R. L. Hadfield, *Sea-Toll of our Time* (1935); Humfrey Jordan, *Mauretania* (1936); E. R. Benstead, *Atlantic Ferry* (1936); Boyd Cable, *A Hundred Year History of the P. & O.* (1937); David B. Tyler, *Steam Conquers the Atlantic* (1939); Commander C. R. Vernon Gibbs, *Passenger Liners of the Western Ocean* (1952); N. R. P. Bonsor, *North Atlantic Seaway* (1956); D. Lobley, *The Cunarders*

Preface

(1969); K. C. Barnaby, *Some Ship Disasters and Their Causes* (1970); J. M. Brinnin, *The Sway of the Grand Saloon* (1971); Colin Simpson, *Lusitania* (1972).

It is perhaps not generally known that on several occasions the Company commissioned the writing of an official history. As early as 1886, a privately published history of The Cunard Steam Ship Company was extracted from *The Illustrated Naval and Military Magazine*. In the late 1930s, Captain Taprell Dorling (known by the pen-name 'Taffrail') was asked to write a complete history of the Company. The manuscript was largely concerned with specifications of ships and ignored the commercial aspects of the Company's business. Secondly, Mr Tom Hughes prepared a manuscript covering the Company's history from 1839 to 1906; the manuscript was never completed. Thirdly, Mr Charles Graves, brother of Robert Graves, wrote a history of the Company's achievements during the Second World War. Though this was actually printed by an American publisher, it was not circulated and the whole edition was eventually pulped. Finally, Henry Eaves, a Secretary in the Company, produced an 800-page typescript giving a year-by-year account of the Company's history from 1840 to 1957. The author made full use of the annual reports and accounts and the work as a whole contains much valuable information not only about the ships but also of the use of resources by successive boards of directors and chairmen. Though this typescript could not be published in the chronological form in which it had been written, one must pay tribute to the vast amount of research involved in its compilation; it is a mine of information on almost every aspect of the Company's affairs.

As will be seen from the following pages, the story of Cunard's endeavour on the North Atlantic is highly complex and difficult of interpretation. For this reason the book has been sectionalised in order to give comprehension to the various threads of development in both policy and action which, when woven together, make up patterns on a wide historical canvas. The whole picture thus presented is one of sustained struggle in an attempt to build and manage ships economically, to sustain competitive advantage over both British and foreign shipping companies, to engage in a growing partnership with government for the safeguarding of mercantile supremacy in time of national emergency and to make effective the use of resources in the service of the ocean traveller.

Preface

The terms of reference governing the writing of this book were reasonably flexible, though stress was laid on the need to investigate the changing scope of successive managements in the accumulation and use of resources and in the solution of problems inherent in the nature of a great shipping enterprise. In a strict sense, this book is not a business history, though the subject matter is largely concerned with financial and business management. In this context, it has not been possible or relevant to give details of the performance of individual ships in Cunard's fleet. To those readers who are interested in such details, therefore, the author expresses his regret and hopes that other information about the management of the Company may act as compensation. As far as possible, within the terms of reference, this book is definitive in compass; to have written both a comprehensive and definitive study of all Cunard's activities over a period of 130 years would have required the production of several large volumes. For those who are interested in aspects of the Company's history not fully covered in this volume, reference should be made to the Cunard archives which, through the generosity of the Cunard Board and that of Trafalgar House Investments Ltd, have now been put on loan in the library of the University of Liverpool. The access thus provided will stimulate further research not only into the history of one of Britain's internationally famous passenger steamship companies, but also into the more comprehensive elucidation of maritime history as a whole during the course of the last century.

University of Liverpool   FRANCIS E. HYDE
March 1975

Acknowledgements

During the writing of this book the author has received much help and kindly criticism from a large number of persons interested in the history of The Cunard Steam Ship Company. Sir Basil Smallpeice, as Chairman of Cunard, initiated the project and made it possible with the permission of the Cunard Board for a free examination of Cunard archives. These archives, as stated in the Preface, through the generosity of Trafalgar House Investments Ltd, have now been placed on permanent loan in the Harold Cohen Library of the University of Liverpool. In pursuance of continuity in the writing of this book, the author is most grateful to Mr Victor Matthews, Chairman, and to Mr Norman Thompson, Managing Director of The Cunard Steam Ship Co. Ltd, for their agreement to proceed to publication. To the late Mrs Lois Rae, granddaughter of Charles MacIver, the author owes a special debt of gratitude for free access to many important MacIver papers in her possession and for her most generous action in donating these papers to the University of Liverpool. This second gift of papers, complementary to the vast bulk of the Cunard archives, will help future historians in their elucidation of the Company's history before 1880. Such benefactions ensure that future research into the maritime history of this Company may be carried on in the port of Cunard's origin and service. It was through the kindness of Mr W. H. P. Piper of the Royal Insurance Co., Liverpool that the author was put in touch with Mrs Rae.

The author has received the greatest possible help from past and present members of the Cunard Company, including Mr F. J. Whitworth, former Managing Director of the Cunard Line, Mr Frank Leach, Secretary to the Cunard Board, Mr H. M. Goulden, former Secretary to The Cunard Steam Ship Co. Ltd, Mr W. D. McKinlay, former Assistant Accountant to The Cunard Steam

Acknowledgements

Ship Co. Ltd, Mr Kendrick Williams, Assistant Secretary, Mr J. G. Dalton, Operations Manager, Cunard Line Ltd, Southampton and Mr D. K. J. Conway, Chairman, North Atlantic Westbound Freight Association. They not only made all existing Cunard records available but gave much valuable assistance in the discovery of complementary sources of information. Mr Ivor Jones, formerly of the General Manager's Office and, later, Property Manager for Cunard, who was asked by the Board to help the author in the task of collecting relevant information from the vast bulk of archives, has been energetic in his quest. The author acknowledges his willing service, especially for the many long hours of labour in his search for information in the Board Minutes and in the mass of paper stored in the vaults of the Cunard Building, Liverpool. He was also responsible for the compilation of the fleet lists contained in the Appendix. Mr R. Leslie Adam of Hill, Dickinson and Co., the Company's solicitors, placed his unrivalled knowledge of maritime history and, in particular, his great experience of the financial management of the Company, freely at the author's disposal. The book has been given a greater accuracy as a result of his careful reading of the first six chapters and his subsequent comments on style and presentation.

Most large companies have their own historians. In the case of Cunard, one must not overlook Henry Eaves, a former Secretary. As already stated, his unpublished history of Cunard, drawn largely from Board Minutes and Chairmens' Reports, has been of considerable assistance in the provision of source material. It is, however, to Mr T. Laird, former General Manager of the Company, that the author owes his greatest debt of gratitude. His wide knowledge of Cunard's history and his critical appraisal of events have been constantly made available to the author; to him should most properly be ascribed the title of Cunard's historian.

Mr Laird spent the whole of his working life with Cunard. His loyalty to management (of which he ultimately became a part) to staff and employees, is evident in all his pronouncements. Yet he is not uncritical of Cunard's failings. His work with the Company covered the time of peak achievement during the inter-war years, the Second World War and the post-war period of some twenty years up to 1965. During this long period he acquired an unrivalled knowledge of ships and their management. He became an expert in Conference matters and, during his term of office as General

Acknowledgements

Manager, he was responsible along with many of his colleagues for the reorganisation of the Company, and the initial planning of *Queen Elizabeth 2*. He witnessed the decline of the Company's fortunes after 1957 and was not unaware of the causes. His experience and knowledge of those unhappy years are reflected in the final chapter of this book, though it must be emphasised that all the opinions expressed are solely those of the author. Mr Laird has read the whole of this book in successive drafts. It is hoped that, in its final form, it will not disappoint one who has for so long been a participant in shaping the Company's history.

The author wishes to express his thanks to the late Mr A. Douglas Lobley who, having read the drafts of some of the early chapters, presented the author with a wide range of comments and information on Britain's maritime development in the nineteenth century; to Mr Basil Greenhill, Director of the National Maritime Museum, Greenwich, for information about Samuel Cunard's early shipping activities; to Mr Mungo Conacher, formerly Chief General Manager of Martin's Bank for permission to use records relating to the Company's account with that Bank; to Mr P. Cotterell, now of the Department of Economic History in the University of Leicester, for extracts from the Glyn, Mills papers; to Mr B. L. Anderson of the Department of Economic History in the University of Liverpool for information relating to Cunard's insurance policy during the 1870s and to drawing the author's attention to John Burns's evidence before the Royal Commission on Unseaworthy Ships; to Miss Pauline Round, Department of Geography in the University of Liverpool for checking contemporary maps of New Brunswick; to members of the photographic section in the Department of Geography for the excellent reproduction of plates in this volume and to Mr R. Bastin for permission to use material from his M.A. thesis on Cunard and the Emigrant Trade 1860–1900.

The subject matter of Cunard's history is wide-ranging, touching as it does on spheres of interest in both governmental and international affairs as well as those concerned with rival shipping companies. In this context the author has been most fortunate in receiving letters and documents from numerous correspondents all over the world. In particular, he wishes to thank Mrs Eleanor Sparks Davison, daughter of Sir Ashley Sparks, Cunard's Resident Director in New York, for letters, telegrams

Acknowledgements

and newspaper cuttings relating to her father's important service to the Company; to Mr E. Reford for information about his firm's long-standing connection with Cunard; to Commander H. E. Morison – whose great-aunt, Mary Ann Morison, married Charles MacIver – for information about his career with Cunard; to Mr Patrick Howarth, Public Relations Officer to the R.N.L.I., for information about Cunard's interest in the Life-Boat Service and documents relating to the provision of a life-boat by the Cunard Company in 1930 and to Miss Frances Gutteridge for sending to the author a series of original illustrations of past Cunard and White Star ships.

The onerous task of typing the text, checking the footnotes and preparing the final copy for publication was efficiently undertaken by Mrs J. Irons. No words can adequately express the author's gratitude to his wife, Ann Elizabeth, for the patience which she showed during the writing of the book, to the willingness which she always gave to the reading of successive drafts and for the encouragement which was forthcoming whenever difficulties arose. It is to her that the book is justly dedicated.

I
Foundation, Capital Structure and Control of the Company 1840-80

I SAMUEL CUNARD: EARLY BUSINESS ENTERPRISE: SECURING THE MAIL AND SHIPBUILDING CONTRACTS

Samuel Cunard, founder of the British and North American Royal Mail Steam Packet Co., (subsequently known as The Cunard Steam Ship Co. Ltd) was born in Halifax, Nova Scotia, on 21 November 1787. As this book is concerned primarily with the business activities of the Company in various stages of development, it is not proposed to enter into an examination of the genealogical controversy surrounding the origins of the Cunard family.[1] It is sufficient to know, as a starting point for this history, that Samuel was the son of Abraham Cunard who, after the War of American Independence, had emigrated to Halifax where he had established himself in his trade as a master carpenter. In this capacity, Abraham had found employment in the dockyard at Halifax and from this relatively humble beginning had laid the foundation of a prosperous business and the background to future enterprise.

In 1783 Abraham had married Margaret Murphy. Her family, all staunch Empire Loyalists, had also emigrated to Halifax from South Carolina. There was, therefore, a common political background uniting Samuel Cunard's parents, a fact which undoubtedly influenced the attitudes of Samuel and his brothers, Henry and Joseph, in their future business relationships. Samuel, however, did not immediately engage in his father's trade; for a time he went into government service and thence to Boston where he learnt the business of shipbroking.[2] This apprenticeship gave him both an interest in shipping and a taste for merchanting; there is no doubt that he engaged in this latter capacity for, at the age of twenty-five, he received from the Lieutenant Governor of Nova Scotia permission to trade with any port in the United States, at a time when that country was engaged in a bitter war with Britain.[3] Following the war of 1812, young Cunard further strengthened his contact with the United States by starting a service in 1815 for the carriage of H.M. mails between Halifax, Newfoundland, Boston and Bermuda.[4] The available evidence suggests that this service was undertaken at his own financial risk and to the entire satisfaction of the Government[5] – an enterprise which, in effect, established the reputation and acumen of this young man of twenty-seven.

Samuel Cunard's father and brothers had played no small part in the family's growing prosperity. Under the title of A. Cunard and Son, family enterprise had expanded outwards from the dockyard. The initiation of activity outside Halifax had, no doubt, been prompted by the removal in 1819 of the dockyard from Halifax to Bermuda, a decision which adversely affected the economy of Halifax. In 1820 Joseph and his brother Henry had gone to the Miramachi (or Miramichi) to start a lumbering and fishing business for Samuel Cunard and Company. The brothers prospered and with the backing of Halifax financiers opened branches at Richibucto, Kouchibouguac and Bathurst. The centre of this enterprise lay in the evolving mercantile community in the small town of Chatham.[6] The eventual failure of these operations in 1848 is said to have caused 'a crash that ruined the Miramachi and nearly wrecked the Cunard line'. This may or may not be a correct assessment but it may help to explain some of Samuel Cunard's preoccupation with financial matters outside the range of his trans-Atlantic company during the 1850s and 1860s. The Cunard associates assumed full responsibility for the financial obligations involved in the crash and it was not until 1871 that all the debts were cleared.[7] In this context, the success and failure of the Cunard brothers had a direct bearing on the early financial arrangements concerned with the initiation and the promotion of The British and North American Royal Mail Steam Packet Company.

Side by side with the enterprise of his brothers, Samuel Cunard's shipping interests had continued to grow. In 1813 he had purchased *White Oak*, a prize ship which he put under convoy in the trans-Atlantic service. Through the operation of this ship, Samuel Cunard enlarged his horizon as a deep-sea shipowner. During the next fifteen years, his acquisition and command over resources grew at a rapid rate. Between 1820 and 1825, he was appointed

Commissioner of Lighthouses, changed the name of his father's firm from A. Cunard and Son to S. Cunard and Company, bought tracts of land in Prince Edward Island and became associated with the ironworks at Clementsport, engaged in the whaling trade, became a founder member of the Halifax Banking Company and was appointed agent for the East India Company. In this latter capacity, he became the distributor of China tea for British North America. This was followed by an active interest in the development of inland waterways, particularly in the promotion of the Shubenacadie Canal Company. These various business interests not only increased his command over resources but earned for him a reputation as a man of standing in the community; in 1830 he was appointed to the Legislative Council. At this time, it was estimated that his company's assets amounted to £200,000.[8] This sum probably included many of the 41 ships which were registered as built by Joseph Cunard before 1848, besides others which were owned by the family. Apart from shipping, however, Samuel Cunard increased his interests during the 1830s by becoming the Halifax agent for the General Mining Association, which ran the Cape Breton coal mines at Sydney.[9] This was a highly profitable arrangement for, at a later date, Cunard ships could be assured of supplies of relatively cheap coal from this source.

The preceding facts are background to the important initial event of this book, namely, the foundation of the Cunard line. It was one thing to have command over resources, it was another matter to know how to use those resources in the most profitable way. To Samuel Cunard's far-sighted vision the answer lay in the promotion of a trans-Atlantic steamship service. In 1831 Samuel and his brothers had taken a financial interest in a steamship, *Royal William*, which went into service on the Halifax–Quebec route. She was a paddle steamer and, in 1833, made a successful crossing of the Atlantic from Pictou to London. A full fortnight before *Royal William* had sailed, however, the steamship *Cape Breton*, had made a crossing of the Atlantic from Britain to Nova Scotia. This latter ship eventually became part of the Cunard family's fleet in 1838.[10] The advent of steamships on the Atlantic, especially with the later crossings of *Sirius* and *Great Western*, fired Cunard's imagination. Thus it was, in 1839, that he came to England determined to seek out and exploit the possibility of a steamship service. There is no doubt that he was influenced by a government advertisement offering a subvention for the carriage of trans-Atlantic mails.[11] The provision of fast steamships was, therefore a corollary of government initiative.

By the 1820s, despite the removal of the dockyard, Halifax was growing into an important packet port. It was usable all the year round and was a focal point for the increasing correspondence between Canadian and British merchants. Most packet captains, however, were unwilling to sail into Halifax during winter months and the only all-the-year service was provided by Admiralty brigs on a monthly sailing schedule.[12] The branch services to Bermuda, Boston and Newfoundland, as we have already stated, were undertaken by Cunard. With the crossing of the Atlantic by steamships in the 1830s, there was still no eagerness to start steamship mail services, even though sailing ships shuttled back and forth between Liverpool and New York carrying mails under various types of contract. The Admiralty brigs, however, did not have a high reputation as good sailers. Cunard himself referred to them as 'coffin' ships, a term in general use, though this disparaging epithet was used by him in juxtaposition and as part of his argument to prove that steamships were more reliable.[13] Despite Cunard's active promotion of the idea, however, it was to another Nova Scotian, Joseph Howe, that due credit must be given for involvement of government in a new type of steamship mail contract.

Joseph Howe was the son of a Loyalist who had left Massachusetts during the revolution and had settled in Halifax.[14] As a token of approval for his allegiance, the elder Howe had been rewarded by the grant of a licence as King's Printer and with the office of Postmaster General of the Maritime Provinces and Bermuda.[15] His son, Joseph, was imbued with his father's passionate interest in improving mail communications and, like Samuel Cunard, had been greatly impressed by the successful trans-Atlantic voyage of *Sirius*.[16] On reaching England in 1838, Joseph Howe was responsible for the submission of an Address to the Colonial Secretary in which was stressed the imperative need for steamship links with British North America. He argued that the line of packets between the mother country and North America should be put on a more efficient basis and that, accordingly, the steamship was the obvious choice for the carriage of mails. As a result of persistent effort, the Admiralty, in whom was vested at that time the arrangements for postal contracts, published an advertisement in the autumn of 1838 asking for a tender of service between England and Halifax, with an additional link between Halifax and New York.[17] Samuel Cunard received a copy of this tender in November. The specifications laid down the use of steam vessels of not less than 300 h.p., the ships to be run on a monthly schedule. The home port was to be chosen from one of five: Liverpool, Bristol, Plymouth, Falmouth or Southampton.[18]

Two tenders were submitted in response. The first was from the St George Steam Packet Co., owners of *Sirius*, offering a service from Cork and connected by a feeder service with Liverpool by smaller vessels than used on the Atlantic crossing. Smaller vessels would also be used on the link between Halifax and New York.[19] The second tender came from the Great Western Steamship Co proposing the use of ships of 1000 tons if made of iron or of 1500 tons if made of wood, on a monthly service between Bristol and Halifax.[20] The company put forward plans for building two new ships and stated that they would be ready to start the service in two years' time. The service, thus proposed, was to Halifax only as the company had no additional facilities for extending it to New York.

Neither of these tenders satisfied the specified conditions and they were declined. It was at this precise juncture that Samuel Cunard took the initial step to secure the mail contract. He arrived in England in February 1839 with the express purpose of entering into negotiations with the Government and of securing support from his friends. By 11 February he had submitted a tender to provide three ships by 1840. 'I came to England', he wrote at a later date, 'with the express purpose of submitting a plan of my own. Although I am a Colonist, I have many friends in this country. I arrived just about the time the Government was perplexed about the tenders that had been made.'[21] There is reliable evidence in substantiation of the help which he received from his friends. In her *Record of a Girlhood*, Fanny Kemble throws light on some of Cunard's early contacts. One of these contacts was Mrs Norton whose association with Lord Melbourne brought her into the society of members of the Cabinet. Mrs Norton was then living with her uncle Charles Sheridan: 'She came often to parties at our house', wrote Fanny Kemble, 'and I remember her asking us to dine at her uncle's, when among the people we met were Lord

Landsdowne and Lord Normanby, both then in the Ministry, whose goodwill and influence she was then exerting herself to captivate on behalf of a certain shy, silent, rather rustic genleman from the far away province, New Brunswick, Mr Samuel Cunard.'[22] Such help undoubtedly gave Cunard an *entrée* which, perhaps, the other steamship company promoters lacked. In any case, Cunard was much too shrewd a man to duplicate the errors of his rivals. From the start, he intended to offer a service *par excellence*; his ships were to be ordered for early delivery and were to be of a number sufficient to cater fully for the trade. His plan of campaign was simple and effective. He proposed to have a contract with a shipbuilder in his pocket as an inducement to the granting of a mail subsidy by the Government.[23]

Cunard's friend, James Melvill, Secretary to the East India Company, gave him an introduction to the firms of Wood and Napier in Glasgow, firms who had already undertaken a shipbuilding contract for the East India Company. Undaunted by the advice of his friends in Liverpool and London who were mistrustful of the growing shipbuilding industry on the Clyde, that he would have 'neither substantial work nor completed in time', he entered into negotiations with Napier.[24] He made his initial approach on 25 February 1839 through the intermediary of Halifax friends who had started business in Glasgow under the title of Messrs William Kidston and Sons.[25] He asked them to interview Wood and Napier on his behalf, explaining that he would require vessels of the 'very best description', of such quality as would pass inspection by the Admiralty, plain and comfortable 'not the least unnecessary expense for show'.[26] If they were interested in such a proposition, he would go immediately to Glasgow to arrange a contract.

Robert Napier was already possessed of a high reputation as a marine engineer. For some ten years, he had built stout engines for the coastwise and Isle of Man packets.[27] In this work he had, by 1839, developed and greatly improved side-lever engines. John Wood, whose firm was eventually absorbed into the Napier organisation, had, in conjunction with other builders, provided Napier with first-class hulls. Complementary to each other they had achieved a position of pre-eminence in the craft of shipbuilding. A reflection of this growing reputation was seen in the building of the steamship *Berenice* for the East India Company.[28] She was highly successful in operation and this fact may have induced James

Melvill to put Cunard in touch with Wood and Napier. It was, therefore, no fortuitous accident that Cunard should have sought their assistance. Indeed, one of their ships, *Queen of the Isles*, served as model for the first Cunarder.[29] Moreover, Napier himself had strong convictions as to the possibility of a trans-Atlantic steamship service. As early as 1833, he had been engaged in correspondence with Patrick Wallace of London concerning the establishment of a steamship line between Liverpool and New York.[30] With shrewd foresight he had already worked out the principles of steamship management and had stressed the importance of catering for emigrants as well as for cabin passengers and cargo. His ideas were much too far advanced for London businessmen to entrust their capital to him and it was not until Cunard gave him the opportunity that he was able to fulfil his ambition.

With the same prime objective, Napier and Cunard were secure in the establishment and maintenance of a successful collaboration. Napier sent Cunard a favourable reply and the latter went immediately to Glasgow. Their first meeting found them in such ready agreement that a contract was speedily drawn up and signed on 18 March 1839. This provided for the construction of three good and sufficient wooden paddle-wheel steamships each not less than 200 feet long, not less than 32 feet beam between paddles and not less than 21 feet 6 inches depth of hold from top of timbers to underside of deck amidships.[31] The ships were to be properly finished in every respect, the cabins appointed in a 'neat and comfortable manner' for the accommodation of from 60 to 70 passengers. Each vessel was to be fitted with two steam engines, having cylinders 70 inches in diameter and 6 feet 6 inches stroke. 'The said Robert Napier hereby binds and obliges himself to finish and complete, to the entire satisfaction of the said Samuel Cunard, equal in quality of hull and machinery to the steamer *Commodore* or the steamer *London*, both constructed by the said Robert Napier and equal to the *City of Glasgow* steamer in the finishing of the cabins.'[32] These Cunard ships were to be of 960 tons each with motive power of 375 h.p. at a cost of £32,000. 'I have given him the vessels cheap', wrote Napier to Melvill concerning Cunard's contract 'and I am certain that they will be good and very strong ships.'[33] In the event, these ships were never built. While Napier was engaged in finishing the engines for *British Queen*, Cunard was making fresh approaches to his friends in London and, as a consequence of the outcome of these approaches, Napier once again altered the original shipbuilding specifications.

Through Mrs Norton, Samuel Cunard had established amicable relations with some members of the Government, and through them the way was opened for him to begin discussions with the Lords of the Admiralty. He started with the clear advantage of having a shipbuilding contract in his pocket, and was therefore confident in his assurance to the Government that his ships would be 'the finest and best ever built in this country'.[34] The outcome was that on 4 May 1839, the first of a long series of contracts was signed for the carriage of mails with all possible speed from Liverpool to Halifax and from thence to Boston.[35] This latter requirement to carry mails to Boston was a variant from the original Admiralty terms. In addition, Cunard agreed to provide a service to Quebec during the months that the St Lawrence was open to shipping, the mail steamers to start from Pictou. The vessels used on the Boston and Quebec routes were to be of 150 h.p., half the power of those originally envisaged for the Atlantic crossing. With an eye to the likely development of steamship technology, a significant clause was inserted to the effect that such changes in construction and machinery should be made 'as the advanced state of science may suggest'.[36] The mail contract was to last for seven years with a subvention of £55,000 per annum.

This mail contract was a fundamental point of initiation for future development. Cunard had assured himself of the services of a first-class shipbuilder and marine engineer; he now had the backing of government and the prestige which such support afforded. It remained for him to raise the necessary capital to found the company, build the ships and make the whole enterprise effective.

II THE FOUNDATION OF THE BRITISH AND NORTH AMERICAN ROYAL MAIL STEAM PACKET COMPANY: THE BURNS AND MACIVER BROTHERS: THE ORIGINAL PARTNERS AND THE NEW CO-PARTNERSHIP CONTRACT

It must be emphasised that in the long series of negotiations which took place during 1839 and early 1840, leading to the foundation of the British and North American Royal Mail Steam Packet Company (later known as The Cunard Steam Ship Co.), the original proposals for the mail contract, the shipbuilding specifications and the capital structure of the new company were constantly changed

Foundation, Capital Structure and Control 9

and modified. The mail subsidy, for example, was increased to £60,000 per annum and the design of the ships was altered in both size and power. Further amendments were made by the Admiralty requiring the services of four ships instead of three and that regular sailing dates should be written into the agreement. As a *quid pro quo* to these more onerous stipulations, the payment was raised from £60,000 to £80,000 per annum from 1 September 1841. The four ships, *Britannia, Columbia, Acadia* and *Caledonia*, had brig lines with three masts and one funnel; each ship was approximately 1150 tons, powered by Napier engines of 420 h.p. (740 indicated h.p.) with accommodation for about 100 passengers.[37] A great deal of space was left for fuel as it was proposed to carry twice the amount of coal necessary for the Atlantic crossing. Furthermore, the Government exercised a right which applied to other shipping companies, that Cunard should carry officers and men in military service at special rates.[38]

It was, however, in the initial capital structure of the company that this government relationship was given a stronger emphasis. In order to understand this, we must trace the efforts of Samuel Cunard in the process of raising capital. Again, we must remind ourselves of the sequence of events. Cunard's original order for three ships had made it possible for him to secure the mail contract; with the contract as an inducement, he believed that it would be possible for him to raise money to pay for even larger ships than those laid down in the first Napier contract, a change of plan necessitated by his prospective view of growing competition.[39] Even so, he received very little encouragement either in London or in Liverpool for his project to start a trans-Atlantic shipping company. He therefore went once again to Glasgow where Napier, for the second time, came to his aid. Napier had long been associated with George Burns who, with his brother James, had been engaged in running a small fleet of coastal steamers to Liverpool. In competition with them had been two other Glasgow merchants, David and Charles MacIver. Napier was confident that if Cunard were to offer the MacIver brothers the Liverpool agency for his ships and the Glasgow agency to the Burns brothers, they might agree to invest in his enterprise and become his partners.[40]

George Burns met Samuel Cunard and David MacIver at Napier's instigation but unexpected difficulties arose at this meeting. It is true that both Burns and MacIver were attracted by the possibility of founding a trans-Atlantic service of steamships and that the mail contract was a powerful inducement; but, in this contract, Cunard had committed himself to paying the Admiralty, in addition to sundry fines, the sum of £500 for every 12 hours deviation of his ships from the prescribed fortnightly schedule from each side of the Atlantic.[41] Burns and MacIver calculated that, under such prescriptions, an average of only one day's delay for each sailing during the year would cancel all revenue contingent upon the subsidy.[42] Moreover, the uncertainties of the trade and the growth of competition were such that additional revenue from passengers and cargo were unlikely to be sufficient to cover costs and return a profit. With such doubts in mind, MacIver informed Cunard that 'the thing would not suit them'.[43] This seemed to be an unhappy conclusion to the negotiations. Napier, however, was not to be gainsaid. He invited all three men to breakfast next morning and a fresh discussion took place on details. To every objection came a satisfactory answer and great stress was laid upon Napier's own undoubted reputation as a builder of reliable engines. In fact, the engine was the key to a regular and strictly timekeeping service. In addition, the rapid westward expansion of America was an economic fact which could not be ignored. Emigration from Europe was bound to increase and the flow of cargo would rise in direct proportion to the growing potential of new settlement. These arguments were of sufficient weight to convince Burns and MacIver that, despite risks, Cunard's venture was likely to succeed. They therefore agreed to join forces, so bringing into effect a remarkable combination of attributes: these were Samuel Cunard's energy and imagination, his diplomacy and personal charm; George Burns's shrewdness and Scottish solidity coupled with attention to detail; David MacIver's prodigious energy for business, a knowledge of men and discipline which maintained at a high level the morale and the efficiency of the whole concern.

The manner in which the original capital was built up and brought within the control of the new company is at once complicated and confusing. In his unpublished history of the Company, Henry Eaves, a former Secretary of the Company, goes far towards unravelling the tangle of events.[44] It is, however, fortunate that the first minute books give us an accurate picture

Foundation, Capital Structure and Control

of the successive moves in the process of capital formation. As we have already seen, the Admiralty contract for the carriage of mails was signed on 4 May 1839, under which Cunard was to receive an annual payment of £55,000 for the service. Ten days later (14 May 1839) Cunard took George Burns and David MacIver into partnership to the extent of one half in the mail contract and in the steam vessels to be employed.[45] The price paid by Burns and MacIver for this half interest was £25,000. In addition, the right was given them to assume others into their share of the partnership.[46] Accordingly, by 23 July 1839, a contract of co-partnership was concluded (incorporating previous contracts of 4, 6, 7, 18 and 25 June and 23 July 1839) between Burns, MacIver and 19 other Glasgow merchants, all associating themselves into a company under the title, 'The Glasgow Proprietory in the British and North American Royal Mail Steam Packets, established for the purpose of carrying mails, passengers, specie and merchandise between Britain and certain North American ports'.[47] These original 21 proprietors took up 165 shares of £500 each, which, when fully paid up would bring in £82,500. Shortly afterwards, however, Samuel Cunard was brought into the co-partnership and the subsidy from the mail contract was taken over as part of a new capital definition. This was effected in May 1840 with the signing of a new co-partnership contract between Samuel Cunard and the proprietors named in the first deed together with some 11 additional subscribers (7 from Glasgow and 4 from Manchester).[48] This document was, in effect, the first real archive of the Cunard line. The capital of the partnership was fixed by a first call on 28 May 1840 at £270,000 consisting of 540 shares of £500 each, of which amount Cunard was allotted 135 shares representing a contribution to capital of £67,500.[49] On 23 December 1840 each original share was converted into five shares of £100 each, the deeds providing that the trustees (George Burns and David MacIver) should have power of pre-emption whenever the shares of any partner should be offered for sale. One clause stated that no shares should be sold outside the partnership without the consent of all members.[50]

It is interesting to estimate Cunard's personal involvement in the capital structure of the venture which was ultimately to bear his name. As a *quid pro quo* for his making over the whole of the mail subsidy to the partnership, he received a 'bonus' of £50,000 standing as a credit in the books of the Company.[51] When the mail subsidy was increased to £60,000 an additional £5000 was made available by way of 'bonus'. He disposed of £12,500 worth of his original holding of £67,500 thus leaving himself with £55,000 or 550 shares.[52] Against this, his credit was sufficient to cover his holding.

The capital holding in the new Company is shown in the following Table on page 13.

The amounts are expressed in share units of £100 each. By 31 December 1841, it had become necessary to raise an additional £30,000 bringing the total to £300,000.[53] It is interesting to see that some twenty-one of the original co-partners found the extra cash and that it was not necessary to bring in additional subscribers from outside. The holdings shown in the final column provide a source for an interesting comment. There was no overall control by the managing partners Cunard, MacIver and Burns. This group owned 28 per cent of the shares, while those holding more than 100 shares each, owned a fraction less than half the total capital. There was, therefore, no tightly knit family holding as in the case of so many other steamship companies founded later. It proved, however, to be an equitable distribution and presented little inhibition to the various functions which each managing agent was henceforth to perform. George Burns was left in Glasgow to supervise the construction of the four new ships; MacIver went to Liverpool to organise the Liverpool terminus, while Cunard himself, sailed for New York to establish the Boston and Halifax branches of the Company. The new Company had been put on a sure foundation. Each managing partner had, through experience, developed skills in the management of ships. This was a common bond linking a diverse range of characteristics and dominant personalities. The success of the venture as a whole depended on the complementary nature of their respective roles and on their natural goodwill to preserve a harmonious system of management.

III BURNS AND MACIVER FAMILY BACKGROUNDS: THE MEDITERRANEAN AND LEVANT TRADES: CONTROL AND THE DIVISION OF CAPITAL IN THE ATLANTIC AND MEDITERRANEAN COMPANIES

Before entering upon any analysis of the operation of the Cunard shipping interests, it would appear to be logical to trace the antecedents of Samuel Cunard's managing partners, David and Charles

Foundation, Capital Structure and Control

Table 1.1

	First capital authorisation of £270 000		Second capital authorisation, raising total to £300 000		
Name	No. of shares	Capital £	Additional Shares	Additional capital £	Total capital £
Samuel Cunard	550	55 000	60	6 000	61 000
James Donaldson	160	16 000	20	2 000	18 000
James Browne	116	11 600	—	—	11 600
James Wright	116	11 600	14	1 400	13 000
Thos Buchanan	116	11 600	14	1 400	13 000
James Campbell	60	6 000	—	—	6 000
Robt Hinshaw	109	10 900	—	—	10 900
Alex Downie	55	5 500	15	1 500	7 000
Wm Brown	116	11 600	—	—	11 600
Robt Napier	61	6 100	14	1 400	7 500
Robt Rodger	116	11 600	—	—	11 600
Wm Campbell	56	5 600	—	—	5 600
Wm Leckie-Ewing	116	11 600	14	1 400	13 000
Archie MacConnell	20	2 000	6	600	2 600
Wm Connal	116	11 600	—	—	11 600
James Burns	51	5 100	24	2 400	7 500
Geo Burns	55	5 500	20	2 000	7 500
David MacIver	40	4 000	15	1 500	5 500
Chas MacIver	40	4 000	15	1 500	5 500
Alex Fletcher	116	11 500	4	400	12 000
Execs of Alex McAslan	105	10 600	—	—	10 500
Wm Stirling	116	11 600	14	1 400	13 000
Elius Gibb	64	6 400	11	1 100	7 500
Alex Glasgow	64	6 400	26	2 600	9 000
James Merry, Jr	37	3 700	3	300	4 000
David Chapman	15	1 500	5	500	2 000
Alex Bannerman	21	2 100	—	—	2 100
John Bannerman	21	2 100	—	—	2 100
Henry Bannerman	21	2 100	—	—	2 100
David Scott	16	1 600	—	—	1 600
James Martin	15	1 500	—	—	1 500
James McCall	13	1 300	2	200	1 500
Alex Kerr	7	700	4	400	1 100
	2,700	270 000	300	30 000	300 000

MacIver and George and James Burns. It was in the hands of these three families that the control of the Company, before 1878, became vested. In order to understand what happened after 1880 it is therefore necessary to explain not only how capital accumulated during the first forty years of the Company's history, but how the control of that capital passed from the generation of pioneers to their sons. In this context, it is also pertinent to examine the means whereby a system of controlled inheritance was devised ensuring equality of ownership. In this process the interests of the thirty-three original subscribers were ultimately concentrated into the hands of four men.

George Burns was born in December 1795. In 1818 he and his brother James began business as general merchants in Glasgow; by 1824 they had become joint owners, with Hugh Matthie of Liverpool, of six sailing vessels.[54] Shortly afterwards, these sailing ships were replaced with steamships powered by side-lever engines and driven by paddle-wheels. In 1829, some of these ships were put into service in a highly competitive trade between Glasgow and Liverpool; others were employed on the route between Glasgow and Belfast.[55] This latter trade was also highly competitive but by 1830 the firm of J. & G. Burns had managed to secure a firm hold, by purchasing the interests of their principal rival John Gemmill.[56] In 1834, however, the competitive struggle was renewed when ships owned by Messrs Thompson and McConnell were put on the cross-channel service between Glasgow and Belfast.[57] It was not until the middle 1840s that the Burns brothers began to secure a significant share of the trade and not until the 1850s that they were able to buy out Thompson and McConnell, their rivals, and create a monopoly.[58]

The MacIver family's interest in shipping began in the eighteenth century, in particular with the exploits of John MacIver, Captain of the armed brig *Swallow*.[59] John's brother David, who also commanded a ship during the Napoleonic wars, was the father of David and Charles MacIver, the subjects of this history. In 1829 David MacIver the younger became the Liverpool agent for the New Clyde Steamship Company and, in the following year, he founded the City of Glasgow Steam Packet Company to run ships between Liverpool and Glasgow on his own account.[60] The pioneer steamer, *City of Glasgow*, inaugurated the service on 25 April 1831 and ran in opposition to the Burnses' ships.[61] Three other vessels were shortly afterwards added to the fleet and these were, in turn, supplemented with *Commodore* and *Admiral*, reputedly the fastest steamships afloat in the late 1830s and early 1840s.[62] In 1835 Charles MacIver joined his brother and the style of the firm was altered to David MacIver and Company. Unfortunately, however, the MacIver ships did not bring in the returns anticipated and, on George Burns's suggestion an amicable agreement was made for the sharing of the general trade. Under this agreement MacIvers were allocated two-fifths and the Burns brothers three-fifths together with control of the concern. After David's death in 1845, Charles took over control and enlarged the firm's shipping operations. By the early 1850s the Burns and MacIver interests were working in harmony within the framework of the British and North American Royal Mail Steam Packet Company. Accordingly, in 1853 their rival Liverpool and Glasgow services were amalgamated, the joint line being represented in Liverpool by Charles MacIver and Company and in Glasgow by G. and J. Burns, the style of this latter firm having been altered in 1842.[63]

We must now return to the inauguration of the North Atlantic service by the British and North American Royal Mail Steam Packet Company. With the promise and ultimate subscription of the initial capital of £270,000 Cunard was able to proceed rapidly with his plans. The first four ships, *Britannia, Columbia, Acadia* and *Caledonia*, were put in hand, while he himself took passage for New York on *Great Western* to inaugurate the Halifax and Boston end of the service.[64] He was, however, back in Liverpool by July 1840 to take passage on the maiden voyage of the Company's first ship, *Britannia*.[65] She sailed from that port on 4 July 1840 and reached Halifax on the 17th and was off Boston light by the next day. In actual fact, she was not the first Cunard ship to cross the Atlantic, a small vessel, *Unicorn*, having been sent ahead of *Britannia* to make the necessary dockage arrangements in Boston. She sailed from Liverpool on 16 May 1840 with twenty-seven passengers and was later put on the Pictou–Quebec route.[66] Nevertheless, *Britannia* was symbolic of a new age of steamship enterprise and her crossing inaugurated the service of a pioneer line for the carriage of mails across the Atlantic.

In spite of the fears expressed by Burns and MacIver in their first conversation with Cunard, the ships maintained a precise and regular schedule of sailings. Between July and December 1840 the

4 ships made 8 voyages and twenty-one in the following year, the average duration of each voyage being 13 days outward and 11 days 5 hours homeward. The shipbuilding programme was pushed ahead and two further ships were added to the fleet, *Hibernia* in 1843 and *Cambria* in 1844. Both *Hibernia* and *Cambria* were of similar construction to *Britannia* but exceeded her in size and speed.[67] The maintenance of a year-round service, however, was not without hazard. In February 1844, for example, *Britannia* was icebound in Boston harbour. She was freed by the Bostonians themselves who, jealous for the reputation of their newly acquired mail service, cut a channel seven miles long through the ice.[68] A serious loss in the 1840s was *Columbia*. She was wrecked on her homeward voyage off Cape Sable in 1843, but though the Company thereby sustained depletion to its fleet, there was no resulting death or injury to passengers and all the mails were saved.[69] Approximately nine-tenths of the capital value of the ship was recovered from underwriters and one-tenth was debited to the Company's own underwriting account.[70] In accordance with the capabilities of the Company, however, and sometimes under political or economic pressure, amendments and adjustments were made to the services from time to time. The branch service to Quebec was discontinued in 1845; those to Bermuda and Newfoundland were strengthened and, in 1851, a branch was extended from Bermuda to St Thomas in the West Indies.[71] In the meantime, however, a direct link between Liverpool and New York had been started in January 1848, though *Hibernia* had, in fact, gone from Boston to New York in December of the previous year.[72] This extension of service to New York was, as we shall see later, a consequence of the renewal of the mail contract and was given added significance because it brought Cunard into competition with other steamship companies serving that port.

The development of the Company's North Atlantic services in relation to shipbuilding policy will be given more detailed treatment in the following chapter. It is necessary, at this point, to examine the introduction and expansion of the Company's interests in a new area of operation, namely the Mediterranean. After the repeal of the Navigation Laws in 1849, it became possible to tranship French goods via a British port to America and to Mediterranean ports. In 1849, therefore, Charles MacIver chartered *British Queen* on his own account for the purpose of entering the

Mediterranean trade.[73] Impressed by the results of this new venture, Samuel Cunard and George Burns decided to support MacIver and, in 1851, *British Queen* was bought outright and taken into Cunard service.[74] So owned, she sailed from Liverpool on 26 April 1851 and together with *Margaret* and *Shamrock*, inaugurated Cunard's services with the Levant and Constantinople. These ships formed the nucleus of a new fleet in direct competition with existing Mediterranean lines such as Moss, Dixon and Bibby. The lowering of duties on fruit in 1853 was an immediate incentive to the growth of this trade and justified MacIver's further expenditure of capital in *Teneriffe, Taurus, Karnak* and *Melita*, all of which were shortly transferred to the British and Foreign Steam Navigation Co.[75] This venture was not only important in securing a new direct trade, but was equally important in that these ships acted as feeders of both passengers and cargo to the main line trans-Atlantic ships. Another diversification of service was that proposed between Liverpool and the West Indies. The iron-screw steamships, *Alps* and *Andes*, later reinforced by *Jura* and *Etna*, were originally built for this route though, as we shall see later, this service was seriously interrupted by the diversion of ships into government service following the outbreak of the Crimean War.[76]

The first ships engaged in the Mediterranean and Levant trades were, as a matter of convenience, despatched under the title of Burns and MacIver.[77] It was made clear, however, that this was not a partnership in the strict sense of the term; 'it has no stock, assets or estate' and there 'is no commission'.[78] As the profitability of the Mediterranean trade increased it became necessary to have a formal organisation for the allocation of resources in the building of new ships and the regular assessment of capital employed. Accordingly, a co-partnership between James Burns, George Burns, John Burns, Charles MacIver and Samuel Cunard was instituted to operate from 1 October 1855 under the title of the British and Foreign Steam Navigation Company.[79] The capital stock was divided into 1000 shares as follows: James Burns 167 shares; George Burns 167; John Burns 167; Charles MacIver 312; Samuel Cunard 187.[80] The ships assigned to this company were registered in compliance with the provisions of the Merchant Shipping Act of 1854, and consisted of *Damascus, Lebanon, Karnak, Melita, Teneriffe, Taurus, British Queen, Alps* and *Andes* – all screw steamships.[81] It was a company with a tightly-knit interest and made the more so by the provision that any partner wishing to withdraw should be bound to offer his shares to the rest of the partners at a price determined by the current value of the vessels.[82]

Thus, by 1855 the capital resources of the Cunard, Burns and MacIver families, were employed in two separate companies, the first, The British and North American Royal Mail Steam Packet Company, trading across the Atlantic and the second, The British and Foreign Steam Navigation Company, operating between the United Kingdom and Mediterranean ports. From the point of view of the management and control of resources, the disposition of the assets in the Mediterranean company has significance because the guide lines laid down for the holding of shares in this company ultimately affected the holdings and the division of assets in the Cunard organisation as a whole. There is evidence that, by 1856, the Burns brothers were facing serious problems of liquidity.[83] These problems were exacerbated by the financial crisis of 1857 and both James and George Burns found themselves with depleted resources and were forced to realise assets.[84] Furthermore, their difficulties had not been relieved when in 1856 Samuel Cunard, with the support of Charles MacIver, had devised a scheme to start a line of steamships to Australia.[85] This project merely increased the Burns brothers' desire to withdraw from the Mediterranean business. On 3 September 1856, George Burns wrote to MacIver: 'You will not be surprised that I should say that rather than go into any of the transactions proposed, (i.e. the proposed service to Australia) involving further outlay of capital to a large extent, I am prepared to co-join with you and others towards a winding up ... For my own part I would be most heartily willing to retire from all business if it were practicable.'[86] These views were not well received, MacIver replying in a characteristic and forthright manner. He sent a copy of his reply to Samuel Cunard in which he declared: 'It will be quite time enough for any partner to ventilate the "winding up" idea after he has given his partners a fair chance of carrying on the business by first offering to them his stock and interest.'[87]

The terms of partnership in the British and Foreign Steam Navigation Company were therefore amended allowing the partners to transfer their shares to their sons. Charles MacIver had, at first, opposed this principle of family succession contending that any shares falling in from partners should, in accordance with the original agreement, be offered in the first instance to the other partners.[88] In this case, the persuasive powers of Samuel Cunard were used to good effect in preventing what might have developed into a rift between the partners. 'We have now been nearly 20 years connected in business' he wrote to MacIver 'a large portion of an ordinary life and we have been most providentially protected. See how many great houses have fallen around us during the last year, who were at the commencement of the year in affluence.'[89] The implication of such advice was well understood, but when George and James Burns retired from the British and Foreign Steam Navigation Company, MacIver still continued to insist that the letter of the agreement be upheld especially concerning the division of commissions.[90] Samuel Cunard was equally insistent that George Burns should be allowed to retain his former rights. 'We should not forget that Mr Burns, our partner and old friend, is in trouble', he wrote. 'It is our duty to come forward and do all that we can to assist him. Now to call on him to resign his commission, leaving it to you to remunerate him as you may think proper is not, in my opinion, the correct mode to be adopted. Mr Burns should be allowed to transfer his shares to his sons (or any portion of them) and he should retain his commissions with or without shares as he may wish.'[91] Again, as late as 9 November 1858, he wrote to MacIver: 'We should assist Mr Burns in his distress . . . do not turn your thoughts to law pleadings. You will in the end thank me for my apparent obstinacy.'[92] Fortunately, Charles MacIver was eventually influenced by Cunard's good advice and the question of transferring shares to the sons of the partners was settled amicably.

George and James Burns retired from the British and Foreign company as from 30 September 1857, Charles MacIver taking 95 of James's shares, the remainder being divided equally between George's sons John and James Cleland Burns.[93] The whole of George Burns's 167 shares were transferred to James Cleland Burns, thus making the new holding in the company: John Burns 203 shares; James Cleland Burns 203; Charles MacIver 407 and Samuel Cunard 187.[94]

On 24 August 1859 George Burns also resigned his partnership in the British and North American Royal Mail Steam Packet Co, having previously relinquished the agency on 30 June.[95] This retirement necessitated changes in the composition of management and in the succession of agencies and commissions. Samuel Cunard became a manager in George Burns's place, the qualification for such office being in future the holding of 200 shares.[96] It was further agreed that George's agency and commissions should pass to his two sons John and James Cleland. At the same time, provision was also made for the succession of James Burns's interests as manager and trustee to pass to John Burns or, failing him to James Cleland Burns.[97] Similar entitlements were also given to Samuel Cunard to provide for his sons, Edward and William, and to Charles MacIver in respect of his sons, David and John.[98] The powers of successive agents, however, were controlled and made subject to the governance of the managers.[99] It is perhaps of relevance to note that in the event of James Burns ceasing to be a partner, his commissions should be shared, one-half to John and James Cleland Burns and one-half to Charles MacIver, these shares to be subject to the agreed rights of succession.[100] In short, not only was the basis of future control in both companies established between the three families, but there was also by virtue of this control, a fixed quantity in the holding of shares.

These agreements remained in force until 1866. By this latter date two factors had emerged necessitating a reappraisal of capital resources. The first followed from the death of Sir Samuel Cunard in 1865 and from the growing strength and profitability of the Mediterranean and Levant trades; the second from Cunard's entering into the North Atlantic emigrant trade. The point linking the two factors was that there seemed to be a reasonable prospect of developing an emigrant trade from Mediterranean ports as well as that direct from Liverpool. In such an eventuality it would be of advantage if the Mediterranean ships under the control of the British and Foreign Steam Navigation Co, could be worked in liaison with those of the British and North American Royal Mail Steam Packet Company.[101]

There followed a series of legal documents which reconstituted the capital structure of the Mediterranean and the Atlantic companies and gave equality in both capital holding and management to the Cunard, MacIver and Burns families. In the first place, the British and Foreign Steam Navigation Co, the creation of Charles MacIver with the later participation of Samuel Cunard and George Burns, was brought to an end.[102] In its place a new company was created to operate from 13 September 1866 under the

Foundation, Capital Structure and Control

same title but with a different capital structure. The old company's stock, as we have seen, had consisted of 1000 shares which were then held in the following proportions: Charles MacIver 407; John Burns 203; James Cleland Burns 203; Sir Edward Cunard 70 and William Cunard 117.[103] In the treaty for the new Company, however, it was arranged that there should be an equality of interests between Charles MacIver, the Cunard brothers and the Burns brothers. Accordingly, the 1000 shares of the old company were redivided as 1200 in the new and were reallocated to the partners: Charles MacIver receiving 400; John Burns 200; James Cleland Burns 200; Sir Edward Cunard 200 and William Cunard 200.[104] The manner in which capital transfers were subsequently made will be shown hereafter. It is sufficient to state here that the value of the old shares was estimated at £450 per unit and changed hands at that price, thus giving a total anticipated capital valuation (including goodwill) of the British and Foreign Steam Navigation Co of £450,000.[105]

The next step was to secure a similar proportionate interest among these five partners in the British and North American Royal Mail Steam Packet Company. On 22 July 1867 an agreement was entered into whereby the interests of the partners in the British and North American and the British and Foreign companies were declared identical.[106] Henceforth, the ships of the Mediterranean and Atlantic fleets were to be used in common 'and employed indifferently for the trade of both companies and the trade of either of them'.[107] The earnings of the two companies were to be placed in one common purse and the net profits arising from the employment of the ships should accrue to and be divided between the two companies as the partners might determine.[108] All transactions were to be recorded in one set of 'business books'.

These arrangements were embodied in a new deed of partnership.[109] The Memorandum of Agreement dated 31 July discontinued the title of the company founded in 1840 and consolidated control in the hands of the Cunard, Burns and MacIver families. Of the original 3000 shares 2130 were held by Charles MacIver and the Burns and Cunard sons, the remaining 870 being held as follows: James Burns 502; Sir James Campbell 150; John James Kerr 72; John Bannerman 73; Henry Bannerman 73.[110] These latter subscribers were bought out at a price of £198 6s 8d per share and their holdings transferred to the remaining sole proprietors. Under the rearrangement the stock of the old British and North American Royal Mail Steam Packet Co. came to be held as follows: John Burns 500; James Cleland Burns 500; Charles MacIver 1000; Sir Edward Cunard 500; William Cunard 500.[111] It will be noted as a point of historical reference that with the death of Sir Samuel Cunard in 1865 and the retirements of George and James Burns, the interests of these original partners had now passed to the second generation, Charles MacIver alone retaining his increasing interest. The new agreement made the position abundantly clear by stating that the five holders of the shares were 'the only remaining partners in the proportions already specified and in these proportions sole proprietors of all the stock and estate whatever of the old company'.[112] On the basis of a calculated anticipated value (including goodwill) of £198 6s 8d per share, the capital of this company now stood at £595,000.

As a result of these various reconstructions, the capital of the two companies was equally divided between the three family interests and, though remaining for the time being separately accounted for, was worked in common under the title of the British and North American Steam Packet Company. By September 1867, therefore, the division of interests may be estimated as follows:

Name	B. & F.S.N. Co. No. of shares	Value £	B. & N.A.R.M.S.P. Co. No. of shares	Value £ s d	Total £ s d
Charles MacIver	400	150 000	400	198 333 6 8	348 333 6 8
John Burns	200	75 000	200	99 166 13 4	174 166 13 4
James Cleland Burns	200	75 000	200	99 166 13 4	174 166 13 4
Sir Edward Cunard	200	75 000	200	99 166 13 4	174 166 13 4
Wm. Cunard	200	75 000	200	99 166 13 4	174 166 13 4

In 1873 Charles MacIver assessed the capital value of the concern as a whole (i.e. the Mediterranean and the North Atlantic interests) at £1,063,566[113] and in 1874 at £1,102,320;[114] by 1878, when incorporation took place, the figure had reached £1,369,034.[115] The 1873 and 1874 figures provided a real valuation for the assessment of shares. In 1878, however, certain liabilities had to be met, giving a somewhat less amount as a net figure.

On the death of Sir Edward Cunard in 1869, his shares were taken over by his brother William. Charles MacIver, however, held firmly to his one-third interest, despite the fact that his two sons, David and John, were closely associated with him in management of both Cunard and D. and C. MacIver affairs. The persistence of the father in retaining control within his own hands led to a series of family disagreements. David held strong views about the type of ship his father continued to use in the Mediterranean trade. 'I have for years urged persistently', he wrote, 'that the class of vessel on which my father prides himself had "run its day" as far as the Mediterranean is concerned. I have no shadow of doubt that the present class of Cunard steamer (*Nantes* type excepted) is destined to be "elbowed out" of the Mediterranean by such steamers as I propose to build.'[116] In pursuit of his aims he sought to acquire to himself the Mediterranean agency and this seemed to be within the realms of possibility when, early in 1874, his father was forced to leave Liverpool and take up residence in Malta in order to recover his health. Much to David's chagrin, however, his father exercised just as much control from Malta as he had done in Liverpool.[117] David, therefore, severed connection with Cunard and threatened to start a new company of rival steamships to the Mediterranean.[118] For a time father and son were scarcely on speaking terms and it was only through the persistent efforts of the family adviser, A. Squarey, that matters were patched up. David's original plan for running a line of his own ships required financial help from his father. When this proved difficult of realisation he broached a second plan under which his father and some of his partners should hold shares in *Tuscany* and other vessels held by David and that, in return, he (David) should hold shares in ships held by them.[119] 'All these vessels', wrote A. Squarey to David in an explanatory legal opinion, 'should be worked under your management in the Mediterranean or some other trade.'[120] Unfortunately, this scheme met with opposition from Charles MacIver's other partners and David left the Mediterranean business to his father and younger brothers and started a new line of steamships from Liverpool to Bombay under the title of David MacIver and Company.[121] Shortly afterwards, however, he abandoned his shipowning activity and embarked upon a political career, entering parliament as a Member for Kirkdale.

IV INCORPORATION AND THE AGREEMENT OF 1880: ROLE OF THE MANAGING AGENTS AND REORGANISATION OF CAPITAL

Thus, by 1878, the year in which Cunard was incorporated, the lines of succession in the holding of shares as envisaged in the 1859 and 1867 agreements, had been altered. By this date the Cunard family interests were represented by William, the Burnses interests by John and James Cleland and those of the MacIver family by Charles senior. These four partners were, therefore, the sole vendors of the assets to the newly incorporated company under the style of The Cunard Steam Ship Co. Ltd.[122]

By an agreement dated 21 May 1878, provision was made for the sale of assets by the four partners to the new Company and, on 4 March 1880, the final apportionments of shares in the new Company were ratified.[123] Under the terms of the 1878 agreement the new Company, in return for the transfer of assets, was required to take over all existing liabilities and contracts and indemnify the vendors against debts and other charges. It was further stated that 'the residue of the consideration for the said sale should be £1,200,000' which should be paid by the allotment to the vendors of 12,000 fully paid shares in The Cunard Steam Ship Co Ltd.[124] Finally, the partners agreed to provide the new Company with the services of managing agents and that these services should continue for a period of at least five years from the date of incorporation. The firms of D. and C. MacIver and Burns and MacIver were appointed as managing agents in Liverpool, that of W. and W. S. Cunard in London and the firm of G. and J. Burns in Glasgow.[125] In these various ways the former functions and control of the three families were transformed and incorporated into a new organisation. They had relinquished a fair degree of sovereignty in the process of change. In particular they had agreed not to engage in any shipping business in competition with that of The Cunard Steam Ship Co. Ltd for a period of fourteen years from the date of the final agreement. As we shall see later, the limiting nature of such a commitment eventually caused disagreement and led to time-wasting and costly litigation.

In working out the financial terms of this agreement, the basis for valuation had been taken as that existing at 31 December 1879. The value of all vessels on 10 February 1880 was put at £1,161,000.[126] To this had to be added the sale price of four other vessels together with the value of wharves, plant, stores and other property, the total of which was £1,369,034. The difference between this estimated value and the £1,200,000 paid to the vendors, represented the liabilities of the old company outstanding at that date. This total of £169,034 was, therefore, made over to the new Company by the partners. In addition, it was agreed that the vendors 'will place at the disposal of the Company, and will transfer at par . . . to such persons as the directors shall designate, share capital of the company to the amount of £533,340 part of the fully paid shares pursuant to the said cited agreement'.[127] This capital was to be found by the vendors in the following proportions: Charles MacIver senior £177,780; William Cunard £177,780; John Burns £88,890 and James Cleland Burns £88,890.[128] It was also stipulated that, for a period of five years, they should retain at least £500,000 in the Company in the proportions: William Cunard (or William Samuel Cunard) £166,680; James or John Burns £166,680; Charles MacIver senior (or Charles MacIver, the younger and Henry MacIver) £166,660.[129] Thus, the Cunard Company brought into association the third generation of the Cunard family and the second generation of the MacIvers.

The allocation of the 12 000 fully paid shares of £100 each in the new Company was made as follows: Charles MacIver senior 3500; William Cunard 3900; John Burns 2000; James Cleland Burns 2000; Charles MacIver the younger 250; Henry MacIver 250 and William Samuel Cunard 100.[130] In this way, the old principle of maintaining parity of interests between the three families was embodied in the capital structure of the new Company; this, at least, was true until the new issue of shares was thrown open to the public.

So ended the first forty years of a steamship enterprise in which capital accumulation, control and management had involved the efforts of the principals. That such enterprise had been successful may be judged by a range of varying criteria. By itself, the extent of capital accumulation may be accepted as an indicator. The original capital of £270,000 had increased by 1880 to £1,369,034 giving an accumulation of £1,099,034, approximately a four-fold increase in forty years. If this is expressed in terms of constant prices, the whole of this increase was virtually a real one. Behind this simple quantity, however, there lay the managerial skill of shrewd men of business, the competitive service of the ships which they employed and the judgement in opening up new trades. In these functions lay the real causes of success during the formative phase of Cunard's history.

2
Men, Ships and Mails 1840-80

I THE INAUGURATION OF THE ATLANTIC SERVICE: IMPROVEMENT
IN DESIGN, POWER AND SIZE OF SHIPS

The successful operation of The British and North American Royal Mail Steam Packet Company during the first forty years of its history was governed by a diverse range of economic, financial and political influences. These influences, in turn, helped in shaping policies relating to the building of new ships, in maintaining mail contracts and services; in entering new trades and in ordering the conduct of business within the framework of a strict code of discipline. The continuous endeavours of the managing partners to meet and overcome successive problems arising from the expansion of steamship services, created lines of policy which, in course of time, came to be regarded as traditional in the conduct of the Company's affairs. What service was achieved in the first formative years has to be set against a background of both opposition and of the growing technical competence of other steamship companies. Even with government backing (or, perhaps, despite such backing) Cunard could not afford to be complacent. In commercial matters there is much evidence for the belief that the managers were equal in all respects to their rivals; but in technological development they were inhibited by varying degrees of conservatism and by the need to conform to official directive. As a result, Samuel Cunard and Charles MacIver left to others the costs of innovation and adopted improvements only when others had tested their reliability by experiment. What they saved in capital outlay, therefore, they might, in technological terms, have lost in competitive advantage.

This relationship between competition and innovation was a constant theme of Cunard management throughout the whole of the nineteenth century; but it was never more insistent than in the first forty years of the Company's history. Before 1860 Cunard had very little incentive to induce experiment. The mail contract provided the Company with an income from all services, of nearly £190,000[1] and, as long as the ships were able to meet the requirements imposed upon them, there seemed to be little advantage in undertaking costly schemes of innovation. This attitude was maintained in face of increasing pressure for improvement during the 1840s and 1850s. In fact, some of the fever of speculation normally associated with railway development at that time seems to have spilled over into trans-Atlantic shipping. Many companies were promoted, but few survived because they were uneconomic in operation. Of such companies, perhaps the Galway line was the most notorious. There was widespread ignorance among investors concerning the problems involved in maintaining a year-round trans-Atlantic service. As such pioneers as Cunard and later Collins and Inman well knew, it was a business which exploited weakness. Even the more technically sound enterprises such as the Great Western Steamship Co. (1838–46) foundered under the cost and adverse publicity resulting from accidents and breakdowns; these facts were given even more dramatic illustration in the failure, at a later date, of the Collins line. Thus, the high incidence of failure among the early steamship companies only served to confirm the leading position held by Cunard. By implication, the rate of failure also confounded the audacity of those who believed that they could experiment on so dangerous an ocean as the Atlantic.

Was this the real reason why Cunard continued to use wooden-hulled paddle steamships powered by side-lever engines for more than a dozen years on the Atlantic crossing? Following the introduction of steamships on the Atlantic, the first major development in a technological sense, was that of iron-hulled, screw-driven ships.[2] Although sound in technical detail, Brunel's *Great Britain*, built in 1843, did not prove to be a financial success. It was another five years before the commercial potential of this type of ship began to be used and fully exploited by the Inman line. Unlike the Cunard management, Inman and his fellow directors were prepared to experiment with new ideas and to act on principles enunciated, executed and tested by scientific skill and inventive genius. Their *City of Glasgow*, which entered service in 1850, might perhaps be regarded as the prototype of all succeeding liners. The wisdom of such a policy was, nevertheless, often brought into question, because the Inman line ships were prone to accidents.³ In general, however, the iron screw-driven ship was eventually accepted because it was stronger and lighter, less easily damaged and more quickly repaired than wooden ships. More important was the fact that, by the middle of the nineteenth century, a limit had been reached to the size of wooden ships. Iron ships, on the other hand, could be built to virtually any size, a factor which was of relevance in accommodating the increasing flood of emigrants after 1850. Coupled with this was the added advantage that, by increasing capacity, lower fares could be charged and, as a consequence, steamship travel could be brought within the financial means of the humblest traveller. Against this background, it soon became obvious that the paddle steamship, with its limited cabin capacity, was uneconomic as a means of ocean transport, unless supported by large mail subsidies. By introducing the iron-screw ships to its regular services in 1850, the Inman line took the first of a series of important steps which eventually changed the course of Atlantic shipping. What, in fact, Inman demonstrated was that screw-driven ships could match the paddle steamships in both speed and manoeuvre and could earn a profit without the prop of a mail subsidy. This in turn opened the Atlantic to non-subsidised liners and facilitated changes in the design of ships and their engines.

Though it is arguable that Samuel Cunard and his partners remained stubbornly in favour of paddle steamships for some time after their effectiveness had been surpassed, it would be erroneous to imply that they refused to accept change. In accordance with the terms of their original contract, requiring the ships to be improved in direct relation to advances in the state of scientific and technical knowledge, they made a continuous series of improvements to the size and design of their paddle steamships.⁴

One or two interesting facts emerge from an examination of their fleet list between 1840 and 1852. The size of Cunard's wooden-hulled paddle steamships engaged on the North Atlantic was doubled and the motive power of the engines was quadrupled.⁵ The same expansive tendency is observable when, after 1852, Cunard turned over to iron hulls and single-screw ships, the size being nearly trebled and the motive power more than quadrupled. This phase lasted until the building of *Persia* in 1856 and *Scotia* in 1862. These were built of iron but were the last paddle steamships built by Napier for Cunard.[6] *Persia* was of 3300 tons having engines with an indicated horse-power of 3800 and *Scotia* was of 3871 tons powered by engines of 5000 I.H.P. Thereafter, the Company reverted to smaller iron-screw ships of from 2200 to 2600 tons with less than 3000 I.H.P.[7] It seems reasonable, by way of confirmation of the view already expressed, to conclude that the Cunard Company did not accept iron-screw ships into their services until both the technical and commercial feasibility of such ships had been adequately demonstrated. In this respect, they were subject to government decision. The Lords of the Admiralty refused to accept the evidence of the superiority of the screw.[8] 'Scientific theorists had informed the Board that the invention was based on erroneous principles and full of practical defects.' In 1853 they gave reluctant permission to P. and O. to build a screw steamer but did not give permission to Cunard until 1862. In that year *China* was the first screw steamer laid down for the Atlantic mail service though iron-screw steamers were accepted into Cunard service from 1852 and were employed in the Mediterranean and ancillary services. Once accepted, however, it is rather more difficult to explain why the design and power of these iron ships was so drastically reduced after 1857.

One logical explanation of Cunard policy is to be found in the growing diversity of service and in the impact of political events on Cunard's development. As we have seen, Charles MacIver was beginning to extend the Company's business in the Mediterranean. This trade required the operation of a smaller type of ship than that employed on the North Atlantic. Consequently, resources were diverted into the construction of Mediterranean ships of limited size and power. It was only in the following decade when the ships of the Mediterranean and Atlantic fleet were used in common, that the size of the Mediterranean ships was increased. There was, however, a more important cause for the disruption of continuous development in Cunard's shipbuilding policy. The outbreak of the Crimean War in 1854 not only disrupted normal commercial relationships but diverted a large amount of tonnage to war requirements. *Alps* and *Andes*, together with several other Cunarders, were requisitioned for government service; *Niagara* and *Cambria* were taken over as transports – *Jura*, *Etna*, *Europa* and *Arabia* were also commandeered.[9] This withdrawal of tonnage so dislocated the trans-Atlantic mail service that, in order to sustain the minimum number of sailings, *Emeu* had to be purchased and diverted from her original Australian route.[10]

It seems likely that these efforts to extend Cunard capabilities in new trades, coupled with the taking over of ships, and the subsequent elimination of competition on Atlantic mail services following the collapse of the Collins line in 1856, had a direct effect on Cunard's building policy. Charles MacIver virtually substantiated such an hypothesis in a letter of 12 April 1857, by declaring that smaller iron-screw ships were far more efficient and less costly to run than the larger vessels of their competitors.[11] At the same time, the Company could only ignore the increasing flow of improvements at their peril. Undoubtedly, by making safety a main criterion of policy, Cunard management often missed initial opportunities for worthwhile innovation.

While the introduction of the compound engine had its teething troubles, the continuous discussion over its merits went on long after the value of the engine had been firmly established. Indeed, Alfred Holt, who had done so much to improve its efficiency and to put the engine to commercial test over long ocean distances, was impelled to state that 'it is a matter of reasonable speculation whether the compound may yet not be abandoned and a return made to the single cylinder engine, modified in details to suit high pressure steam'.[12] It is evident that the Cunard Company held back from its use through fear that great loss of life might result from the explosive hazards of the high steam pressures required to drive such engines. It is true that the danger was a real one for, between 1854 and 1884, working steam pressure increased from 25 lb per square inch to 110 lb. It was not until Siemens's open-hearth steel became available after 1865 that reliable and safe boilers could be put aboard ship. There was also the added inhibition in the minds of certain Cunard partners that a more complicated engine, such as the compound, was necessarily more delicate and therefore, more likely to suffer breakdowns at sea.[13] These views were probably fundamental to answering the question why the Cunard Company continued with small, low-powered ships long after their competitors had gone into other forms of construction. The Company's first compound-engined ship was *Batavia* which was put into service in 1870.[14]

In fairness to the Cunard management, however, it must be pointed out that some of the other British lines, such as National, deferred the change-over to compound engines, not through lack of enterprise, but from the simple fact that they could not raise sufficient capital to do so.[15] Their hands were only eventually forced by pressure of competition. In Cunard's case, the conversion, when it came, went far beyond the bounds of current practice. In 1885 *Etruria* and *Umbria* were brought into service. They were the most powerful single-screw ships built to date, having compound engines of 14 500 I.H.P.[16] They were costly in operation and only returned a profit when carrying upwards of 70 per cent of passenger and cargo capacity.[17] The enormous engines in these ships consumed over 300 tons of coal per day and needed 112 firemen and trimmers to maintain them.[18] It became obvious that if the Cunard Company were to re-equip the fleet with such ships, the whole of their Atlantic service might be rendered unprofitable because of excessive fuel consumption. Other shipping companies, including some of their competitors, having faced this problem, were already in process of solving it by turning over to triple expansion engines. The first Atlantic liners fitted with these engines had been those of North German Lloyd in 1886, though P. and O. had fitted out two ships with such engines in the previous year.[19] The new motive power proved 'as superior to the compound engine as the latter had proved superior to the simple expansion engine'.[20] Economy in fuel and greater power were achieved with a significant reduction in the actual size and weight of the engine. This led to criticism from Cunard shareholders that the Company should have had *Etruria* and *Umbria* fitted with compound engines.[21] The two ships had cost a total of £616,000; they were virtually obsolete by the time they were launched.

In yet another important technical improvement, Cunard was unduly belated in acceptance. This was the introduction of twin screws. Since the inauguration of screw propellers, the fracturing of shafts and blades had occurred with damaging regularity. Although most passenger ships continued to be fitted with auxiliary sails until well into the 1880s, these were of little use on large steamships of the post-1870 period, serving only to keep the ship's bow into the wind in the event of an engine failure. The financial losses involved in breakdowns from broken shafts and propellers were extremely heavy. 'Constant breakage of the propeller blades', wrote T. H. Ismay of the White Star Line, to Harland and Wolff in 1872, 'is becoming a question of the most serious importance to us, not only on account of the great expense entailed thereby, but also as affecting the prestige of the line which must suffer if these accidents continue.'[22] Made of cast steel, both shafts and blades were unable to withstand the strains put upon them as the power of engines increased. Experiments were made with tougher and more expensive metals. For a time manganese bronze was widely used for blades. At £115 per ton, it cost Cunard a total of £16,559 to refit their trans-Atlantic ships with new blades in the two years 1889 to 1890.[23] With regard to shafts, improvement in design and the widespread use of nickel steel did much to overcome frequency of fracture. Twin screws came in with the Inman line's ship *City of New York* in 1888. The advantages were immediately obvious – if only for the single fact that the hazard from breakdown caused by shaft failure was diminished.

Once again, however, Cunard allowed its competitors to discover the technical difficulties as well as the economic advantages before adopting such an innovation. It was not until 1893 that the Company adopted twin screws in *Campania* and *Lucania*. Even so, there was still much to be learnt from the performance of these new ships, as the following extract from an (1892) article in *The Times* indicated: 'In view of recent experience', it was stated, 'the twin screw, except for purposes of safety, is still on trial. The arrangement is more costly since every part of the means of propulsion is doubled. The inertia is also doubled and the effective power developed in the two screws is discounted by the troubled water each makes for its neighbour. The performance of the *Campania* may throw new light on these points.'[24] The succeeding trials showed that *Campania* suffered from excessive vibration, a fault which would not have been serious in a cargo ship, but one which had to receive immediate attention in a passenger liner. For Cunard, the matter was of such serious import that they considered taking legal action against Fairfields, the builders.[25] On the advice of their solicitors, however, the action was not pressed and Cunard withheld final payment until the defect had been put right.[26] To do this necessitated a series of tests and adjustments, while the ship was in service. It was not until the middle of 1894 that a solution was found by adjusting the pitch of the propellers, a device which kept the revolutions below the point where vibration began.[27]

Apart from the above measures designed to increase the power and safety of engines, there was a wide range of improvements concerned with better methods of lubrication, stronger bearings and a wider use of steel, all making for safer ocean travel. Technical devices were also buttressed by an increasing intervention from the State. After 1870 the provisions of the Passenger Acts were paralleled by a code of rules covering varying types of marine machinery and enforced by periodic Board of Trade surveys. Such enactments did not greatly affect the Cunard Company's position as their ships had always been designed to secure the highest possible factor of safety. Their policy in this respect had been reiterated by Charles MacIver in 1873 when giving evidence before the Royal Commission on Unseaworthy Ships. '"Classification" could not be of any advantage to us, because in everything, I believe, we are over the strengths.'[28] He was probably right in his assertion and, by saying so, unwittingly provided a simple answer to the peculiarities of Cunard's shipbuilding policy in relation to competition which characterised the first sixty years of the Company's history.

II MAIL CONTRACTS AND COMPETITION

We must now retrace our steps in order to examine the nature of the early competition experienced by Cunard in the maintenance of its mail contract. Other shipping lines, most of them carriers of mail, were strongly opposed to the granting of a government subsidy to Cunard. They vied with Cunard in laying down vessels which could compete successfully in the provision of mail services, hoping thereby to attract to themselves a share of government assistance. Apart from British companies, however, Cunard had to face growing opposition from American and French-owned shipping lines all of which were in receipt of congressional or government support. The impact of the ensuing struggle to maintain the subsidy was not only a reflection of divided opinions in maritime terms but also brought into relief a division between the Admiralty, which supported an efficient shipping line in the interests of national security, and the Post Office, which required the mail service to pay its way.

In 1843 the Great Western company had, as we have seen, added a most remarkable ship, *Great Britain*, to their fleet. Her hull was of iron instead of wood and she was fitted with a screw propeller instead of paddle wheels. With a length of some 300 feeet and a tonnage of 3200, she was nearly three times the size of *Britannia*. Although in the event *Great Britain* proved to be uneconomical in operation, her presence in 1845 was sufficient to rouse a lively anticipation in the minds of Great Western directors that the Government might look favourably upon their claim for subvention for the carriage of mails between Bristol and New York.[29] It was, therefore, not without some expression of alarm that one of Great Western's directors, in giving evidence before the Committee on Halifax and Boston mails, should have referred to the reports that New York was to be made the terminus of the Cunard line. He emphasised that for a number of years, *Great Britain* had sailed between Bristol and New York carrying mail without the slightest assistance from government.[30] Various memorials, including some from Birmingham business men, supported Great Western's case for subsidy. As part of the case it was claimed that the Cunard line had frequently attempted to kill competition by lowering rates whenever *Great Britain* sailed at the same time as a Cunarder – a claim which Cunard himself could not deny.[31] Such action was 'not done with his concurrence. I regretted it as it looked like an opposition'.[32] Samuel Cunard insisted that he had always had it in mind to go to New York and, by 1847, the necessity to do so had become urgent because 'I saw that the American Government was giving encouragement to a mail line that would interfere very much with me.'[33] In spite of the fact that proposals were made in the Committee for opening the contract to public tender, Cunard was given a renewal. The new contract was, in fact, signed in July; it provided for a service to New York in addition to the Boston–Halifax service and was to be run on alternate Saturdays for eight months, April to November, with a monthly sailing in winter.[34] In 1852 the service was made weekly throughout the year, the vessels leaving Liverpool on Saturday of each week alternately for the two American ports.

Thus, within a few years from *Britannia*'s first voyage, Samuel Cunard had won from the Admiralty a variety of contracts increasing the subsidy to his line from £55,000 to £173,340 or, if the branch services be added, to £188,040 a year.[35] This figure was maintained until the 1860s despite frequent pressure from shipowners and merchants alike that such subsidies were generally harmful to commercial expansion. The arguments, however, were not confined to the commercial plane; Samuel Cunard found himself in the process of sustaining his contract between the cross-fire of the Admiralty and the Post Office. The latter government department rejected Cunard's oft-repeated assertion that his large subsidy was completely covered by the postages paid on the mails that he carried. When in 1853 an enquiry was made into the whole process of mail packets, the Committee under the chairmanship of the Postmaster General, Viscount Canning, commended the regularity of Cunard service but denied the claim that postage revenue equalled the subsidy.[36] Against some £188,000 paid out only £121,000 had been received. Nor did the Committee accept the principle that large and continuous subsidies were necessary. So much so that in 1857 the Post Office opposed the renewal of the Cunard contract.[37] Fortunately for the Company, however, the Admiralty and the Treasury were on its side. 'The best course for ensuring a satisfactory performance', wrote the Secretary to the Admiralty, 'will be to prolong the contract. Keeping the superiority of the British line appears to My Lords to be of national importance.'[38] The Admiralty thereupon renewed the contract – an action which was to have repercussions. Three years later a Committee on Packet Contracts ruled against the Admiralty function and returned to the Post Office the power to contract for sea-going mail services.[39] This power was in fact returned in 1860 by Act of Parliament.

The persistent anxiety concerning the mail contract was perhaps overshadowed by the very real fear which Samuel Cunard experienced as a result of the growth of competition from across the Atlantic. With the opening of the New York direct line, his son, Edward, had moved to New York as agent and supervised the building of new piers at Jersey City. Shortly afterwards supplies of bunker coal began to arrive from Liverpool.[40] It was not long before this new route assumed a position of major importance in the Company's sailing schedules. As R. G. Albion has shown, the duties on Cunard cargoes collected at New York amounted to some $10,500 in 1848 as against $29,500 at Boston. By 1850 the total at New York was $118,000 compared with $63,000 at Boston.[41] By this latter date, however, the Cunarders were beginning to experience some of the most persistent competition ever recorded in maritime history.

By 1845 public opinion in America was becoming insistent in the determination to win back the prestige which their sailing ships had held before the advent of steam. The first attempt was made by two ships, *Washington* and *Hermann*, by providing a service to Bremen in 1847. They were slow and uneconomical and had to be supported by a subsidy from Congress.[42] A second line out of New York began in 1849 under the title of the New York and Havre Steam Navigation Co. This company, also aided by a subsidy, ran two ships, *Franklin* and *Humboldt*. These, however, were scarcely the type of ship that could drive the Cunarders off the Atlantic, though Samuel Cunard was somewhat apprehensive of their competitive strength. 'If we were to relax now in the power and size of our vessels', he stated, 'the whole service would fall into the hands of the Americans which (*sic*) are well sustained by their Government.'[43] His fears were shortly justified, for in the ensuing ten years he had to meet and overcome the challenge of a formidable rival, Edward Knight Collins.

III THE COLLINS LINE AND INTENSIFICATION OF COMPETITION

Collins's meteoric rise and fall as a shipowner is reasonably well known.[44] He was a well-known American shipowner who, for a period of twenty years, had operated sailing packets, first to Vera Cruz, then to New Orleans and, until 1847, with his Dramatic Line to Liverpool.[45] Part of his success was due to the lavish accommodation and food provided for passengers on his ships. It is likely that the aura of success enabled him to win a subsidy contract from the U.S. Postmaster General on 1 November 1847. In return for an annual payment of $385,000, Collins agreed to build four fast ships 'capable of beating the Cunarders'.[46] Supported by the financial backing of James and Stewart Brown he organised the United States Mail Steamship Co., popularly known as the Collins line.[47] As R. G. Albion has shown, the four new ships were given the best possible hulls and engines; the hull contracts being placed with the yards of Brown and Bell and William H. Brown and the engine and machinery contracts with Allaire and the Novelty works.[48] Commodore C. Perry was brought in as adviser because the ships were to be built as potential cruisers.[49]

The first Collins ship, *Atlantic*, opened the service from New York to Liverpool and, by 1850, she had been joined by *Pacific*, *Arctic* and *Baltic*, all of some 2800 tons, approximately 1000 tons larger than the average Cunarder. Speed was to be the essence of success and these new ships made the crossing nearly one whole day faster than the Cunarders.[50] The race was on and within a few months Charles MacIver was estimating that Cunard had lost some £30,000 of business to the new line as a result of increasing competition for passengers, cargo and mails.[51] Worse was to follow. In February 1852 came Collins's master stroke in lobbying, whereby he secured an increase in his mail subsidy to $853,000.[52] The prospect that increasing resources would inevitably lead to more intense competition from larger and faster ships undoubtedly spurred the Cunard Company into an acceptance of iron-screw ships and to many modifications in the building of their large paddle steamship *Persia*.[53] The fact remains, however, that following the first flush of success, the Collins line did not overwhelm Cunard. The latter Company continued to carry more mail; in 1851, for example, Cunard carried 2,613,000 packets; Collins 843,000; the Bremen line 313,000 and the Havre line 139,000.[54] In passenger traffic, however, the speed and comfort of the Collins liners were inducements, particularly to American travellers. In the first eleven months of 1852, Collins carried 4306 passengers against Cunard's 2969.[55] Competition was, therefore, finely balanced and it appeared that the strict regulation to all Cunard captains to couple speed with safety might yet prove to be ill-judged in face of Collins's avowed intention to drive Cunard ships off the Atlantic.

In the last resort, it has always been claimed that speed was the key to the outcome of the struggle.[56] The enforced speed of the American ships not only meant heavy coal consumption, but strained the engines so that, according to rumour, secret repairs had to be made by Allaire and Novelty engineers, following each crossing of the Collins ships.[57] The steady regularity of the Cunard service which went on all the year round through ice and fog, produced dividends: Cunard made money, Collins did not. In the eight checkered years of this line's history not a single dollar was returned to shareholders.[58]

When disaster came it struck with fatal severity. On 27 September 1854 Collins's ship, *Arctic*, was in collision with a small French steamer, *Vesta*, and eventually foundered with the loss of over 300 lives including the wife, son and daughter of Collins.[59] The line managed to survive this loss; orders were placed for a still larger ship, *Adriatic*, and other ships were chartered to take the place of *Arctic*. Then on 23 January 1856, *Pacific*, while crossing from Liverpool went missing without trace. She was racing *Persia* on this leg of the voyage and it is likely that, in fog, she struck an iceberg, for when *Persia* finally reached New York, she not only reported ice but showed visible signs on her plates of having encountered it.[60] This was the beginning of the end of the Collins line. Congress immediately reduced the subsidy in 1856 and discontinued it completely in 1858; the *Adriatic*, costing $1,200,000, after making only one or two voyages had to be sold to meet the claims of creditors and finally, the whole line collapsed in financial ruin.[61]

IV SECRET AGREEMENT BETWEEN CUNARD AND THE COLLINS LINE: THE FIXING OF RATES AND POOLING OF EARNINGS

There was, however, another side to this struggle between the Cunard Company and the Collins line. The facts, so far described, have always been generally accepted as a logical interpretation of events. A recent discovery of key documents proves that far from engaging in a life-and-death struggle, the two companies had a secret working arrangement for the pooling of earnings on the carriage of passengers and cargo. The arrangement did not obviate the possibility of competition in service between the companies, but it helped to maintain levels of rates and iron out fluctuations in earning capacity.

As we have already seen, Samuel Cunard, by the late 1840s, was alive to the prospective threat of competition from other steamships on the North Atlantic. Though he was not greatly perturbed by the incursion of steamships belonging to French companies – 'their ships were built as men-of-war and will be strong and heavy and not fast'[62] – he was much more apprehensive of the effect of competition from American companies particularly from the newly created United States Mail Steamship Company. On 1 May 1847 he said, '... the American ships will be different. They will introduce all our improvements together with their own.'[63] This forecast was correct particularly with regard to carrying capacity, motive power and passenger accommodation. 'We shall also have national prejudices to contend with', added Cunard, 'so that every attention will be required to meet them; but I do not despair of getting our fair share and the intercourse between the two countries will yearly increase.'[64] Again, he was correct in his assessment, although the fair share of the traffic was to be achieved by agreement rather than by the cut and thrust of rate warfare. The clue to future policy lay in Cunard's final paragraph. 'It will behove us to think of any measures that may be considered improvements as the Americans will be alive to everything.'[65]

At a somewhat later date when the ships of the United States Mail Steamship Company (the Collins line) were beginning to threaten Cunard's position, Charles MacIver recalled Samuel Cunard's words. It was impossible, at the beginning of 1850, for the British ships to match the technical superiority of the new Collins ships, *Atlantic* and *Pacific*, and MacIver had to resort to other methods as a means of ameliorating the sharpness of competition. Accordingly an agreement was reached and signed on 29 May 1850 (to operate as from 25 May) between Charles MacIver, representing Cunard and Messrs Brown, Shipley and Co., representing the Collins line.[66] The essential clauses provided for the fixing of minimum rates on the carriage of both passengers and cargo: £35 for adult First Class cabin passengers and £20 for Second Class passengers from Liverpool to America and $120 and $70 respectively from America to Liverpool.[67] Each company was permitted to charge higher rates and retain the difference; the prohibition applied only to charging a lower rate than that agreed. The rate for cargo was fixed at £7-7-0 per ton including primage; individual parcels not paying less than 10 shillings and all parcels paying less than 21 shillings had to be prepaid.[68] The most interesting part of the agreement, however, was that concerned with the pooling of earnings in order that subsequent allocation might be adjusted equitably in accordance with variations in the earning capacity of the steamships. This device became standard practice during the latter part of the century, the working of this particular agreement was probably one of the first, if not the very first, of its kind between rival steamship companies on the North Atlantic.

It was accepted that the American ships had a greater capacity for the carriage of passengers and cargo than the Cunarders and that there were balancing advantages and disadvantages. The British ships, because of their high reputation in Liverpool, were likely to carry more and consequently earn more on westbound passages whereas the American ships, because of their high reputation in New York, would probably have an advantage on eastbound voyages. For these reasons a pooling arrangement was established based on a triple voyage pattern. On the westward route the earnings from cargo and passengers of one American ship were to be set against those of two British ships; on the eastbound route the pooling arrangement applied only to the carriage of passengers.[69] If the gross annual earnings of the American ships were less than one-third of the aggregate of all the voyages of the two companies, Cunard was required to pay to the Collins line 'such sum as shall increase the gross receipts of the American company to one-third of such aggregate'.[70] On the other hand, if the American ships earned more than one-third of the aggregate receipts, the American company would pay to Cunard 'such sum as shall increase the gross receipts of the British company to two-thirds of the aggregate'.[71] The receipts from the carriage of specie and other goods paying an *ad valorem* freight were to be simply divided, one-third to the American line and two-thirds to Cunard 'without reference to the carrying capacity of any of the vessels'.[72] A fairly generous allowance of £7 for each passenger was to be deducted from the excess account 'comprised in such excess for the expense of provisions and keep' and two shillings was also allowed per ton of cargo 'for the expense of loading'.[73] Finally, it was agreed that any transhipment cargoes from MacIver's Havre steamers carried westwards in American ships should be so carried free of managerial charge. The freight collected on such cargoes was to be placed to the credit of the Havre steamers. As a *quid pro quo* the Cunard Co. agreed to credit their transhipment of Havre cargoes in the same way and add the receipts from this trade to those collected on cargo from Havre to Liverpool . . . 'if any profit shall appear thereon (after charging the current expenses of working) such net profit shall be divided between the American company and the British company rateably and in proportion to the number of voyages performed'.[74] In case of any loss being incurred in the operation of the Havre steamers, it was agreed that Cunard should be solely responsible for coverage. In other words, the Agreement provided for a semi-pooling arrangement on the working of the Havre steamers as well as that upon the working of the trans-Atlantic ships.

This Agreement was operative from 25 May 1850 to 1 January 1852; it was renewed and lasted until 24 February 1853 when it was again renewed and revised. The last settlement was made on 31 March 1855.[75] By the following year the loss of *Pacific* made it difficult for Collins to adhere to the terms of the Agreement and

MacIver, on behalf of the British company, agreed to a suspension until the new Collins liner, *Adriatic*, could be put upon the berth.[76] In fact, the Agreement was never again renewed for, as we have seen, Collins was shortly to be engulfed in financial difficulties and finally forced out of business. Shortly before this happened, however, there is evidence that, in 1857, both Collins and Cunard were beginning to feel the effects of competition from German lines and they were forced to reduce rates for cabin passengers from £35 to £30.[77] Nevertheless, for a period of five years, the two supposedly rival steamship companies worked in reasonable harmony agreeing freight and passenger rates and ironing out inequalities arising from differences in service and tonnage discrepancies. In historical terms, the existence of such an agreement is most important as it overturns preconceived ideas about the nature of the competition supposedly existing between Cunard and the Collins line. Furthermore, if in the strict sense of the term, this Agreement cannot be considered as a Conference arrangement, the details of its operation were certainly embodied in many later Conference agreements. The conclusion must therefore be that both British and American shipowners were alive to the means whereby competition might be alleviated and that Cunard management, in particular, was aware of methods designated to offset the worst effects of competition and was, perhaps, in advance of other British steamship managements at this precise date.

It is fortunate that sufficient material has survived for us to examine the working of the Collins–Cunard agreement. There were times when each accused the other of not abiding by the terms. On 13 December 1853 James Brown, President of the American company, wrote complaining that Cunard had put on a screw ship in direct competition with *Atlantic*, delivering goods in New York at a cut-price of £3 per ton whereas the agreed rate at that time was £5.[78] Brown was even more outspoken at the prospect of a second Cunard screw ship being run in competition with *Pacific*. 'I have seen Mr Collins', he added, 'and he agrees with me that if Mr MacIver pursues this course we see no remedy but dropping our rate for freight, as it will not do to come away with but half cargo. We desire to act in good faith and each expects the same from Mr MacIver.'[79] The fact that the Cunard screw ships were despatched to Jersey City rather than to New York did not dispel the suspicion in Brown's mind that MacIver was attempting to extract an unfair advantage and, in so doing, was setting aside the terms of the agreement. After further remonstrations, the screw ships were withdrawn and harmony was restored. On the reverse side of the coin, MacIver had occasion to complain that the Americans were breaking the passenger agreement. He discovered that American passengers from New York were being offered cut rates as an inducement to travel on Collins rather than on Cunard ships. Alternatively, when cut rates were agreed the Collins line sometimes charged full rates without declaring them. 'See whether you can devise a plan', wrote MacIver to F. A. Hamilton, a signatory to the original agreement, 'to put our passenger arrangement on some such basis as the cargo ... for it is quite evident to me that under no circumstances that I can contemplate would our Company be likely to be worse off without an agreement at all than with the present. No bargain can be expected to exist which is not to conduce to mutual benefit.'[80] Despite such outbursts the operation of the Agreement seemed to work to the satisfaction of both companies. Competition, apart from that in service, was reduced to a minimum and earnings were maintained as the figures show:

EARNINGS FROM NORTH ATLANTIC SHIPS

Year	Earnings by Cunard £ s d	Earnings by Collins line £ s d	Total £ s d
1850 To 31 December	115 485 9 10	62 351 16 0	177 838 5 10
1851 To 31 December	218 729 5 1	141 402 19 0	360 132 4 0
1852 To 31 December	233 477 2 6	162 707 12 1	396 184 14 7
1853–4 1 April–31 March	323 509 10 6	215 733 14 9	539 243 5 3
1854–5	311 685 13 3	219 227 8 11	530 913 2 2

Source: MIP Earnings from Atlantic ships.

The yearly settlements were variously adjusted in relation to changing circumstances. In 1851, for example, there were months when British ships ran a weekly service and American ships a fortnightly service. This pattern necessitated some change in the distribution of earnings.[81] Between 1854 and 1855, a distinction had to be made to cover differences in sailing schedules for periods when both companies ran ships on their regular days from each side and when both companies ran ships on alternate weeks from each side.[82] The Havre agreement was also modified from time to time as in 1850 and 1853–4 when it was claimed that certain ships had been guilty of 'shutting out British goods'.[83]

After making allowances for such variations, the pooling arrangement showed the following results. In 1850 the estimated one-third share of joint earnings amounted to £59,279. To this amount had to be added some £4500 representing one-half of the surplus on the Havre trade (instead of the one-third as agreed) as a consequence of 'one of the ships shutting out British goods'.[84] The portion due to the Collins ships was, therefore, £63,779. Their actual one-third share of the earnings amounted to £62,351, so that the British and North American R.M.S.P. Co. (Cunard) had to pay the United States Mail S.S. Co. the sum of £1427.[85] In 1851 a balance of £13,184 was due to the British company on the working of the schedule whereby the American ships ran a fortnightly and the British ships a weekly service. Against this, however, had to be set £2348 due to the American company for the alternate weekly service.[86] This left a balance of £10,836 from which amount had to be deducted a sum of £4078 representing freights on goods from Havre allowed by Charles MacIver.[87] The net balance payable to the British company on the year's working was, therefore, £6758. After making provision for a similar range of adjustments, the balance due to the British company was £5215 in 1852, and, under the revised agreement, the sum of £5000 to the British company in each of the years 1853–4 and 1854–5.[88] This must surely imply that the American ships had a decided superiority in speed and service over the Cunarders despite the fact that in aggregate terms the American company continued to maintain their share of approximately two-fifths and the British company three-fifths of the total trade by value.

So ended an exciting and, as it turned out, a not-unprofitable chapter in Cunard's management of the North Atlantic trade. For the Collins line the story had an unhappy ending; Cunard, on the other hand, had greatly strengthened its position on the North Atlantic. The Company was secure in the monopoly of its mail contract and had greatly improved the technological direction of its shipbuilding policy. Its prestige, based on regularity of service and the safety of its ships, had been fortified. It remained for management to direct resources into new and lucrative trades in order that earning capacity might increase with the growth of new trades and new opportunities. In this context, it was a logical and, perhaps, an inevitable decision to take the Company into the emigrant business.

V CHARLES MACIVER'S MANAGEMENT OF THE SHIPS

In the exercise of this increasing power, the scope and quality of managerial responsibility were prime factors. Sir Samuel Cunard (knighted in 1859) and his son Edward, took control of the Halifax, Boston and New York end of the business. They were responsible for eastbound cargoes and passenger bookings together with the servicing of the ships in Canadian and American ports. They also represented the Company in all negotiations with the American Government relating to the operation and renewal of mail contracts. Charles MacIver appears to have exercised sole control in Liverpool with regard to the servicing and management of ships, though he obviously had, during the 1860s and 1870s, a wider responsibility over shipbuilding policy and a continuously increasing direction of rate-fixing and allied commercial matters. The Burns brothers (and later George's two sons John and James Cleland) were concerned with ship construction and the often tedious business of negotiating successive mail contracts with the British Government.

In the realm of safety at sea, discipline and general ship management, Charles MacIver was given a wide discretion from a very early date. 'We rely on your keeping every person attached to the ship', he wrote in his orders to captains in 1848, 'both officers and people throughout the several departments, up to the highest standard of discipline and efficiency which we expect in the service.'[89] While admitting that the charge of the ship was put in the hands of the captains, he proceeded to enunciate certain limitations to the free use of authority. The speedy and safe delivery of the mails was given first priority. 'You must not stop or delay the ship on the passage for any purpose, without previously consulting the Admiralty agent and having his sanction. Treat the Admiralty agent as a respected passenger' . . . 'The mails require the captain's best attention. Have them always ready to hand at the respective ports in England and in America as the first duty after the ship is secured.'[90] Again, while the safety of the ship at sea was acknowledged to be the responsibility of the captain, Charles MacIver did not scruple to issue precise instructions on this point. 'The trust of so many lives under the captain's charge is a great trust. It will require great vigilance day and night.'[91] Other precautions listed were concerned with the prevention of fire both at sea and in dock. In the maintenance of strict voyage schedules it was essential that personnel should be trained to the highest pitch of efficiency. 'Good steering', it was stated, 'is of great value. Pick out some of the best helmsmen for this duty. Let them steer the whole voyage out and home – such sailors to be paid five shillings per month extra wages ranking as quartermasters – but not to be so rated in the ship's articles.'[92] Canvas was not to be used except for the purpose of steadying the vessel in a gale. Furthermore, the officer on watch was required to count the revolutions of the engines every two hours.[93] Amidst a host of further instructions relating to the management and discipline of the crew, the cleanliness of the ship and the maintenance of adequate ventilation, MacIver laid great stress on the safeguarding of vessels when icy conditions prevailed at Boston and New York. The frequent use of soundings was another matter which greatly exercised MacIver's mind. 'It is to be borne in mind', he wrote, 'that every part of the coast board of England and Ireland can be read off by the lead and ships from abroad making their landfall should never omit to verify their position by soundings. But masters eager to obtain the credit of making a short passage rather than lose a few minutes in heaving the ship to, will run the risk of losing the vessel and all the lives on board.'[94] It must not be forgotten, however, that such instructions, however wisely and carefully prepared, could not have been effective without the full co-operation of masters of Cunard ships. In this context, the name of Captain Judkins, Master of *Persia* and later Commodore of the fleet, needs to be mentioned. He served for thirty years and acquired a reputation, second only to that of Charles MacIver himself, for devotion to the interests of his Company.[95]

Enough has been said to underline the careful attention to detail, having as a prime objective the safety of the ships at sea and the preservation of life on board. In 1848 Cunard, in an endeavour to prevent collisions, introduced a system of lights, green on starboard, red on port and white at the masthead, a system which was subsequently adopted by the Board of Trade.[96] In the matter of working out safe tracks for the ships to sail on, Charles MacIver was insistent that everything possible should be done to avoid ice and icebergs during the winter and spring months. The disaster to the Collins ship, *Artic*, inspired Lt M. F. Maury of the United States Navy to publish in 1855 a statement about steamship lanes.[97] His suggestions were adopted by order of the American Government, as a means of preventing collisions in fog. The outward lane lay to the north beyond the influence of the Gulf Stream, the homeward lane to the south in the strength of the current.

There is some evidence that the Cunard ships, under MacIver's instructions, were following so-called safe tracks some years before Maury's plans were published.[98] Writing to Samuel Cunard in 1850, he confirmed the practice of following safe routes.[99] Some twenty-five years later, in 1875, MacIver attempted to obtain a more general acceptance of safe routes by other shipping companies. He drew up a series of tracks which Cunard ships were, henceforth, to follow and the added safety which was implicit in these negotiations encouraged many other British lines to follow suit.[100] It was, however, more difficult to obtain co-operation from foreign companies. Accordingly, it was not without some feeling that T. A. Bellew, Secretary to the Cunard Board, wrote to the Board of Trade: 'They (the directors) have no doubt whatever that if all vessels confine themselves to one specified course for the outward and another for the homeward voyage, for all seasons of the year, the chances of collision would be most materially diminished.'[101] He added that some years previously (i.e. 1875) after having failed to secure unanimity of action among the lines, Cunard had published the routes followed by their ships. 'I am to state', he concluded, 'that whether adopted by other lines or not, the Cunard Company intend continuing the route which 38 years of experience has proved safest for their steamers.'[102] Despite continuous efforts to establish a firm agreement between maritime nations, no decisive step was taken until 1913–14 when a more precise definition was given to a series of safe tracks.[103]

Finally, it was in the economical management of the ships that Charles MacIver's personal characteristics were consciously demonstrated. In this function he was both strict and fair though his general outspokenness often earned for him something more opprobrious than the title of martinet. There are many examples of his forthright directives but two will suffice for our purpose.

Having laid down a series of regulation bills of fare for officers and crew, he was, on occasion, highly incensed when variations occurred. On 20 January 1847 he wrote generally to the officers' mess enclosing the regulation bill of fare. 'There has never been any other', he stated, ' . . . each of the officers had better make up his mind whether that bill of fare is agreeable to him or not. I shall be very happy to receive the resignation of anyone who is not satisfied with it.'[104] He was at pains to clarify his determination. 'Wherever I find a set of men', he added, 'rating themselves only by what they can stow away in their bellies, I have *prima facie* evidence that they are not the men for the British and North American Royal Mail service.'[105] In particular the Christmas festivities on board *Cambria* greatly outraged MacIver's sense of propriety. 'Disgraceful to the parties concerned', was his comment, 'wanton and extravagant waste of the Company's victualling stores and subversive of specific rules.'[106] Accordingly, he ordered that full charge at passenger rates be made to officers and crew 'together with the wines drawn on that day' as a cover for the 'uncalled for' expenditure.

On another occasion he learned that the seamen both ashore and afloat had requested a half day's holiday on Saturday. Writing to Captain Leitch he expressed himself on this issue. 'With vessels getting ready to sail on Monday . . . it follows that the services of men who choose to make a holiday of Saturday after 1 o'clock have to be supplied by others who may not be seamen, as the world has to go round all the same, notwithstanding the few who would like it to stand still at 1 o'clock on Saturday.'[107] He reminded the captain that from the moment a seaman signed articles he came under the jurisdiction of the 'Mercantile Marine Act' and that consequently, he could not be absolved from any duty as and when the need arose. 'My own time of working is nine hours a day without a break for meals or anything else and that Saturday, from the circumstances of vessels sailing early in the week, is one of the busiest days . . . It goes to show that if this Saturday's work were neglected by me and half-holiday reigned through every department, there would be many hands left idle and with nothing to do on more days than Saturday.'[108]

Against such a man few could prevail. His strongly held business principles became an inflexible guide to conduct and it was probably for this reason that W. B. Forwood pronounced him to be one of the outstanding shipowners of the 1850s and 1860s.[109] Charles MacIver undoubtedly stamped the imprint of his personality on the course of Cunard's shipping policy for nearly forty years. To him must be ascribed a major part of the success and, perhaps, not a little of the failure during this period. Without his strict guidance over the management of ships and the direction of commercial affairs, the Company would not have acquired the merited reputation and high prestige based on the quality and safety of its service.

VI JOHN BURNS AND THE NEW MAIL CONTRACT

By comparison with Charles MacIver, the managerial function of the Burns brothers was less dramatic. Preoccupied as they were, in Glasgow, with the management of their own coastal shipping interests, they were outside the main stream of commercial events stemming from the rapid growth of Liverpool's trans-Atlantic trade. Nevertheless, their experience as shipowners, coupled with their proximity to the Clyde yards, gave scope for their administrative skill in directing Cunard's shipbuilding policy. This function, however, had always tended to be circumscribed by the requirements laid on the Company by the terms of successive mail contracts. Accordingly, George Burns (and later, his sons John and James Cleland) had, perforce, to maintain a close liaison with government departments in negotiating terms concerning both size and speed of ships and the financial guarantee for the maintenance of mail services. Their long experience as shipowners undoubtedly gave them an advantage in this particular aspect of Cunard management. In this context, the events which occurred between 1866 and 1869 concerning the renewal of Cunard's mail contract, throw considerable light on the nature of John Burns's function as a manager.

It is not necessary to go into detail about the protracted negotiations between the British and United States Post Offices to secure a lowering of postage rates. A principal cause of difference had been concerned with the actual amount to be paid for the sea postage. Rowland Hill had requested 4¢ for the sea carriage since, in his view, the subsidy paid to Cunard 'much exceeded the postage'.[110] It was not until 1867 that agreement between the two Post Offices was reached; a combined rate of 6d was to be charged on letters sent across the Atlantic, a rate which went into effect on 1

January 1868.[111]

This charge of 6d did not satisfy the opponents of mail subsidies. They contended that large subventions hindered the acceptance by government of the principle of cheap ocean postage and urged the Post Office to carry letters by any ship willing to carry mail at cheaper rates. These views were strongly expressed in the evidence before the Committee of 1869 set up to enquire into the contracts recently negotiated with Cunard and Inman.[112] These two companies had combined to obtain a fixed subsidy in reply to the request of the Post Office for tenders on the actual mail carried. In fact, the National and Guion Lines had offered to carry the mails virtually for a 1d per ounce (i.e. a rate of 1d a letter) but the Treasury rejected both submissions.[113]

It will be remembered that since 1847 Cunard's annual subsidy for the carriage of Atlantic mails amounted to £173,340. On 8 February 1866, the Postmaster General wrote to the Lords Commissioners to the Treasury stating that the contract for the conveyance of the North American and Bahamas mails was terminable in January 1868 (if 12 months notice be given to the contractors immediately after the 1st January 1867'.[114] In a subsequent communication dated 4 April 1866, the Commissioners were authorised to inform Burns, MacIver and Cunard that notice of termination would be served upon them. The Government had decided to throw open the new contract to competition and to dispense with the old type of subsidy.[115] Henceforth, as already stated, payment was to be made in accordance with the weight of mail carried. 'Payment should be made for the mails', it was stated, 'equal to the whole sea postage if the voyage be performed in a certain time, and equal to a smaller sum according to a fixed scale in cases of overtime.'[116]

This change of attitude on the part of government came as an unwelcome surprise to the Cunard partners. The fact that they had brought new ships into service and were in process of laying down others capable of meeting the requirements of the mail contract, is evidence of anticipation that a renewal would be made in their favour. John Burns strenuously opposed any alteration to the principle of a contract system on the grounds that only because of an annual subvention guaranteed for a term of years, could shipowners devise and continue a systematic shipbuilding policy. In addition, the proposal to open up the mail service to competition for government assistance was a direct threat to the privileged position which Cunard had held since 1840.[117]

In the event, a temporary compromise was reached. A contract was negotiated with the Postmaster General for a period of one year beginning on 1 January 1868, whereby Cunard, in return for a payment of £80,000, was to continue the carriage of mails to New York and Halifax. At the same time, however, the principle of throwing open mail services to competition was implemented by the introduction of sea postage contracts with the Inman line and with North German Lloyd.[118] The Cunard partners were not only apprehensive about their traditional role as carriers of mails following the prospective termination of this one year contract, but were alarmed by the support which the Government were now prepared to give to their rivals. The effect of these events was to induce a reappraisal of policy which, in the short run, led to a consideration of the complete abandonment of mail services.

After a consideration of all the implications of the new proposals, therefore, the Cunard partners decided not to submit a tender for a new contract after 31 December 1868.[119] The background to this decision has to be traced over a period of two preceding years. In a subsequent letter of explanation to the Post Office, John Burns made it clear that he had consistently advocated continuation of mail contracts involving direct payments to the Cunard Company, in contradistinction to payment for sea postage.[120] If such contracts were brought to an end, it would be 'futile to expect us, or anyone else, to go on building expensive and powerful steamships only suited to the special requirements of that service'.[121] The partners were forced to take unprecedented action when, on 10 April 1866, notice had been received informing Cunard that it was the intention of the Postmaster General to terminate their existing contract on 31 December 1867. 'When we received that letter', wrote John Burns, 'the *Russia*, specially built for the mail service, was in course of construction. She was completed in May 1867; but on our receiving the intimation referred to, no other course was open to us but to prepare ourselves for a total abandonment of the contract service upon the date mentioned and simultaneously to relinquish all idea of building any more *Russia*'s.[122] This statement might well provide a reason for the words 'Royal Mail' having been omitted from the title of the new company created in 1867; it certainly provides additional evidence of the influences directing Cunard's shipbuilding policy.

The Post Office were both surprised and perturbed by Cunard's refusal to tender. On 24 October 1867 the Postmaster General wrote to the Lords Commissioners of the Treasury summarising the existing position.[123] There were four regular mails each week between Britain and the United States; Tuesday outward from Southampton by North German Lloyd; Thursday outward from Queenstown by the Liverpool, New York and Philadelphia Steamship Co. (Inman line); Friday from Londonderry by the Montreal Steamship Co. and on Sunday from Queenstown by Cunard. The homeward mails from America were carried by Cunard on Wednesdays; on Tuesdays by North German Lloyd; on Saturdays by Inman and the Montreal Steamship Company. It was obvious that if Cunard withdrew from this pattern of services the balance of regular mail deliveries would have been greatly disturbed. Representations were accordingly made to John Burns that Cunard should tender on the basis of a subvention rather than on that of payment for sea postage.

As a result of this less rigid attitude on the part of the Post Office, John Burns was able, without embarrassment, to submit a tender on behalf of Cunard. He insisted on a contract similar in form to those which had previously been negotiated.[124] As a *quid pro quo* for concessions in this matter, he was forced to offer a service at a greatly reduced subvention and a reduction in the term of the contract from ten to seven years. Referring to this offer the Postmaster General wrote 'they (Cunard) are, in fact, now paid at the rate of 11s 4d per mile, but the sum which they ask would give (when the Halifax service is abandoned) 6s per mile'.[125] He concluded his remarks with the warning that if the Cunard offer were to be rejected, the new arrangement beginning in mid-winter would place the other tendering companies at 'an even greater disadvantage than in the summer. I beg very earnestly to advise acceptance of the offer of Messrs Cunard, Burns and MacIver conjointly with the tenders of North German Lloyd and the Liverpool, New York and Philadelphia Steamship Co.'[126] This advice was taken and three contracts were issued to take effect from 1 January 1869.

John Burns had thus been successful, at least on behalf of his own company, in negotiating for the maintenance of the annual mail subvention, albeit at a greatly reduced amount. The new Cunard contract embraced a service twice a week from Liverpool, calling at Queenstown, by vessels 'of not less than 2,000 tons, having a speed of 12 knots'.[127] This was an undoubted advantage as the ships of the Atlantic and Mediterranean companies were now being worked in common. Thus, some of the smaller Mediterranean ships could, on occasion, be used for the carriage of mails. For Inman, the contract required a service of once a week from Liverpool, calling at Queenstown, with ships of similar tonnage and speed to those used by Cunard. Both contracts were to run for a period of seven years with a year's notice of termination. The respective subventions were £70,000 a year to Cunard for a twice weekly service and £35,000 to Inman.[128] The contract with North German Lloyd, however, was different in every respect. It provided for a weekly service from Southampton by means of 'good substantial and efficient steam vessels of adequate power and speed'.[129] It was terminable at any time on six months notice served by the Postmaster General on the contractors. The payment to the contractors was based on the weight of mails carried, viz. 1s for every ounce of letters, 3d for every pound of newspapers and 5d for every pound of book packets or packets of trade patterns conveyed by their vessels.

In reviewing the conduct of these negotiations perhaps the last word may be left with John Burns. It is obvious that he was not satisfied with the drastic reductions in the subvention but 'there was a certain degree of stability in the proposal which was acceptable to us, inasmuch as it enabled us as prudent men, to contemplate the building of steamers which would meet the exigencies of the public service'.[130] He was, however, still apprehensive about the length of the contract which had been reduced to seven years duration. In his opinion, seven years was not long enough to lay down ships specially adapted for postal requirements. In this view he was strongly supported by William Inman.[131] Finally, one may judge the nature of John Burns's own function in relation to that of his partners. 'Now as regards myself', he wrote, 'I am perhaps, the only one of our firm who most tenaciously clings to a contract service, influenced in some degree by my being individually so mixed up with the negotiations which have led to the continuance of the contract service.' . . . 'As long as my exertions are of use', he concluded, 'in tending to bring about arrangements for the material advantage of my partners, and the public service in this matter, I shall steadily continue my endeavours.'[132]

VII FINANCIAL PROGRESS AND GROWTH 1840–80: THE ASSUMPTION OF CONTROL IN NEW HANDS

How can one measure the extent of the Cunard Company's growth during the first forty years of its history? Unfortunately, there are no series of accounts or other allied statistical sources of evidence to enable precise calculations to be made. One has, therefore, to collate various isolated facts in an endeavour to arrive at a conclusion.

In 1840 the Company owned 4 ships of 8200 tons displacement. By 1880 the fleet had grown to 28 ships of 136,493 tons displacement and of these 19 were operating services on the North Atlantic and 9 to the Mediterranean.[133] In capital terms, the rate of progress since foundation in 1840 had been both continuous and reasonably consistent with Cunard's widening range of activity. At the general meeting held on 11 July 1844, the stock had been valued (against an authorised capital of £300,000) at £248,400, giving a share value of £82 16s 0d.[134] By 31 December 1879, the value of the Company's property (including the fleet) had reached £1,369,034 against a subscribed capital of £1,200,000.[135] This gave a share value of £456 7s. on the original basis of calculation. In actual fact, as shown in Chapter 1, the original 3000 shares had become concentrated in the hands of the Cunard, Burns and MacIver families and, by 1880, consisted of 60,000 shares of £20 each. Whatever criterion of measurement is used, the capital stock of the Company had been increased something more than fourfold.

Another useful, though strictly limited, indicator of Cunard's business activity can be gauged from the receipts from the services which the ships operated. By 1879 there is a fuller statement of profit and loss for the two main sections of the Company's business; though this particular year cannot be regarded as representative of normal trading as it coincided with the end of a prolonged depression in the emigrant trade. In the Prospectus for 1880, the accountants stated that in the preceding eleven years there had been a net return of 8 per cent per annum after allowing for insurance, maintenance and depreciation charges.[136] The return for 1879 was only marginal. Nevertheless, the figures quoted for this latter year are interesting if only for the details given on page 55.

To obtain a closer approximation of the profitability of each service, one would need to allocate the remaining income of £51,500 between the services according to their entitlement and, on the

Receipts 1878-9

From:	£	s	d	£	s	d
Atlantic trade	489 139	5	2			
Mediterranean trade	227 462	11	7			
Havre trade	35 774	9	2			
				752 376	5	11

Other income:			
Postal service contracts	25 085	17	10
Government charters	21 898	17	0
'Marathon' voyage for White Star Company	1 131	9	6
Commissions, etc at Havre	3 433	5	1
Total Income	£803 925	15	4

Expenditure 1878-9

From:	£	s	d	£	s	d
Atlantic trade	478 503	7	9			
Mediterranean trade	170 188	0	1			
Havre trade	37 276	12	6			
				685 968	0	4

Other expenditure:						
General administration at home and abroad:	£	s	d			
Office expenses	24 986	13	2			
Law expenses	73	15	6			
Managing agents	33 222	12	1			
Salaries of Secretary and marine and engineering superintendents	2 175	0	0			
				60 458	0	9
Expenses of steamers laid up				4 433	8	11
Special repairs and renewals				23 560	11	8
Collisions and other accidents				14 141	8	1
Total expenditure				£788 561	9	9

other side, charge the services with their proportion of the items shown under the expenditure £102,600. The significance of these figures, however, lies in the comparatively low net voyage profits. Whereas the Atlantic trade reflected the state of prolonged depression and returned a mere £11,000 profit, that from the Mediterranean trade was some £57,000. One possible explanation of these differences lies in the fact that the Mediterranean trade was, at this time, primarily a cargo trade, but there was the additional factor that, in the Atlantic trade, Cunard still lagged behind other companies in the carriage of emigrants. It is further proof, if any were needed, that without government charters and the mail subvention, this area of the Company's business would have been wholly unprofitable. Finally, one cannot escape the conclusion that, in relation to Cunard's future development, the Company was not replenishing resources adequately to meet increasing commitments. It is probably true that the Company had reached a point where normal depreciation and retained profits were insufficient to meet the prospective demand for the larger and more costly ships, which the Chairman envisaged would be required for the maintenance of Cunard's competitive strength in the 1880s. In this may lie the explanation why the partners sought incorporation and why they, in turn, were required to maintain their capital to the extent of £500,000 within the Company for a period of five years and also why some £533,340 of their capital stock was made available to the public after 1880.[137]

It is possible to find other corroborative evidence for the above statements. In 1870 Cunard's share of Atlantic passenger traffic was approximately 15 per cent. The ships laid down to cater for this trade, such as *Siberia* and *Samara*, were all under 3000 tons, with relatively low-powered engines. They had accommodation for about 800 steerage passengers. *Parthia*, delivered in 1871 and fitted with compound engines, but still relatively low powered, could carry 220 saloon and over 1000 steerage passengers. It was not until the depression in the mid 1870s and the ensuing sharpness of competition, that the Company was induced to alter its policy regarding the size and power of its ships. *Bothnia* and *Scythia* were the first Cunarders over 4000 tons with engines of over 3000 I.H.P.[138] They could carry about 300 saloon and 1200 steerage passengers. Though they increased the carrying capacity of the Line, their operational costs were high with the result that profit margins were very narrow. The partners were, therefore, faced with the dilemma of having to improve the quality of the fleet in order to meet increasing competition, from relatively scarce resources, at a time when the returns from trade did not justify such outlay.

Profit and loss, however, are not the only criteria by which to measure the growth and development of a shipping line. Though, by comparison with other shipowners, the Cunard partners may have exercised a conservative attitude in their shipbuilding policy, they managed to keep the fleet in a continuous, if not exciting process of reconstruction. In the ordering and management of the ships at sea and in the provision of commercial opportunity, the partners were undoubtedly efficient. This was certainly true in the 1850s in the offsetting of opposition from the Collins line and, in the 1860s, by their management of negotiations for the renewal of the mail contract. If their command over resources was diminished after 1874, this was relative only to the pressure of competition in a falling market.

Sir Samuel Cunard died in 1865, Charles MacIver in 1885 and George Burns in 1890. The control of the pioneers so efficiently exercised over a period of forty years had now passed to other hands. In the long term of historical development the accomplishment of Sir Samuel Cunard, no less than that of the other partners, was but a prelude to more than a century of further endeavour.

3
Cunard and the Emigrant Trade 1860—1900

I LIVERPOOL AS FOCAL POINT FOR THE EMIGRANT TRADE: COMPETITION BETWEEN LIVERPOOL BASED SHIPPING COMPANIES: FLUCTUATIONS IN THE TRADE

The British and North American Royal Mail Steam Packet Co., having survived the first threat of serious competition and having widened the scope of its operations through its associated company by opening up trade with the Mediterranean, now turned to the problem of increasing returns from the North Atlantic trade. It was a fact well understood by most Liverpool shipowners that the evolution of the steamship could not have taken place without the increase in demand for cargo and passenger accommodation. It was a prime reason why, in 1860, the Cunard partners decided to enter the steerage business. By that date it had become obvious that the profits accruing from the Government Contract to carry mail and that from high-class cabin traffic and freight, could not sustain expansion; that in fact, despite the hazards of competition, a more lucrative form of enterprise would henceforth lie in the carriage of emigrant traffic across the Atlantic.

The particular concatenation of circumstances which made Liverpool into a focal point for emigration westbound, has been the subject of many investigations.[1] Since 1800 the growing trade between Liverpool and the United States had vastly increased the volume of American tonnage using the port. The rising tide of cotton, tobacco and later wheat, provided a constant incentive to improve and extend the Liverpool dock estate. Furthermore, the initiation and extension of a railway network linking the port with all parts of the country made Liverpool into a terminal with advantages particularly adaptable to the changing needs of the North Atlantic sea route. This was especially true of the rail link with Hull which provided a quick and cheap line of communication for

Scandinavian and north German emigrants. Above all, however, Liverpool was now seeking every opportunity of amassing capital not only for the extension of services by sailing ship, but more particularly for transforming Liverpool into the foremost steamship owning port of the United Kingdom.[2] The growth of the American economy was a prime attribute in this commercial expansion. In the half-century from 1840, the population of the United States quadrupled and total trade increased more than sevenfold. Inherent in this growth was what has been described as a push–pull effect on the flow of emigrants from Britain and Europe to America. In the decade from 1840, total immigration into the United States amounted to 1·713 million and in the next decade, the figure had been increased by 50 per cent to 2·598 million.[3]

If Samuel Cunard had been a pioneer in creating his steamship company, it was left to others such as William Inman, Thomas Ismay and Alfred Holt, to carry the steamship revolution into a stage of technological efficiency. Thus it was that Liverpool became a centre for the development of the change from wooden to iron hulls, from the paddle wheel to the screw and in the inauguration of more powerful motive machinery through the acceptance of the compound tandem and, later, the triple expansion engine. These factors, among others, helped to turn Liverpool into a cargo and passenger liner port *par excellence*, at least during the years from 1860 to 1900.

By 1860 the Liverpool emigrant trade was not only a well-organised part of the port's activity, it had become subject to a high degree of competitive rivalry. The large returns which Inman had made from the trade since the establishment of his line in 1850, did not go unobserved and by 1871 there were four other major British lines engaged in it and sailing from Liverpool; these were Cunard, Guion, National and White Star lines. This may indicate some measure of the extent of business; but it should not be assumed from this attraction of lines into the trade that it was either an easy or highly profitable source for the employment of ships. In all aspects it was hazardous, fraught with unimaginable difficulty and on occasion, subject to financial loss. The real point to grasp is that it was the steamship which changed the whole nature, organisation and profitability of the trade. The technological revolution which followed the inception of the steamship as an ocean carrier, solved many of the problems which had previously faced the poor unfortunate emigrant.[4] By 1870 therefore, he was able to cross the Atlantic in relative safety, at a reasonable price and, in spite of the weather, in a scheduled time.[5] The provision of such service by the steamship owner required a high degree of managerial skill, the control of large blocks of capital to enable him to maintain technical efficiency in the continuous rebuilding of his fleet and competitive strength through the attraction of passengers. This latter endeavour could not always be sustained as the traffic was subject to degrees of periodic fluctuation both seasonal and long term.[6] Apart from this, the Liverpool shipowner had to meet increasing competition from German and later American lines and this, together with fluctuations in the levels of the trade, tended to keep fares low and to hamper the operation of Conference agreements. Such factors demanded newer attitudes of mind and greater flexibility in the use of resources than those customary among earlier generations of shipowners. In these circumstances, it is not surprising that there was a high rate of failure among shipping companies; of the five major British lines engaged in the passenger trade, only Cunard managed to survive into the twentieth century.

In spite of the general attributes so far mentioned, which contributed to the rise of Liverpool as an emigrant port, there were certain other complementary factors emanating from the nature of Liverpool's own trade. Until about 1855, most of the emigrant trade had been undertaken by American sailing packet companies such as the Black Ball and White Diamond lines, all of which provided bigger and faster ships sailing on regular schedules. As Liverpool's import trade grew, however, and local companies were founded to deal with it, the supply of British shipping space increased and surplus capacity westbound was available for the carriage of human cargo. This fact, coupled with a determined policy on the part of railway companies serving Liverpool to capture emigrant traffic by offering reduced rates with pre-paid tickets, led to a high concentration in the flow of emigrants through Liverpool.[7] Liverpool shipping companies also profited from the extension of Continental railway networks, though after 1880, this lucrative source of revenue was greatly curtailed by the incursion of German passenger lines, which were able to short circuit the flow to Liverpool at the ports of Hamburg and Bremen. Finally, the basic experience of men such as William Inman, T. H. Ismay and Charles MacIver senior, and many others like them, facilitated the transfer of resources from sailing ships to steamships and provided close personal supervision over the ordering and regulation of emigrant vessels.

Against this background we must now examine the various changes in the composition and level of this new and lucrative Liverpool trade. Official United States figures show that the total numbers of immigrants entering that country were as follows: 1861–70, 2·314 million; 1871–80, 2·812 million; 1881–90, 5·246 million; 1891–1900, 3·687 million.[8] Of this total of approximately 14 million, about 80 per cent came from Europe and, of these, some 5½ million sailed from British ports, Liverpool accounting for the largest flow of some 4¾ million.[9] In aggregate, therefore, (and discounting the Canadian traffic) Liverpool handled about one-third of the total entering the United States from all sources. As Robin Bastin has shown, the bulk of the emigrants, (at least until 1867) were Irish, many of whom were enabled to make the crossing as the result of remittances or prepaid passages from America.[10] Some 20,000 to 30,000 such emigrants passed annually through Liverpool. In fact, the focal point for the collection of Irish emigrants remained in Liverpool long after the introduction of the Queenstown call by both the Inman and Cunard lines in 1859, and by many other lines over the following years. For some years after 1867, however, the English rather than the Irish became the largest national emigrant group.[11] Most of the English emigrants came from urban areas; by the 1880s they were mostly drawn from the building, coal mining and metal working trades. They were undoubtedly attracted by the opportunities offered in the vast territories in the west of the United States, which, after the Civil War, were linked by trans-continental railroads and developed through the active participation of the Government.[12] After 1875, however, the heavy importation of foreign wheat produced such distress in the corn-growing areas of England, that thousands of small farmers and agricultural workers were forced to emigrate.

Apart from these categories, however, the Liverpool emigrant lists in the 1860s contained many Continentals, especially Germans and Scandinavians.[13] These were channelled through Liverpool by steamship agents in the countries of origin. In attracting emigrants they placed great stress on the shorter sea journey from Liverpool. For the Scandinavian emigrant the great advantage of the rail link between Hull and Liverpool was effective in providing a quick, short and relatively cheap route. Bastin discovered some Guion line records in Sweden which throw much interesting light on the organisation of the traffic in the 1880s.[14] As competition between the shipping companies was extremely fierce, desperate measures (often involving sharp practice) were adopted to induce intending passengers to buy through-tickets on a particular line. In country districts it was customary for the clergy to be used to act as agents for Guion.[15] The use of advertisements in terms quite at variance with reality, antedated modern practice by 100 years and was extremely forceful in its appeal. For example, the route across the North Sea to Hull was an induced crossing, but reception facilities at Hull were, more often than not, quite inadequate for the flood of emigrants continually passing through on their way to Liverpool.[16] Conditions became so chaotic that in 1882 a government enquiry had to be instituted to investigate hardship caused by lack of co-ordination between shipping and railway companies.[17] Chaos, confusion, ill-treatment and the fleecing of travellers had become synonymous with the very word emigration. Nevertheless, despite such conditions increasing numbers of travellers continued to use this route from Scandinavia to America. In 1887, 68,819 aliens arrived in Hull out of a total of 92,994 foreigners embarked from United Kingdom ports to the U.S.A.;[18] in other words, more than two-thirds of the foreign emigrants passed through Hull to Liverpool in that year.

From the point of view of the shipowner, the fluctuating character of the emigrant trade posed serious managerial problems. The whole trade depended on levels of activity in both Europe and America, its flow could not be calculated from one year to another. The graph of emigration from Liverpool to the United States shows four major troughs and three high peaks during the years from 1860 to 1900. The first trough occurred during the Civil War, the second from 1875–8, the third between 1883–6 and the fourth from 1892–7; the years of maximum activity were in the early 1870s, from 1880–2 and from 1887–91. These fluctuations were a particular feature of the traffic across the North Atlantic; the deep trough in the carriage of emigrants to America between 1875 and 1878 did not have a parallel in the emigration from Britain to any other part of the world.[19] The range of instability in the American trade from 1880 to 1886, can be judged from the following figures, the percentages given being those denoting change from the previous year.[20]

	LIVERPOOL		LONDON	
Year	To all parts	To U.S.A.	To all parts	To U.S.A.
1880	+55·5	+66·3	+18·9	+159·3
1881	+24·8	+24·6	+16·3	+ 37·4
1882	+ 2·4	− 4·1	−12·3	− 34·1
1883	−23·7	−21·2	+11·0	− 20·5
1884	−13·7	−13·4	− 8·6	− 42·4
1885	−11·1	− 4·6	− 7·1	− 74·7
1886	+31·8	+32·4	+16·0	+133·8

By virtue of the strength of Liverpool in this trade, only a comparatively small number of emigrants were carried from London; accordingly, although the percentage rate change may have been greater in some years than that for Liverpool, the percentage of fluctuation in aggregate terms affected the earning capacity of Liverpool shipowners to a far greater extent. Consequently, the Liverpool shipowner was faced with an accentuated series of problems in a highly hazardous business.

Essentially, it was the extent and timing of the fluctuation which presented the greatest threat to the earning capacity of ships. In 1863 and again, in 1880, there was an increase of 64,000 passengers; by the latter date, the largest trans-Atlantic liner could carry 300 Cabin and 1200 Steerage passengers and a round voyage to New York took about a month.[21] Furthermore, the high peak density occurred in the six months April to September. Thus it happened that, for the spring and summer months, there was usually insufficient tonnage and overcrowding in years of high emigration, whereas for the remainder of the year there was surplus tonnage, rising costs and low receipts. In years of falling emigration, this situation was greatly aggravated. In 1874 traffic from Liverpool to the U.S.A. was 55,000 less than in the previous year and ships of the White Star line were sailing two-thirds empty; in fact, all the passengers carried by the line in 1874 could have been shipped by two of the seven liners in the fleet.[22] Surplus capacity and its attribute, increasingly fierce competition, became commonplace in the North Atlantic trade after 1880. When emigration from Liverpool declined by 77,000 between 1892 and 1894, the result was a damaging rate war which, as we shall see later, cut fares to a bare cost minimum and eliminated company profits.[23] It is true that compensatory movements of emigrants eastbound from the U.S.A. to Europe occasionally took place; but inevitably such advantage was usually outweighed by larger falls in the westbound traffic. Nevertheless one cannot ignore the important element of returning emigrants if only to counter the common fallacy that all emigration was outwards from Europe. An estimate made in 1875, divided the passengers returning to Liverpool as 7 per cent tourist, 23 per cent business men and 70 per cent disappointed emigrants.[24] During the latter thirty years of the century, the flow of British emigrants back to their native soil greatly outnumbered all other nationalities. It has been estimated that from 1869, the exodus was approximately 50,000 a year, and from 1885 to 1894 approximately 100,000 a year.[25] The proportion of departures to arrivals varied with the ebb and flow of business cycles, being low in good years and high in bad years. Thus in good years, the proportion was 12 per cent (1870), 8 per cent (1882) and 21 per cent (1888). In the depression years, the proportion was as high as 47 per cent (1875) and 53 per cent (1894).[26] After 1894 one cannot exclude from the figures a fair proportion of seasonal migrants; indeed the speed and cheapness of the crossing encouraged many skilled workmen to travel in response to economic conditions and rising wage rates.[27] They usually went out in spring and returned in autumn. As round-trip passengers they represented a welcome addition to total numbers carried.

The vast numbers transported and the sharpness of competition inevitably resulted in low fares. In 1860 it cost £8 8s to cross the Atlantic, but the decline in emigration caused by the American Civil War and the rapid increase in tonnage, reduced fares to £6 6s by 1863.[28] The rate changed very little for the next twenty years. After 1883, however, fierce competition for passengers together with difficulties involved in maintaining a North Atlantic Conference, forced steerage fares down to £4 4s.[29] It was only in the 1890s that the rates were able to be raised to £5. Cabin rates were approximately double those for steerage.[30] The low rates had important implications for the Liverpool liner companies. Above all, large numbers had to be carried in order to cover rising costs and provide a modest return on capital. Herein lay an adequate reason for a steady increase in the size of ships, an increase which averaged 3000 gross tons in each succeeding decade.[31] Not all of the extra tonnage went into the provision of additional berths; a fair proportion provided luxuries in the form of libraries and smoking-rooms solely for the benefit of cabin class passengers.

Apart from the economic limitations suffered by shipowners by virtue of the need to make a fair return on capital and by the rigours of competition, there were inhibitions on the free use of resources imposed by the State. Allegations of overcrowding, insanitary conditions and poor food on board ship were given additional emphasis by more serious complaints of inhuman treatment of passengers by shore officials and ships' crews.[32] Accordingly, in 1855 the Government endeavoured to impose controls; an Act was passed regulating conditions under which passengers could be carried.[33] This was an important and comprehensive instrument in that it codified much of the existing legislation and provided the means for enforcement. Under this Act (and the amending statute of 1863) the general comfort of travellers was improved, particularly by the requirement of additional space per passenger on lower and upper decks. The reduction in the age of a state adult from fourteen to twelve years and the enumeration of two children below the age of twelve counting as one adult, had the effect of alleviating overcrowding. Not more than one person could be booked per berth apart from husbands and wives or women and children. All unmarried males above the age of twelve had to be accommodated in the fore part of the ship; separate water closets had to be provided for women and ventilation in all passenger quarters had to be of a standard satisfactory to emigration authorities.[34] Much care and thought was given to the improvement of catering arrangements, improvements which eventually made it unnecessary for emigrants to travel with their own stores of food. All aspects of shipping operation were subject to inspection, and final clearance depended on a medical check on both passengers and crew; in fact, any ship carrying more than 300 passengers was required to sail with a doctor on board.[35] These drastic provisions transformed the whole process of carrying emigrants; by implication, their very necessity gave credence to the dreadful conditions which must have prevailed before the Act was passed. In the course of time, the standards imposed by the Act of 1855 were improved by the sharpening of competition and, in addition, were further supplemented by the acceptance of similar provisions in America.[36]

There is little doubt that shipowners regarded the intervention of the State with alarm. Angry protests were raised at the extra financial burdens resulting from the imposition of regulations. 'In the case of the last new steamer which we built', stated William Inman, 'it made a difference of some eighty tons in our cargo which, at £2 per ton and other things, is about £400 per trip, and that is about £3000 per steamer.'[37] One can better understand the force of Inman's argument when applied to current conditions; for in the 1860s German ships, not subject to regulation, began calling at Southampton – competing for traffic which predominantly sailed from Liverpool.[38] Opposition among Liverpool shipowners took the form of a 'memorial' which stated quite bluntly that as a consequence of being obliged to conform to the rules and regulations of the Board of Trade – 'your memorialists are obliged to incur much greater expense in the building and equipping of their steamships than is incurred in the foreign steamships with which they have to compete'.[39] In 1874 Charles MacIver of Cunard organised a protest through the Liverpool Steam Ship Owners' Association against further regulations by the Board of Trade requiring shipowners to declare which of their passengers intended to remain in the United States.[40] This necessitated bringing passengers on board some two to three hours earlier in order to obtain the information and so increased operational costs. One direct aspect of these additional imposed costs was the elimination of many small shipping companies and the eventual concentration of business in the hands of the larger and better organised firms.

II CUNARD'S PARTICIPATION IN THE EMIGRANT TRADE AND GOVERNMENT INVOLVEMENT IN THE MAINTENANCE OF SERVICES

Having dealt with some aspects of the emigrant trade as a whole, we must return to Cunard's participation in it. As already stated, the Company entered this business in 1860. It was not a propitious time to have done so, even allowing for the fact that the trade was obviously a lucrative source of income with only one serious British competitor – the Inman line. The unsettled political situation eventually led to Civil War in the United States and adversely affected the flow of emigrants. The fall in traffic was so serious that, in August 1861, Cunard was forced to suspend the emigrant service. It was not until March 1863 that the flow of passengers began to revive, and it was only in the following years that the Company made real and determined efforts to capture a reasonable share of the traffic. Five new screw steamships – initially used in the Mediterranean trade – were put on to the Atlantic crossing; these were of 1800 gross tons, having an average speed of 10 knots and providing accommodation for about 500 steerage passengers.[41] But Cunard now had to face and solve fundamental problems relating to the size and type of ship suitable for the emigrant trade.

In the first twenty years of the Company's history, the wooden-hulled paddle steamships had been more than adequate for carrying mails and a relatively small number of cabin class passengers. Compared with this type of sedate business, entry into the steerage trade had all the marks of a reckless gamble. It demanded that capital resources should be utilised to keep the risk from fluctuating traffic at a minimum. This in turn posed the all-important question as to the type of ships to be built and when to build them. In the new circumstances, past experience was not necessarily a good criterion for management. The solution to the problem was perhaps the obvious one – that of building bigger and faster ships. During the decade of rising emigration, 1863–73, Cunard was thus engaged, adding about 44,000 gross tons to its fleet.[42] In the same period the Company sold some 20,000 gross tons, including all but one of the old paddle steamships. By the mid-1870s Cunard's Atlantic fleet was well over 60,000 gross tons, outstripping Inman's fleet by at least 20,000 tons, and the National line by 10,000 tons. Apart from *Scotia* and *Russia*, all Cunard's ships were now designed to carry steerage passengers. In other words, within the space of a dozen years, Cunard had not only changed the whole course of its policy, but had reorganised its assets so that it had become the largest and most powerful steamship company on the ocean.

It might be supposed that so great and so rapid an expansion might have led to weakness in both economic and financial terms; that, with most of its eggs in one basket, the Company would be vulnerable to depression in trade and other diverse factors affecting the flow of emigrants. The prophets of disaster had not long to wait; for between 1874 and 1878, depression in America reduced the emigrant trade to a mere trickle. All shipping companies were badly hit, but Cunard suffered much less from over-expansion than most of the other Liverpool lines. In this one fact the real strength of Cunard can be assessed.

First, the mail contract (re-negotiated in 1868) brought in an annual £70,000; a valuable and stabilising element in the Company's revenue which continued until 1876. After this date, the Post Office instituted a system of payment depending on weight of mail carried.[43] At the same time there were obvious disadvantages in being tied to a contract which demanded regular all-the-year sailings, particularly in time of falling emigration and low freight rates such as occurred after 1874. Despite this there can be little doubt that the mail subsidy helped to balance operating costs during periods of falling revenue. Second, the high-class nature of Cunard's cargo and cabin accommodation acted as a hedge against risk in time of depression. The safety and regularity of service which the Company offered, and which the owners of high-value cargo demanded, secured high rates of freight even though depressed conditions prevailed in other branches of the trade. Furthermore, although the number of emigrants carried during the 1870s fluctuated over a wide range, figures for cabin class passengers remained steady.[44] This intense competition for steerage traffic pushed fares down at one period to as low as £2 before a new rate agreement was negotiated in 1875.[45] Cabin fares, however, remained unchanged throughout the whole period. In the context of Cunard's strength in depression, the income from cabin fares remained relatively inelastic and provided an element of stability. Other companies, such as Inman, National and Guion, which depended mainly on steerage receipts, found themselves in a bleak and intractable financial position. The real advantage which Cunard had over other lines derived from the breadth of its interest in service. Any surplus capacity occasioned by depression over the Atlantic could usually be diverted to other routes; the Mediterranean, for example, where Cunard had existing trading connections. This procedure avoided the laying-up of ships and enabled tonnage to be reintroduced on the Atlantic as and when conditions improved. In particular, many of the Company's 'B' class emigrant ships engaged on the Liverpool–Mediterranean run, such as *Atlas*, *Kedar* and *Tarifa*, were well able to be adapted to this kind of transfer.[46]

Thus, despite difficulties arising from political and economic crises, Cunard's entry into the steerage trade was, for the reasons stated above, not attended by the disastrous consequences once readily anticipated by her rivals. Nevertheless, the period from 1875 to 1880 was one of enforced retrenchment. The two chief competitors, Inman and White Star, possessed better ships, superior in speed, passenger accommodation and operational efficiency. The competitive problem posed could only be solved in one way, namely, by eventual modernisation of the fleet. The adoption of such a policy could not, however, be put into effect in the conditions prevailing before 1880; in fact, only one new ship was ordered.[47] The current programme involved the selling of some 35,000 tons of old ships and the adaptation of the remainder.[48] The Atlantic ships were lengthened and refitted with compound engines. This cost approximately £100,000 a year, and so great was the strain on Company finances that further problems concerning the nature and structure of the whole Cunard organisation had to be met and solved. In order to secure more capital it was decided to form a joint-stock company in 1878 and to go public in 1880.[49]

All these changes were not achieved without considerable strain on the existing management. Despite attempts to become more competitive the essential problem could not be solved by tinkering with ships and scrapping old tonnage. The very nature of the business required a well devised plan for the continuous building of new ships. This had become obvious by the early 1880s; the only question outstanding was – how many to build and when precisely to lay them down?

There had been signs of disagreement between the managers as early as 1873 over the building policy. Giving evidence before a Royal Commission in that year, Charles MacIver stated 'any vessel that we build will carry passengers; and when we lay her down, it is not determined whether she is intended to carry passengers or not'.[50] He went on to say that he held a decided opinion that any ship over nine beams in length was a 'misconception of the science of shipbuilding'.[51] It is interesting to note that this measurement had already been accepted by another Liverpool shipowner, Alfred Holt. Charles MacIver, however, was at some pains to absolve his fellow partners from sharing his opinion. It is clear that MacIver had already been persuaded against his better judgement to accept a majority ruling, for he also declared in evidence that Cunard was then building two large ships, *Bothnia* and *Scythia*, with a length of ten beams.[52] The controversy on building policy died down during the years of depression after 1874, but when the emigrant traffic revived in 1879 the argument was renewed. Although by 1880 Charles MacIver had retired from active management his policy was continued by his two sons, Charles and Henry. Although supported by some of the shareholders they were no match for the dominant personality of John Burns, first Chairman of the new Company established after the incorporation. Burns not only persuaded the directors of the necessity to build ships capable of competing with other lines, but forced the MacIver brothers into resignation in 1883.[53] At a stormy shareholders' meeting on 11 April 1883, Burns outfaced strong criticism of such action and refused to satisfy demands for information about the disposal of the MacIver interests in the Company. Part of their holdings had in fact been purchased by Burns and some of the other directors.[54]

With the benefit of hindsight, it is now possible to state that Burns had seriously miscalculated future trends in the emigrant trade. As a consequence his policy to rebuild the fleet after 1880 led to an over-expansion of tonnage in relation to demand and, as we shall see later, to rising costs.[55] The plans laid down in 1880 envisaged the addition of 53,000 tons to the Cunard fleet by 1885. This expansion constituted the largest increase in tonnage undertaken by a British passenger company in the nineteenth century, exceeded only by North German Lloyd.[56] Unfortunately, Burn's programme was based on a misconception. It was generally anticipated that although the emigrant trade was subject to wide fluctuations, each successive peak of activity would be higher than the last.[57] This, in fact, proved to be a correct assessment, apart from the peak in 1882. Cunard's attempts to meet such expectations, however, were often beset with frustrating difficulties. Deliveries of new ships to Cunard were delayed, freight rates tumbled in 1881 and 1882, an unfortunate series of accidents and losses at sea reduced Cunard's competitive strength and, most alarming of all, a declining trend in emigration resulted in a serious short-fall in the potential carrying capacity.[58] After 1881 there were only seven years of increasing traffic against thirteen years of falling traffic. As a consequence, the following twenty years to 1900 saw diminishing receipts and ships sailing half empty. Cunard's policy of expansion had been mistimed; the

Company found itself in possession of too much tonnage in relation to demands for service and the increasingly fierce competition for declining numbers of emigrants, reduced receipts from this source and the ultimate return on capital. Between 1883 and 1886 Cunard was unable to pay a dividend, was compelled to draw on capital reserves and had to borrow from its bankers.[59] At face value these adverse facts would not seem to be supported by the general financial statements. In the twenty years referred to, shareholders received a dividend on fourteen occasions and no dividend for six years; the debenture and other debts which had totalled over £700,000 in 1885 were repaid in 1888; by 1900 the Company's liquid assets totalled £328,000, with £500,000 in reserve.[60] We shall endeavour to make a deeper analysis of this financial situation in a subsequent chapter.

The problem, so pertinent in the 1870s, of knowing what type of ship to build, had by the 1890s been solved by the inexorable pressure of competition. In the last resort the only possible way for shipping companies to remain in the passenger business was through the provision of large, fast, expensive ships, a provision which involved them in an equally expensive course of technological leapfrog. These circumstances would have presented difficulties even in times of prosperous and increasing traffic, but when set against declining trends, they proved to be insuperable in the absence of outside support. In such a context the Government was faced with the necessity of maintaining passenger and mail services within the compass of national interests. It was forced, as a matter of policy, to underwrite new construction partly in the belief that prestige was at stake and partly in an endeavour to stave off the growing threat of American and German competition. The net effect of government involvement in Cunard's affairs will be considered in a subsequent chapter.[61] It is sufficient to make the point here that without such support it is very doubtful whether Cunard could have survived the worsening conditions after 1900.

The above statements need some qualification lest a wrong impression be conveyed that Cunard acted supinely in the face of events. The two new ships, *Campania* and *Lucania*, put into service in 1893, were of 12,950 gross tons and cost approximately £600,000 per ship.[62] They were each equipped to carry 1400 passengers; assuming 11 round trips a year they had a joint carrying capacity of 30,800 passengers from Liverpool to New York. This figure was only a few thousand short of the average number carried annually by all Cunard ships during the 1890s.[63] It was obvious that within such commercial limitations working costs would be unnecessarily high and voyage profits unnecessarily low. Expenditure on coal, wages and provisions were large items of a fixed nature and could only be readily offset by a buoyant revenue. In Cunard's case, the failure to keep costs stable resulted from the decision to construct an uneconomic type of carrier. The lesson was eventually learnt, though many years were to elapse before steps were taken to eradicate this source of weakness; in the two last ships built for Cunard in the nineteenth century, *Invernia* and *Saxonia*, attempts were made to bring ship design more into line with the fundamental economic requirements of the passenger carrying business.[64] The two ships were only slightly larger than *Campania* and *Lucania* but they were five knots slower. Coal consumption was reduced by 30 per cent and more space was made available for passengers and cargo. There was also a significant increase in steerage accommodation.[65] It was a brave but ineffective experiment. The putting of these ships into service was followed by a steep rise in the price of coal, and any cost advantage was swallowed up and their erstwhile competitive strength accordingly weakened.[66] By 1905 new and more formidable pressures were reasserted. The need for high speed and greater size had returned in an accentuated form.

III CHANGES IN THE DIRECTION OF THE TRADE: EFFICIENCY AND GOODWILL OF AGENTS

The goodwill of a first class shipping line does not, however, depend entirely on its ability to meet and overcome financial and economic difficulties. A reputation for safety and reliability of service are as much the assets of a company as figures in a balance sheet. In much the same way the efficiency and reliability of agents throughout the world add to the smooth operation of a company's business. One has to consider the implications of these additional factors on the operation of a firm just as much as those concerned with speed, size and comfort of ships and the interaction of competitive pressures.

It has already been demonstrated that from the beginning of Cunard's history, the Company was fortunate in having skilled and experienced men in the management of its business. It is also generally accepted that under their inspiration the line built up an enviable reputation for dependability. The fact that Samuel Cunard himself had agreed in the first mail contract to accept a tight time schedule for his ships under heavy penalty for delay, was a pointer to the enforcement of a strict system of discipline on board as well as to a high degree of managerial efficiency in the running of the ships. As we have seen, every precaution was taken to safeguard both passengers and ships; a policy which often had a two-edged effect, especially after the entry of the Company into the emigrant trade. Indeed, the rigid insistence on safety-first became something of a standing joke among Cunard's competitors; so much so, that there is truth in the oft-quoted line that 'they never lose lives, only passengers'.[67] In purely technological terms this insistence on safety had obvious drawbacks. As a result of a constant fear that mechanical breakdowns at sea would place their mail contract in jeopardy, new types of engine were rarely installed until their reliability had been adequately tested by other lines. This may well have saved Cunard many of the initial costs of innovation, but it was a policy fraught with disadvantage in the highly competitive conditions of the 1860s and 1870s.

It is a nice point to argue whether reducing losses to a minimum and acquiring prestige for safety adequately compensated for years of low profitability. Nevertheless there is evidence that other shipping lines were envious of Cunard's record.[68] Some less generous spirits attributed Cunard's safety record to good luck rather than to good seamanship. Perhaps a more accurate explanation was given by John Burns in 1869. 'We have even made the question of profit subordinate to the question of safety, but, in the long run I believe such a policy has paid.'[69] It would undoubtedly be cynical to suggest that any company which based its policy on such a proposition would inevitably find itself in financial straits in periods of intense competition.

On the North Atlantic there had long been an inherent contradiction facing shipowners between speed and safety. Even in the days of sailing ships there had been a tendency for competing lines to regard the ocean as a race-course. The coming of the steamship, as R. G. Albion has shown, stimulated an intense interest in relative speeds and performance on both sides of the Atlantic.[70] In pandering to public interest both shipowners and ships' captains were guilty of culpable negligence. Ships on tight time schedules were driven at high speed through fog and ice-fields without due regard for hazard. The result had been a tragic series of disasters and an appalling loss of life.[71] Despite this no company was able to ignore the publicity value of an especially fast crossing. While Cunard disavowed any intention of competing for the Blue Riband, the Company was always careful to emphasise the link between fast ships and the carriage of mails.[72] In the last resort the constant demand for speed came largely as an emotional response to public opinion; for there is very little evidence that the majority of travellers were unduly influenced by it. Most of the emigrants had insufficient knowledge of the relative technical merits of ships to determine their choice; they were in no position to have clear-cut opinions about the operational skill of particular shipping companies. Bastin has shown from a survey of passengers carried in Liverpool ships in 1882 and 1883 that faster ships attracted no more bookings than slower ships of the same line.[73] Available evidence suggests that general conditions on board were much more important as an inducement than half a day clipped off the crossing.[74] On the other hand speed was important to the shipowner because it secured certain, albeit dubious, economic advantages. Fast ships might, in favourable conditions, make an extra voyage a year, lower operating costs and secure additional revenue from the carriage of extra passengers. A fleet of fast ships *caeteris paribus* might earn as much as £30,000 by way of marginal revenue. But in Cunard's case there was little correlation between revenue and the overall speed performance of its ships. The important point to notice here is that speed enabled Cunard to run a weekly service with four ships instead of five in the 1880s, three ships instead of four in the 1900s, and later, with the advent of the 'Queens', two ships instead of three.[75] This led to reductions in costs and an increase in revenue by virtue of the larger carrying capacity of the new ships.

Between 1860 and 1900 the average time of crossing from Liverpool to New York was ten days, though some ships were crossing in seven days.[76] This was an appreciable time to have large numbers of passengers under care and management. For this reason alone, good food and comfort might well be regarded as an antidote to unpleasant conditions. Inman and Guion had been the first British, and Collins the first American, companies to recognise this fact. Cunard alone withstood the demand for more luxurious treatment and remained stubbornly spartan in its provision of food and accommodation. (Witness the publicity given to these shortcomings by William Chambers and the extent of the improvement recorded by Charles Dickens between his first voyage in 1842 and his later trip in 1867–8.)[77] Small cabins, lack of public rooms and illumination by candle-light were no match for the attractive features provided for emigrants by the Inman line in the shape of saloons, iced water, set meals and information printed in three languages.[78] It took Cunard a long time to accept such frills – frills which by the 1870s were bringing to cabin class passengers conditions normally experienced in the best hotels of the time. The fact that in the early years Cunard did not offer a high degree of luxury did not unduly worry the partners; they treated complaints in a somewhat cavalier fashion: 'going to sea was a hardship', wrote Charles MacIver senior to a dissatisfied traveller; 'the Company did not undertake to make anything else out of it'.[79] On all counts this attitude was astonishing, particularly since it was made at a time when competition was acute. Such attitudes, however, were not confined solely to passengers. The Company took longer than the other Liverpool lines to bring its ships up to the standards laid down by the Board of Trade in 1881; pertinent criticism from agents was ignored and shareholders who voiced concern for the unfortunate emigrant were given short shrift.[80]

Attempting to assess this curious and peculiar facet of Cunard management one is tempted to suspect that, compared with the management of the partners before 1878, the directorate after 1880 had tended to become complacent, and that they had very little personal experience of the actual conditions on board ship. Some recognition of this fact was made by Sir William Forwood after his visit to America in 1897. He advised his fellow directors to see more of the Company's ships both in port and at sea.[81] The innate conservatism in management was also reflected in the maintenance of business methods which had changed very little over a period of forty years. The reiterated view put forward by John Burns in 1869, that emigrants would always choose the line which offered the lowest fare, may have been true in a strictly limited sense but showed some lack of perception of the nature of competition.[82] The range of fares between the major lines differed very little; real inducement was provided by such things as standards of comfort and the general treatment of passengers.

Recognition of this point came painfully and slowly to the Cunard directors. The essence of the whole argument was not that Cunard provided sub-standard accommodation but that passengers expected something better from so famous a Company.[83] Obviously some Cunard ships provided better standards of comfort than others; *Campania*, for example, was rated as a 'superior' ship and the newest Cunarders could generally be given fair comparison with the ships of the White Star Line.[84] Nevertheless it was not until 1903, when competition became really sharp, that the necessity to raise standards in both food and accommodation for steerage passengers began to exercise the minds of management. One of the most serious complaints was made by a steerage passenger after crossing on *Lucania* in 1903. His experience epitomised a growing volume of dissatisfaction. He began by stating that Cunard's agents had given him inaccurate information about the voyage; secondly, steerage accommodation was dirty, overcrowded, offensive to the smell and allocated in a haphazard manner. He also claimed quite rightly that steamship companies made more money out of emigrants than from any other class of traveller because they received less attention and were given less space and poorer food.[85] The sting came in his final criticism. He asserted that the average steerage passenger was made to feel that the 'Company was doing him a personal favour in conveying him across the Atlantic'. As with most complaints this was probably coloured by a single unfortunate experience and should not be given undue weight by way of generalisation. Nevertheless, it is perhaps significant that shortly afterwards Cunard's Liverpool traffic department was better organised and directed towards the service of the customer.[86] Furthermore, the whole agency system was reviewed, many new agents were appointed and given more precise instructions in the handling of passengers.[87] In retrospect, these changes proved to be essential preliminaries to the putting into service of the fast new liners, *Lusitania* and *Mauretania*. It was a long and, perhaps, increasingly hard struggle in an endeavour to achieve excellence in all branches of service. In the last resort, the effort paid high dividends for, in the years before the outbreak of the First World War, Cunard had established an invaluable reputation as Britain's premier passenger line.

In the business of attracting passengers, a shipping company was very largely dependent on the efficiency and goodwill of its agents. This was especially true for steerage passengers because they were generally more responsive to skilful sales talk than cabin class travellers. By 1860 Cunard had developed a widely strung system of agency business serving its needs. The most powerful agents were in New York, Boston, London, Glasgow, Liverpool, Queenstown, Le Havre and Gothenburg. As a means of facilitating its entry into the steerage trade in 1860, the Company had appointed two well-known Liverpool companies as agents. These were James Baines and Company, owners of the Black Ball line of packets to Australia and Messrs Williams and Guion, owners of the Black Star line.[88] Both companies had been engaged in the steerage trade for several years and both were established with a network of agencies in strategic ports of the world. At a time when Cunard's own agents were concerned solely with cabin passengers, the advantages of this new connection must be obvious. The two packet companies, for their part, were equally attracted by the prospect of additional revenue from agency work as they were in process of losing business to the new steamship lines.[89] In fact, Williams and Guion made such a success of recruiting steerage business on Cunard's behalf that in 1866 they decided to enter the steamship business themselves. Within four years Guion was carrying more steerage passengers across the Atlantic than Cunard.[90]

By the 1880s two new factors emerged which had the effect of increasing the importance of the agency function. There was a rapid growth in pre-paid passages and the extension in Europe of new areas of emigrant supply. In aggregate, the balance of emigration shifted from north and west Europe to central and southeastern Europe.[91] Shipping companies had, therefore, to compete for traffic in Germany, Poland, Hungary, Austria, Italy and Greece. This was heightened by the fact that in 1893 control stations had been set up on the German borders and put under the direction of the German shipping lines.[92] This had the effect of diverting traffic to these lines. Various corrective measures had, therefore, to be adopted by the British lines. An increasing number of agents had to be maintained on both sides of the Atlantic and expenditure on such service was greatly augmented. By 1890 the German line, Hamburg–Amerika had about 3200 agents in America alone;[93] throughout the 1890s Cunard spent an average of £50,000 a year on home and foreign agencies; by 1911 this figure had more than doubled.[94] Cunard had also established a special emigrant department in the Liverpool Office during the 1880s, from which information sheets, guide books and tickets were issued to agents all over Europe and America. The firm of Vernon Brown and Company of New York, specialists in emigrant business, provided a vital link between Head Office and provincial agents.[95] The files of correspondence between Cunard's General Manager, David Jardine, and Brown, contain a mass of detail on the day-to-day running of the trade especially during the difficult years of the 1890s.[96] This firm was alive to all the pressures, such as under-cutting by other lines, trends in traffic and relative competitive conditions. The exchanges between Brown and Jardine are, therefore, valuable sources of information, giving an insight into the complicated nature of the trade. They also underline the importance of employing first-class agents in the direction of such business.

In strictly managerial terms Cunard's experience in the steerage trade before 1900 was fraught with hazard and uncertainty. A case could be argued that by comparison with the efforts of their competitors Cunard's long-term decisions, based upon expectation of future profitability, were sometimes ill judged. They did not enter the steerage business until ten years after Inman and this incursion was immediately followed by years of Civil War, a period in which westward emigration from Europe was curtailed.[97] There was similar misjudgement in the early 1870s when larger carriers were put into service to cater for a rapid expansion of the trade. In fact, from 1874 to 1878 there was a steep and continuous decline in emigrant numbers.[98] Again, in the early 1890s a large capital outlay in the laying down of fast ships was followed by some years of decline in the European emigrant trade as a whole.[99] This misconstruing of events, (which was not confined solely to Cunard management, as the failure of other companies clearly illustrates) threw the whole cost structure of the Company out of gear and profitability at certain periods could not be sustained. Above all, the attitude of management towards the steerage business as a whole (particularly during the 1890s) was not always helpful. From available evidence one suspects that there were times when the carriage of emigrants was regarded as a distasteful necessity and that other considerations, excellent in themselves, such as comfort and safety at sea, had a depressive influence on potential earning capacity. That such attitudes were eventually altered was attributable to wiser management no less than to common sense; but this does not allay the possible suspicion that there were many years before 1890 when Cunard, given the more forthright policy of an Inman or an Ismay, might have captured a greater share of the market when conditions were adverse.

Against such contention must be set the fact that ships were put into service for at least twenty years. In calculating the possible return on the initial outlay of capital, some account must have been taken of fluctuation in the levels of earnings from one year to another. With the operation of fast expensive passenger liners, it may be calculated that in good years such ships would earn more than anticipated and, in so doing, would offset the results of poor years. In such a context, therefore, the timing of an entry into a trade or the introduction of new ships into a falling market had less relevance than might be supposed in the calculation of marginal profit. As we shall see later, this was certainly the case with the operation of Cunard's more powerful ships.[100] If mistakes were made in the years before 1900, their effect was much less harmful in the long rather than the short run. To Cunard's shareholders, at least, some comfort may have been derived from the knowledge that the Company's fine record and prestige in maritime terms did not depend entirely on the carriage of human cargo, though the steerage business was a most important element in earning capacity at certain periods of the Company's history.

IV RELATIVE PROFITABILITY OF THE TRADE

Having examined some of the more important secular influences affecting earning capacity in the carriage of emigrants, it is now relevant for us to determine the relative importance of such trade to Cunard's total activity. This involves some discussion of the more profitable sections of the Company's business and, by implication, some account of comparative costs between one section of the carrying trade and another. While the question of aggregate costs will be dealt with in a subsequent chapter, it is necessary here to examine their make-up in some detail. From the data it may then be possible to arrive at some conclusions about the nature and profitability of the enterprise in relation to Cunard's total commitment.

Before 1850 the number of passengers carried by Cunard was very small, being an average of seventy per ship in each direction.

In 1846 the cabin fare to Boston on a Cunarder was 39 guineas and £24 for the homeward voyage.[101] The chief reason for this difference was that, on the eastbound run, steamships had to meet stiff competition from fast sailing ships. At the same time, while Cunard was able to charge £7 a ton for cargo carried from Liverpool to New York, it was only on rare occasions that cargo could be obtained for carriage homewards,[102] and during the winter months very little cargo was carried at all. In such circumstances the mail service, supported by subvention, was of particular importance in sustaining profitability. Thus, during the conditions prevailing in 1846, the average earning capacity per voyage was made up as follows:[103]

	£
Passage receipts	4546
Cargo	1050
Mails	3295
Total	£8891

The cost of sending *Britannia* on a round trip was approximately £4200.[104] This figure included all sea-going expenses, insurance, repairs and harbour charges but did not include depreciation or interest on capital. The latter items would have brought total costs chargeable against revenue to just over £5000, an amount just about covered by passage money and freight. It is clear, therefore, that without the mail subvention, Cunard could not have returned a profit. If further proof were needed of the truth of this statement, one could cite the experience of other companies either supported or unsupported by a mail subsidy. The Great Western Company, which had no subsidy, had collapsed in 1846, as did the Collins line in 1858 shortly after its mail subvention had been halved. Thus, in the early days of steamship enterprise on the North Atlantic, government aid provided a hedge against commercial hazard.

After 1850, however, this balance in the coverage of Cunard's voyage costs was changed. The entry into Mediterranean trade broadened the scope for the allocation of resources and consequently for the offsetting of costs by virtue of a diversification of interests. Nevertheless in the Atlantic trade there was a somewhat narrower definition. The coming of iron, screw-driven ships, powered by compound engines after 1850, did much, as we have already seen, to inaugurate cheap ocean travel. These innovations, coupled with the flooding flow of emigrants westwards, gave a new emphasis to the relationship between costs and receipts. Furthermore, in Cunard's case, the very great reduction in mail subvention after 1868 meant that this part of the Company's service was henceforth barely capable of covering costs.[105] There was, therefore, very little surplus from this service for reallocation. At the same time cabin traffic remained relatively small until after 1880 and when increase did occur costs rose disproportionately to revenue for this class. This part of the trade was highly inelastic as it was influenced less by changes in the level of fares than by general conditions of accommodation, service and safety. In other words, the great changes, both technological and commercial, which took place on the North Atlantic between 1860 and 1880, are explicable only in terms of the emigrant traffic. This was especially true for Cunard in the years between 1863 and 1873 when their ships and those of Inman's line were carrying about half the passengers from Liverpool to America. It was less true when other British lines began to compete in the trade and, at a later date, when German and other Continental lines began to take advantage of the geographical change in the sources of emigrant supply.

The financial benefits deriving from this trade and the change in emphasis of a shipping company's earning capacity can be judged from a few examples. In 1861 Cunard had earned a gross revenue of £114,000 from the carriage of cabin passengers to and from America while the Inman line had received £184,000 for both cabin and steerage passengers.[106] By 1870 the four principal British lines, Cunard, Inman, Guion and National, were carrying about 90 per cent of the traffic from Liverpool. As there had been a fourfold increase in traffic since 1861, such volume ensured a gross revenue to those lines of just under £1 million from outward sailings alone, some three-quarters of this total being earned from steerage passengers.[107] By 1880 despite intervening years of depression Cunard was earning just short of £800,000 from the carriage of cabin and steerage passengers – approximately three-quarters of the gross revenue.[108] By contrast some 60 per cent of the National Line's gross revenue in 1873 came from passenger bookings; but in 1874, the first year of the depression, the percentage dropped to less than 45.[109] While freight earnings remained relatively stable, the number of passengers declined from 32,425 in 1873 to 19,088 in 1874.[110] As a result total profit fell from £148,000 to £15,000. In other words, passenger trade had become the definitive element in the National Line's earning capacity. This was also generally true of other lines and any serious fluctuation in revenue from this source was a controlling factor over the level of profit. It was because of this that the important part of any Conference agreement was that concerned with steerage rates.

There was sound economic sense in this, particularly in the context of profitability. The cost of carrying emigrants was relatively small; they were provided with a low standard diet which, according to estimates contained in correspondence between Cunard directors in 1886, averaged about one shilling per day for a single passenger.[111] Very little service was required. On *Servia*, for example, the full steerage fare was £3 3s during periods of intense competition. On a single voyage 637 adults and 38 children were carried for a total of £2014.[112] At a shilling per head for victualling for eight days, total food costs (children half-price) amounted to £263. Costs for overheads applicable to steerage service came to £45. There was an additional charge of two shillings Head Money at New York for adults amounting to £64, so that total costs chargeable against steerage passengers were £372, leaving a working profit of £1642. Although this is an isolated example, it provides some indication of what shipping companies expected by way of return from the steerage trade. In this particular case, steerage fares were very low as, in 1886, they had been pushed down by a fierce rate war. In years of higher rates, the revenue from 637 adult steerage passengers might have been well over £3000 on the outward voyage.

By contrast the carriage of cabin class passengers was individually less remunerative. Various itemised lists for *Etruria* in 1887 give the following provisions for cabin class consumption;[113] 850 lb of lamb, 350 lb of veal, 600 fowls, 300 chickens, 100 ducks, 50 geese, 80 turkeys, 200 brace of grouse, 11,500 eggs, 220 quarts of ice-cream, 1100 bottles of champagne, 2500 bottles of porter, 850 bottles of claret, 640 bottles of various spirits and 4500 bottles of mineral waters. By taking various voyage accounts for the fast ships during the 1880s, one can arrive at an average of £1600 for the food bill and £1400 for the wages bill per voyage.[114] The total of £3000 represented about 27 per cent of average aggregate costs per voyage. In the apportionment of food and wages costs, however, there was a considerable discrepancy between cabin and steerage classes. The reason for this discrepancy was that services and facilities for cabin class passengers were disproportionately high. Such things as curtains, carpets, furniture and crockery all needed frequent replacement; more staff were needed to cater for passenger needs, especially as more luxurious conditions were demanded. By 1886 just under half of an average crew of 220 for large liners, such as *Servia*, were concerned with services and catering for the cabin class.[115] This meant that from an average wages bill of £1400 per round trip, some £650 could be attributable to the maintenance of cabin class facilities. If we add £900 as the average cost of feeding cabin class passengers, the total of £1550 represents the average aggregate costs for this class or about 18·7 per cent of total voyage costs; by comparison, the proportion for steerage passengers (after making allowance for the cost of food consumed by the crew) was about 6 per cent.

There were other important factors which have to be taken into account in any consideration of the relative profitability of cabin and steerage traffic. A disproportionate amount of space had to be made available for cabin passengers. New Cunarders laid down in the 1880s provided some 60 per cent of total net tonnage for this accommodation compared with 20 per cent for steerage. Moreover the latter accommodation was usually of a temporary nature and was frequently cleared to make way for cargo;[116] cabin class space, on the other hand, was permanent. All other things being equal, therefore, cabin space was more likely to be under-utilised for longer periods. During the first three months of 1885, Cunard, White Star and Inman ships, each equipped to carry 200–300 cabin passengers, were sailing from Liverpool with an average of 50.[117] Though the lowness of this figure can be attributed to seasonal factors, it must be obvious that at such levels unit operating costs were greatly increased beyond the point where gross revenue could possibly cover them. This fact was accepted because the potential revenue provided during the summer season was sufficient to wipe out the winter losses and also secure a margin of profit.

Another relevant factor deriving from cabin class accommodation was the relationship between such accommodation and apparent obsolescence of a ship. The high rate of obsolescence was caused primarily by the constantly changing demands for cabin traffic. The strength of competitive pressure led to a fairly continuous improvement in size and design of cabins and in the level of luxury provided. It was a costly type of innovation and one which increased rather than diminished capital charges. Furthermore, more expensive cabin design and lay-out increased insurance costs. The differentiation between receipts and initial operating costs can be judged from the following figures (average receipts and costs per voyage) for the ships in Cunard's North Atlantic fleet for the three years 1884–6.[118] The year 1884 was one in which regular rate agreements were in operation, but in 1885 these agreements had been broken and a fierce rate-cutting war had developed. As we have already stated steerage rates were cut to £3 in 1885 and were not restored to £5 5s until August of that year, by which time the peak of the season had passed. These circumstances are reflected in the earnings and the profitability of the ships as shown in Table 3.1. By 1886 normal conditions again prevailed.

It must be emphasised that the figures in Table 3.1 for average voyage receipts and expenditure are for years in which the Liverpool emigrant trade was in depression. Furthermore the figures for disbursements include only initial operating costs such as fuel, wages, ships' stores, handling charges and port and general charges. They make no allowance for depreciation, insurance and other overheads. Despite this, however, certain facts emerge from a consideration of the figures as a whole which are of particular interest. At a time when Cunard was beginning to experience severity of competition in the emigrant trade, particularly from Continental lines, the balancing factors between costs and revenue were again in process of change. For the fast ships, *Umbria, Etruria, Servia* and *Aurania*, receipts from cabin passengers could generally be expected to cover initial costs, leaving those from steerage passengers and freight to return a working profit. In odd years, when there was an adverse fluctuation in passage money, both cabin and steerage receipts might cover costs, leaving freight to secure a profit on the voyage as a whole. For the rest of the fleet, under conditions prevailing between 1884 and 1886, the combined receipts from cabin and steerage rarely covered costs and it was only the freight which on average gave a first profit.

One salient point is that for all the ships in the Atlantic fleet, there was a reduction in costs between 1884 and 1886. Examination

Table 3.1

AVERAGE RECEIPTS AND EXPENDITURE PER VOYAGE
(£)

	1884	1885	1886
Umbria			
Cabin	5934	6349	11 023
Steerage	1184	1867	1816
Freight	1981	1119	1566
Voyage costs	9780	9286	8647
Profit or loss	− 681	+ 49	+ 5758
Etruria			
Cabin	—	12 078	12 653
Steerage	—	1433	1829
Freight	—	1805	1549
Voyage costs	—	9043	8777
Profit or loss	—	+ 6273	+ 7254
Servia			
Cabin	10 233	9080	6057
Steerage	1473	1784	2026
Freight	3102	2994	3046
Voyage costs	9238	8263	7667
Profit or loss	+ 5570	+ 5595	+ 3462
Aurania			
Cabin	9426	8196	6715
Steerage	1273	1853	1934
Freight	3045	2702	2785
Voyage costs	9028	8105	7687
Profit or loss	+ 4716	+ 4646	+ 3747
Gallia			
Cabin	5757	4004	2798
Steerage	852	1136	1814
Freight	2642	2455	1927
Voyage costs	6626	6052	5508
Profit or loss	+ 2625	+ 1543	+ 1031
Cephalonia			
Cabin	2096	1532	1841
Steerage	1604	1417	2118
Freight	3270	2853	2871
Voyage costs	5615	5128	4821
Profit or loss	+ 1355	+ 674	+ 2009

Table 3.1 (continued)

AVERAGE RECEIPTS AND EXPENDITURE PER VOYAGE
(£)

	1884	1885	1886
Catalonia			
Cabin	746	554	768
Steerage	1588	1328	1827
Freight	3455	3201	3189
Voyage costs	5067	4690	4558
Profit or loss	+ 722	+ 393	+ 1226
Pavonia			
Cabin	1886	1294	1473
Steerage	1669	1285	1839
Freight	2953	2756	3148
Voyage costs	6023	5313	5015
Profit or loss	+ 485	+ 22	+ 1445
Bothnia			
Cabin	2945	1351	1916
Steerage	1054	1101	1959
Freight	2788	2225	2133
Voyage costs	5452	5265	4767
Profit or loss	+ 1335	− 588	+ 1241
Scythia			
Cabin	2007	1193	1331
Steerage	1486	1435	2409
Freight	2532	2070	2089
Voyage costs	5363	4751	4675
Profit or loss	+ 662	− 53	+ 1154
Samaria			
Cabin	229	213	41
Steerage	1390	1069	477
Freight	2243	2081	2657
Voyage costs	3344	3293	3091
Profit or loss	+ 518	+ 70	+ 84

of the cost structure for the four fast ships (*Oregon* excluded), shows that while port and general charges and loading charges fluctuated within narrow limits, big savings occurred in fuel and wages. For *Umbria* there was a total reduction of £1133, of which fuel and wages accounted for £821; the corresponding figures for *Servia* were £1571 with fuel and wages showing a reduction of

£715.[119] For the remainder of the ships in the fleet, *Gallia* and *Cephalonia* may be singled out. *Gallia*'s average costs per voyage were reduced by £1118 of which £341 could be attributable to reductions in fuel and wages, and for *Cephalonia* there was a fall of £794 of which fuel and wages accounted for £340. The general inference from this must be that in times of adversity, when it became necessary for Cunard to temper costs to receipts, there was a greater margin for reduction in fuel and wages costs in the larger and faster ships than in those on the smaller.

Though these figures are those for the average per voyage, a better perspective may be gained by reference to the annual number of voyages made by each ship. *Umbria* made only 1 voyage in 1884, 2 in 1885 (the ship having been taken over by the Government for some months in this year) and 10 in 1886;[120] *Etruria*, 9 in each of the years 1885 and 1886; *Servia*, 9 in 1884, 9 in 1885 and 13 in 1886; *Aurania*, 8 in 1884, 11 in 1885 and 12 in 1886.[121] Whereas total average voyage costs for *Umbria* had decreased by £1133 between 1884 and 1886, total passage money had increased by £5721 of which £5089 was accountable from increased cabin receipts.[122] This item added to the reduction in costs more than covered the average voyage profit of £5758. In the case of *Etruria* which made the same number of voyages in 1886 as in 1885, the marginal differences were much narrower, though the receipts for the carriage of cabin passengers more than covered average costs and, in addition, contributed to more than half the average profit.[123] Despite the fact that *Servia* increased the number of annual voyages, cabin receipts (which had covered costs in 1884), fell by approximately £4000 and about two-thirds of a decreased profit in 1886 was due to a reduction in average costs and an increase in steerage traffic. A similar pattern is observable for *Aurania* which also increased the number of annual voyages. With the remainder of the ships in the fleet (*Samaria* excepted) the balancing factors were identical; the increase in the receipts from the carriage of steerage passengers coupled with a decrease in costs were sufficient to cover adverse fluctuations in cabin and freight receipts and thus enable a profit to be declared.

From the evidence so far presented, it may be deduced that by the mid 1880s the importance of the emigrant trade to Cunard's earning capacity had become less than in the early 1870s. Though emigrants were carried on the faster ships, the greater part of their revenue was derived from the wealthy cabin traveller. This is obvious from the figures given for *Umbria, Etruria, Servia, Aurania* and *Gallia*.[124] The inference must therefore be drawn that the continued high level of receipts from cabin class passengers acted as a hedge against undue fluctuations in emigrant traffic. As might be expected the slower ships carried a much higher proportion of emigrants, but freight was generally the largest item in average gross earnings. In short, the receipts from the emigrant trade were now no longer the principal determinant of profitability; this fact was obviously a source of strength in the conditions which prevailed during the 1890s. Nevertheless Cunard made efforts to increase revenue from steerage passengers as competition became more stringent. In common with other lines they introduced an intermediate class. Under normal conditions rates for this class ranged from £7 to £8 from Liverpool to New York, though at times when rate-cutting was in operation, these amounts might be reduced below £5.[125] For the extra money passengers were provided with bedding and eating utensils and greater space was allocated per person. The amenities were still spartan, but much less rigorous than those for the lowest steerage rate. In general this new class proved to be popular as many were prepared to pay a little extra to avoid the discomforts of steerage passages. Some indication of the relative importance of this new class to Cunard can be judged from the fact that, in the 1890s, it accounted for one-third of total passengers carried on the outward voyage and one-quarter on the homeward.[126]

These facts considered against the background of rising building costs per ton and high capital charges, indicate that there was very little leeway for improving levels of profitability, especially at periods of low loading capacity. From the evidence cited above, it is reasonable to assume that if the large, fast and costly ships could be run to full capacity, the better able would Cunard be to offset the effects of adverse fluctuations in both the volume of, and the rates charged for, the emigrant traffic. During the 1890s, however, the number of cabin passengers carried by all lines remained relatively stable, whereas second class and steerage fell drastically. 'The marked feature of the year', wrote an observer of the year 1894, 'was the great decrease in emigration which from Europe to New York was less than half that in 1893, and this despite a reduction of more than 50 per cent in fares during the last half of the year. The deficiency upon outward traffic alone by all lines sailing to America was upwards of £1,250,000 compared with 1893.'[127] In fact, from 1894 to 1899 the level of emigration from Britain to America was approximately half of what it had been during the 1880s.[128]

In such a context the various attempts by Cunard and other lines to secure stability of rates by means of Conference agreements, and the many endeavours by Cunard, in particular, to reduce items of expenditure, assumed a more than usual emphasis. Under conditions in which gross revenue fluctuated widely from one year to another and *average* earnings per ton changed very little, any increase in the various items of expenditure bore directly against an inelastic income factor and, as a consequence, profit margins were reduced.

We shall examine the working of the various Conference agreements and the relationship between costs and revenue in the two subsequent chapters. For the purpose of the present stage of our analysis, it is of relevance only to draw a conclusion from the changing impact of the emigrant trade upon Cunard's financial resources. As already stated, the earnings from emigrant traffic after 1860 effectively replaced the mail subsidy as a balancing factor in the profitability of Cunard's various services. By the mid 1880s steerage trade was accounting for about one-quarter of gross receipts, though if costs attributable to emigrant traffic are deducted net receipts were probably about 30 per cent of net revenue. In the 1890s, under conditions of severe and adverse fluctuation, the percentage fell to less than 15.[129] By virtue of the numbers carried and the low costs involved it was a lucrative form of service, but although it continued to be so at least until 1914 its relative importance as an element in Cunard's total earning capacity grew less with each succeeding decade after 1880. This is probably one reason why Cunard survived, whereas other companies, such as Inman, Guion and National, which were so heavily dependent on this trade, were submerged by the pressure of competition from German, French and other Continental lines.

4
Cunard and North Atlantic Conferences 1860–1914

I THE GROWTH OF COMPETITION AND THE NEED FOR AGREEMENT

The nature of the trans-Atlantic passenger trade was such that it became extremely difficult to regulate unrestricted competition. This was because conditions affecting the levels of traffic were subject to rapid and unexpected fluctuations, so that when agreement between competing lines had been negotiated, the regulation imposed quickly became out of date. The result was that Conferences proved to be fragile instruments and were generally unsuitable except for short periods when it was absolutely necessary to mitigate the effects of intense rate wars.

There were, however, two fundamental reasons why agreement was essential to a smooth working of the trade. The first arose from the necessity to secure some form of harmonious relationship between British steamship companies, especially during years of depressed trade. The prime function of a passenger Conference agreement was to ensure the maintenance of agreed levels of rates. Passenger traffic was always seasonal, being light during the winter months, particularly from January to March. It was therefore in the interests of the various lines to see that rates were maintained during the slack periods as well as during the summer season. In such circumstances competition between the British lines was based essentially on quality of service. The second reason arose from the need, particularly after 1880, to protect British lines as a whole from the incursion of Continental and American shipping interests. At first this necessity was temporary in character, but after 1900 British lines had to come to a more permanent arrangement with the Continentals. These agreements were not solely concerned with the carriage of passengers. They often included clauses fixing rates of freight on the carriage of cargo, this latter being important as a source of revenue needed to cover high fixed charges at times when receipts from passengers fell off. Nevertheless by far the most important traffic agreements were applicable to the steerage business, for it was in this branch of a company's activity (at least until 1880) that the highest rewards were gained and, conversely, the greatest loss might be sustained.

In the 1860s, as we have seen, leadership in the development of the steerage trade had come from William Inman. Recognising the strength of Cunard in such services as mails and cabin class, he concentrated his resources on the provision of adequate accommodation for the large and growing number of emigrants. He not only had a head start in this type of business, but was by nature of his experience in a strong competitive position when rival steamship companies were founded to engage in the trade. He was painstaking in his efforts to find out and meet the needs of his passengers. He welcomed technical innovation, his line being the first to operate iron-screw steamships on regular crossings; he was also one of the first shipowners to accept compound engines; he was adept in the chartering of ships to increase his carrying capacity when boom conditions prevailed.[1] It was an efficient start to a great enterprise, and by 1870 his company was carrying an average of 40,000 emigrants a year.[2] The real strength of operation, however, was tested in the relationship between total capacity and traffic available. Inman and Cunard were the first real contenders for the steerage trade under conditions of increasing traffic, but this simple division of enterprise was soon broken by the incursion of three new Liverpool lines, National, Guion and White Star.[3] The balance of interests was upset and competition between rival British companies became an established feature of the passenger trade as a whole.

Both the National and Guion companies specialised in the carriage of large number of steerage passengers and cargo between Liverpool and New York. At first they were content to allow Cunard and Inman to compete for express cabin class traffic.[4] By the early 1870s, however, National and Guion had built up fleets with a combined total of some 60,000 tons – an expansion which was largely in response to the increasing volume of emigration to America. The average number of passengers carried per ship rose from 300 in the early 1860s, to just under 400 by the end of that decade and by 1870, 95 per cent of all emigrants travelling to

North America went by steamship.[5] It was in such optimistic circumstances that the White Star line was founded in 1869. In some respects this new foundation was similar to the Inman line. They were both the creations of men who had gained their experience of shipping operations in the management of sailing ship companies. Their reputation was established by the adoption of new standards in ship design and passenger accommodation. The formidable personality of T. H. Ismay, founder of the White Star line, was equal in stature with that of many other powerful Liverpool shipowners of the time, such as Alfred Jones, Alfred Holt, James Harrison, John Swire and Alfred and Charles Booth.[6] He had also been a director of the National Steam Ship Company, and the new company which he formed in 1869 had all the marks of successful inauguration. An important financial link between White Star and the Belfast shipbuilding firm of Harland and Wolff enabled Ismay to obtain excellent ships on a favourable cost–plus basis.[7] As a result the first six ships which were built for the company between 1871 and 1872 embodied the latest innovations and were so well equipped that they rendered existing tonnage out-of-date. The new ships had a hull ratio of 10:1. They were fitted with compound engines and had comfortable cabin and saloon accommodation.[8] In other words, White Star presented a challenge to the other Liverpool companies which was difficult to meet and overcome.

The virtual overcrowding of the North Atlantic by so many companies and by so much tonnage could only sustain profitable operation under conditions of increasing trade. Even so there were difficulties arising from relative competitive strengths during boom periods such as that existed before 1874. Well-established lines such as Cunard experienced short periods of acute embarrassment, while the newcomers had to face a whole variety of non-economic inhibitions. There was, for example, the physical difficulty of finding adequate berths for the ships of the companies in the Liverpool docks system. Ismay had long and complicated negotiations with the Mersey Docks and Harbour Board before White Star ships were eventually allocated a berth in 1872, in West Waterloo dock.[9] As far as Cunard was concerned there was the prospect that the new fast ships of rival companies might not only reduce their Cabin traffic, but that the Government might be persuaded to transfer the mail contract.[10] In fact the claims of the new steamships for a share of the mail subsidy became so persistent and dangerous that Cunard was forced into a programme of modernisation.

As we have seen, opposition to change had led to a crisis among the partners. Nevertheless the threat to the mail subsidy was a real one. It had long been regarded with envious eyes by Cunard's rivals, for when translated into terms of capacity it represented the annual carriage of some 10,000 steerage passengers from Liverpool to New York. Such a cushion may, as some critics remarked, have reduced Cunard's incentive to improve and modernise its ships; the more pertinent observers claimed that so large a subsidy protected the Company against the full force of competition.[11] In his evidence before a Select Committee in 1869, T. Wallace, the Southampton Agent for North German Lloyd stated: '... it is an established fact that Messrs Cunard have kept cutting down the freight very low from Havre for years; sometimes they had been taking goods from Havre to New York for 20s a ton measurement. The expenses of getting the goods from Havre to Liverpool cannot be less than half that money and, as everybody interested in shipping must know, 10s per ton from Liverpool to New York is not only not a paying, but it must be a losing game.'[12] The inference was that it was the mail subsidy that was making it possible for these low rates to be charged.

This statement, coming as it did from the representative of a company which had just been given a mail contract, induced a strong reply from John Burns. After preceding his remarks with the declaration that it was the fierceness of the competition which had compelled Cunard and Inman to co-operate, he went on to announce the existence of what must have been one of the earliest forms of shipping conference on record. 'To show the necessity for people to look for self-preservation', he stated, 'there is, at this moment in Liverpool, what they call a Steam Conference of all the British steamship owners in Liverpool and Glasgow, whereby all the rates of freight are regulated at that Conference whether by subsidised or nonsubsidised lines ... The National and Guion's company [sic] are parties with Mr Inman and my own Company to this arrangement. Therefore, the question of subsidised companies being able to carry at less rates of freight is a gross fallacy.'[13] This was, indeed, a revelation of importance, because though it is reasonably well known that bilateral agreements were in operation in the 1860s, there has been little evidence to substantiate the belief that a Conference involving a number of competing lines existed before the early 1870s.[14] The real significance of this disclosure does not lie in the historical chronology of the Conference system as such, but in the fact that by this early date shipowners (including the owners of new steamship lines) had devised a scheme for their mutual protection. The obvious question which follows is what, at this precise time, these owners were protecting themselves from; certainly not the pressure of foreign competition. It is, therefore, necessary to make a more detailed examination of this Conference arrangement in order to understand the nature of the particular conditions which called it into being.

II THE LIVERPOOL STEAMSHIP CONFERENCE: CONTROVERSY ON RATES FOR SLOW AND FAST SHIPS: THE DEPRESSION 1874–8: GROWING STRENGTH OF GERMAN LINES

The available evidence suggests that in late 1867 or early 1868, Cunard and Inman entered into a working agreement fixing rates of freight.[15] They were joined by National, Guion, Allan and Anchor lines. Besides cargo rates the arrangement also covered minimum passenger fares. This could not have been a protective device against foreign competition, for in 1870 the four Liverpool companies, Cunard, Inman, National and Guion, carried 96 per cent of the passenger traffic to America.[16] In the same year some 184,000 emigrants and other passengers were carried in British ships from the United Kingdom to America, whereas only 4800 were carried in foreign ships.[17] It was not until some fifteen years later that North German Lloyd and Hamburg–Amerika were involved at levels of traffic likely to cause difficulty for British companies. Furthermore a series of investigations by the Board of Trade in 1868–9 disproved the generally accepted belief that German ships calling at Southampton had an unfair advantage over British ships, by not coming under the regulation of British legislation.[18] In fact German ships were subject to their own national regulation and discipline as stringent as that imposed on British ships.[19] Moreover the German vessels, having been laid down in British shipyards, were just as well built as those of their British rivals. These facts must have been known by Liverpool shipowners at that time and it is therefore difficult to understand why it was generally believed that rate agreements amongst themselves protected them from foreign competition. If, however, the British lines entered into agreements strictly as instruments for their mutual protection, it is relevant to enquire into the nature and effectiveness of such devices.

It is always difficult for an historian to get inside the minds of persons who lived in the past and, in particular, to make an objective appraisal of motives. In this case perhaps one can best attempt to understand why the bogy of foreign competition was raised by putting it in the context of prevailing political and economic opinion. Modern research into Continental industrial systems has done much to alter the perspective of Britain's own industrial achievement. Although the 1860s was a time of rapid commercial expansion within the framework of free trade and Gladstonian finance, there were already signs that Britain's commercial lead had been narrowed.[20] The fear of the foreigner had been transferred from the purely political into that of an economic environment. In the field of shipping foreign competition was at first a convenient scapegoat; but it later became an effective basis for pressure to be exerted on the Government to obtain reductions in the irksome passenger regulations. In the state of opinion ruling in the 1860s, there was a widespread fear that such phenomena as railway monopolies and associations among shipowners might threaten the existing political system.[21] In these circumstances any agreement having as its main purpose the fixing of prices had no better disguise than that of a defence against the unscrupulous foreigner.

The real nature of the Liverpool Atlantic Conference, however, was made manifest during the depression in the Liverpool –American trade between 1874 and 1878. For more than five years the Conference had worked reasonably well within the general framework of harmonious relations. Under the agreement the lines had been placed on a relatively equal footing in competing with each other for the trade available, though there had been considerable differentiation in frequency of sailings and in quality of service; but with the onset of falling traffic and falling receipts strains and weakness in the Conference structure began to appear.

On 1 May 1874 the National Line left the Conference, an action which was based on the grounds that the other members had refused to allow National to charge lower rates to compensate for its slower ships.[22] In actual fact they had found it impossible to match the superior quality of the Cunard ships. Their reason for breaking with the Conference was a valid one and, as we shall see later, the principle was accepted that older and slower ships should be allowed to charge a lower rate than newer, faster ships.[23] The Chairman of the National Line, by way of further explanation, voiced a general grievance that the Government subvention paid to Cunard made it impossible for his company to offer the same kind and quality of service as the other lines were able to provide under the agreed rates.[24]

There was also another cause of potential dissension between National and Cunard over the latter's defence of its Boston trade. Cunard had always regarded this trade as its own preserve, but it would seem that the high railroad freights from the west into Boston (particularly on grain) had seriously and adversely affected the cargoes for shipment from that port.[25] It is true that since Cunard had developed an alternative service to New York in 1848, that port had accommodated a growing share of the Company's traffic. During the 1850s the volume of Cunard's business with New York was approximately twice that with Boston, and with the entry into the steerage business the ratio was increased in New York's favour. Nevertheless the Boston trade continued to be a substantial part of Cunard's activity. By the early 1870s, however, Boston had become a relatively high cost port and the Company considered the advisability of removing all its steamships to New York.[26] On learning this National began despatching ships to Boston much to the annoyance of Cunard. There followed a fierce rate-cutting war, not only between Cunard and National but also between all the other lines.[27] The Conference had disintegrated and for a period of thirteen months there was intense competition for both passengers and cargo. Steerage fares fell as low as £2, freight rates were halved, receipts fell sharply and all the companies suffered severe financial loss.[28]

In such circumstances the need for a renewal of agreement became an urgent necessity and negotiations between the competing lines were opened. By September 1874 some form of compromise seems to have been reached, but it was rendered null by both National and Guion who complained that the advantage allowed to them was not sufficiently remunerative.[29] Mr Lamport, a shipowner and member of the Liverpool Steam Ship Owners Association, was instrumental in acting as a mediator throughout these difficult negotiations.[30] His good offices were in constant demand, but his task was made virtually impossible by Cunard's bitter resentment of the National Line's incursion into the Boston trade.[31] This resentment was so deep-seated that Cunard refused to attend meetings designed to effect a settlement. By May 1875, however, Charles MacIver was so worried by the worsening situation that he assumed the role of mediator himself.[32] The disagreement between the fast and slow lines was contentious and intractable of solution and when MacIver published the correspondence between Cunard and the National Line, the rift grew deeper.[33]

It was, therefore, surprising and unexpected that harmony was able to be restored on 4 June 1875.[34] The solution involved the acceptance of differential rates; steerage fares were to be £5 5s on fast ships and £5 on certain slower ships owned by National and Guion.[35] A rate of 40s per ton measurement was fixed for fine goods and primage was reduced to five per cent for slower ships.[36] It is interesting to note that these new rates were lower than those ruling under the first Conference. Another bone of contention was removed by a general agreement that no line should henceforth have a preserve in any trade or port. Unfortunately the time was not propitious for the exercise of good intentions; the depression in America got worse, and as a consequence there was a drastic reduction in the flow of emigrants from Europe. Average numbers of passengers carried per ship fell from 340 in 1874 to 210 in 1875.[37] Even so, rock bottom had not been reached. In the following year, the Chairman of the National Line reported that 'all the steerage passengers that we took from Liverpool in 1876 could have been taken over in three steamers. The falling off has been nearly from 40,000 to 6000 and the resultant loss of profit to the Company on that one item alone exceeds £100,000'.[38] This was certainly no augury for the expectation of profit which had caused the size, capacity and number of passenger ships on the Atlantic to be doubled within a decade.

It was obvious that in order to tide over such a period of adverse fluctuation, drastic remedies would have to be applied outside the operation of rate-fixing agreements. Expenditure had to be cut; the directors of National, for example, accepted a 50 per cent reduction in fees; lines not bound by the terms of mail contracts reduced the number of sailings and some laid up ships.[39] These expedients, however, did not effectively reduce costly overheads which had to be met as long as a company remained in business. Cunard and Inman adopted a policy of retrenchment and sold off many of their older and less profitable ships.[40] For three years no new vessels were brought into service. The final act of humiliation came when National and Guion, in an attempt to diversify the range of their business, converted some of their ships to cattle carriers.[41] Even Cunard succumbed to this expedient; but the difficulty of getting rid of the smell of cattle caused them to abandon the trade.[42] White Star diverted some of their ships to the Far East trade and Cunard some of its smaller and slower ships to ports in the Mediterranean. For the larger, faster and expensive liners, built especially for the carriage of large numbers of passengers, these measures were not appropriate. There was no substitute for the emigrant traffic. Financial losses suffered by the Liverpool lines were more than ample proof of this fact.

With the recovery of the emigrant trade in the early 1880s, and more particularly with the increasing flood of Continental emigrants after 1885, the threat of new competition to the established Liverpool lines came from three sources; the first from British interlopers, the second from the two powerful German companies North German Lloyd and Hamburg–Amerika and the third from an attempt to revive an American mercantile marine. The impact of all three was to intensify the need for protection and to emphasise the importance of agreement within the structure of a Conference system.

As occasion demanded new ships were brought into service by the existing Liverpool lines after 1880; but there was also an increase of tonnage from small companies which were created on the expectation of a quick profit. Liverpool was predominant among other ports in being a centre for single ship companies.[43] This phenomenon was not necessarily a reflection of mushroom growth, as several large established lines trading to the Far East, South America and Australia contained such companies within their structures. Nevertheless there is every indication that an increase in tonnage was induced by the expectation of high returns from the emigrant trade. Among newcomers in Liverpool were Papayanni Bros, Warren and Co., British Shipowners Co. (founded by James Beazley), Flinn, Main and Montgomery, Beaver, Dominion and Allan lines. The influx of new tonnage from these sources into a trade already over-supplied was but a short-term consequence of particular economic conditions. It added to the competitive difficulties of the main line companies, but usually the dangers inherent in the threat from pressure of surplus capacity was short-lived. The wide fluctuations in the level of traffic were to drive non-specialist services on to other routes and into other trades.

A more serious threat, however, was posed by the growth of a powerful German opposition together with parallel attempts by certain American shipping lines to make a more effective entry into the North Atlantic trade. As long as the bulk of European emigrants had passed through Britain, Continental shipping lines had very little chance of breaking into a trade almost wholly served by British companies. In the 1880s, however, the passage of emigrants from Germany, Austria and Eastern Europe through Hamburg and Bremen, provided North German Lloyd and Hamburg–Amerika shipping lines with the same basic financial springboard which had enabled their Liverpool rivals to prosper and expand after the 1860s. There is also the additional fact that from the 1880s the flow of emigration had shifted to South and Eastern Europe, where the two German lines had a marked geographical advantage apart from their control of the frontier stations after 1894.

The further fact that German shipyards were, as yet, ill equipped to provide the right type of vessels was no real deterrent to entry into the emigrant business, for the majority of the German ships were built on the Clyde. In the course of time the growth of industrial potential at home and the acquisition of territories overseas greatly stimulated the development of a German mercantile marine, by producing both passengers and cargoes.[44] These factors were essential for growth, but the real driving force promoting successful shipping enterprise came from the inspiration and organisational skill of managers such as Albert Ballin of Hamburg–Amerika and Herr Lohmann of North German Lloyd. If one accepts the assertion by D. H. Aldcroft that 'German shipowners had few marked economic advantages over their rivals' the implication must be that success was achieved by dynamic management.[45] The two German lines were given aggressive leadership which sought to exploit any opening likely to yield a high return on capital. North German Lloyd made a successful bid in 1886 to carry British mail from Southampton, and as a means of overcoming the seasonal fluctuations in the emigrant trade, Hamburg–Amerika instituted winter cruises in 1891.[46] Perhaps the best indication of encroachment by the German companies into the Atlantic trade before 1900 can be made from the following relative figures, both companies being well placed to cater for the increasing flow of passengers from Austria and Russia through German ports.

Westbound North Atlantic steerage traffic (excluding Mediterranean) carried by major lines in 1891[47]

Line	Passengers	% of Total
Norddeutscher Lloyd	68 239	15·3
Hamburg–Amerika	75 835	17·0
White Star	35 502	7·9
Cunard	27 341	6·1

III THE USE OF THE CONFERENCE SYSTEM BY THE GERMAN LINES: CONFERENCE AGREEMENTS AND RATE WARS: CUNARD LEAVES THE CONFERENCE: THE ATLANTIC POOL

Both German lines used the Conference system mainly as a weapon to undermine the power of British companies.[48] As we shall see later, they also entered into an alliance with the Morgan combine of American shipping interests specifically for the purpose of waging both a defensive and an offensive war against Cunard. In short the rapid inroads which these German lines made into the North Sea and North Atlantic trades were, at one and the same time, dangerous and difficult to overcome. It was eventually left to Cunard, alone among British companies, to find a means of alleviating this new and forceful competition.

In these developments one must not overlook movements in the United States to re-establish mercantile power. The effects of the Civil War not only caused a decline in American shipbuilding, they also retarded any early effort which might otherwise have been made in reducing Britain's lead in steamship technology. Furthermore it was not until the basic capital needs of expansion in such industries as oil, railroads and steel, had been met, that the American entrepreneurs began to look once again at ocean shipping.[49]

As far as passenger services were concerned the most successful

United States company (and the most serious competitor to British lines) was the International Navigation Company. This firm had been established in Philadelphia in 1873 and had been largely financed by Pennsylvania Railroad money.[50] The objective was for the steamship company to channel emigrants into Philadelphia, the Atlantic terminal of the railroad. In order to acquire British ships and British know-how, a bid was made for the Anchor Line, but the attempt was unsuccessful.[51] Subsequently the aim of securing the fruits of British technology was achieved by a relatively easy conquest, made possible by the collapse of the Inman Line. William Inman died in 1881 at a time when his line was experiencing growing misfortune. The line had been obliged to borrow heavily in the United States and the International Navigation Company had become a major creditor.[52] When the Inman Line found it impossible to continue, the American shipping line offered to buy out the company and there was no alternative to acceptance. It is true that T. H. Ismay of the White Star offered to support the Inman Line by a large loan. It was Ismay's belief that it was unwise to allow a weak company to go out of business because it made room for a much stronger competitor to enter the trade; but Ismay made his offer conditional upon other Liverpool shipowners joining in the salvage operation.[53] The outcome was that the Inman Line passed into American hands. Henceforth the firm was known as the Inman and International Line, though when the organisation was reconstituted in 1893 the whole went under the simpler name of the American Line.

For Cunard and White Star the emergence of this new competitor across the Atlantic was cause for renewed anxiety. The Americans controlled large capital resources and brought to the shipping business their own thrustful kind of competition. They worked the ships extremely hard in an endeavour to bring to their investors the greatest profit in the shortest possible time. This may have proved to be a successful policy in the days of the famous Yankee Clippers, but when applied to the operation of steamships it had unexpected results. As speed and the number of voyages increased, aggregate costs rose sharply. Moreover American managers demanded a quick turn-round in port with the result that servicing was more often than not either negligent in detail or ill supervised in essentials.[54] The net effect of this was that breakdowns at sea became more frequent, voyage schedules were disrupted and reputations suffered. Merchants thereupon began sending their cargoes by more reliable companies. Nevertheless there was small consolation for British lines in witnessing American mismanagement. It seemed to have little effect on the number of passengers carried. It is a matter for reiteration that the ocean traveller was induced to choose one line rather than another, not by profitability but by quality of food and type of accommodation provided. The evidence suggests that in these latter respects, the American lines were superior to their British competitors.[55] The continued grounds for misapprehension by British shipowners were therefore justified. By providing more luxurious and more comfortable services throughout the whole range of accommodation, the American lines presented a real threat to the mainstay of the trade; namely the traffic on the route between New York and Liverpool.

There were three ways of moderating such persistent and stringent competition. The first was by counter amalgamation. Several tentative attempts had been made in the 1890s to explore the possibility of Cunard and White Star joining forces; but these had always foundered on the rock of personal antipathy and pride in family achievement.[56] At a somewhat later date an abortive attempt by Sir John Ellerman was made to secure control of Cunard. Between 1898 and 1900 a series of approaches made by intermediaries indicated that Ellerman was prepared to offer £1,400,000 as purchase price.[57] At that time Cunard's assets were about £2 million and consequently Lord Inverclyde refused to give serious consideration to the proposition.[58] The whole correspondence relating to these negotiations was placed before Cunard directors on 27 March 1900 and the Chairman's action in declining the offer was given unanimous approval.[59]

The second course was that of inducing a competitor to take his services elsewhere. This, in fact, was the successful plan agreed on in 1891 by both Cunard and White Star. They persuaded Clement Griscom, President of Inman and International to make Antwerp, rather than Liverpool its European terminal.[60] Southampton was to be the British port of call. In return Ismay and Burns agreed to indemnify the American Line for moving to Southampton, White Star paying £20,000 and Cunard £10,000 per annum for a period of five years.[61] These amounts were readjusted after further negotiation, and in 1893 the American Line transferred its services to the Antwerp–Southampton–New York route.

The third method in the process of combating new competition was through the reorganisation and redevelopment of Conference agreements and procedures. By the last decade of the nineteenth century most shipowners had accepted the Conference system as the only sensible instrument for the mitigation of cut-throat competition. For some lines it provided the only safeguard for maintaining themselves in business. As far as the Liverpool companies were concerned, however, there had always been considerable difficulty in sustaining mutual action. Both Cunard and White Star were consistent in their objection to any scheme which involved the pooling or sharing out of passenger revenue, claiming that under such an arrangement the more efficient lines would continuously subsidise the less efficient.[62] As a consequence the agreements which eventually found acceptance were based on highly complex systems of differential rates for the various lines within the ring. The whole situation was further complicated by the fact that some Liverpool lines were carrying passengers and freight from German, Scandinavian and Mediterranean ports as well as from Liverpool. This necessitated a wide range of agreement and involvement in various short-lived Conferences; but for Cunard the most important of them all related to the carriage of steerage passengers from Liverpool to New York and Boston.

For the most part Conference agreements were mainly of importance at times when rate wars demanded common action. Between 1884 and 1885, for example, emigration from the United Kingdom dropped by as much as 60,000 on the figure for the previous year. Steerage rates were cut to £3, and following this collapse unrestricted competition caused the break-up of the existing rate agreements.[63] In fact, Cunard was the first to withdraw from agreed commitments. Rate cutting was widespread, though on this occasion White Star would seem to have been under less pressure than Cunard in reducing fares.[64] Nevertheless by February 1885 a worried White Star agent in Chicago wrote, 'we are losing trade in the west and not getting our share of the pre-paid business . . . As far as I can learn, the Cunard are doing more than double the amount of pre-paid business than we are at present . . . Cunard agents are able to offer and sell pre-paid tickets one dollar below our net rate . . . The Inman people are now, and have been ever since the Conference was dissolved, paying extra commission.'[65] It is even more surprising that White Star should have adopted a complacent attitude, particularly at a time when the company had to face increasing pressure from new Cunnard tonnage. Without precise information as to the various sources of Cunard revenue, Ismay could only make judgements at face value and he was convinced that the new Cunarders, operating under conditions of falling returns, would never pay their way.[66] To a somewhat incredulous Ismay, Cunard also cut steerage rates below those of White Star. The fare from Liverpool to New York was cut from £4 to £3 on the faster ships in May 1885.[67] This was a desperate bid to capture traffic, because at this rate voyage costs would not be covered. A settlement had to be reached, and by the end of August the steerage rate had been restored to £5 5s. But it came too late to catch the peak of season traffic and was no inducement for complete and loyal adherence to existing agreements, especially during the winter months when seasonal shortage of emigrants led to reduced sailings and the laying up of ships.[68] Consequently fresh agreements had to be negotiated to adjust rates, sailing schedules and agents' commissions. For the next ten years this pattern of dissension, agreement, negotiation and companies opting out, became common practice. It was not a happy atmosphere in which to conduct steamship operations. Bitter recrimination was a constant sequel to self-interested action. 'Mr Ismay has, of late years, assumed the rights of a free-lance . . . The White Star people seem disposed to rule or ruin . . .'[69] Unilateral rate cutting was rife and lack of any consistent policy between lines meant that there was very little real resistance to the determined and united opposition, especially when it came from American and Continental lines.

By contrast with agreements among British lines, those among Continental companies were much more formidable in their effect, being primarily designed to give German lines the greatest possible advantage over their rivals. The general background from which such agreements sprang was that German lines should cease competing with British ships in British ports in return for a similar regulation restricting the services of British companies in Continental ports.[70] Rates from the United Kingdom and from the Continent were to be approximately the same. The first attempt to negotiate an agreement with Continental lines occurred in 1885. Two Conferences were formed in this year. The first was a North Atlantic Conference composed of British lines with headquarters in New York, entitled The North Atlantic Passenger Conference

(N.A.P.C.); the second was a Conference of North European Steamship Lines, the result of a meeting held at Cologne in April 1885.[71] The European lines invited the British lines to participate in joint discussions about the regulation of rates. It is possible that the approach was prompted by Albert Ballin's attack on the British lines' monopoly of Scandinavian traffic to New York.[72] This was to be effected by the establishment of a line between Stettin and the U.S.A. In the event of this project failing, Ballin made it clear that Hamburg–Amerika would invade British ports and carry steerage passengers from Liverpool via Le Havre and from Plymouth via Hamburg.[73]

Cunard's directors were greatly exercised by this threat of opposition in their home port, and in 1886 an agreement was signed under which Ballin withdrew the Scandinavian service, though as a *quid pro quo* his company was given access to certain British ports for the carriage of steerage passengers.[74] Minimum passenger rates were approved and a clearing office was established in Hamburg for the distribution of passengers between British and German lines. Aldcroft asserts that for a time this agreement worked reasonably well.[75] This was probably true of British lines apart from Cunard. The directors of this Company had given but a grudging acceptance to membership and they were highly suspicious of Ballin's motives.[76] Under his active management cohesion was given to this cartel, similar in many respects to that which John Swire had brought to the various Far Eastern cargo conferences. In a particular sense, the Cunard directors felt they had been outwitted by Ballin; having been forced to enter the Conference it became extremely difficult for them to pursue a policy of rate cutting as and when occasion demanded.[77] Furthermore it soon became clear that Cunard was becoming apprehensive about the operation of the agreement as a whole. The directors complained that the Company was not receiving the share of this traffic to which it was legally entitled.[78] They were also doubtful whether Hamburg–Amerika had withdrawn from the Scandinavian trade. Cunard was first to leave the European Conference, an action which undoubtedly influenced other British lines to follow suit.[79]

The break-up of this first European Atlantic Conference was greatly resented by Ballin. Having been thwarted in his first encounter with Cunard he tried a different tactic. He had long cherished the idea of pooling the Atlantic traffic, a proposition which had more than once been rejected by both Cunard and White Star.[80] Ballin's chance, however, came unexpectedly with the prospect of a depletion in the trade caused by cholera in Europe and depression in America. It became obvious that a desperate struggle for passengers would ensue, rates would tumble, ships would be laid up and heavy losses would be sustained by every line. The future seemed to be so foreboding that it was enough to bring a 'pool' into being. This creation was known as the Nordatlantischer Dampfer Linien Verband (N.D.L.V.) and included North German Lloyd, Hamburg–Amerika, Holland–America and Red Star lines.[81] Provision was made for British and American lines to join but they showed no great enthusiasm during the initial stages of the new organisation. The participants, however, received a share of the westbound steerage traffic from North European ports, 'plus or minus movements in a line's tonnage or passengers, being met by compensatory adjustments in the levels of quotas and fares'.[82] Though British companies were invited to join, they eventually refused on being informed that their share of Continental traffic would be only 14 per cent.[83] So fragile was the state of negotiation that it only needed the effects of a falling market to spark off a damaging rate war with the German lines. Once again the steerage fare from Liverpool to New York slumped to £3, a rate which persisted through 1893. 'The low rate of steerage', complained a Cunard director bitterly, 'has so far not increased the numbers outwards ... It is very mortifying to have to carry them for such miserable pay.'[84] Conditions remained depressed throughout the first half of the following year, and by August 1895 fresh approaches from the Continental lines resulted in yet another form of agreement to which British, American and European lines subscribed.

Under the provisions of the 1895 Declaration of Intent, the main heads of proposals were that the Continental lines should withdraw from the Finnish and Scandinavian berths, the British lines (apart from Anchor) should retire from the Italian trade both outwards and homewards, while retaining six per cent of outward passages from Libau to Le Havre; finally the Continental lines agreed to retire from the British traffic outwards and homewards.[85] The significant difference between this agreement (which was to last for three years) and the 1892 proposal was that British lines were allocated only six per cent of Continental traffic. Other consequential arrangements were to follow; in 1896 minimum cabin fares were fixed on both fast and slow ships;[86] the summer season was defined as running from 1 May to 31 October. In 1898 agreement was reached by fourteen lines allocating east and west-bound steamship routes across the Atlantic.[87] Within the terms of this agreement the German lines undertook to leave Scandinavian traffic to the British lines and to the Danish Thingvalla Line. It appeared that at last common sense was prevailing; internecine strife between rival companies engaged in the Atlantic passenger trade would become no more than an unhappy memory. Alas for such hopes! At the very time these apparently harmonious meetings were taking place, Cunard and other British companies were becoming more and more dissatisfied with their small share of Continental business.[88] The dissatisfaction was further exacerbated by their mistrust of the methods employed by foreign lines to capture their traffic. The whole Conference structure, so laboriously built up over the preceding three years, began to disintegrate in face of another adverse fluctuation in the level of emigration in 1898, though Cunard did not break all ties with the Agreement until 1903.[89] It was but a reflection of events that the Cunard report for 1898 should contain the ominous note – 'the present war in passenger rates will be bound to affect our revenue.'[90]

This brief review of the frequent attempts first by rival British companies, and later by British and foreign lines, to find a solution to the intense and bitter warfare which frequently broke out in passenger carrying, does not make edifying reading. The fact that the trade was volatile, and that solutions when found proved to be ephemeral, undoubtedly caused a vast waste of resources. Too much capital was poured into what proved to be an unstable and, at times, unprofitable venture. Mutual mistrust leading to a lack of a common policy resulted in rate wars and increasingly to low rates of return on capital employed.[91] During the first few years of the twentieth century these difficulties were increased by a change in emphasis, caused primarily by the emergence of large-scale amalgamations which raised the strength of competition from a purely local and individualistic plane to one of international dimension. As a result the struggle involved the intervention of government in the maintenance of a British mercantile marine. Despite this, however, Conferences still remained as a source of co-operation during periods of depression, though for Cunard their effectiveness was much less evident after 1906 than for the difficult decades at the end of the nineteenth century.

In this context it is necessary to refer to cargo agreements. The first thing we must clearly understand is that Cunard, in common with most other passenger lines, depended at certain times on freight earnings to cover operating costs. The carriage of cargo was an important source of income, especially when passenger traffic was reduced. There were periods between 1860 and 1914 when receipts from cargo made up one-third of total earnings.[92] In this respect, therefore, the adjustment of freight rates was of considerable concern to Cunard management. In general cargo liner agreements were subjected to the pressure of outside competition in much the same way as were passenger liner agreements; on the whole, apart from certain disruptions in the 1880s, the former were relatively permanent structures and worked in the interests of harmony among shipowners. Unfortunately for cargo liner operators, however, the trend in freight rates was steadily downwards for the period 1860–1908. As unit rates declined volume became important, and in gross terms it was more lucrative to carry bulk cargoes of wheat, cotton, linseed and sugar. Though passenger ships were specifically designed to carry cargo, they normally transported high value, low volume merchandise. If bulk cargoes were dealt in they were usually accommodated under charters, but at times when high value, low volume cargoes were scarce, bulk shipments such as wheat were carried.[93] Furthermore, the possibility of creating a separate Atlantic Conference for cargo was inhibited by the simple fact that the severity of competition on the various Atlantic routes ruled out the use of a rebate system;[94] without such a system shippers had little or no incentive to send bulk cargo in ships belonging to passenger lines. Consequently there was greater incentive to cut rates, and although most passenger rate agreements contained clauses relating to the carriage of cargo, these proved to be much less effective in preventing rate warfare than did the agreements entirely devoted to the carriage of cargo on other routes.[95]

The most serious upheaval in the Atlantic cargo trade occurred in 1889. The *Liverpool Journal of Commerce* reported on the intransigence of Liverpool companies in the following terms: 'Advices from New York state that the White Star company has made a sensation in commercial circles by a cut of 50 per cent in freight rates. They assert that all the other lines have been secretly cutting rates and that it is better to have a sharp rate war than to do a cutthroat business. The Cunard Company says it can do business as low as, if not lower than, any other line and will meet and beat the White Star cut.'⁹⁶ In short, the cargo agreements among the Liverpool companies trading on the North Atlantic, were no wit less uncertain than passenger rate agreements. They disintegrated as soon as trading conditions began to worsen; thus freight capacity was adversely affected and, in this respect, an important part of a company's revenue and profitability as a whole was jeopardised.

In all aspects the Conference structure was an imperfect defence mechanism for Liverpool shipping passenger lines. Time was running against them and the initial advantages which had given them an unrivalled lead were being eroded, not only by changes in the source and type of North Atlantic traffic, but by their own mistrust, complacency and apparent wilful ignorance. As larger ships came into operation, other ports benefited at the expense of Liverpool because of the inhibitions imposed by the natural and physical handicaps of the Mersey estuary and the Liverpool dock system.⁹⁷ Moreover foreign lines, possessing large capital resources and directed by prescient management, were now setting the pace in ways calculated to undermine the once dominant position held by companies such as Cunard. It needed strength of purpose, a cool head and foresight for Cunard's successive chairmen to extract the Company from the enmeshing and frustrating difficulties of the time; it needed a carefully planned policy based on long-term strategy to make the Company into a profit-making concern.

IV ALLIANCE OF MORGAN COMBINE AND GERMAN SHIPPING COMPANIES: THE IMPACT OF THIS ALLIANCE ON CUNARD: THE FRANKFURT CONFERENCE AND THE CONTINENTAL POOL: THE 1908 AGREEMENT: ATTEMPT BY UNITED STATES TO BREAK CONFERENCE AGREEMENTS

The creation of the Morgan combine of American shipping interests in alliance with North German Lloyd and Hamburg –Amerika, posed a serious threat to Cunard's position as a competitor for passengers on the North Atlantic. The details of negotiations leading to the formation of this combine will be discussed in the following chapter. We are only presently concerned with the effects of this new source of competition on the trade in general and the structure of Conference agreements in particular. Primarily, however, we are interested in the impact of the changing pattern of trade on Cunard's ability to survive as an independent company and to make an adequate return on capital employed.

The first effect of the Morgan intervention on the North Atlantic was felt in October 1903. A sharpening of competition forced Cunard to reduce rates for first class passengers and to lower rates for third class passengers travelling on *Umbria* and *Etruria*.[98] The latter reductions, amounting to 5s for British and 10s for Scandinavian passengers, were designed to offset the lower rates of German lines allied to the International Mercantile Marine. By the middle of 1904, however, the rate war intensified. Ships in the Morgan combine carried third class emigrants from London westbound for as little as £2.[99] At a board meeting on 11 June 1904 it was agreed that as from 13 June the following rates should be charged on westbound third class traffic: *Campania* and *Lucania*, £3; *Umbria, Ivernia, Etruria* and *Saxonia* £2 15s; *Carpathia* and *Aurania* £2 10s; all Continental westbound rates £3 off, and first class rates from Rotterdam, Paris, Antwerp and Bremen to be the same as those from London.[100] Eastbound rates were left at the discretion of their New York agents to reduce as circumstances should dictate. The Morgan group replied by reducing their rate for steerage passengers to something over 30s.[101] As a result, Cunard was forced, in August, to instruct the New York office to lower immediately the eastbound cash minimum to £12 for saloon fares, second class cabin £8 for *Campania* and *Lucania* and all other ships to £10 for saloon passengers and £6 for second class cabin accommodation.[102] In other words, having failed in his bid to secure control of Cunard, Morgan and his associates were now attempting to drive Cunard ships off the North Atlantic by instigating one of the fiercest rate wars in history. It was a situation which could not be long maintained. No shipping company, however well protected by legal sanction or by subsidy, could withstand such competition. Though Cunard managed to attract more passengers and increase gross earnings by over £50,000, total direct running costs increased by £217,000 thus reducing net income by approximately £160,000 in 1904.[103] It is true that a small part of the £217,000 was devoted to the inauguration of the New York –Fiume service and that this was, therefore, a development cost;

but the general position was that marginal revenue was not increasing at a rate sufficient to bring increasing returns. There is also evidence that most of the constituents in the Morgan combine were making comparable losses.[104] Not least among these were the German lines and, as a consequence, a Conference was called at Frankfurt in August 1904, at which Cunard and the Continental lines were represented.[105]

In order to understand the significance of the Conference at Frankfurt, it must be made clear that Cunard had built up a reasonably prosperous business in the carriage of Hungarian and Austrian emigrants from the port of Fiume to the United States, a trade in which the German lines participated. The rate war had undoubtedly adversely affected the German companies, and in order to alleviate the chaotic conditions arising from unrestricted competition, Albert Ballin, on behalf of the Continental lines at the Frankfurt Conference, suggested that Cunard should, in respect of its Hungarian business, become a member of the Continental Pool.[106] This suggestion was in the nature of an olive branch as, by implication, it would have given Cunard a share of other Continental business. In practice, however, the share of traffic was to be based on the ratio between the number of Cunard sailings from Fiume and that of the other Continental lines. This worked out at 26 sailings per annum, or 5·27 per cent of the total Continental business; for any number of emigrants carried in excess of this percentage, Cunard would be required to pay a specified sum per head into the Continental Pool; conversely, the Company would be paid *pro rata* for any number under that percentage.[107] Cunard, however, could not agree to such an arrangement as it would have involved a loss on every sailing. As a counter proposal they put forward a new percentage designed to give them a minimum of 40,000 passengers per annum.[108] This in turn was subjected to further amendment by the Chairman of the Conference to the effect that Cunard should be entitled to carry from Fiume and Liverpool a number of passengers equivalent to two-thirds of the Hungarian emigration; but if such numbers should be less than 26,000 the Continental lines should pay to Cunard on such shortage a fixed rate per head.[109] If the number exceeded 40,000, however, Cunard should pay to the Continental lines the same rate on the excess; also, if the total number of Continental passengers should be reduced in any year below 300,000, the above-mentioned minimum should be reduced *pro rata*, and if the figure exceeded 40,000 the maximum was to be proportionately revised.[110] This offer, which was somewhat more to Cunard's advantage was, however, rejected by the Continental lines.

Nevertheless, despite frustrations, some progress was made and it was reported to the Cunard Board on 17 November 1904 that provisional agreement had been reached with the German companies, and this agreement was approved by the Hungarian Government in December.[111] Accordingly, the rate war was terminated in January 1905 and passenger rates were maintained at normal figures. There was, perhaps, a reflection of this return to normality in the fact that, for 1905, Cunard's revenue at £1,773,268 was the highest so far recorded in the Company's history. This was attributable to the restitution of normal fares and better homeward freights.[112] By March Lord Inverclyde was able to make a full report on the negotiations over the past year and indicate the agreed rates to be charged for first and second class passengers.[113] It was a somewhat uneasy truce. On 13 April Lord Inverclyde made a further statement on the negotiations with the German lines and the Morgan combine, stating that, in his opinion, better terms could have been arranged had the Company fought longer 'and if there had been not so great a desire to make peace'.[114] He also accused the International Mercantile Marine of failing to carry out tentative agreements made between themselves and Cunard on 14 January – agreements upon which all the other contracts were contingent. Cunard therupon informed Albert Ballin and the International Mercantile Marine that they considered themselves 'absolutely free both in regard to rates and in every other respect'.[115] The rate war continued in a desultory fashion and regularity of service from the Mediterranean was affected; so much so that the Hungarian Government put forward proposals in December 1905 to form a national company to take over the agreement with Cunard for the carriage of new emigrants to the United States. This proved abortive as the Hungarian Government could not raise the necessary capital to purchase the Mediterranean ships and goodwill of Cunard's fleet.[116] The whole confused situation was further complicated in 1907 by the financial crisis in the United States, which directly affected the emigrant trade from Europe and exacerbated the already declining trend in the traffic from Liverpool.

The competitive struggle so far referred to was a direct result of the alliance between the Morgan combine and the Continental lines. This alliance was both offensive and defensive in operation and was mainly directed against Cunard's control of the carriage of emigrants from Mediterranean ports.[117] 'It is true', stated Cunard's Chairman at the Annual General Meeting of 1905, 'that the Continental companies were annoyed with the arrangements which we had made with the Hungarian Government for a service between Fiume and New York but as I said last year, it was a simple matter of business which we or anyone else were quite free to enter into, and the Continental companies have no right to object to our opening up a new route or developing new business just as they themselves had done.'[118] This firm attitude was not designed to bring amelioration to a situation which was fast deteriorating, especially when it became known that the German lines had sought the assistance of the companies in the Morgan combine to add to the competitive pressure against Cunard.[119] The opposition took various forms; pressure on the Hungarian Government to terminate the agreement with Cunard; intimidation of Cunard's agents in Fiume, (the Adria Sea Navigation Co.) by inflicting heavy losses upon them in their purely local trade; and threats to agents in the United States that they would suffer boycott should they book passages on Cunard ships.[120] 'With the result', continued the Chairman, 'that in many instances, agents have been alienated from us and we have been obliged to find and appoint new ones.'[121]

Against this unhappy background must be set both the cyclical pattern and the trend in emigration across the Atlantic. Such adverse influences were sometimes subject to mitigation, as in the autumn of 1907, for example, by the maintenance of westbound cargo freight rates.[122] This year, as a whole, marked a peak in the carriage of emigrants westbound amounting to some £1,116,000. Nevertheless despite various means of alleviation, the earning capacity (particularly that in relation to tonnage employed) of most passenger lines, was seriously curtailed by purely economic factors, the wasteful effects of cut-throat competition adding unnecessary aggravation to a general worsening of conditions in the following year. By the beginning of 1908 it had become clear to Cunard's competitors that agreement on rates was vital to the continuation of all services. These views were strengthened by the drastic fall in the number of emigrants carried; only 335,000 booked passages in 1908, representing a fall of some 70 per cent over the figures for the previous year.[123] At this juncture the German Emperor was induced to take a hand in bringing the two sides together. 'The Emperor', stated William Watson, Cunard's Chairman, 'had said that he was going to tell Mr Ballin that he must settle things with the Cunard; that it was absurd this fighting and cutting of rates and throwing away money.'[124] Accordingly, 'the fierce and unnecessary rivalry was stopped and, by agreement, all rates were restored. This agreement we hope', stated William Watson on 23 April 1908, 'will work satisfactorily for the next few years.'[125] The advent of peace was given added significance through the putting into operation of *Lusitania* and *Mauretania*. These new fast leviathans were put into service with either *Lucania* or *Campania* on a three-ship instead of a four-ship voyage pattern, leaving Liverpool on Saturdays and New York on Wednesdays. This enabled the Company to inaugurate a further service with four other ships sailing from Liverpool on Wednesdays and from New York on Saturdays.[126] This indeed was wise and economical management designed to make the best and most efficient use of resources. It was also a sign of Cunard's technical superiority over her rivals. With such superiority the Company could adopt a less intractable attitude towards the Continental lines.

What, then, were the more favourable prospects which induced Cunard to come to an agreement with its competitors in 1908, and what were the ensuing advantages arising from the creation of a more comprehensive conference structure for the regulation of the North Atlantic passenger trade? There is little doubt that Cunard was in process of achieving superiority over its competitors, at least in prestige and in the technical efficiency of its ships. Compared with some forty years earlier when the fleet was unable to meet the challenge of Inman's emigrant service or of Guion's perfection in speed and luxury, the Company's closest rival and the one which posed the greatest threat in the realm of prestige was the White Star Line; but though the latter company's ships *Teutonic*, *Oceanic* and *Adriatic* were engaged in an express service from Southampton to New York, they were no real match for the new crack Cunarders, and the *Olympic* and the 'unsinkable' *Titanic* were, as yet, scarcely beyond the embryonic stage of the drawing board.

Thus, taking all factors into consideration, Cunard was induced to adopt a somewhat less intractable attitude towards the Continental lines. On 31 January 1908, a meeting of all companies engaged in the trans-Atlantic trade was held in London. The agenda included consideration of agreements on rates for first and second class passengers and a pooling arrangement for third class emigrants.[127] As already stated, it was confidently hoped that peace might once again be restored between all competitors. In tracing the course of events over the past five years, Albert Ballin referred specifically to the difficulties caused by the agreement between the Hungarian Government and Cunard 'by which a service was formed which seriously interfered with the business of the Continental lines'.[128] He also referred to the large carrying of European passengers by British lines over and above the six per cent which they had accepted in the agreement of 1898. First class rates were then examined, the rates for *Mauretania* and *Lusitania* being taken as a basis for the fixing of a graduated tariff for various classes of ship.[129] A minimum of £25 for first class and £12 for second class was agreed. Proposals relating to the third class pooling scheme met with considerable difficulty, though it was agreed that Cunard should carry 13·7 per cent of both eastbound and westbound traffic with complete freedom for its Fiume service westbound.[130] All non-Hungarian passengers carried on Cunard's Fiume service, however, had to pay compensation to the general pool. On eastbound sailings Cunard was required to enter the pool in respect of the carriage of non-Italian passengers to Trieste, on the basis of their average carryings for 1906 and 1907.[131] As an overall measure of commitment Cunard agreed to limit their westbound sailings to twenty-six regular and four extra crossings. Should they increase this number they would compensate the pool for the additional numbers carried. All the above proposals were to take effect from 1 March 1908.

It is sufficient in this present context to note that peace in the competitive struggle was achieved for a period of approximately three years, adjustments to rates being made by general consent in accordance with the levels of demand for service. After 1911 competitive pressures were contained by a series of short-term extensions of existing agreements. In the six months before the outbreak of the First World War, however, the German lines broke with the Conference. This breach was caused primarily by disagreement between the two German lines, Ballin and Heineken of

North German Lloyd quarrelling openly over control of the Austrian frontier stations.[132] This quarrel was pursued to a bitter conclusion and there was a short but sharp rate war between the German lines and the rest of the Conference. A further cause of anxiety at this time originated from proceedings which were taken by the United States Government against Cunard under the provisions of the Sherman Anti-Trust Laws. In fact Cunard was but one among a number of defendants, the majority, with one or two exceptions, being the principal lines engaged in the steerage traffic between the United States and Europe. The charge was that the steamship companies 'had combined and conspired to restrain a part of the trade and commerce of the United States' with foreign nations and 'to monopolise the same'.[133]

In their petition, the American Government charged the shipping companies with executing a contract generally known as AA. The crux of this contract, it was stated, permitted companies to guarantee to each other a percentage participation of the entire steerage traffic forwarded from all European ports to and via the United States and Canada.[134] It was agreed that the public suffered by reason of the combination of the defendants, not by virtue of inferior service, but through the charging of excessive rates; that furthermore it was the combination that made excessive rates possible. It was also claimed, and to an extent proved, that Agreement AA was intended to operate by giving various lines the share in the steerage traffic which they had previously enjoyed and to maintain their previous percentages in the trade.[135]

This action had implications far beyond the pronouncement of a judgement. It led to an investigation of the whole process of Conference agreements comparable in some respects with that of the Royal Commission on Shipping Rings. In their defence the shipping lines acknowledged entering into an agreement but denied that such an understanding was in violation of the Sherman Anti-Trust Act. They also denied charging arbitrary rates and in their submission showed that Agreement AA did not, and could not, make an arbitrary division of the available business.[136] They pointed out that there had been constant competition among the defendant lines since 1908 and that the percentages fixed by this Conference agreement were subject to revision at short periods. Furthermore it was claimed, with a certainty that could not be gainsaid, that the lines tried constantly to increase their earnings with a view to obtaining better percentages on their increased business. The only real effect of Agreement AA was to enable each company to protect its allocated share of the traffic; in particular, that which it had been able to get and keep.[137]

The evidence and conclusions compiled by a Committee of Congress were passed to the Supreme Court. After making some distinction between monopolistic combines in land transport and those combinations existing in sea transport, the court declared that 'it is not claimed by the defendants that oceanic carriers may combine for the purpose of destroying a competitor; but it is claimed that, under the laws of the United States they may legally combine for the purpose of avoiding rate wars and to avoid the evil consequences to themselves, to their passengers and to the public which would result from unrestricted and destructive competition'.[138] The concluding judgement was that by virtue of the conditions ruling in passenger sea transport, shipping companies must be allowed some reasonable degree of self-government. Special reference was made to evidence given by Mr Lister, Cunard's Passenger Manager, in contending that Conference agreements were not designed to destroy competition; that in fact, when lines went into bankruptcy it was generally the result of their own mismanagement.[139] Furthermore by pointing to the level of charges which had existed over the past twenty years, it could not be maintained that Conferences had been the cause of arbitrary or excessive rates, but that by contrast Conference lines had furnished to the public facilities for ocean travel with a high record of safety and a continuous level of improvement.[140] The judgement of the Supreme Court was consequently not unfavourable to the existence of Conference agreements.

Thus, by 1914, the structure of Conference agreements had achieved a degree of acceptability on both sides of the Atlantic. For Cunard the evolution of procedures had been inherent in a constantly changing policy to maintain the Company's strength under conditions of fluctuating trade and changes in the patterns of that trade. From the first pooling agreement with the Collins line in 1850, the regulation of competition for the emigrant business in the 1860s and 1870s had come within the scope of a Liverpool agreement. This had subsequently been extended to a more comprehensive arrangement with Continental and American lines and the institution of an Atlantic pool. With the advent of the Morgan combine, however, the emphasis had changed and the fierceness of the ensuing struggle had underlined the necessity of applying agreements to all categories of passenger traffic carried by all lines. The 1908 Conference was probably a most successful attempt to secure agreement among so wide and disparate a body of competitors. It worked reasonably well for five years, and although by 1914 the structure was once again beginning to disintegrate, the lesson which such co-operation had taught would not be forgotten in future to regulate the trade. It is difficult to make any assessment of the advantages which Cunard might have enjoyed by being a member of successive Conferences before 1914. It is probably true that substantial advantages came not so much from Conference regulations as from the efforts of her own management in securing maximum revenue at the lowest possible cost. This is an aspect of the Company's direction which we shall endeavour to analyse in the next chapter.

5
Costs, Revenue and Returns 1880—1914

I THE NEW SHIPBUILDING POLICY: RESIGNATION OF MACIVER BROTHERS

We must now return to the early 1880s. John Burns had become Chairman of the recently incorporated Company and the keynote of new activity was sounded by him in his speech at the Ordinary General Meeting on 27 April 1881. 'The steam navigation of this country', he declared, 'like almost every branch of industry, is carried on under circumstances of keen competition and, for any company to succeed, it must be possessed of the best boats with which to do its work efficiently . . . coupled with which there has to be the strictest observance of economy in details.'[1] Against the background of such an objective it was proposed to apply the Company's reserves to the building of large powerful ships while at the same time reducing liabilities and working costs. By such a policy it was hoped that more than adequate facilities would be provided for meeting likely changes in the pattern of trade. In retrospect this was a bold decision, designed as it was to offset prospective loss and increase competitive strength in those branches of the trade likely to be subjected to fluctuating conditions.

The immediate effect of this new direction was to precipitate a managerial crisis. It will be remembered that the MacIver brothers, Charles and Henry, were appointed as managing agents of the new Company and that they had agreed to serve in such capacity for a period of not less than five years.[2] Furthermore they had given an undertaking should they cease to be managers, not to engage in shipping activities which might offer direct opposition to Cunard. Finally all the managing owners of the old Company had accepted the proviso, on the establishment of the new Company, that they would retain at least £500,000 of their capital in the new Company, the MacIver interest being represented by a figure of

£166,660.³ For about two years, the managing agents under the designation of D. and C. MacIver and Burns and MacIver of Liverpool, worked in harmony with the new directorate; but by the early months of 1883, it was clear that dissension had occurred between the MacIver brothers and John Burns. The former complained that their powers as managing agents had been curtailed, that their advice had been ignored and that interference with their decisions made it increasingly impossible for them to perform their duties as outlined in their terms of appointment.⁴

Apart from the question of maintaining managerial power and status, the younger MacIvers disagreed with the projected policy of the directors in building new, large and expensive ships. In this view they were undoubtedly influenced by their father, Charles MacIver who, by 1875, had come to the conclusion that the most profitable type of ship for the North Atlantic service was around 4000 tons, designed to carry both cargo and passengers and driven by relatively low-powered engines.⁵ In the light of subsequent events, however, it is a moot point whether such a type of ship would have been effective in the competitive conditions ruling in the 1880s. It was within the context of the growing pressure of competition that in 1883 the directors were persuaded by Mr William Pearce, of John Elder and Company, to build two large, fast ships (*Umbria* and *Etruria*), a decision subsequently justified by the Chairman of Cunard in 1884.⁶ This action heightened the controversy between the directors and the managing agents, for the MacIver brothers were convinced that such large ships could never be run at a profit.⁷ In general terms this view had some substance, for as we have seen, although large ships did return an initial operating profit, offsetting charges for overheads and depreciation more often than not turned this profit into a loss. It was only by strict application of the managerial function to the reduction of costs that such a situation could be rectified. In 1880 and 1881, however, the directors – as distinct from the managing agents – were convinced that the operation of large powerful ships was an essential element in maintaining Cunard's competitive position.⁸ Accordingly the protestations of the managing agents were ignored and, by implication, their powers as decision-takers greatly diminished.

In effect the disagreement about the type of ship to be built led the MacIver brothers to a reassertion of functions which they considered had been impugned. In a letter to the directors they stated that their responsibilities involved administration, operating matters and direct control of agents.[9] Although they did not include the question of shipbuilding policy in their letter, it is clear from additional evidence that they expected to be consulted in all matters concerned with the operation of the ships.[10] The directors, however, refused to meet the MacIver brothers on the points raised and the latter had no option but to resign from their office on 28 March 1883.[11] This resignation, be it noted, was some two years before the agreed date of the expiry of their term. 'We trust that it will be well understood', wrote Charles and Henry MacIver to the Cunard Board, 'that, in withdrawing from the Company, we are not actuated by any feeling of hostility towards it and that we shall act, not merely upon the letter, but in the spirit of the 9th clause of the agreement of 4 March 1880.'[12] Despite the provocation which the MacIver brothers felt they had received at the hands of John Burns and his fellow directors, there is no doubt that their declaration of intent was sincere and made in good faith. The events which followed, therefore, must be regarded as the result of misunderstanding and suspicion, finally causing a complete break in association between the MacIver family and The Cunard Steam Ship Company Limited.

In August 1883 it became known that William MacIver (youngest son of Charles senior) was proposing to start a line of ships to the Mediterranean under the title of the City of Liverpool Steam Navigation Co., managed by D. and C. MacIver.[13] When it further became known that Charles MacIver senior had advanced capital to William for this project and that the two brothers Charles and Henry, lately Cunard's managing agents, had also joined in the formation, the Cunard directors jumped to a number of conclusions.[14] The first was that this new line was being established in opposition to Cunard and was, therefore, in contravention of the agreement made and signed by Charles MacIver senior with the new Cunard Company on 4 March 1880. The second was that Charles MacIver senior, again in default of the agreement, had fraudulently advanced capital to his youngest son from proceeds realised by the sale of some of his Cunard holdings.[15] The reaction was swift and, perhaps, unwise. Cunard's solicitors were instructed to seek an injunction preventing any member of the MacIver family from trading under the title of Burns and

MacIver.[16] The next step was to disassociate the new Cunard Company from the two firms Burns and MacIver and D. and C. MacIver, 'informing all Mediterranean ports and anyone else who dealt with these companies, that this had taken place'.[17] For his part, Charles MacIver senior strongly denied that he was in breach of contract. He had not realised assets held by the Cunard Company though he admitted advancing funds to William after July 1883, funds derived from his private fortune and made to his son as a personal gift.[18] As for William setting up a line in opposition to Cunard's Mediterranean interests, his reply was characteristic. 'I do not consider that my son William's action', he wrote, 'which I should add is entirely uncontrolled by me, is a breach either of the agreement of 4 March 1880 or of the assurance of 28 March last. I think it right to inform you that neither I nor my sons, the signatories to the agreement . . . are directly or indirectly concerned or interested in the success or failure of the Mediterranean scheme which Mr William MacIver is promoting.'[19]

It is not necessary to follow the twists and turns of the ensuing litigation. As the Cunard Board of Directors was not able to accept Charles MacIver's explanation of events, recourse to law was inevitable. One can only record this with regret as it brought to an end more than forty years of close personal and trusting relationship between the Cunard, Burns and MacIver families; but Charles MacIver had never been averse to fighting for what he believed were his legal entitlements and, in this case, his credibility and good faith had been impugned. Moreover Cunard's case was weak, partly because they had no positive proof that the MacIvers had acted in defiance of their agreement and partly because they had insufficient documentary evidence in support of their plea.[20]

On 12 January 1885 a motion in the Chancery Division of the High Court was made before Mr Justice Pearson on behalf of the plaintiffs (Cunard) for the production of further documents. It was explained that the action was being brought by Cunard to restrain the defendants who, with one exception, had been members of the 'old' Cunard Company, from interfering with the plaintiff Company's business.[21] The whole argument turned on the submission of documentary evidence that Charles MacIver senior and his sons Charles and Henry had advanced capital to William for the purpose of enabling him to start a shipping line to the Mediterranean in direct opposition to existing Cunard services. The MacIver case was that William had never been a member of the 'old' Company and consequently had not been party to any covenant forbidding him to enter into competition with the plaintiff Company.[22] The defendants strongly denied having made capital available to William to enable him to start an opposition line. In the absence of direct proof it was difficult to sustain the charges despite doubts about the actual intentions of William MacIver and his brothers. In the end common sense prevailed. On 19 March 1885 the Liverpool press reported that agreement had been reached. 'The long pending dispute between the Cunard Company and Messrs D. and C. MacIver', it was stated, 'has at last been settled to the mutual advantage of all the parties concerned.'[23] Under the terms of a private understanding Cunard waived any objection to William MacIver's new line entering the Mediterranean trade provided that his ships did not compete directly in those ports served by Cunarders. Should MacIver ships wish to engage in trans-Atlantic services, they were to be confined (until the agreement expired in 1894) to ports on the eastern seaboard of the United States, south of Charleston.[24]

So ended the active connection of the MacIver family with Cunard shipping interests. The MacIver capital in the Cunard Company, retained under the 1880 agreement, was eventually bought by John Burns and some of the directors, a procedure which caused annoyance to some shareholders, who claimed that such shares ought to have been made available for general purchase.[25] Nevertheless despite the rights or the wrongs of the issues raised, one potent cause of dissension had been removed. The MacIvers with all their expertise in the management of ships had gone. It was left to the directorate to engage the Company's resources in such manner that enterprise could be sustained. In this context new men with new ideas were probably a prerequisite for the successful management of the Company in the difficult conditions which faced British ships on the North Atlantic for approximately thirty years before the outbreak of The First World War.

II THE BUILDING PROGRAMME AND TRADE FLUCTUATIONS: ADMIRALTY AGREEMENTS: FLUCTUATIONS IN COSTS AND RECEIPTS: THE PROBLEM OF LARGE SHIPS AT LIVERPOOL

The implementation of Cunard's building programme went

rapidly ahead after 1881. Beginning with *Servia* (Cunard's first steel ship) and *Catalonia*, the process of modernising the fleet made progress with methodical regularity.[26] 'To meet the large and increasing trans-Atlantic business of the Company', it was stated, 'contracts have been entered into for the construction of three additional steamships of great size and power . . . and will be named respectively *Aurania, Pavonia* and *Cephalonia.*'[27] In part payment for this new construction the builders (Messrs J. and G. Thomson of Glasgow) took over two old Cunarders, *Hecla* and *Olympus*; both had been in service since 1860.[28]

Despite earlier optimistic reviews of prospects by the directors, however, trading conditions in the Atlantic and the Mediterranean areas of the Company's business grew steadily worse in 1881 and 1882. This was partly because of falling freight rates in the homeward trades and partly because of intense competition in the Mediterranean services. Indeed, by 1884, as we have already shown, most of the Mediterranean ships were barely covering voyage costs and returned no profit at all if depreciation charges were offset against receipts.[29] The answer to this deteriorating situation was given by the action of the directors in embarking more capital in two large steel screw ships 'of improved type and design' to be built by Messrs John Elder and Co. of Glasgow.[30] These were *Umbria* and *Etruria*, the two older vessels, *Parthia* and *Batavia*, now no longer profitable in operation, being taken by the builders in part payment.[31] To meet a portion of the cost of these new ships, debentures were issued to the extent of £250,000. Nevertheless trade continued to be depressed and profits were retained at relatively low levels.[32] 'To those who are acquainted with shipping', ran the Report for 1884, 'this reduction in the profits, which prevents the directors from adding to their insurance fund or recommending the payment of a dividend, will not be surprising.'[33] In an endeavour to increase competitive strength, therefore, the Company purchased *Oregon* at a cost of £220,000. She was a large ship, originally built by John Elder and Co. for Cunard's competitors, the Guion line, well built with a speed of 18½ knots and specially equipped for the carriage of cabin passengers.[34] The idea was that *Oregon* should become the fourth fast ship in a weekly service.

Despite the effects of generally depressed conditions which, for Cunard, lasted into the first months of 1886, there were two mitigating factors which helped to stimulate profitability. The first was a continuous reduction in working costs, and the second the leasing of ships to the Government.[35] In the spring of 1885, for example, *Umbria* and *Oregon* were chartered by the Admiralty for a period of six months. This was a precautionary measure taken as a result of a short-lived scare that Britain might be involved in a war with Russia.[36] The two vessels were completely armed and fitted out under the superintendence of Admiralty officers. In 1886 an agreement was made with the Admiralty whereby the five fastest vessels in Cunard's fleet should be held at the disposal of the Government for a period of five years, an annual retaining fee being paid for *Umbria*, *Etruria* and *Aurania* as part of the arrangement.[37] The Admiralty realised that to take over liners in a haphazard manner might lead to a waste of public money. The passenger liner companies for their part were only too ready to receive a subsidy in peacetime which would enable them to build fast ships for their trans-Atlantic services.

Cunard was not slow in recognising the advantages of such an arrangement. Accordingly they signed a treaty by which they undertook to keep *Aurania*, *Etruria* and *Umbria* running in such a way that they would be immediately available to the Admiralty as cruisers should their services be so required.[38] Furthermore they agreed to build gun platforms on their decks, to undertake the maintenance of gun mountings, to see that half their crews were R.N.R. ratings and to guarantee that they would fit these ships out as auxiliary cruisers in less than a week should an emergency arise. In return the Company received annually an estimated minimum of £20,000 per ship, a sum which when added to the mail subsidy, represented a considerable offsetting safeguard against loss in years of adverse trading conditions.

From the point of view of entrepreneurship, there is every sign that although the Cunard directors were successful in reducing costs, there was little prospect of achieving profit maximisation. We must now examine the fluctuations in working costs and receipts in greater detail. The two main items in working costs were fuel and wages. These amounted in the 1880s to approximately 53 per cent of total operating costs for trans-Atlantic voyages, whereas for the smaller class of ship engaged in the Mediterranean trade these same items accounted for less than 50 per cent.[39] Despite this difference, however, it was the Atlantic trade by virtue of volume alone that was the principal source of revenue and, ultimately, of profit. In practice, as already stated, it was the interaction of freight and passenger receipts which attracted resources into the Atlantic services – an interaction which the earlier Mediterranean trade (largely a produce trade) did not possess. The impact of a carefully planned building programme, whereby modern ships were constantly in process of replacing older and less efficient vessels, was of importance in determining the level of costs. Improvements in speed, design and accommodation enabled Cunard not only to take advantage of any increase in trade but were essential either for the reduction or stabilisation of unit costs at certain periods. If, for example, aggregate costs are expressed in costs per gross ton a definable pattern emerges. (See Table 5.1.)

Table 5.1
Costs per gross ton 1880–1914[40]

Year	£	Year	£
1880	15·5	1898	9·3
1881	13·4	1899	9·1
1882	11·9	1900	8·5
1883	11·3	1901	10·4
1884	9·3	1902	9·6
1885	9·9	1903	8·5
1886	10·4	1904	8·7
1887	10·6	1905	8·0
1888	11·7	1906	9·4
1889	12·1	1907	7·9
1890	12·3	1908	7·1
1891	11·9	1909	10·0
1892	11·2	1910	9·4
1893	9·1	1911	8·4
1894	10·0	1912	9·3
1895	8·3	1913	8·9
1896	9·1	1914	8·8
1897	9·1		

The high cost per gross ton in 1880 can be accounted for largely by the growing obsolescence of the old fleet. Thereafter until 1885 the effect of the introduction of new tonnage coupled with a determined policy of reducing operating costs is discernible. From 1886 to 1890 the continuous rise was caused by factors not entirely related to growth in activity, though between 1890 and 1896 there would appear to be some inverse correlation with fluctuations in trade. From 1896 to 1899 costs were kept relatively stable largely owing to the negotiation of favourable long-term coal contracts.⁴¹ In the years of acute competition from 1902 to 1905 there was a fairly consistent reduction. After 1906 the introduction of *Mauretania* and *Lusitania* obviously affected the picture, though the degree of variation from one year to another can be explained only be reference to the impact of disparate and external influences.

The favourable trend in the reduction of costs between 1881 and 1884 was, however, subsequently marred by two countervailing factors. The first was by the heavy incidence of accident and loss at sea. The new ship, *Aurania*, had to be withdrawn for six months in 1883 during the busiest season of the year; *Sidon* was lost in 1885 and the recently purchased *Oregon* early in 1886; *Demerara* was sunk without trace in 1887; *Nantes* was lost through collision on 7 November 1888 and *Malta* was stranded and lost on the coast of Cornwall in October 1889.⁴² Apart from the capital loss sustained by this heavy chapter of accidents amounting to approximately £350,000 (of which about 60 per cent was covered by outside insurance) the earning capacity of the fleet was thereby adversely affected. This, when coupled with the second factor, rising costs of coal and wages, added to the Company's difficulties for certain years, in maintaining stability in the level of costs. This, in turn, helps to explain the relatively high costs per gross ton during the years 1886–9.

There is evidence that the directors made strenuous efforts after 1890, particularly through the initiative of Sir William Forwood, to reduce coal costs. Coal contracts in the United States were renegotiated and a fresh approach was made to suppliers in North and South Wales and in Lancashire.⁴³ Nevertheless the gains which were made by these efforts were shortly dissipated through the employment of relatively faster and high-cost ships, such as *Campania* and *Lucania*, which were added to the fleet in 1893. There were signs, however, that the directors were reasonably successful in keeping costs within limits, particularly in relation to the changing age and composition of the fleet. In the 21 years to 1900, there were 11 years in which costs were above £10 per gross ton, whereas in the 14 years after 1900 there was only one such year. Alternatively, there were 9 years in the former period when costs were below £10 per gross ton and only 2 years in which they were below £9, in the latter period there were 12 and 8 respectively. In other words, the policy of the directors in keeping costs at a minimum was achieving a greater measure of success in the course of time. This would also imply strict control over all branches of expenditure and a generally consistent relationship between aggregate costs and growth of tonnage.

After 1900 Cunard's fuel costs rose sharply. A warning note was sounded at the Ordinary General Meeting for 1899 when it was stated that 'the advance in the price of coal increased the working expenses of the fleet'.[44] In fact average costs per ton had risen on the various contracts negotiated in the 1890s from 14s in 1890 to 17s 6d in 1898.[45] The fact was given further emphasis in 1902: 'When it is remembered', declared Lord Inverclyde, 'that the Company uses from 400,000 to 500,000 tons of coal in the year, it will be seen that an increase in the price of only 1 shilling per ton, means over £20,000 additional expenses and, as a matter of fact, the price of coal in this country went up a good many shillings last year. In 1900, when prices began to rise more rapidly, we were helped by our contracts, but during a considerable part of 1901, we had to bear the brunt of prices being at their highest. In fact, during 1901, the average price of coal being put upon our steamers in Liverpool, was 37 per cent higher than the average price for the five previous years.'[46]

In such circumstances, it was obvious that a change of policy was required and, as a countervailing influence to sole dependence on a high cost fuel, the Superintendent Engineer was asked on 11 December 1901 to report on the probable cost of altering *Tyria* to an oil-burning vessel.[47] As a more immediate and, perhaps, more practical step towards a reduction of coal consumption, efforts were made to obtain more information about the relative economy of turbines, compared with that of reciprocating engines. Tests were carried out with two sets of engines, one at Wallsend-on-Tyne and the other on the London, Brighton and South Coast Railway's steamers, *Arundel* and *Brighton*, the former set having reciprocating, the latter turbine engines.[48] From the point of view of costs, the shore tests showed that at full speed the turbine was 23 per cent more economical than the reciprocating engine; at nine-tenths speed, 16 per cent more economical and only became less efficient when speeds approached three-quarters or less.[49] In the prevailing opinion of the time, economy in operation was a priority, and the evaluation of relative advantage which the turbine had over the reciprocating engine at high speed could not be faulted.

Accordingly *Carmania* (1904) was fitted with three turbines and triple screws, and the new large, fast ships were powered by turbines.[50] In the case of *Lusitania* (1907), *Mauretania* (1907) and *Aquitania* (1914), each had four turbines and quadruple screws.[51] All other things being equal, these new ideas, once put into effect, helped in achieving a stabilisation (and in certain years a lowering) of unit costs, even though aggregate costs increased by reason of the added size and power of the fleet.

There were, however, other influences at work tending to offset economies produced by increasing applications of technical skill and engineering know-how – influences which were not always within the competence of the Company to control. As passenger liners became larger their very size, within the compass of current port facilities, precluded efficient handling either within the dock system at Liverpool or at New York. There were two chief causes of dis-economy, the first being the inadequate provision of dock space at Liverpool, and the second, insufficiency in the depth of water at the Bar of the Mersey estuary 'which at times causes much delay and expense as well as annoyance to passengers'.[52] This expense and annoyance was also prevalent at New York where, until the Ambrose Channel had been cut, no passage for very large ships into or out of the harbour could be made between sunset and sunrise.[53]

The lack of facility for large passenger liners at Liverpool had been a bone of contention since the early 1890s. The cargo liner owners, led by Alfred Holt, had resisted the efforts of passenger liner companies to secure larger and deeper docks, believing that Liverpool's future lay in the handling of bulk cargo rather than the servicing of passengers.[54] In this context it had been calculated that cargo ships had reached a foreseeable optimum size. As early as 23 November 1893, John Burns had engaged in a somewhat acrimonious correspondence with the Mersey Docks and Harbour Board, complaining that the two new Cunard mail ships, *Campania* and *Lucania*, had to be worked in the river as it was impossible for them to find accommodation in the docks.[55] The expenses of loading and discharging were thus greatly augmented. John Burns estimated that, for the four fast ships, *Umbria*, *Etruria*, *Campania* and *Lucania*, Cunard had incurred an additional cost of £12,000 in 1893 because these ships had to be moored and serviced in the river instead of at the Company's berth. Furthermore, Burns pointed out that under the terms of the 1858 Act, the Dock Board was empowered to keep the river free for navigation and to impose a penalty of up to double rates on ships moored in the river.[56] Cunard found itself in the position of having to pay rates for accommodation which it was unable to use and becoming liable at the same time to heavy penalties for servicing Cunarders in the river. The Dock Board were, rather surprisingly, unsympathetic to Cunard's case, replying by implication that the Company ought to have refrained from building large ships until adequate berthing space had been made available.[57] It was only when Burns made it known that Cunard might consequentially be driven to transfer the mail ships to another port, that a compromise was reached.[58]

With the building of *Lusitania* and *Mauretania*, however, the problem of adequate accommodation once again became urgent. 'Further serious cost in the working of these large ships', stated Cunard's Chairman in his report for 1908, 'is incurred owing to *Lusitania* and *Mauretania* being frequently unable to enter the docks at Liverpool owing to want of water or, when having entered, to leave when loaded. In consequence, the ships, more often than not, had to remain in the river from the time of arrival to time of departure, carrying out all the work of loading and discharging at high cost.'[59] At this time Canada Dock was the only dock with sufficient depth of water to cater for these large ships, but access was difficult as entrance could only be made through Sandon Basin and the Huskisson passage. This latter passage was but 90 feet wide, a limitation which obviously placed an inhibition on the size of ship to be laid down. This in turn was a fact which, in the prevailing opinion of 1910 to 1912, was not acceptable to passenger liner owners. The White Star Line, for example, after persistent efforts to persuade the Dock Board to deepen some of the docks to at least 18 feet below Old Dock Sill and also to deepen the river channel and cut the Bar, had already taken decisive action.[60] Their crack liner *Majestic*, being unable to use Canada Dock, had been removed together with other of their fast ships, to Southampton in 1907. The process of dredging the channel and of cutting the Bar was a continuous one, that of deepening the docks could be achieved only by the construction of a new system.

The whole vexed question of sufficiency of water and size of docks at Liverpool came to a head with the prospective building of *Aquitania*. This Cunard ship took three years to complete, having a

Costs, Revenue and Returns, 1880–1914   131

length of 867 feet 7 inches and a beam of 97 feet and a total gross tonnage of 45,647. This was by far the biggest ship built for the Company. Her beam gave but a 3-foot clearance through the river gates into Canada half-tide basin and was 7 feet wider than the Huskisson passage into Canada basin. Under these circumstances, therefore, the Cunard directors were faced with the dilemma either that they could build no ship beyond a certain size or that, like White Star, they would have to transfer the base of their mail service to Southampton. 'We lay this difficulty before the Liverpool Dock Board', stated Alfred Booth, 'and they got to work at once to see how it could be overcome.'[61] The solution seemed to be in completion of Gladstone graving dock 'which will be completed, as far as human foresight can provide, shortly before *Aquitania* is ready for sea'.[62] The graving dock referred to was the first part of a much larger system. It was opened on 11 July 1913, and *Aquitania* was delivered from John Brown's on 18 May 1914.

III CUNARD'S EARNING CAPACITY AND ALLOCATION OF RESOURCES: PURCHASE OF THOMSON LINE

If we now turn to Cunard's revenue earning capacity for the period 1880–1914, it is evident that passenger and freight receipts were determined by two main factors. The first was the effectiveness of management in allocating resources into new tonnage in order to check the ageing composition of the fleet; the second was through measures designed to offset cyclical fluctuations in trade either by the alleviation of competition within the framework of Conference agreements or by direct government subvention.

The figures in Table 5.2 give the gross earnings per ton of shipping employed. The revenue is that for both passengers and freight for all services including Atlantic and Mediterranean, together with receipts from the carriage of mails.

Table 5.2.
Earnings per gross ton[63]

Year	£	Year	£
1880	18·5	1886	12·4
1881	15·2	1887	13·5
1882	14·5	1888	15·2
1883	12·9	1889	16·0
1884	10·2	1890	14·8
1885	12·0	1891	14·1

Earnings per gross ton[63]

1892	12·8	1904	9·1
1893	10·6	1905	9·7
1894	9·9	1906	12·4
1895	9·4	1907	10·1
1896	11·2	1908	10·1
1897	10·9	1909	12·9
1898	11·4	1910	13·5
1899	10·6	1911	11·5
1900	12·7	1912	13·8
1901	12·1	1913	12·8
1902	11·8	1914	12·8
1903	10·3		

It will be seen that there was a downward trend in earnings from 1880 to 1885. The causes of this decline have been analysed in Chapter 4. From 1886 to 1889 there was considerable recovery. Thereafter until 1895 (and again for reasons already discussed) there was a decline consistent with other indicators in the general levels of economic activity. From 1895 to 1899 the somewhat better results were undoubtedly caused by Cunard entering the North Atlantic pooling agreement. The effect of rate cutting during the years from 1903 to the middle of 1905 when Cunard was in open contest with the Morgan combine and their German allies, is clearly discernible; the years 1907 and 1908 reflected the poor state of the American economy, but from 1909 to 1914 the earning capabilities of the larger and faster liners, combined with efforts to reduce costs, were adding weight to higher and relatively more stable returns. An additional element in this improvement was provided by Cunard's entry into the Canadian trade.[64]

Although earnings per gross ton fell between 1880 and 1885, costs also fell so that net margins were reasonably well maintained. Alternatively, costs rose between 1886 and 1890, but earnings also rose at a faster rate, consequently margins were again well sustained. In the 1890s, though costs were generally maintained at low levels, earnings fell sharply from 1890 to 1895. Thereafter, until 1899, they fluctuated on a slightly rising trend. If one excludes the year 1895, in which costs exceeded earnings, the margins were lower for the decade 1890 to 1899 than for the preceding ten years. After 1900 (which was an exceptionally good year) the margin between costs and earnings showed little sign of real improvement, and in 1904 earnings barely covered costs. The rate war was temporarily suspended in 1905 and there was a consequential increase in voyage profits. From 1908 to 1909 the margin rose to about £3 per ton and from this latter date until 1914 the average was about £4 per ton.

Behind this catalogue lies a series of determined efforts on the part of Cunard management to maintain profitability despite adverse trading conditions at some periods and despite intense commercial rivalry at others. We shall examine the full range of Cunard's accounts in the final section of this chapter in an endeavour to discover the volume of funds available for allocation and the rates of return on capital employed. For the present it is sufficient to take the broad view that, during the period under review, Cunard never failed in aggregate terms to make a gross profit. Dividend policy was conservative and no dividends were paid in poor years or when the directors considered it inadvisable to do so. Reserves were fully used and replenished in good years. Thus, in the early 1880s, the reserves were put wholly to the rebuilding of the fleet and a debenture debt of £450,000 was incurred by 1885 in addition to some £300,000 of other liabilities.[65] Yet by 1888 the Chairman was able to report that the debentures had been repaid and, by 1891, reserves had been built up to £700,000.[66] This was wise management because, in the lean years from 1892 to 1895 these reserves were used to improve the competitive strength of the fleet. From 1898 reserves were again built up and by 1900 liquid assets were £328,000 and reserves £550,000.[67] This policy was continued until 1914. It is therefore possible to express the view that although Cunard experienced considerable difficulty at certain times in the years from 1880 to 1914, the Company not only managed to survive, but remained financially stable. This opinion must, however, be qualified by the fact that the Company was in receipt of government subvention and, as we shall see further in section IV, was given special consideration and financial backing from the Government after 1902.

How, in physical terms, did the directors attempt to meet the economic problems of fluctuating costs and revenue? As already stated, the 1880s were years in which Cunard management tried to overcome the ageing composition of the fleet by a planned programme of rebuilding. The effectiveness of such a policy was blunted after 1885 by rising fuel costs, higher wages and costs of materials, additional expenditure for the implementation of the Merchant Shipping (Life Saving Appliances) Act of 1888 and losses incurred by the dock strike of 1890.[68] The two new powerful liners, *Campania* and *Lucania*, introduced in 1893, did not immediately justify expectations as high income earners simply because the timing of their initiation coincided with a down-swing in trade. They were therefore unable to realise the full potential of their earning capacity.

Next came the allocation of resources to the cargo side of Cunard's business. Two new cargo ships, *Sylvania* and *Carinthia*, were put into service in 1895 and were worked to reasonably full capacity by taking advantage of improving conditions in trade.[69] Furthermore, in the expectation of a likely improvement in trade after 1900, a twin-screw cargo steamship named *Ultonia* of 8056 gross tons was added to the fleet in 1898. She was bought on the stocks from Messrs Swan, Hunter and Co. and fitted with berths for third class passengers, thus serving as a dual-purpose vessel.[70]

For the same kind of trade two other twin-screw ships, *Ivernia* and *Saxonia*, together with new cargo ships for the Mediterranean trade, were ordered.[71] In short, the directors were applying resources and bringing ships into service capable of meeting a more precise demand, in the hope that unit costs could be kept at a minimum and earning power increased. Unfortunately, however, neither *Ivernia* nor *Saxonia* (twin-screws, 10,000 I.H.P.) introduced in 1900, achieved this end. In 1901, for example, the greatest shrinkage in aggregate receipts occurred in homeward freights earned for the previous year 'although the volume of the cargo carried by the Company was greater than ever before'.[72] Implicit in this statement was the fact that rates per ton for 1901 were far below those for many years past. In this case, therefore, the anticipation of the directors was not fulfilled. In the same year, first and second class passenger traffic was somewhat below that for 1900 though third class earnings showed some increase.[73] In this latter fact, perhaps, there was reason to believe that the introduction of the dual-purpose ship fitted for cargo and third class passengers, might provide more flexible facilities in the interest of profitability.

Nevertheless, for the first four years after 1900 conditions on the North Atlantic were such that fears were constantly expressed by Cunard's shareholders that the laying down of new ships, when the fleet as a whole was being worked below full capacity, might be a costly and hazardous policy to pursue.[74] By 1905, however, levels of trade were beginning to show signs of improvement. Homeward freights increased and passenger traffic became more stable; the emigrant trade, on the other hand, was large and showed signs of increasing. There was, therefore, at this time, justification for putting into service two ships *Carmania* and *Caronia* (1905) and, under the provisions of the 1903 agreement with the Government, for continuing with the laying down of *Lusitania* and *Mauretania*. Thus, the directors were guided by strategic and commercial pressures in maintaining an up-to-date fleet, so designed that it could take every advantage of changing conditions on the North Atlantic. In so far as the intervention of the Morgan combine affected Cunard's earning capacity, it strengthened the directors' resolve to secure a more intensive working of the faster ships, to adopt a more positive attitude towards the removal of uneconomic services and the substitution of more profitable ones, to sell old ships and replace them with dual-purpose carriers and to eliminate waste in all branches of the Company's activities.

The year 1909 was in many respects a turning point in Cunard's struggle to attain a greater measure of efficiency. Emigration to the United States increased considerably, although receipts from such traffic did not rise proportionately as eastbound passages were less than in 1908.[75] Nevertheless as a result of the Conference agreement concluded between all the main passenger lines in this latter year, both the North Atlantic and Mediterranean tariffs were maintained at normal rates. Earnings were therefore fairly buoyant and the Company's financial position was greatly strengthened. There was, however, some check to earning capacity through the stranding of *Slavonia* off the Azores and her subsequent abandonment as a complete loss;[76] there was also an outbreak of fire in *Lucania* whilst she was in dock at Liverpool, the damage being so severe that it was necessary to put her into the hands of the Underwriters.[77] Both vessels, however, were adequately insured and net loss was kept at a minimum. The steamships *Etruria*, *Aleppo*, *Cherbourg* and *Saragossa* 'being no longer suitable for the trades in which they were employed' were sold; while in order to maintain the Mediterranean cargo trade, three suitable ships were purchased and renamed, *Phrygia*, *Thracia* and *Lycia*.[78] A new contract was placed with Swan, Hunter for a ship of 18,000 tons gross to be called *Franconia*, intended for the Boston trade.[79]

The whole point about these various changes in the composition of the fleet was that they formed part of a deliberate policy based on a far-sighted premise. 'A great change has been coming over the Atlantic freight business', so ran the Report for 1909, 'a change which, today, must be clearly recognised and faced. On the one hand, we find that the rapidly growing population of the United States will, before very long, absorb that country's entire production of foodstuffs; on the other hand, while twenty years ago the passenger steamer had to be supplemented by the cargo steamer, today the modern type of steamer of moderate power in proportion to her larger size, is able to do the work of both. There does not, therefore, appear to be much further prospect of profitable employment for purely cargo steamers at such ports as Boston and New York.'[80] Accordingly the *Sylvania*, the last cargo vessel in the fleet, was put up for sale. It is a matter of some relevance that as a result of these various changes, the working costs of the fleet as a whole were reduced by approximately £190,000 in 1909 and by a further £42,000 in the following year.[81]

One further development needs to be mentioned. In 1911 direct contact with Canada was established through the purchase of a passenger and cargo business owned by the Thomson Line. 'We have felt for some time', stated the Chairman, 'that an extension of our business to Canada was eminently desirable and I am glad to say that our entry into the trade has been received in a most friendly spirit by the other lines with which we shall be cooperating.'[82] From the start, weekly cargo service was established by running certain cargo steamers of the Cairn Line in conjunction with Cunard's own fortnightly passenger sailings. This venture was not only relevant in the context of Cunard's earning capacity, but it affords yet another example of the extension of Cunard's strength in the new conditions prevailing after 1909.

In these ways the Cunard directors sought to bring varying degrees of stabilisation to the cost–revenue equation of the Company. These efforts obviously have to be viewed within the deeper perspective of financial management as a whole; but before doing this we must return to the *political* aspect of management, a function no whit less important than commercial or purely economic aspects of the Company's direction. In 1902 the stakes were raised by Cunard's rivals. Company prospects became a matter of international diplomacy involving government decisions as to future development.

IV THE MORGAN COMBINE AND THE 1903 AGREEMENT

The foregoing analysis of costs and revenue has been made within the context of Cunard's ability to adjust policy to meet the changing conditions of trade subject to their own competence in the allocation of resources. In 1902, however, a series of events occurred which were not only relevant to a consideration of the elements determining future profitability, but which also raised national issues of policy related to foreign competition. Before we engage in any further consideration of Cunard's financial management, therefore, it is necessary to have some understanding of events in 1902 if only to confirm the conclusion that the ensuing changes in the financial structure of the Company marked a turning point in Cunard's history.

In April 1901 J. Pierpont Morgan and Co., American bankers and railroad financiers, purchased the ordinary shares of Frederick Leyland and Co. (1900) Ltd, a company which was, at that time, part of the Ellerman group of shipping interests.[83] This purchase was only the first part of a much larger scheme. On 4 February 1902 a provisional agreement was entered into between J. P. Morgan and Co., and the Oceanic Steam Navigation Co. Ltd (White Star line, Ismay, Imrie and Co.), the British and North Atlantic Steam Navigation Co. Ltd (Dominion line), the Mississippi and Dominion S.S. Co. Ltd, the International Navigation Co. (American line), the Atlantic Transport Co. of West Virginia (Atlantic Transport line). The combine came into being in 1902 when the International Navigation Co., successor to the old Inman line, changed its name to the International Mercantile Marine Co. The capital of the new Corporation was increased from $15 million to $120 million, half of which was in ordinary shares on which a dividend was limited to 10 per cent while debentures were still outstanding, and the other half in 6 per cent cumulative preference stock.[84] In addition the Corporation had authority to issue $50 million collateral trust debentures bearing 4½ per cent per annum.

At first glance this was a most formidable combine of shipping interests, engaged in the North Atlantic trade under a centralised direction. This over-capitalised organisation provided a direct threat to Cunard's position on the North Atlantic, not so much from the scope and range of competitive shipping activities, for these existed before the combine was formed, but from the fact that it could adopt a comprehensive policy on freight rates and put new tonnage on to routes which, even in time of general shipping depression, were relatively profitable. Furthermore the overall power of the new group was augmented by purchases made by individual members; for example, the Atlantic Transport bought Cunard's old rival, the National Line, and White Star gained control of the Shaw Savill Line of New Zealand; with the Leyland Line had gone the West-India and Pacific Steam Ship Co., also the Wilson, Furness, Leyland connection.[85] As a further measure of intention the scope of the combine's power was enlarged by the inclusion of the Red Star Line. The attractive influence of so great a combination went even further. The formidable Albert Ballin, guiding spirit of the Hamburg–Amerika line, recognising the difference which this array of companies would make to North Atlantic trade, came to a ten-year agreement with the promoters. This agreement provided for a regulated interchange of shares and certain communities of interest, Ballin undertaking at the same time to persuade North German Lloyd to come into specific agreements designed to promote harmonious working relations with the new group.[86]

It would be an understatement of fact to infer that the advent of the Morgan combine created a stir in British shipping circles. In Liverpool and London wildest speculation fed by rumour prevailed, both as to the intentions of the group and as to the possible repercussions on British shipping interests as a whole. In the first place the British Government was directly involved because, under existing agreements between White Star and the Admiralty, certain ships were retained as armed cruisers. The prospect of the White Star fleet being taken over by an American-owned company, therefore, raised problems as to the future status of these ships.[87] Questions were asked in Parliament expressing concern as to the future handling of these ships once they had passed under American ownership; a concern which was not altogether allayed even when assurances were given that only the shares of White Star had been transferred.[88] The ships would continue to sail under the British flag. In fact, the British Government's right to take over White Star ships was made binding in a further agreement with the shipping combine, signed on 1 August 1903.[89]

This somewhat bald statement of fact, however, hides many interesting moves which went on behind the scenes. The first fact to get clear is that the creation of the Morgan combine virtually coincided with the death of John Burns, first Lord Inverclyde. Rightly or wrongly it was anticipated that his holding of capital in Cunard might become available for purchase and that Morgan might endeavour to secure such shares should they come on the market.[90] This led to speculation that the Company as a whole might eventually be taken over. From this point, therefore, it is necessary to clarify the course of events. Rumour was to some extent supported by apparent evidence when by the spring of 1902 at least five approaches had been made to Cunard. First, towards the end of 1901 feelers were put out by a firm of London solicitors. Under instructions from a financier and company promoter named H. Osborne O'Hagan they made an offer for shares 'on behalf of the American shipping combine';[91] secondly, T. A. Bellew, who had previously been associated with Cunard, renewed a former proposal on behalf of his 'anonymous clients';[92] thirdly, the stockbrokers acting for the trustees of the late Lord Inverclyde's estate were approached on 18 March by a firm of Glasgow Stockbrokers (Messrs Watson and Smith) with an offer to take up an unlimited quantity of Cunard shares at the highest price paid during the previous ten years – £20 per share;[93] fourthly, on 14 March hearing of the possibility of an unknown (probably American) bidder, the engineers and shipbuilders, Messrs Vickers, Maxim and Co., expressed their willingness to take up a large block of the Company's shares 'which execution of the late Chairman's estate had brought on to the market';[94] finally, Sir Christopher Furness, a Cunard shareholder and Chairman of Furness, Withy and Co., revived a plan which he had earlier proposed for taking over the Company.[95]

Some of these manifestations of interest must have seemed curiously unrealistic to the Chairman, the second Lord Inverclyde, for it was only on 8 March that he had heard of the Morgan agreement which had been signed on 4 February.[96] On learning the details he immediately informed Lord Selborne, First Lord of the Admiralty. The implications of the preceding moves were not really understood, but both Inverclyde and Selborne were alive to the possibility that Cunard's shareholders might sell out to Morgan at tempting prices.[97] Furthermore as the Burns family no longer held a controlling interest, it would be possible for Cunard to pass out of British ownership. Selborne replied expressing himself as 'disturbed and uneasy' and, after consulting his ministerial colleagues, he had an interview with Lord Inverclyde on 17 March asking him as a first step, to consider adding a pre-emptive clause to the current Admiralty contract; this would prevent the transfer of any of the Company's reserve ships to a foreign owner without the Admiralty's consent during the term of the existing agreement.[98] In the interests of his shareholders Inverclyde rejected this request. He also pointed out that the Company, no less than the Admiralty, were aware of the dangers of allowing American shipping companies to outbuild British companies, but that Cunard could not lay down and operate economically fast, large ships without adequate government support.[99] As a counter proposal he offered to hold thirteen named vessels at the disposal of the Admiralty in return for an increased subvention,[100] but the offer was declined by Selborne. These exchanges marked the opening of a protracted series of negotiations between Cunard and the British Government which were to last until the end of August 1902.

It now became necessary for the two sides to define their respective positions. In a particular sense, the creation of the Morgan combine had raised issues requiring some revision of government policy regarding rights over and subvention of armed merchant cruisers. There was already in being a revived Parliamentary Committee on existing steamships subsidies and it was Selborne's opinion that the work of this Committee should be kept separate from any future government subvention for cruiser building.[101] Selborne was therefore not prepared to act until he had the full backing of his ministerial colleagues, together with the findings of yet another committee on the future policy of the Government on cruiser building. It was estimated that such information would not be available for at least a year. In the meantime Selborne had to safeguard the Admiralty's vessels. Any further subvention must, therefore, be considered as a separate question.[102]

With the full support of his fellow directors Inverclyde had no option but to insist that consideration be given to the impact of events on his Company's position as a whole, including its future development. In this context, it was not possible to distinguish between payment of existing subsidies and the building of new ships, for the number, type and design of the latter must inevitably determine the size of the fleet which Cunard could profitably operate.[103] This point of view was reinforced by figures (supplied by Inverclyde) showing the relative costs of building and working large, fast ships on the North Atlantic. Comparing the mail subsidies paid by the U.S. Government to their shipowners and referring to the subsidy Bill then before Congress, he was able to show that American shipowners were not only receiving more than the subvention plus subsidy which Cunard was now suggesting, but that the new Bill before Congress would greatly increase this.[104] Cunard could not, therefore, bind itself more tightly to the Admiralty until it knew what the British Government were prepared to offer in return. By the middle of April 1902 it was stalemate between the two sides.

But there were signs that pressures were beginning to build up. Several Cunard shareholders at the Ordinary General Meeting on 10 April showed a lively interest in the offers which had been made to purchase shares.[105] At the same time a sixth prospective purchaser appeared in the shape of Henry Wilding, bearing instructions from C. A. Griscom, President of the American Line, to enquire whether Cunard would be prepared to enter the Morgan combine.[106] The inducement offered was on the basis of £18 per share value for 55 per cent of the shares, but the offer was declined. There is some evidence that before declining Cunard indicated that purchase might be acceptable at £20 per share.[107] Inverclyde's account of this particular negotiation is given in a letter which he wrote to Bruce Ismay on 18 May 1905. Referring to the price offered by Wilding, Inverclyde said: 'In reply I stated that neither the basis on which the offer had been made, nor the price indicated commended themselves to me. Further, that unless the offer was for the Cunard Company as a whole, I must be satisfied before placing it before the shareholders, that the proposed combination would have as much interest in keeping up the Cunard Company as in developing any other section of the syndicate.'[108] As the Morgan combine were not prepared to take over the whole of Cunard's assets, they withdrew from the discussions.

This approach, however, strengthened Inverclyde's hands in negotiating with the British Government. It was at this juncture that questions were asked in Parliament about the subsidised vessels in the White Star fleet about to enter the Morgan combine, and the formation of the Mercantile Cruisers Committee was announced. But the fear still remained that Cunard's shareholders might dispose of their holdings to the highest bidder, and Lord Inverclyde was accordingly urged by Selborne not to commit Cunard without previous notice to the Government.[109] The serious nature of the problem was now fully realised, so much so that control of the situation became vested in the hands of a three-man committee of the Cabinet, Lord Selborne, Joseph Chamberlain and G. W. Balfour.[110]

On 2 May 1902 the Government took a fresh initiative inviting Lord Inverclyde to issue a new statement of his Company's proposals. These proposals (which were afterwards reported to the Mercantile Cruisers Committee) were briefly that the Government should enter into a twenty-year agreement with Cunard by which it would provide the Company with a loan of £5·2 million at 5 per cent for the laying down of nine fast ships (of which the Government should be mortgagee) and that the Admiralty subvention should be increased as these ships became operational.[111] The *raison d'être* of the proposal was that by such subventions Cunard's shareholders would be guaranteed an annual 5 per cent dividend; in return the Government would be getting the benefit of the fastest vessels afloat, and be secure from take-over by a foreign power.[112] This was the end of a phase in the negotiations and, for the next three months, interest was shifted to a new series of proposals put forward by another would-be purchaser.

Some time between 22 March and 12 April, Sir Christopher Furness offered to purchase Cunard shares with an implied desire to take over control of the Company.[113] There followed a somewhat obscure passage of move and countermove in which each side sought to win advantage; Inverclyde, for his part, always having an eye on possible repercussions on the Government. On 31 May he sent a circular to all shareholders stating that negotiations affecting the future position of the Company were in progress. 'It is not possible, however, to make any more definite statement at present, or until progress based on these negotiations has been submitted to H.M. Government.'[114] Amongst the shareholders themselves, speculation about the nature of the negotiations was ill-founded and inaccurate in deduction. Subsequent to this circulation rumours were rife that Cunard might be preparing to enter the Morgan combine – a thesis which we have discovered was entirely without foundation.¹¹⁵ Alternatively, it was thought that Cunard was planning a countermove to Morgan through the promotion of a rival combination of British shipping companies. There were grounds in support of the speculation for moves were taking place for the purpose of forming such a combination.

There is evidence to suggest that this new conception sprang from an embryonic idea of that shrewd Liverpool shipowner, Sir Alfred Jones. In a letter to J. B. Ismay, Chairman of White Star, Clinton Dawkins, a member of the London Board of the International Mercantile Marine, added facts by way of elucidation. 'I understand', he wrote, 'that attempts are being made to organise a rival combination embracing the Cunard, the Elder Dempster and the Allan lines and that Lord Inverclyde's circular refers to these negotiations. It has nothing to do with the combination into which the White Star has entered (i.e. the Morgan combine). I believe that Sir A. L. Jones is the moving spirit in this attempt and it is expected – but I do not know with what warranty – that the British and Canadian Governments will assist with subsidies.'¹¹⁶ Ismay's concern was evident from the strenuous attempts which he made to uncover the facts. 'Do you know anything about the Cunard deal', he wrote to the Rt Hon. W. J. Pirrie, Chairman of Harland and Wolff, 'if so, you might let me know. We can get no information of an authoritative nature. Rumour has it that your friends Jones and Furness are at the bottom of it.'¹¹⁷ Correspondence with many other shipowners confirmed Ismay's fears. Jones was known to have ready access to Joseph Chamberlain and other members of the Cabinet, a relationship which was regarded with suspicion by many British shipowners.¹¹⁸ 'The genesis of the rival British combination I learn from the Government', wrote Dawkins, 'is as follows: the Government has been frightened by unauthorised language used by certain people to the effect that our (Morgan) combination is to be rapidly expanded and is to be used either to absorb all the other lines in the Atlantic or to clear them off the sea. I need hardly say that there is no such intention on the part of our friends and, indeed, the Government perfectly realise that Mr Morgan cannot be credited with any such intention . . . In order to obviate any such possibility the Government are favouring the consolidation of the outstanding lines in the Atlantic, viz. the Cunard, Allan and Elder Dempster . . . There is no question of the Government giving this new combination exaggerated subsidies, though there may be some small improvement on existing subsidies.'[119]

In fact, the account of this whole episode contained in the Cunard files testifies to the general accuracy of Dawkins's information. It is clear that the Government became disturbed by the possibility that Cunard might be taken over by the Morgan combine. Selborne had made it clear, when he wrote to Inverclyde, pointing out that there were three possible courses open to the Company. Cunard could join the American combine ('to this', added Selborne, 'we strongly object and will do all we can to assist you to justify yourself to your shareholders for not doing so'); secondly, that the Cunard Company should remain exactly as it was and fight the combine single-handed ('only with increased assistance from the Government in some form'); lastly, to enter into some kind of co-operation with other British shipowners ('which, if feasible, we should distinctly prefer').[120] This statement was considered by Lord Inverclyde to be unsatisfactory and he replied bluntly: 'I think the time has come when you should say what you intend to do with regard to the Cunard Company and not continue on the present indefinite course.'[121]

At this juncture Sir Christopher Furness submitted his plans (referred to above) for a combine of British lines and there were grounds for believing that the Government would assist him. Within a week of Furness's proposal the news was made public of the proposed sale of White Star shares to Morgan, with the terms of the alliance between the American lines and the two German shipping companies, Hamburg–Amerika and North German Lloyd.

At face value this was not only a formidable threat to Cunard and other British companies trading across the Atlantic, it was also a danger to national interests which the Government could ill afford to ignore. In view of the importance of the issues raised, therefore, it is surprising that the Government should have dragged its feet. It was still within the bounds of possibility that Cunard's shareholders would be tempted to sell out to Morgan. For the time being, however, the prospect of a possible link-up with the Furness combine seemed to Lord Inverclyde the only immediate course to pursue.[122]

On 10 June 1902 Inverclyde attended a meeting at which were

present Sir Ernest Cassel (representing Government opinion), Sir Christopher Furness and Sir Alfred Jones. A memorandum was prepared setting out the details of the proposed new combine. This was to be based on a capital structure of £20 million and was to include the Cunard, Elder Dempster and Beaver lines. Some £6,750,000 was to be set aside for building new tonnage in return for a subsidy of £350,000 additional to the existing mail contracts.[123] Two days later Sir Christopher Furness was asked by Lord Selborne, Joseph Chamberlain and G. W. Balfour to modify the proposals.[124] Though revised estimates were submitted, it had become evident by the end of June that the Government were not prepared to underwrite the scheme.[125] When finally Sir Alfred Jones insisted that the Canadian part of the scheme involving the Beaver line must be kept separate from the rest of the merger, the whole proposal, lacking both Government support and no real enthusiasm from the intended participants, collapsed without regret or recrimination.[126]

The next move in the negotiations was taken by Lord Inverclyde. On 30 July he had another meeting with Sir Ernest Cassel and Joseph Chamberlain at the Colonial Office, but he was unable to obtain any satisfactory assurance that the Government would take a decision about Cunard; he was told that a decision could not be made until October.[127] Thereupon, Lord Inverclyde wrote to Chamberlain outlining the very serious position into which the shareholders of the Company had been placed, largely because of repeated delays arising from the inability of the Government to come to a decision.[128] He made it clear that if the Government were to do nothing, the Company would be faced with either absorption or annihilation; the situation in which Cunard now found itself was a direct result of Lord Selborne's insistence that the Company should not join the Morgan combine and he (Lord Inverclyde) now had to justify his action to the shareholders for not taking such a step.[129] Accompanying this forthright statement were further proposals for immediate consideration. They were as follows:

1. A Government loan to the Company of £2,400,000 at 2½ per cent to provide for two large new ships.
2. An annual subvention of £150,000 as soon as the new ships were built.

3. The then existing annual subvention of £20,000 to be raised to £66,000 pending the completion of the new ships.
4. The payment for mails to be continued at not less than the present rates.
5. The Cunard Company to repay this loan at not less than 5 per cent per annum.

This letter and the new proposals had the desired effect, Chamberlain replying immediately that the Government were prepared to renew negotiations.[130] The Cabinet met on 7 August and on the same day Balfour wrote to Lord Inverclyde that the meeting had been strongly against paying any additional subsidy until the two new ships were ready, and as a *sine qua non* the Government should have, as security for the repayment of the loan, the general assets of the Company in addition to the two new ships.[131] In all other respects, the proposals put forward on 1 August were satisfactory. Agreement was ultimately reached and the terms were published in a speech which Mr Balfour delivered at the Cutler's Feast in Sheffield on 30 September 1902.[132]

In essence the agreement confirmed the loan for the building of two fast, new ships, the loan to bear interest at $2\frac{3}{4}$ per cent; security for the loan was to be a first charge on the two new vessels, together with the existing fleet and general assets of the Company. The whole was to be repaid within a period of twenty years. In return the Government was to pay Cunard an annual subvention of £150,000 instead of the existing Admiralty payment. Perhaps the most pertinent clauses, in view of the attempt by the Morgan combine to take over British shipping firms, were those in which Cunard pledged itself (during the term of the agreement) to remain a British concern 'and that under no circumstances shall the management of the Company be in the hands of, or the shares of the vessels of the Company held by, other than British subjects'.[133] Furthermore, during the currency of the agreement Cunard was to hold at the disposal of the Government the whole of its fleet and all other vessels as built. There was also a further undertaking that the Company should not unduly raise freight rates or give preferential rates to foreigners.[134]

One might presume that sufficient safeguards had been established in both the interests of Cunard and the International Mercantile Marine; but it must also be remembered that, side by side with the negotiations which the Government had been conducting with Lord Inverclyde, were those which were taking place with J. P. Morgan for the acquisition of Ismay's White Star Line. In the event only the share capital of White Star was transferred to the Morgan combine, the Government insisting on continued use of vessels for naval, military or postal services, as and when required; but it was also stipulated that 'vessels of uncommercial speed (i.e. especially fast vessels) which H.M. Government may require to be constructed and which were primarily designed for service in time of war, were not included in this agreement'.[135] The majority of directors in British companies within the Morgan combine were to be British subjects; no British ship in the combination nor any ship built for a British company was to be transferred to a foreign registry without the written consent of the President of the Board of Trade. All British ships were to be officered by British subjects, and sailors and crews were controlled by a ratio laid down by the Government. The Admiralty also exercised the right to purchase or hire any British ships in the combine on terms similar to those already in existence between the Admiralty and the White Star Line. Finally at least one half of any new tonnage built for the combine was to be for British companies in that group.[136]

It has been necessary to give a detailed account leading to the formation of the International Mercantile Marine and its effect upon the Cunard Company. As we have already seen in the previous chapter, the commercial repercussions were serious. Cunard was now faced with the formidable threat of a unified competition across the Atlantic and also from the two German lines in alliance with the American combine. In political terms, however, it seems obvious that by an adroit manoeuvre the expertise of Selborne, Chamberlain and Balfour had extracted the last scrap of advantage from the negotiations with Morgan and his representatives. They had retained the fleet of Cunard and partly that of White Star in required national service and had, as far as possible, acquired safeguards over areas of future development.

No less important, however, had been Lord Inverclyde's adept handling of his Company's interests. He had exerted pressure at the right time and given little in return for an assurance of future security within the framework of a virtual Government partnership. By contrast Bruce Ismay had emerged from the negotiations weakened in strength and prestige. His firm, Ismay, Imrie and Co., ceased to exist and he was henceforth to hold a relatively minor position within the power structure of the new combine.[137] It is also difficult to understand what long-term benefit Morgan had gained from taking over the share capital of White Star. The British Government's insistence on retaining White Star ships under the British flag inhibited any extension of American control, apart from that of a financial nature. The flow of White Star resources to the International Mercantile Marine made it necessary for White Star to seek overdrafts from their bankers, Glyn, Mills and Co., in order to finance certain shipbuilding requirements.[138] As a result Cunard emerged as the premier British passenger line, secure in its position and recognised by the Government as a national asset.

Although Cunard had successfully overcome a crisis of first magnitude in political and financial terms, it still had to face the commercial effects of stronger competition in the North Atlantic passenger trade. This was reflected in the rate of return on capital employed and in the flow of resources available to management. Within this compass costs bore a high proportion to revenue – at least until the new ships under the 1903 agreement came into service. As a final exercise, therefore, we propose to examine the availability of funds and the return on capital employed for the whole period 1880–1914. In this analysis the short-term effect of Morgan's intervention should be discernible as well as the capability of Cunard, in the longer term, to achieve recovery.

V THE RETURN ON CAPITAL

The events so far described in this and preceding chapters had an obvious bearing on Cunard's general financial position from year to year throughout the whole period before 1914. We propose, therefore, to make a more detailed examination of the Company's accounts to obtain a better understanding of financial policy and management. In particular we shall endeavour to establish a more precise relationship between the fluctuating fortunes of the Company and the control which the directors exercised over the allocation of resources. Finally it is hoped that from the figures available an estimate of rates of return on capital employed may be made. By such indicators definition may be given to the relative success or failure of the directors in meeting and overcoming adverse pressures on the general levels of financial stability.

Costs, Revenue and Returns, 1880–1914

The following analysis is necessary in the interests of accuracy. Table 5.3 shows the operating position of Cunard, giving gross income from passengers, freights and mails in column 1; operating expenses are given in column 2 and depreciation and inventory adjustments in column 3.[139] If columns 2 and 3 are deducted from column 1, the balance as shown in column 4 is net operating profit.

Table 5.3

(£000)

Year	Gross income (1)	Operating expenses (2)	Depreciation and inventory adjustments (3)	Net operating profit (4)
1880	1138	955	60	123
1881	1002	863	67	72
1882	1118	917	90	111
1883	1075	937	93	45
1884	1026	937	87	2
1885	1100	907	141	52
1886	1134	952	138	44
1887	1214	950	135	129
1888	1338	1030	135	173
1889	1382	1045	131	206
1890	1286	1064	126	96
1891	1222	1033	125	64
1892	1111	974	126	11
1893	1199	1028	154	17
1894	1117	1028	177	— (88)
1895	1163	1204	180	— (41)
1896	1321	1076	185	60
1897	1302	1088	167	47
1898	1313	1064	172	77
1899	1368	1088	173	107
1900	1612	1074	196	342
1901	1395	1199	168	28
1902	1325	1078	159	88
1903	1437	1188	165	84
1904	1489	1427	140	— (78)
1905	1773	1465	182	126
1906	2270	1717	220	333
1907	2499	1944	255	300
1908	2497	2324	297	— (124)
1909	2821	2171	377	273
1910	3068	2110	471	487

Table 5.3 (continued)

(£000)

Year	Gross income (1)	Operating expenses (2)	Depreciation and inventory adjustments (3)	Net operating profit (4)
1911	3081	2265	455	361
1912	3584	2430	501	653
1913	3660	2535	444	681
1914	4079	2811	550	718

Many of the implications relating to gross income and gross expenditure have already been referred to in previous chapters and no further comment is necessary apart from the fact that operating profit virtually doubled between 1911 and 1914. Fluctuations in the allocations for depreciation bear directly on changes in the age composition of the fleet.

To the figures for net operating profit, however, have to be added those for net non-operating income. Such income consisted of sundry receipts and the balances of interest from reserve investments.

Table 5.3 (continued)

(£000)

Year	Non-operating income (5)	Non-operating expenditure (6)	Net non-operating profit or loss (7)	Total net income Col. (4) + Col. (7) (8)
1880	10	—	10	133
1881	21	—	21	93
1882	18	—	18	129
1883	8	—	8	53
1884	15	15	—	2
1885	—	27	− (27)	25
1886	1	22	− (21)	23
1887	3	13	− (10)	119
1888	6	2	4	177

Table 5.3 (continued)

(£000)

Year	Non-operating income (5)	Non-operating expenditure (6)	Net non-operating profit or loss (7)	Total net income Col. (4) + Col. (7) (8)
1889	13	—	13	219
1890	24	—	24	120
1891	32	—	32	96
1892	38	—	38	49
1893	29	—	29	46
1894	5	1	4	— (84)
1895	5	2	3	— (38)
1896	5	—	5	65
1897	8	—	8	55
1898	12	—	12	89
1899	15	—	15	122
1900	15	—	15	357
1901	30	—	30	58
1902	16	—	16	104
1903	23	—	23	107
1904	18	—	18	— (60)
1905	14	16	— (2)	124
1906	11	36	— (25)	308
1907	59	57[1]	2	302
1908	122	133	— (11)	— (135)
1909	15	134	— (119)	154
1910	36	212	— (176)	311
1911	83	112	— (29)	332
1912	117	109	8	661
1913	152	105	47	728
1914	149	102	47	765

[1] Includes cost of temporary shed accommodation at New York of £4774.

It should be noted that the figures for non-operating income are largely made up by interest on reserve investments and generally reflect the state of Cunard's reserves; conversely, the non-operating expenditure consists of interest payments on borrowed money including, after 1907, repayment on Government advances.[140]

Having arrived at a series of figures for net income, it now becomes possible to see how the directors appropriated these funds. These latter items included payments of direct taxation, dividends to shareholders, additions to general reserves and insurance fund.

Table 5.3 (continued)

(£000)

Year	Direct taxation (9)	Dividends to shareholders (10)	Additions to general reserve (11)	Net additions to insurance fund (12)
1880	3	82	18	30
1881	1	48	11	31
1882	2	64	10	50
1883	2	—	—	50
1884	2	—	—	—
1885	1	—	—	24
1886	—	—	—	23
1887	—	40	—	78
1888	1	64	23	87
1889	2	96	20[2]	96
1890	5	64	—	43
1891	5	48	—	39
1892	4	32	—	8
1893	3	32	—	7
1894	2	—	—	(88)
1895	—	—	—	(39)
1896	—	40	—	23
1897	1	40	—	13
1898	2	56	—	29
1899	4	80	—	34
1900	6	128[1]	89	119
1901	11	64	(25)	6
1902	11	64	—	24
1903	7	64	—	30
1904	1	—	(75)	7
1905	—	64	50	3
1906	—	80	50	124
1907	5	80	100[3]	7
1908	5	—	(50)	(94)
1909	—	—	80	67
1910	—	80	470[4]	100

Table 5.3 (continued)

(£000)

Year	Direct taxation (9)	Dividends to shareholders (10)	Additions to general reserve (11)	Net additions to insurance fund (12)
1911	1	96	100	47
1912	10	121	100[5]	42
1913	17	121	100[6]	60
1914	20	185	—[7]	69

[1] Bonus dividend of 48,000 + ord. div. of 80 000.
[2] The £20 000 is a transfer to boiler fund to meet exceptional repairs etc.
[3] £100 000 is amount specially written off cost of new ships.
[4] Includes £400 000 transferred from insurance fund.
[5] £300 000 was transferred from profit and loss account to a separate repair and renewal account—this has not been included as a reserve figure.
[6] £300 000 was transferred from profit and loss account to a separate repair and renewal account—this has not been included as a reserve figure.
[7] £350 000 was transferred from profit and loss account to a separate repair and renewal account—this has not been included as a reserve figure.

We have already seen how reserves were built up and used before 1905. From 1906 to 1908 the level was unchanged at £200,000 in the general reserve and about £500,000 in the insurance fund, but thereafter there was a fairly rapid increase, so that by 1914 total reserves stood at £1,181,000.[141]

Table 5.4

(£000)

Year ending 31 December	Operating profit (1)	Operating profit after tax (2)	Total capital employed (3)	Return on capital employed (4)
1880	123	120	1749	6·86
1881	72	71	1780	3·99
1882	111	109	1840	5·92
1883	45	43	1971[1]	2·18
1884	2	—	2303	—

Table 5.4 (continued)

(£000)

Year ending 31 December	Operating profit (1)	Operating profit after tax (2)	Total capital employed (3)	Return on capital employed (4)
1885	52	52	2303[2]	2·22
1886	44	44	2213[3]	1·99
1887	129	129	1913[4]	6·74
1888	173	172	1910	9·01
1889	206	204	2000	10·20
1890	96	91	2002	4·55
1891	64	61	2037	2·99
1892	11	7	2040	0·34
1893	17	14	2044	0·69
1894	(88)	(90)	1972[5]	—
1895	(41)	(41)	1984[6]	—
1896	60	60	1913	3·14
1897	47	46	1923	2·39
1898	77	75	1946	3·86
1899	107	103	1971	5·11
1900	342	336	2150	15·63
1901	28	17	2125	0·80
1902	88	77	2132	3·61
1903	84	77	2155	3·57
1904	(78)	(79)	2805[7]	—
1905	126	126	3776[8]	3·34
1906	333	333	4959[9]	6·71
1907	300	295	5756[10]	5·12
1908	(124)	(129)	5420[11]	—
1909	273	273	6170[12]	4·43
1910	487	487	6195[43]	7·86
1911	361	360	6089[14]	5·91
1912	653	643	6227[15]	10·32
1913	681	664	6274[16]	10·58
1914	718	698	6291[17]	11·09

[1] Plus £85 000 loan from bankers.
[2] Plus £450 000 debentures.
[3] Plus £450 000 debentures.
[4] Plus £96 000 debentures.

Costs, Revenue and Returns, 1880–1914

[5] Plus £20 000 loan from bankers.
[6] Plus £75 000 loan from bankers.
[7] Plus £680 000 bankers acceptances on new ships and overdraft of £45 000.
[8] Plus £1 190 000 bankers acceptances on new ships and government advances of £456 000.
[9] Plus £660 000 bankers acceptances on new ships and Government advances of £1 999 004.
[10] Plus £785 000 bankers acceptances on new ships and overdraft of £55 000 together with Government advances of £2 616 000.
[11] Plus £2 470 000 2¾% mortgage debenture stock held by Govt.; £800 000 issued 4½% mortgage debenture stock.
[12] Plus £2 340 000 2¾% mortgage debenture stock held by Govt.; £1 600 000 4½% mortgage debenture stock.
[13] Plus £2 210 000 2¾% mortgage debenture stock held by Govt.; £1 600 000 4½% mortgage debenture stock.
[14] Plus £2 080 000 2¾% mortgage debenture stock held by Govt.; £1 520 000 4½% mortgage debenture stock.
[15] The capital stock of the Company was changed, 5% cumulative preference stock, £1 135 000 issued plus 640 000 ordinary £1 shares; with the addition of £1 950 000 2¾% mortgage debenture stock held by Govt.; £1 440 000 4½% mortgage debenture stock; balance of £30 000 repairs and renewals account and £57 000 overdraft from bankers partly secured by debenture stock.
[16] Plus £1 820 000 2¾% mortgage debenture stock held by Govt.; £1 360 000 4½% mortgage debenture stock; £56 000 repairs and renewals fund; £15 000 loan secured by mortgage on freehold property, Pier Head, Liverpool; £136 000 overdraft from bankers secured by debenture stock.
[17] Plus £1 690 000 2¾% mortgage debenture stock held by Govt.; £1 280 000 4½% mortgage debenture stock; £141 000 repairs and renewals fund; £137 000 loan secured by mortgage on freehold property, Pier Head, Liverpool. £113 000 overdraft from bankers part secured by debenture stock.

It is, perhaps, relevant at this juncture to give an explanation of the policy which Cunard's directors adopted with regard to insurance. This was made clear by John Burns in his evidence before the Royal Commission on Unseaworthy Ships in 1874. He stated that, at that time, Cunard ships were not classified at Lloyds. The Company preferred to rely on their own surveys as to seaworthiness; 'we consider', he added, 'that our ships are so constructed that they would pass Lloyds and even go beyond Lloyds' requirements.'[142] On the other hand, risks arising from errors in navigation involving loss or accident at sea were insured. 'If we had not insured since the commencement of our service', said Burns, 'I suppose we should have put in our pockets over a million of money.'¹⁴³ The premiums had been worth a great deal more than the risk. As the total annual cost of insurance premiums was £60,000 it became a matter of constant vigilance to keep such costs within limits. Consequently the partners themselves assumed some of the risks. John Burns was at pains to explain that the ships were not insured to their full value. There were simple rules of procedure whereby new ships were reasonably well covered, but with depreciation the value was reduced quarter by quarter and year by year so that premiums were correspondingly reduced.¹⁴⁴ After 1880 the Company, through its own insurance reserve, bore the risk of ship values not covered in the market.¹⁴⁵ This was of special benefit during the 1880s when the Company had a series of losses.

Subsequently, when *Mauretania* and *Lusitania* were put into service it became more difficult to obtain cover in the market and the Company was faced with an increasing risk. By 1910 it was not possible to obtain market cover for any individual ship beyond £800,000. Underwriters were tempted to increase their normal rates, 'but even with the underwriting capacity of the marine insurance world stretched to its utmost', stated Cunard's Chairman, 'we have still been left from the first with very large amounts entirely uncovered, amounts quite disproportionately large when compared with our uninsured risks on any other vessels.'¹⁴⁶ While Cunard was the only company owning such high value ships nothing could be done to remedy this situation. As other companies, such as White Star and Hamburg–Amerika added higher cost ships to their fleets, however, it was mutually agreed that uninsured risks should be spread over a larger number of bottoms. Formation of a mutual association to ensure this end was therefore put in hand and Cunard's Articles of Association were amended on 10 April 1913 to make this possible.¹⁴⁷

In such ways, therefore, did Cunard's directors make appropriations from available net income derived from both operational and non-operational sources. As a final exercise we now propose to estimate the returns on capital employed. Although the authorised capital of the Company was £2 million in 1880 only £400,000-worth of shares additional to the original £1,200,000 was taken up. If we add annual amounts transferred to the credit of the reserve fund and the insurance fund together with Government advances and borrowings to the issued capital (the figures given in

Table 5.4, column 3) the total represents long-term funds. Operating profit is given in column 1 (i.e. gross receipts less gross costs plus depreciation as given in Table 5.3, column 4); by expressing this figure (less tax paid) as a percentage of the annual levels of long-term funds, the rate of return on capital employed is determined.[148] It is obvious from Table 5.4 that between 1880 and 1896 the returns on capital employed have a close correlation with the cyclical trends in what is known as the 'great depression'. It is accordingly arguable that at a time when Cunard was meeting increasing competition from Continental lines for passenger traffic, dependence on freight as an alternative source of revenue was being seriously affected by fluctuations in the levels of industrial activity and cyclical movements in trade. The low rates of return during the next ten years (1900 excepted) are explicable only in terms of the increasing fierceness of competition from American and Continental companies. After 1904 however an augmented flow of capital through the Company was being used, though not necessarily employed in bringing in an operational return. As can be seen from the footnotes to Table 5.4 a large proportion of this new money came from Government advances, from banks and from debenture issues. This was the period in which large, fast ships were being laid down and, if one discounts the very poor year 1908, the real effect of their operation on the rate of return was not apparent until after 1909.

What can be learnt from an analysis of the various threads composing this chapter? The first generalisation must be that Cunard's policy – applying successive blocks of capital to the rebuilding of the fleet in an endeavour to achieve technical superiority – did not have the desired long-term effect. The directors were, however, more successful in the short run. They undoubtedly maintained levels of operational profitability (and incidentally ironing out the worst effects of adverse fluctuations) not so much by increasing gross receipts as in making determined attempts at reducing costs. Secondly, as a result of the formation of the Morgan combine, the British Government was eventually induced to make sizeable advances to Cunard. Without such aid it is arguable whether the Company would have survived the difficult years 1903–8. The strength of the competition which they had to meet in these five years would probably not only have reduced receipts below the level of costs, but would, because of the high cost of ships, have wiped out the Company's reserves bringing Cunard to the verge of bankruptcy. That this did not happen was due to the fact that Cunard was able to capitalise goodwill into a national asset. Finally, as a corollary of this, Cunard's increasing strength after 1906 was expressed in terms of technological advantage. This, coupled with the Conference agreement and the cessation of rate cutting after 1908, removed inhibitions on the Company's earning capacity. Cunard had thus survived probably the most difficult period in its history. In both commercial and financial terms, the policy of conservatism eventually began to pay dividends; but a sterner test was yet to come in the shape of four years of destructive warfare and the confusion following the conflict.

6
War, Peace and Depression
1914—34

I CUNARD'S CONTRIBUTION TO THE WAR EFFORT

Dislocation of normal commercial activities due to the outbreak of the First World War was both serious and protracted for Cunard. The 1903 agreement gave the Government the right to take over most of Cunard's ships in time of war for use as armed cruisers, troop transports, hospital or prison ships. The directors were therefore faced with the dilemma of fulfilling their obligations under this agreement and of maintaining some semblance of service for the carriage of passengers, freight and mails. For this reason a significant decision was taken by the Board on the outbreak of war – to retain *Lusitania* in the Company's employment and use her for normal commercial work.[1]

The first impact of the war caused the withdrawal of much of Cunard's operational capital, and although income was received in the shape of subventions from the Government for the use of ships, the income could not be profitably re-employed apart from that engaged in the promotion of controlled wartime activity. In the second place, through the intensification of submarine warfare heavy toll was taken of Cunard's dual-purpose carriers, and it became necessary for the Company to widen the scope of its control over capital by the purchase of shares in other shipping companies. We shall refer to this phase of the Company's policy in due course; for the moment, however, we need only take a general view of the effects of war on the combined fleets of Cunard and the associated members of the group.

The employment by the Admiralty of ships in the Cunard fleet during the war has been the subject of many books.[2] For our purpose it is of relevance to mention but a few of the functions. *Aquitania* was in service as an armed cruiser until 30 September 1914; from May to August 1915 she was engaged as a troopship; from this latter date until Christmas 1916 she was used as a hospital ship. During the whole of 1917 the vessel was laid up but resumed service in March 1918 as a troopship.³ *Caronia* was commissioned as an armed cruiser on 8 August 1914 and attached to the West Indies and North America station. She was fitted with 4·7-inch guns but later, in May 1915, her armament was increased to 6-inch guns. She was engaged in trooping between South and East Africa and India until returned to Cunard service.⁴ For the first two years of the war *Laconia* was an armed cruiser on special service off the East African coast; she took part in the action which led to the destruction of the German armed cruiser *Königsberg* in the Rufigi River. After returning to Cunard's North Atlantic service she was sunk by a German submarine on 25 February 1917.⁵ *Carmania* was fitted out as an armed cruiser in August 1914 and fought and sank the German cruiser *Cap Trafalgar* near Trinidad Island in September of that year. Under command of Captain Barr (who received the C.B.) she was restored to Cunard service in 1916.⁶ *Mauretania* was converted into a troopship in 1915, became a hospital ship in 1916, a transport in 1917 and fitted with 6-inch guns. Her final spell of service was in the repatriation of troops in 1919.⁷ *Franconia* and *Alaunia* were in service as troopships from September 1914 carrying reinforcements from Canada and making voyages to India and the Mediterranean.⁸ Both ships were sunk by enemy submarines in October 1916. *Andania*, *Ascania*, *Ivernia* and *Saxonia* were used as prison ships in 1915 and were afterwards employed as transports to India and the Mediterranean.⁹

This abbreviation of the wartime activities of some of Cunard's ships comprises only part of the total fleet's wartime contribution. It is sufficient, however, to emphasise the somewhat odd interpretation which was, at times and with reference to particular ships, put upon the terms of the 1903 agreement. Despite the desperate need for armed merchantmen as naval auxiliaries, the Government also required large fast ships to carry passengers, freight and mails. For this reason, as we have seen, several Cunarders were returned to the Company after a period of service to perform their normal commercial functions. Let it again be noted that of the three large fast ships, built and financed under agreement with the Government, two were taken into war service and the third, *Lusitania*, was maintained on normal scheduled crossings of the Atlantic. As far as this ship was concerned, the war barely disturbed the pattern of her routine; sailing times were published and passenger lists were open to inspection.[10] What changes there were came from considerations of a commercial nature rather than from the impact of war. Strange as it must appear to us now, the directors viewed the decline in Atlantic travel, together with the increased cost of coal and the difficulty of finding sufficient labour to service so large a vessel, purely as non-profit elements in an otherwise normal cost–revenue exercise.[11] So much so that it was deemed necessary to reduce the steam power of *Lusitania's* propelling machinery by a quarter.[12] This helped in solving the problem of manning the stokeholds but reduced the speed of the ship to 21 knots.

The sinking of *Lusitania* on 7 May 1915 has been the subject of continuing controversy.[13] Certain facts are reasonably clear. The situation on the North Atlantic was changed in February 1915 when the German Government announced their intention of regarding the English Channel and the approaches to the Irish coast as a war zone. Notice was accordingly given that they would endeavour to destroy every merchant ship found in these waters 'without it always being possible to avert the peril which thus threatens persons and cargoes'.[14] Notwithstanding this clear declaration of intent, a declaration which in Britain was regarded as at variance with international law, merchant ships including *Lusitania* continued with scheduled crossings to and from the United States and Canada.

In accordance with prepublished sailing dates, *Lusitania* left New york for Liverpool on 1 May 1915. Her passenger list was well subscribed, a fact which is difficult to explain in view of the ominous warning which had been issued from the German Embassy in Washington prior to the ship's sailing.[15] The warning was couched in blunt terms: 'Travellers intending to embark on the Atlantic voyage', it was stated, 'are reminded that a state of war exists between Germany and her allies and Great Britain and her allies; that, in accordance with formal notice given by the German Imperial Government, vessels flying the flag of Great Britain or any of her allies, are liable to destruction in these waters.'[16] However one may regard such a statement today, it seems reasonably clear that it was not then taken seriously. Opinion generally expressed at the time was that despite the German statements no nation, however desperate the naval or military situation, would flout codes of international behaviour by attacking unarmed ships on the high seas. In such a climate, it became unthinkable that the German naval command should regard the operations of *Lusitania* with suspicion or that her passengers, men, women and children (among whom were many Americans) should be in jeopardy. In view of recent disclosures, however, it is alleged that *Lusitania* was carrying contraband, including ammunition, and that the ship, from a German point of view, was a legitimate target.[17]

Despite the fact that there is evidence to show that *Lusitania's* captain, W. T. Turner, was apprehensive about the voyage, there is reason to believe that, within the limits of the resources available to him, he took adequate precautions. Steam was maintained at the highest pressure, bulkhead doors and portholes were closed, lookouts were doubled and special observers trained in submarine detection were posted.[18] Of her 48 lifeboats with a capacity for 2600 passengers, 22 were carried under davits and swung out for immediate use. The tragedy was that when the ship was hit there developed a concatenation of circumstances which rendered many of these lifeboats unusable. Approximately ten miles off the Irish coast the ship was hit by at least one torpedo. There is some evidence in support of the view that a single torpedo could not have caused the destruction of so powerful a liner in such a short space of time.[19] In the light of recently published documents from American Government archives, it is probable that a single explosion might have caused a further detonation and that this was the prime cause of sinking.[20] The sea rushed in and the vessel began to go down by the head; at the same time she took on a heavy list. Within twenty minutes the great ship had disappeared and of her company of 1962 passengers and crew only 761 survived.[21]

It is not relevant, in this present context, to embark upon an examination of the evidence and the findings of the subsequent Commissions of Enquiry nor to assess the impact of the propaganda and counter propaganda which resulted from this disaster. From a purely business point of view, the loss of so large and fine a liner struck a heavy blow at Cunard's potential strength in carrying on vital commercial links across the Atlantic; and this, when coupled with all the other serious losses of tonnage, greatly weakened the Company's recuperative capacity on the high seas after war ended in 1918.

The overshadowing of these events at sea has tended to obscure the many other contributions which Cunard made to the war effort. Some 900,000 troops were carried in the Company's ships or in those directly under Cunard management together with 10 million tons of cargo.[22] Under the Liner Requisition Scheme the directors were called upon to operate and manage in the North Atlantic trade 180 different ships on account of their owners. They also handled at their various port agencies on behalf of the Wheat Commission no less than 350 vessels engaged in the carriage of vital food supplies.[23] There was wide diversification of effort and capital resources. At Cunard's engine works, for example, besides servicing their own ships, the Company fitted out seaplane carriers and other vessels for the Government.[24] The branch engine shop in Rimrose Road, Bootle, purchased by the Company in March 1915, was converted later in that year into a shell factory employing 1000 persons. Total output of this factory at the time of its closure after the Armistice was 200,000 4·5-inch shells, 175,000 6-inch and 34,000 8-inch.[25] The Company's laundry, having much less ship work to do, was turned over largely to providing facilities for military hospitals in the Merseyside area.[26]

Perhaps the most significant diversion of resources and managerial skill was evinced by the Company's close association with the building of aeroplanes. The foundations of a factory were laid at Aintree in October 1917 and the first aeroplane was built in June 1918. 'This good result would never have been achieved', stated Sir Alfred Booth, 'but for the strenuous efforts of the committee which we formed to supervise the work and assist the manager of the factory.'[27] This committee consisted of Cunard officials under the chief responsibility of A. D. Mearns.[28] By June 1918 deliveries of parts for which subcontracts had been made were coming in and the first machine was finished.[29] At this stage unexpected difficulties arose; 'we found', continued Sir Alfred, 'that we were not given the free hand we had expected, to make the best of the place on commercial lines.'[30] The real issue was that control from London was considered to be necessary and it soon became evident to the Cunard Board that it was useless to try to combine the advantages of commercial management with the centralised system of control instituted by the Air Board.[31] Accordingly, after seeing the venture through its teething troubles the whole supervisory function was discontinued by Cunard and management handed over to the central authority.

It is obvious that the effects of war upon Cunard's function as a shipping company were at one and the same time tragic and disruptive. Apart from the severe loss of operating capital there was a diversion of skills into many forms of national service, yet out of this upheaval came new strength. In the field of management new techniques had been learnt; in technological terms new knowledge had been acquired concerning the high tensile properties of steel and much invaluable information had been acquired concerning the use of oil as a motive fuel. These were assets which Cunard was able to put into effective use when, after the end of the war, the Company was faced with the difficult task of rebuilding the fleet and resuming normal peacetime shipping activities.

II POST-WAR DIFFICULTIES: AMALGAMATION AND EXPANSION

The most immediate post-war problems which the Cunard management had to solve were: firstly, making good the losses in tonnage sustained during the war and, secondly, the establishment of more efficient administrative links with associated companies either acquired prior to the outbreak of war or during the course of conflict. By such means it was hoped that a regeneration of capital assets could be secured and a consequential increase in share capital of the concern as a whole be made more effective. Only by such methods could Cunard make the transition from wartime to peacetime management equipped to deal with the abnormal commercial difficulties facing it in a post-war world.

In order to understand the impact of acquisition on the capital structure of Cunard it is necessary to have a clear picture of the various forms of amalgamation which had taken place since 1911. This involves a catalogue of events necessarily introduced in order to render future reference comprehensible. By an agreement of 31 March 1912 the Cunard Company completed the purchase of the ordinary shares of Anchor Line (Henderson Bros Ltd).[32] The capital consisted of 25,000 shares of £10 each; the price paid was £17 per share of which £10 was paid in cash and £7 secured by an issue of fully paid 5 per cent cumulative preference stock of the Cunard Company.[33] In addition to the ordinary shares of the Anchor Line there were, at the time of purchase, some 32,500 preference shares of £10 each, held by about 1100 persons.[34] These negotiations resulted in certain interlocking directorships and, more significantly, in a direct interest in the Anchor–Brocklebank business from Glasgow and Liverpool to Calcutta. In 1912 Brocklebank had purchased the Calcutta Conference rights of the Anchor Line together with four Anchor ships.[35] In return Anchor had acquired an interest in Brocklebank to the extent of 1000 ordinary shares of £100 each. We shall examine the importance of the Brocklebank link in a subsequent part of this section.

The two most immediate consequences of this merger between Cunard and Anchor were, firstly, to bring an end to a prolonged period of rivalry on the North Atlantic and, secondly, to widen the scope of Cunard's own interests on other routes. Competition between Cunard and Anchor in the New York trade had existed since 1856. In 1862 the rivalry had been extended to the Mediterranean trade; after 1869 Anchor ships were carrying emigrants from Naples to New York.[36] By 1875 Anchor ships began direct services from Glasgow and Liverpool to Bombay. This was followed in 1882 by a direct line to Calcutta. Thus, by taking over the Anchor Line, Cunard had begun a process of diversification through an extension of its influence over sea routes other than those on the North Atlantic. As we have already seen, it had developed services to Canada and now, through Anchor, was prospectively enlarging its influence over a much wider area of trade to the East.

Nor did the upheaval of war inhibit this policy of expansion. In June 1916 an agreement was signed whereby the whole of the share capital of the Commonwealth and Dominion Line was acquired by Cunard.[37] Commonwealth and Dominion was a large private company engaged in the refrigerated and general cargo trade between the United Kingdom, Australia and New Zealand and also between New York and Australasia. The Line had been formed by the amalgamation of the Tiser Line, the Milburn Line (William Milburn and Co.), the Star Line (J. P. Corry and Co.) and the Indra Line (J. B. Royden and Co.). The issued share capital was divided into 1,248,469 ordinary shares of £1 each and 649,075 6 per cent cumulative preference shares of £1 each. As a consideration for the transfer of these shares, Cunard made over 561,811 ordinary shares, £365,000 5 per cent preference stock and £1 million 6 per cent preference stock all of Cunard Company.[38] In addition, as the Commonwealth and Dominion Line possessed a large amount of liquid assets in the form of treasury bills which would accrue to Cunard, a corresponding amount, payable partly in cash and partly in securities (including £1 million 5½ per cent debenture stock of Cunard and redeemable within five years) was added to the purchase price.[39] This new group within Cunard eventually assumed the title of the Port Line. The intention behind this amalgamation was given precise definition by Cunard's Chairman: 'The Company's interests in the past', he stated, 'were centred exclusively on the trade between Liverpool and the United States, with the result that wide fluctuations in earnings were inevitable. By the entry first into the Canadian trade then into the Indian trade and now by the acquisition of a large interest in the overseas carrying trade of the Commonwealth of Australia and the Dominion of New Zealand, I believe that a sound balance has been secured, which would enable the Company to face with confidence, the difficulties and fluctuations in trade after the war.'[40] We shall endeavour to examine whether or not these aspirations were in fact realised.

The process of acquisition continued. In 1916 the Anchor Line became associated with the Donaldson Line and a new company, Anchor–Donaldson Ltd, took over the ships and goodwill of the Clyde to Canada service.[41] In December of the same year, Cunard extended its influence in the agency and shipbroking business by acquiring shares in Funch Edye and Co. Inc of New York, an action which it intended to expand annually until the whole of the Funch Edye Corporation became the property of Cunard.[42] This attempt at rationalisation by controlling their own agency work was given further impetus on 1 January 1919 when Cunard took up an interest in Robert Reford Ltd, general agents of the company in Canada, by purchasing 3000 shares of $100 each, 70 per cent paid up, at a cost of $210,000.[43] All these events are given added weight when put against the general background of Cunard's aspirations to widen the scope of its shipping and business activity. This whole policy was given even greater impetus and perspective in 1919 through a merger with the long-established firm of Thos and Jno Brocklebank. On 6 March of that year Cunard acquired 1500 ordinary shares of £100 each of Brocklebank capital, out of a total subscribed of £250,000, the remaining £100,000 being held (as already stated) by the Anchor Line.[44] As Brocklebank had already sold half the shares in their company to Edward Bates and Sons in 1911, this purchase by Cunard meant that henceforth their relationship with the Bates family would be close and continuous. As we shall see, this relationship assumed a powerful directive force in the Company's history over the next thirty years.

The holders of Brocklebank shares received by way of consideration for the sale, 100 ordinary Cunard shares of £1 each for each £100 Brocklebank share.[45] The other Brocklebank capital consisted of 10,000 non-cumulative preference shares of £10 each, 6000 of which were privately held and 4000 held by the Anchor Line.[46] Thus Cunard had secured a substantial stake in a firm whose history went back to 1770. In this present context it is not proposed to delve into antecedents. The facts about the Brocklebank shipbuilding and shipowning interests are well known.[47] All that need be said here is that, following the abolition of the East India Company's monopoly, the firm (styled Thos and Jno Brocklebank since 1806) began to send ships to Calcutta and became pioneers in general trade to that port. By the 1850s they were trading to both the east and west coast of South America, to Newfoundland and, as an extension of their Indian business, to China and the Philippines.[48] When iron superseded wood the firm ceased to build its own ships and turned to Harland and Wolff.[49] For nearly twenty-five years they used iron sailing ships and it was not until 1889 that they started to employ steamships. The concern was turned into a limited liability company in 1898, all the shares being owned by the Brocklebank family. For some years Brocklebank were joint owners with Royal Mail of the Shire Line trading to China and Japan; but in 1911 they sold their share of the latter company to Royal Mail and concentrated on the Calcutta trade.[50] It was in the same year (1911) that Sir Percy Bates and his brothers became associated with the firm. Their interlocking connection with the Anchor Line has already been mentioned. Apart from these facts the only other point relevant to our theme is that in 1916 Brocklebank obtained an interest in the Well Line, a firm running steamships from Middlesbrough and London to Madras, Colombo and Calcutta.[51]

Enough has been said in the foregoing paragraphs to trace the links between the various shipping companies brought into association with Cunard and the manner in which the financial arrangements were effected. The first and most obvious result of such expansion was a change in the capital structure of the Cunard Company. This structure had remained unchanged from 1880 to 1911, though the shareholding of the Cunard, Burns and MacIver families had passed into other hands. It will be remembered that the original holding of the Cunard, MacIver and Burns families in the Company amounted to 60,000 shares of £20 each, making a total of £1,200,000. In addition there were 40,000 shares of the same denomination, half paid up, totalling £400,000; thus the subscribed capital amounted to £1,600,000. By 1911 the original holding of £1,200,000 had passed, under power of pre-emption, into the hands of the managing directorate, the only remaining link with the founders of the Company being represented in the person of the third Lord Inverclyde. When he died in 1919 the last surviving managerial connection with the Burns family was broken. In view of the growth of Cunard's assets it is perhaps surprising that the capital structure should have remained unaltered for a period of thirty years; but with the coming of expansion through acquisition, it became necessary to secure greater flexibility in the control of resources and a wider representation in management.

Accordingly, on 19 December 1911 a resolution was passed altering the Articles of Association and increasing the capital. The original 60,000 shares were divided each into 20 shares of £1, whereof 720,000 of the new denomination were constituted as preference shares and 480,000 as ordinary shares.[52] The 40,000 shares of £20 each (£10 paid up) were also converted into 10 shares of £2 (£1 paid up) whereof 240,000 were preference shares and 160,000 ordinary shares.[53] The preference shares bore the right to a cumulative preferential dividend of 5 per cent per annum on the amount of capital paid up. Finally the Company capital was increased from £1,600,000 to £2,500,000 by the issue of 900,000 new shares of £1 each divided between preference and ordinary shares, with the proviso that at no time should the preference stock exceed £1,500,000.[54] Furthermore as a result of this process of reorganisation the authorised capital was reduced by extinguishing the liability in respect of the uncalled capital amounting to £400,000 or £1 per share on the 400,000 shares of £2 each, resulting from the subdivision of the 40,000 shares in the Company's original capital.[55]

The foregoing details have been set out in the hope that elucidation may be given to future conversions and to the interlocking holdings of associated companies. The scheme of conversion proposed in 1911 took effect in 1912, whereby £960,000 of preference stock and £640,000 of ordinary shares were issued in exchange for the paid up capital of the Company.[56] There remained unissued £540,000 of preference stock and £360,000 of ordinary shares, thus giving an authorised total of £1,500,000 preference and £1,000,000 ordinary of which £1,600,000 had been paid up. Assets created by the issue of new capital had a twofold purpose. They enabled the managers to shift liability for the Government Debentures (originating from the 1903 agreement) by making such assets cover the first floating charge; secondly, the new preference shares could be used in payment or part payment of mergers with other companies.[57] The process of capital accretion went on apace; with each new amalgamation there was a corresponding addition to authorised capital; by the end of 1919 the total was £6,000,020 (the odd £20 being the Government share) of which £5,470,806 was subscribed.[58] From 31 December 1919, however, the authorised capital was increased by £1 million, of which £6,956,209 was subscribed.[59] In the simple interlocking of capital Cunard owned some 79 per cent of the associated companies' capital, while they in return had acquired 37 per cent of Cunard's.

By the end of the war therefore Cunard's financial position was strongly and broadly based. Within ten years total assets had increased from about £6,600,000 to about £15,000,000.[60] In 1909 the Company owned 275,000 tons of shipping; by the end of 1919 it owned, or controlled through its associated companies, an aggregate of 558,380 tons and there were 426,800 tons under construction for the various companies.[61] Moreover the mortgage debt to the Government had in the intervening period been reduced by nearly £1,300,000.[62] In economic terms the mergers had secured to Cunard control over a vastly increased tonnage which, by comparison with post-war inflated prices, had been acquired at relatively low cost. This in turn, meant low depreciation and capital costs.[63] In short there were good grounds for optimism in the prospective use of resources. 'We begin the new era of peace under very favourable auspices', stated the Chairman, '... [though] it is useless to disguise the fact that the national position is sufficiently serious to shake the confidence of the most optimistic.'[64] These well judged though ominous words were but foresight of impending difficulties. Cunard's history for the next twenty years was bedevilled by fluctuations in trade leading to general stagnation, by dislocations in the Company's normal patterns of business activity and by worsening labour relations. The test for management was as severe as at any time in the Company's previous history. We must therefore seek to answer the question – how successful was Cunard management in attempting to overcome the various problems thrown up during the uncertain inter-war years from 1919–39?

III UNITED STATES IMMIGRATION POLICY AND POST-WAR SHIP-BUILDING PROGRAMME

The first and most obvious task facing Cunard management at the beginning of 1919 was the replacement of tonnage lost during the war. Although by amalgamation Cunard had control over many more ships than before 1914, losses in particular classes of ship had been severe and had resulted in unbalancing Cunard's potentiality in certain trades. There were only eight ships left capable of serving the Atlantic trade, of these *Aquitania* and *Mauretania*, the fastest express liners, were still under requisition to the Government.[65] By comparison with the associated lines the magnitude of Cunard's losses amounted to 22 ships of 220,444 tons gross, or 56 per cent of pre-war tonnage; while Anchor Line lost 7 ships of 69,039 tons; Commonwealth and Dominion Line 7 ships totalling 45,215 tons and Brocklebank and Well Lines 9 ships of 55,155 tons, making an aggregate 45 ships of a total of 389,853 tons gross.[66] By any standard this was a formidable list, but in the case of Cunard and Anchor the incidence of loss fell upon the best type of combined cargo and passenger steamships of moderate speed. To bridge the gap until tonnage replacement could be made 6 'standard ships' were purchased to enable the Company to maintain the Atlantic cargo trade. These together with charters for special demands sustained earning capacity.[67]

But it was already becoming evident that the foundation on which Cunard had established its strength in pre-war years (i.e. on the carriage of passengers and cargo) had been seriously disrupted. No longer could the Company so easily adjust the use of its resources to the exigencies of a fiercely competitive business in an otherwise free market. After 1919 the directors had to face the prospect of adverse pressures on rates, resulting from an oversupply of cargo liner tonnage throughout the world.[68] Passenger services, especially those to Canada and the U.S.A., were inhibited by direct government intervention. The result was that Cunard, in common with many other shipping lines, had to devise new policies and initiate new types of business in an attempt to meet and overcome downward trends in traditional forms of activity. This required new ships capable of catering for a much wider range of demand and, as a consequence, new procedures had to be devised in the allocation of resources in order to secure the greatest possible return on capital employed.

The most formidable and immediate problem affecting Cunard's traditional business was that posed by legislation restricting immigration into the United States. The post-war action of Congress (dating from the summer of 1921) was based upon a restriction to 3 per cent of the total of each nationality domiciled in that country at the time of the census in 1910.[69] The direct effect of this legislation was that although first and second class traffic was reasonably well maintained, third class traffic carried by Cunard westwards was reduced from 49,305 passengers in 1921 to 34,763 in 1922 (total traffic eastbound and westbound fell from 74,663 to 55,324).[70] Relative costs were thus increased as these reduced numbers were accommodated in ships sailing from the United Kingdom towards the end of each month, with the result that 'third class space on many of our voyages went comparatively empty'.[71] There was, however, an indirect effect arising from the operation of the United States Immigration Law. The Italian Government, in the interests of their mercantile marine, restricted the carriage of Italian emigrants (a business in which both Cunard and Anchor had longstanding connections) to Italian ships.[72] To counter the loss of revenue from this move, Cunard, Anchor and White Star combined their separate offices, thereby reducing administrative and other costs.[73] Such action, however, was but a palliative and not a cure for the fundamental nature of the problem.

A main objective required the maintenance of diplomatic and political pressure against the United States Government to ameliorate the harshness of restrictions. It was becoming more than ever essential that the earning capacity of British shipping lines be freed from intervention of a noneconomic character. Under pressure from shipping companies the Governments of Britain and the United States were induced to take ameliorating action. On 7 November 1924 an Order in Council declared a reciprocal agreement with the United States, exempting from taxation the profits earned by the shipping lines of both countries.[74] This measure had the immediate effect of lightening a cost burden on British shipping, a considerable concession as tax relief was made retrospective from 1 May 1923. A further step was taken by Congress in changing the basis of immigration. The census of 1890 rather than that of 1910 was henceforth to be used as the statutory point for percentage computation for the number of immigrants to be admitted.[75] This had the effect of slightly increasing the quota from the British Isles but reduced the aggregate from European countries, except Germany. The net result of this revision was that the number of immigrants admissible from Europe was just over 357,000 in any one year, whereas in 1913 ships of lines belonging to the Atlantic Conference had carried some 1,141,000 third class passengers to the United States.[76]

It had become evident that the former strength of Cunard's business in the emigrant trade had been permanently weakened; as a consequence, new and more flexible policies would have to be formulated in order to sustain the profitability of the organisation as a whole. The process called for greater diversification of function in both the maintenance and ultimate growth of revenue as well as in the control of rising costs. As a pointer to a more realistic appraisal of events, Cunard purchased on 27 April 1921 the whole of the non-cumulative 5 per cent preference shares in T. and J. Brocklebank, thereby acquiring the remainder of the interests of the Brocklebank family and the Anchor Line in that company.[77] As Anchor still held £100,000 worth of the ordinary subscribed capital, control of Brocklebank had thus passed to Cunard and Anchor. Endeavouring to cut costs Cunard acquired on 1 January 1921 an interest in the ship-repairing firm of R. and H. Green and Silley Weir Ltd (London); the agreement was to last for fourteen years. All voyage repairs, renewals and overhaul of vessels belonging to Cunard and associated companies were to be undertaken by Green and Silley Weir.[78] Finally Cunard's potential strength in Europe was given greater effectiveness by the creation of a subsidiary company in Hamburg entitled Cunard See-Transport G.m.b.H. with a capital of 300,000 Marks,[79] and in March 1922 by the formation of a new Hungarian–American Transport Company in Budapest, together with a Roumanian–Cunard company in Bucharest.[80]

These efforts were but the preliminaries to an implementation of new functions. Carriage of emigrants had become a much less

Samuel Cunard, merchant of Halifax

Samuel Cunard, founder of the British and North American Royal Mail Steam Packet Co.

Charles MacIver

George Burns

Britannia in the ice at Boston, 3 February 1844

Persia, 1856

John Burns, First Lord Inverclyde

Cunard advertisement giving Atlantic track, 1875

Sir Alfred Booth

The first *Mauretania*

Sir Thomas Royden

Queen Mary at full speed.

Sir Percy Bates

Queen Elizabeth serving as a troopship

Queen Elizabeth 2

Queen Elizabeth on fire in Hong Kong harbour

important element in Cunard's total earning capacity; new spheres of trade had to be explored, developed and exploited. It was, therefore, a corollary that new ship designs and new shipbuilding programmes should be instituted to meet the exigencies of demand for a different and a wider variety of shipping services. One serious difficulty sprang from the fact that among Cunard's pre-war Atlantic liners only *Carmania, Caronia, Mauretania* and *Aquitania* had survived. To compensate for the loss of *Lusitania*, a half-share (with White Star) in the enormous and, as it turned out, highly uneconomical German liner *Imperator* (re-christened *Berengaria*) had been acquired.[81] These five liners, as compared with the past, constituted but a skeleton fleet quite incapable of meeting the demand for fast express Atlantic services. They could not match the competitive strength of other lines in this specialised type of business; for against them were such ships of the International Mercantile Marine, including White Star's *Majestic* (formerly the German liner *Bismarck*) in which Cunard also owned a half-share, the French line, the United States Line and the United American lines. The United States lines were now running six former German liners including *Vaterland* (rechristened *Leviathan*). Thus the Cunard fleet serving the North Atlantic was not only unbalanced in terms of its former ratio between fast ships and smaller ships of moderate speed, but was in a greatly inferior competitive position. Furthermore, by way of aggravation, Cunard's Canadian service had been totally abandoned during the war and, when it was reconstituted, became subject to immigration controls almost as severe as those imposed by the United States.[82]

The necessity of undertaking an unprecedented building programme was more than obvious if Cunard was to restore its normal relative tonnage and regain its lost trade. The decision-taking process involved both the number of ships to be

	Tonnage	Turbines	S.H.P.
Scythia (1921)	19 503	6	12 500
Samaria (1922)	19 602	6	12 500
Laconia (1922)	19 680	6	12 500
Franconia (1923)	20 158	6	12 500
Carinthia (1925)	20 277	6	13 500

laid down and, more important, the design and type of tonnage capable of meeting a wide range of prospective demand. Apart from the new ships for the Australasian trade (17 vessels laid down between 1919 and 1928), there were five main line Atlantic steamships (designated '600-footers') laid down and delivered as on p. 173.[83]

In addition, *Tyrrhenia* (re-named *Lancastria*) added in 1922, was slightly smaller with a tonnage of 16,243 but with the same S.H.P.[84] All were oil-fired and incorporated the latest equipment for handling cargo and well-designed accommodation for the comfort of passengers. Then came a series of what were called 'A' class ships.

	Tonnage	Turbines	S.H.P.
Albania (1921)	12 767	4	6800
Andania (1922)	13 950	4	8500
Antonia (1922)	13 867	4	8500
Ausonia (1922)	13 912	4	8500
Aurania (1924)	13 984	4	8500
Alaunia (1925)	14 030	4	8500
Ascania (1925)	14 013	4	8500

These 'A' class ships were of moderate power with oil-fired turbines and had capacity for the carriage of both passengers and cargo.[85] The whole programme took just over six years to complete; some initial delays had occurred because of strikes in the shipbuilding yards, *Scythia* having to be sent to France and *Laconia* to Rotterdam to be finished.[86] By 1925 Cunard had in service a relatively effective fleet capable of meeting most foreseeable demands and enabling it to fulfil the obligations of a widening range of activity on progressively developing routes. By 1922 these obligations had been greatly increased compared with pre-war commitments. They comprised the following services:

1. Southampton, Cherbourg to New York including the carriage of mails (which by agreement with the Post Office had been transferred from Liverpool to Southampton in 1919).[87]
2. Liverpool to Halifax, Boston, New York and Philadelphia.
3. London to New York, Philadelphia, Baltimore and Portland.

4. Bristol to New York, Philadelphia, Baltimore and Portland.
5. Antwerp, Rotterdam and Hamburg to New York.
6. Extended services to the Mediterranean, the Levant and the Black Sea.
7. The associated lines' services to Australia, New Zealand and India.

By the time the 600-ft liners and the 'A' ships came into service the passenger services also included:

8. Liverpool, Cobh, N.Y.
9. Liverpool to Montreal.
10. London, Havre, Montreal.

When the St Lawrence was closed London and Liverpool services operated to New York with calls at Halifax. The service Hamburg to New York was unprofitable and ceased to operate.[88]

By a relatively wise use of resources, by a certain degree of foresight based on judgement and by an acceptance of new ideas, Cunard had not only been brought to a point of recovery from the disastrous effect of war, but had been given the capability of expanding its influence in a highly competitive post-war world.

In one sense the whole process of events described above marks a second transitional stage in the Company's history and growth; though if the history be viewed from a purely technological point of view it constituted a third period of transition. Cunard had hitherto tended to lag behind other companies in technological terms. It had therefore been left to a body of remarkable managers at the end of the nineteenth century to keep Cunard ships afloat; it was the second Lord Inverclyde who had been largely responsible in securing the aid of a virtual government partnership when American and German competition had threatened the lifelines of Cunard's earning capacity. Now, between 1919 and 1925, it was the able direction of another shrewd administrator, Sir Alfred Booth, who had set the course of transition from coal to oil and from vast uneconomic carriers to those of moderate size and power. Such changes, it was hoped, would be facilitated by a less rigid capital structure and a determination to widen the scope of business activity. Alas for aspirations and well-laid schemes! The 1920s and 1930s were to throw up such intractable problems that no management, however wise, could have coped adequately with them. This was a fact that affected not only Cunard but all the shipping lines throughout the world.

IV FLUCTUATIONS IN RECEIPTS AND COSTS

An examination of the working of Cunard's fleet in the several branches of trade reveals many interesting sidelights on management in the taking and carrying out of decisions. The two most important problems facing the directors after 1920 were concerned with the means of increasing revenue and the various processes of containing and reducing voyage operating costs. These items apart, there was continuous negotiation in the various Conferences (see Chapter 8) to extract the utmost advantage in order to sustain income. Despite difficult conditions, some signal success was achieved. This was especially true of the years from 1923 to 1929; thereafter the force of increasing depression tended to upset the effect of long-term decisions. Finally, in terms of operational capital, the new ships in operation after 1925 returned sizeable credit balances in each succeeding year to 1929. In fact aggregate net voyage receipts might have been greater had it not been for the relatively high costs incurred by some of the older ships such as *Mauretania* and *Berengaria*. Nevertheless in the maintenance of first and second class traffic the huge, fast ship still had prestige value and this persisted not only as a goodwill asset but was given more concrete expression when at a later date the Company laid down *Queen Mary* and *Queen Elizabeth*.[89]

It is virtually impossible to obtain a series of figures in the 1920s comparable with those already analysed for the period before 1914. This difficulty is inherent in the form and composition of the accounts, as the basis on which items of income and expenditure were classified was repeatedly changed. This fact was emphasised as early as 25 April 1917 when the Chairman explained to shareholders that 'the accounts are presented to you this year in a slightly different form, which has been rendered desirable by the purchase of the Commonwealth and Dominion Line'.[90] The ships of this line were operated as a separate company though owned by Cunard. The earnings from these sources took the form of dividends instead of voyage earnings less disbursements. Henceforth, as a result of changing circumstances, all interest and dividends were brought into the revenue account instead of crediting them to the profit and loss account direct. On the expenditure side of the revenue account, such items as insurance, repairs and renewals, office and agency expenses were no longer stated separately but were merged into the working expenses for the year.[91] 'We do not think that any useful purpose', added the Chairman, '. . . is served by the publishing of the details of these items, while the changed character of the business would, in any case, make any comparison with the past, positively misleading.'[92]

For our purpose, therefore, it becomes necessary to establish certain areas of comparability in the accounts and to supplement information not contained therein by referring to individual items of expenditure shown in the Voyage Books. Having made these qualifications, it is now possible to make some assessment of the earning capacity and annual surplus derived from the operation of the Company's ships. In Table 6.1 the figures in column 1 represent gross income from voyages and cruises together with dividends from associated companies. Column 2 includes all disbursements, both operational (including depreciation) and non-operational such as tax. The figures in column 3, therefore, represent the annual balance of funds (or loss sustained) remaining to the Company on each year's working.

Table 6.1
RECEIPTS AND EXPENDITURE
1922–34

(£000)

Year (1)	Gross Income (2)	Expenditure including depreciation and tax (3)	Balance (4)
1922	8313·3	7918·7	394·6
1923	8627·8	8236·6	391·2
1924[1]	3191·4	2797·4	394·0
1925	3307·1	2974·3	332·8
1926	3057·4	2541·4	516·3
1927	3340·0	2680·0	660·0
1928	3214·0	2663·5	550·5
1929	3628·9	2818·9	810·0
1930	2662·4	2643·8	18·6
1931[2]	5614·3	6167·5	(loss) 553.2
1932	4944·1	5871·4	(loss) 927·3

Table 6.1 (continued)

1933	4619·0	4864·0	(loss) 245·0
1934[3]	448·4	359·3	89·1

[1] In this year the profit and loss account is given in a different form. On the credit side of the acount net receipts are given, i.e. the voyage receipts less the operating expenses of the vessels together with interest, dividends etc, while on the debit side operating costs have disappeared.

[2] There was an operating profit of £396 508, against this had to be set £949 712 for depreciation and other charges, giving a loss of £553 204. In order to make the figures for this and the two following years comparable with those up to 1930, the latter items have been included in the expenditure column.

[3] Including £64 691 repayment of tax deducted from dividends paid to Cunard by subsidiary companies.

The table notes explain the apparent discrepancy in the totals of income between 1923 and 1924. The figures for 1934 are for eight months only and are affected by the changed composition of the account consequent upon the merger with White Star. It will be seen that apart from 1926, the year of the General Strike, earnings were relatively well maintained and that 1929 was a year of increasing returns. As we shall see later, the directors sought to increase earning capacity by introducing special rates for group travel and short-dated tourist round-trips.[93] After 1929 the figures reflect the worsening conditions caused by the onset of world depression. Within this general picture there were four main factors in operation: firstly, the carriage of third class passengers was reasonably well maintained up to 1929;[94] secondly, there were significant alterations made in specific ships designed to reduce working costs and to make accommodation more attractive to all classes of passengers;[95] thirdly, a competitive advantage was upheld against other lines within the operation of Conference agreements and, finally, there was a considerable reduction in the cost of fuel after 1927.

There were both adverse and favourable factors at work in determining Cunard's overall earning capacity. After 1927, for example, there was a continuous fall in the number of first and second class passengers carried both east and west.[96] There was also a fairly regular decline in the volume of cargo carried eastwards amounting to about 500,000 tons, though that carried westwards achieved a peak in 1929 of about 337,000 tons.[97] Earnings from the carriage of mails dropped in 1929, recovered in 1930 but declined again to 1933.[98] It would appear that from the point of view of marginal revenue the third class traffic was of significant importance. For this reason it is of interest to discover the causes affecting this type of business.

There was obviously truth in the view expressed by Sir Thomas Royden in 1926, that when conditions were good in the U.S.A., more Americans took the opportunity of making a trip to Europe;[99] but this class of business in no way compensated for the loss of the old emigrant trade, the flow of which still continued to be drastically restricted by the U.S. immigration laws. To fill up ships and utilise idle capacity Cunard increased the number of cruises both round the world and to the Mediterranean. Though such diversions helped to augment revenue they did not solve the problems affecting the main Atlantic trade. 'To meet this serious loss of business', declared Sir Thomas Royden, 'we have had to devise ways and means whereby the space which our ships have for the carriage of third class passengers can be more fully utilised. To this end, we are developing what is known as the tourist type of travel, where passengers, though paying a normal third class fare (reduced somewhat when a round-trip ticket is taken) can be supplied with some of the amenities usually associated with travel of a more expensive character. Such accommodation has appealed to a large section of the public in America.'[100] The figures relating to the carriage of third class passengers from 1925 onwards, therefore, include tourist travellers.

There was one ameliorating feature affecting the carriage of emigrants after 1925, which undoubtedly helped in swelling the numbers of third class travellers westwards. In common with the other lines in the Canadian business, Cunard, under pressure from government, was induced to make a reduction (amounting to twenty per cent) in third class rates 'in order to encourage immigration into Canada'.[101] The response was disappointing. Consequently, the British and Canadian Governments introduced the principle of assisted passages, prospective applicants for employment and settlement being selected by Canadian Government officials with the object of filling vacancies in either agricultural or other approved forms of employment.[102] For such emigrants a very attractive reduced rate of passage was made available to all parts of

Canada. To facilitate the operation of this scheme, Cunard joined with the Hudson's Bay Co. in establishing the Hudson's Bay Co. Overseas Settlement Ltd.[103] As a result the number of emigrants to Canada began to increase and, in 1926, further incentive was given by an increase in rebates. Towards the end of 1927, however, the whole government scheme was revised, making it possible for an emigrant to cross to Canada for a flat rate of £10, without any restriction on the nature of employment taken up on arrival.[104] The difference between this and the normal rate was absorbed by the Government and the steamship lines on an agreed basis.

Parallel with these efforts to induce emigration by regulation, there was in 1929 a change in the United States' Immigration Law, a change which gave a slight advantage to Cunard's services. New quotas, based on the 1920 census, came into operation in July and had the apparent effect of reducing the immigrants admitted annually from 164,667 to 153,714; but the operation of the new quota in fact doubled the allocation to British nationals, giving an increase of 31,714, while numbers from Eire and Germany were reduced by just over 10,000 and 25,000 respectively.[105] Cunard obtained some slight advantage from this, although compared with the German lines her share of total trade declined marginally.[106] In the varying circumstances, management showed a willingness to accede to change and to identify itself with profitable ventures in a constant struggle to offset the unprofitable sections of activity.

Nor were the Cunard managers at fault in endeavouring to improve all the other classes of service capable of bringing in an increased revenue. 'We have spent a considerable sum of money in altering and improving first class passenger accommodation on our three express steamers (*Berengaria, Aquitania* and *Mauretania*)', it was stated in the Report for 1927. This involved the enlargement of rooms, the provision of private baths, and the installation of hot and cold running water in all cabins. 'With new tonnage being put into the trade by our competitors, it is essential that, for our older steamers, we do everything we reasonably can to see that they do not fall behind in the race.'[107] As a further extension of this desire, passenger accommodation in *Caronia* and *Carmania* was greatly improved. Unfortunately the prospective increase in cabin class traffic did not justify so large an outlay. By 1929 the number of first class passengers had still not reached the level carried in 1909.[108]

V CUNARD'S ATTEMPTS TO INCREASE REVENUE AND REDUCE COSTS

Having considered some of the more important elements affecting the operational income of Cunard ships during the 1920s we must now turn to the changes influencing working costs. The two most important costs were fuel and wages, which in 1925 accounted for approximately 50 per cent of total disbursements. The successful achievement by Cunard management in securing a considerable reduction in total costs was in no small measure due to the effective reduction of fuel bills. The real nature of the achievement can be judged by the fact that, despite some upward movement in individual costs, Cunard ships were steaming an increased mileage with each succeeding year after 1925. Unit costs, therefore, fell sharply and, *caeteris paribus*, net working revenue was increased.

One of the largest savings occurred in the overall cost of oil fuel. The figures show that for this item alone there was a fall from £2,145,400 in 1925 to £1,330,600 in 1930.[109] In achieving this reduction Cunard management had waged a continuous struggle over the intervening years. In 1925, for example, it was stated that the price of oil had risen from £2 8s 3d per ton in the preceding year, to £2 14s 5d per ton. 'This increase in price, together with the fact that our oil-burning ships steamed 1,097,203 miles in 1925, or 193,000 more than in 1924, was responsible for an increased expenditure in oil fuel alone of over £556,000.'[110] On the year's working for 1926, the cost of fuel oil was still a preoccupation of management, though as a counter to the rather rueful comment that 'the cost of fuel oil does not compare favourably with coal', the Chairman was at pains to explain the advantages of using oil. 'The express steamer', he added, 'can make many more voyages under fuel oil than would be possible on coal, owing to the physical impossibility of loading coal as fast as oil.'[111] In fact, the use of oil in 1926, when there was a prolonged coal strike in addition to a general strike, enabled Cunard ships to maintain strict time schedules on all voyages.[112] There was, however, a rather hollow warning in the final statement 'that if oil prices continue to rise we may have to revert to coal for at least part of the fleet'.[113]

The position was not greatly altered in 1927, the contract price of oil remaining relatively high. By the end of the year, however, the problem of high cost fuel had virtually been overcome, at least in relative terms. Many of the ships had been equipped with increased carrying capacity for bunker oil and this enabled the Company to buy more oil in the U.S.A., where prices were lower.[114] New contracts were negotiated under which longer-term arrangements ensured more favourable prices. 'The question of oil fuel supplies has been one of anxiety in the past', said Sir Thomas Royden, 'I am happy to say that, for the next few years at least, this difficulty has been overcome, and we have been able to close a contract for our supplies in the U.S.A. and Great Britain up to the end of 1931 on reasonable terms.'[115] Compared with the reductions in cost of fuel, that for wages was less spectacular, for though aggregates were contained within a stable range between 1925 and 1930, it must be remembered that more voyages were being undertaken and more routes were being served with each succeeding year. Unit costs on wages were therefore being reduced.[116] The aggregate rise in port and general charges was subject to the same factor; the greater the number of ships entering and clearing port, the greater the aggregate cost. The continuous decline in the cost of the two other important items, loading and discharge and provisions for passengers, reflects considerable increases in efficient service, first in the better dockside equipment and secondly in bulk purchase arrangements for victualling the ships. The same factors generally apply to the other extraneous charges.[117]

It is possible to examine the relative effect of reduction in costs in a specific way. If we take the average cost per ton of fuel between 1925 and 1932, there was a reduction of approximately one-half; loading and discharging charges on the other hand increased by about fifteen per cent. If we next apply all the various costs to the working of particular classes of ship and express them as a figure related to every £1 of revenue earned (Table 6.2), it will be seen that of the fast express ships *Aquitania* was the most economical to run and that relative costs increased considerably (as might be expected) when economic conditions worsened after 1930. The 600-foot ships (represented here by *Laconia*) show a relatively low cost ratio compared with the express ships and, during depression, were worked at even lower cost per unit of revenue. In other words, these particular ships were able to show a greater margin of working profit at all seasons and despite adverse fluctuations in trading conditions. By comparison 'A' class ships (represented by *Antonia*) were more expensive to operate and did not return anything like the same amount of working profit during the difficult years. From this one may conclude that the 600-foot ships, by virtue of their adaptability, were capable of sustaining profit margins under changing conditions to a higher level than any other class of ship in the Cunard fleet.

So far we have dealt only with operational costs. It now becomes necessary for us to set the working capacity of the fleet against the wider financial background of the Cunard organisation as a whole. This involves the debiting of many other items in the balance sheet, such as depreciation, overheads, preference dividends, capital and other charges. Unfortunately many of these items are not given separately in the accounts and we have therefore had to extract such information from the voyage books. In aggregate, however, all such charges are included in the total annual expenditure as shown in Table 6.1.

Table 6.2

AVERAGE COST PER £ PASSAGE MONEY AND FREIGHT[118]
(*Expressed in shillings and pence*)

Year	Victualling	Stores	Fuel	Wages	Repairs and Renewals	Total
Berengaria						
1925/26	1/4·92	6.96	5/6·97	1/5·55	1/5·01	10/5·41
1926/27	1/6·10	7·40	5/5.13	1/7·04	2/8·51	11/10.18
1927/28	1/6·30	7·51	4/8·19	1/7·54	1/6·13	9/11·67
1928/29	1/5·38	7·21	3/1·05	1/7·04	1/9·79	8/6·47
1929/30	1/6·21	8·04	3/5·62	1/9·65	1/8·60	9/2·12
1930/31	1/8·39	10·51	5/1·98	2/5·26	2/4·24	12/6·38
1931/32	1/6·10	9·92	4/0·74	2/3·25	1/4·93	10/0·94
1932/33	1/8·75	1/1·20	5/3·69	2/5·48	2/9·62	13/4·74
Aquitania						
1925/26	1/4·09	6·62	4/5·18	1/5·47	1/11·97	9/9·33
1926/27	1/4·29	7·11	4/4·03	1/6·85	2/6·97	10/5·25
1927/28	1/4·31	7·18	3/5·79	1/7·04	1/4·46	8/4·78
1928/29	1/5·12	7·24	2/6·45	1/8·00	1/9·17	7/11·98
1929/30	1/5·69	8·08	2/8·05	1/10·27	1/4·51	8/0·60
1930/31	1/7·04	9·82	3/9·72	2/5·39	11·89	8/9·86
1931/32	1/4·18	9·65	3/3·77	1/11·64	10·69	8/3·93
1932/33	1/7·63	1/0·74	5/6·05	2/7·32	2/7·25	13/4·99
Mauretania						
1925/26	1/5·22	7·09	6/4·49	1/9·17	1/3·63	11/5·60
1926/27	1/7·09	8·26	7/0·17	1/11·81	2/4·28	13/7·61

Table 6.2 (continued)

Year	Victualling	Stores	Fuel	Wages	Repairs and Renewals	Total
1927/28	1/6·51	7·90	6/1·03	2/0·06	1/7·58	11/11·08
1928/29	1/5·85	7·58	4/2·57	1/11·74	2/7·91	10/11·65
1929/30	1/6·56	7·90	4/4·00	2/1·84	1/2·63	9/10·93
1930/31	1/7·40	10·03	5/6·15	2/8·62	1/3·42	11/11·62
1931/32	1/4·79	10·50	4/0·14	2/6·16	1/5·34	10/2·93
1932/33	1/10·14	1/2·89	7/3·60	3/0·77	9·92	14/3·32
Laconia						
1925/26	1/7·63	8·57	4/1·37	2/4·45	6·38	9/4·40
1926/27	1/5·81	7·36	3/10·90	2/4·72	1/9·44	10/2·23
1927/28	1/8·87	7·56	3/9·18	2/7·25	11·77	8/10·63
1928/29	1/8·07	7·25	2/7·75	2/4·88	1/3·85	8/7·80
1929/30	1/7·70	7·21	2/5·46	2/3·52	1/0·53	8/0·42
1930/31	1/9·02	8·09	2/8·56	2/6·80	1/2·62	8/11·09
1931/32	1/4·60	5·23	1/10·48	2/1·28	5·81	6/3·40
1932/33	1/3·84	6·15	2/7·93	2/1·35	10·40	7/5·67
Antonia						
1925/26	1/7·12	9·04	4/2·98	2/7·54	1/0·46	10/3·14
1926/27	1/5·90	8·05	3/8·79	2/2·96	1/2·81	9/4·51
1927/28	1/9·49	10·94	3/11·10	2/9·57	1/2·55	10/7·65
1928/29	1/8·08	10·14	2/11·27	3/0·23	1/2·82	9/8·54
1929/30	1/9·96	11·33	3/3·74	3/7·07	11·68	10/7·78
1930/31	1/10·40	10·73	3/4·74	3/5·27	7·84	10/2·98
1931/32	1/6·54	8·02	2/7·55	2/9·31	6·35	8/1·77
1932/33	1/7·31	9·41	3/7·85	3/4·29	1/0·36	10/5·22

Table 6.3

OTHER EXPENSES
£000

Year	Office expenses	Advertising etc.	Depreciation
1925	885·0	263·0	893·3
1926	866·2	263·2	906·0
1927	928·6	349·4	852·4
1928	977·7	362·8	821·0

Table 6.3 (continued)

OTHER EXPENSES

Year	Office expenses		Advertising etc.	Depreciation
1929	1008·9		326·8	743·6
		FRANCONIA Cruise Special account	30·0	
1930	1102·3		347·3	696·1
1931	1006·6		174·2	675·1
		FRANCONIA and LANCASTRIA	34·4	
1932	1067·5		168·2	720·0
		Special Account	39·7	

Year	'B' operating account	Depreciation sundry properties	Miscellaneous expenditure	Cost of discounting bills
1925	262·9	23·7	168·6	111·2
1926	264·4	35·0	220·3	133·8
1927	232·3	32·5	186·9	88·6
1928	339·5	36·9	203·8	23·3
1929	345·0	34·5	194·3	5·9
1930	114·6	36·6	192·0[119]	—
1931	35·8	29·7	147·1	—
1932	—	26·6	131·3	—

Year	Cunard building mortgage interest	Income tax	Debenture stock interest	Preference stock		Gold notes interest	Total
				Interest	Dividend		
1925	—	12·0	290·0	135·0	—	(6·4)	3051·1
1926	—	12·0	279·2	135·0	—	(77·2)	3192·3
1927	—	50·0	203·1	135·0	—	72·6	3131·5
1928	21·9	20·0	200·0	—	135·0	23·1	3165·0
1929	22·1	22·3	200·0	—	135·0	20·8	3089·0
1930	22·1	—	200·0	—	135·0	—	2845·9

Table 6.3 (continued)

OTHER EXPENSES
(continued)

| 1931 | 22·1 | — | 200·0 | — | 135·0[a] | — | 2460·0 |
| 1932 | 22·1 | — | 200·0 | — | — | — | 2375·4 |

[a] Only £67.500 paid in 1931.

Apart from operating costs the directors made determined efforts to reduce capital charges. On 17 October 1927 a resolution was passed increasing the capital of the Company to £8,100,020, by the creation of 1,100,000 new ordinary shares of £1 each.[120] At that time the funded debt of the Company (dating from the Government agreement in 1903) amounted to about £4 million, the short-term debt to about £1,500,000 and liabilities to ship builders to about the same figure, making in all a total of £7 million.[121] This amounted to the total of issued capital of the ordinary and preference stocks. Incidence of heavy debt charges was obviously an inhibiting factor in the struggle to secure ultimate profitability, and was an item which needed to be reduced in parallel with the other efforts already mentioned to reduce working costs. By increasing capital resources it was hoped that new funds would be made available for improving the efficiency and earning capacity of the fleet. It was argued that with increasing voyage profits there would follow a more flexible allocation of resources leading among other things, to a lowering of outstanding debt.[122] However acceptable this may have been in financial practice, the success of such an operation depended primarily on the level of trading activity and the maximum use of shipping capacity. With the benefit of hindsight, it is perhaps unfair to express too critical an appreciation of such an aspect of management; to the shipowner of 1927 there seemed to be grounds for hoping that conditions would improve and that, in consequence 'in order to obtain the best net profits from an increase in gross revenue it has been necessary to keep watch on *every* item of expenditure'.[123]

Another facet of the directors' determination to reduce costs in line with the above statement can be seen in the various attempts to redeem loans and convert mortgage debenture stock to a lower rate of interest. The original mortgage debenture stock (negotiated with the Government in 1903) at the rate of 2¾ per cent was paid off by annual instalments of £130,000 and fully redeemed in 1927.[124] In 1908 it had become necessary to provide for the consolidation of outstanding liabilities on shipbuilding account, and accordingly there was created £1,600,000 4½ per cent debenture stock, of which £800,000 had already been issued. 'It will be within your recollection', stated the Annual Report for 1908, 'that during the last ten years, we have increased the tonnage of our fleet from 128,000 to 245,000 tons. The cost of this new tonnage including the cost of *Lusitania* and *Mauretania* (which we built under our agreement with the Government) exceeded £6,000,000, and our indebtedness on the shipbuilding acceptances and on open account at the end of 1907, exceeded £1,400,000.'[125] It was, therefore, desirable that this indebtedness should be consolidated on terms which would provide for its liquidation by instalments at fixed dates. These resources sustained the shipbuilding programme including the building of *Aquitania* and the whole of this stock was redeemed in 1919.[126] As an aid to the purchase of the Commonwealth and Dominion Line in 1916, a further £1,000,000 of 5½ per cent mortgage debenture stock was issued. This was eventually redeemed in 1921.[127]

The post-war building programme was secured by transfer from resources and from the issue of a new £4,000,000 7 per cent debenture stock. This was a high rate of interest and bore heavily on the Company's finances during the years of trade fluctuations. In July 1926, therefore, arrangements were completed for the conversion to a like amount of stock bearing interest at the rate of 5 per cent. This had the effect of saving the Company some £75,000 per annum on interest charges alone.[128] Even so the annual interest payments on mortgage debenture stock remained at approximately £200,000 for the next few years. By 1933 the Company still showed an indebtedness of £4,000,000 mortgage stock, no favourable financial opportunity having occurred to liquidate any part of this amount.

Although no new debentures were issued in the late 1920s, the Company did manage to increase borrowing by the use of a relatively profitable expedient. This was through the medium of dollar finance. At the end of 1925 interest rates in New York were favourable, a natural consequence of London rates supporting official policy of maintaining the American exchange at par. Believing that in such circumstances dollar rates would always be lower than those ruling in London, the Cunard management borrowed $7,500,000 in U.S. gold notes at 5 per cent per annum.[129] The loan was for a period of two years 'and I am assured', said the Chairman, 'that if a renewal is desired, it will not be difficult to arrange'.[130] This was a new, albeit short-lived source of finance opened to the Company at a time when every possibility for the reduction of debt charges was being actively pursued. The gold notes were repaid on maturity in 1927 and a new issue of $2,500,000 was taken up at a reduced rate of $4\frac{1}{2}$ per cent for a further period of two years.[131] The arrangements for these loans had been undertaken in New York by Messrs Brown Bros and their associates. 'It is a legitimate source of pride', so ran Cunard's argument, 'that the Company's credit is so high that it is able to borrow money without collateral security at so favourable a rate.'[132] Perhaps so, but it is significant that no further loan of this kind was negotiated following the redemption of outstanding obligations in 1929. This is perhaps explicable in the light of the behaviour of stock markets in that year.

VI ASSESSMENT OF MANAGERIAL EFFICIENCY

In conclusion we must now attempt to make some assessment of success or failure by Cunard's management during the difficult post-war years. We have already seen (Table 6.1) that overall credit balances remained reasonably stable from 1922 to 1924 despite many changes affecting the traditional pattern of trade; after 1925, however, the effect of the new tonnage coupled with the policy of reducing costs can be seen in the augmented balances. Though there was a reduction in these balances in 1928, the figure for 1929 was the highest for the decade. From 1930 onwards, however, the figures reflect the deepening world depression. On the surface it would appear that all previous efforts by management to redress the financial position of the Company, to increase business and sustain earning capacity, were outweighed by the heavy losses sustained after 1930.

By 1932 it appeared to the prophets of doom that Cunard was about to be engulfed in bankruptcy and disappear from the list of British shipping companies. Though there may have been some justification for the belief that Cunard's financial position was deteriorating, the conclusion drawn from that belief was superficially based. The real answer lay in the strength and purpose of management and in the generative power which that management was capable of sustaining. In overall financial terms important remedial measures were being taken to give a more realistic valuation of assets. Influenced no doubt by the effect of the Kylsant disclosures, the directors reduced visible reserves from £1,500,000 to £500,000 in 1930.[133] The balance of £1 million was applied to the writing down of the book value of shares in subsidiary and other companies and in the transfer of £138,696 to the contingencies reserve account. Cunard's interest in the America–Levant Line (acquired during the war to facilitate the prospective carriage of emigrants from south-east Europe to the U.S.A.) was disposed of in January 1931.[134] The objectives designed for this company had never been realised, partly because of the operation of the American Immigration Laws and partly because of American Government competition in the Mediterranean. As a further exercise in the process of revaluation, Cunard was also induced to make a more realistic appraisal of its holdings in the Anchor Line. The Company's investment in this line, a portion of which had been acquired at a considerable premium, had not shown a dividend for seven years and there was no prospect of a return in 1931. After balancing all the circumstances, therefore, it was decided to write down this asset to a figure materially below fifty per cent of its par value.[135] This was a more drastic reduction than that recommended by the auditors, but it was evidence of the determination expressed by the Chairman that 'reserve funds are provided for use and not for ornament'.[136]

It is evident that during the years of intense depression the same spirit of enterprise had prevailed in decision-taking as that which had directed the Company's fortunes during relatively more prosperous years. During the period as a whole (i.e. 1914–34) the enlargement of resources consequent upon acquisition had given added financial strength to the Company structure; the fleet had been rebuilt and equipped with oil burners; markets had been widened and every attempt made to secure as great a share as possible of passenger traffic; earning capacity had been sustained by Conference agreements and operating costs together with debt liabilities had been reduced; yet despite these efforts the Company found itself in a worse financial position at the end of the period under review. Outstanding liabilities were still a heavy burden, operating receipts failed to cover costs, overheads and depreciation. As a result, heavy losses in each successive year between 1931 and 1933 weakened any effort which Cunard might have made to overcome the adverse cyclical influence of world-wide depression. It seemed that the dynamic energy displayed during the 1920s had achieved little more than a temporary respite in Cunard's progress towards eventual bankruptcy.

In such circumstances prestige and goodwill could prove to be valuable assets; new types of trade had to be sought, new policies evolved and new capital resources made available if the Company was to survive. The answer seemed to be in the laying down of new ships of immense size and power which would at one and the same time sustain prestige and increase trading capabilities. *Queen Mary* and *Queen Elizabeth* were therefore in conception not only revolutionary in the development of the shipbuilders' craft, but also the anticipated instruments of salvation.

7
No. 534 and the formation of Cunard White Star Limited

I EVENTS LEADING TO MERGER

The events between 1925 and 1934, leading ultimately to the merger of The Cunard Steam Ship Co. Ltd and White Star Line (Oceanic Steam Navigation Co. Ltd), are extremely complicated and difficult to follow. This arises from the fact that there were three areas of controversy each impinging on the other, involving at times separate and at other times joint, matters for negotiation. Firstly there was the growing involvement of the White Star Line with the mounting financial difficulties of the Royal Mail group of which this company had become a part, difficulties which were undoubtedly aggravated by the adverse trading conditions at the beginning of the 1930s. Secondly, there was the promotion of policy by The Cunard Steam Ship Co. to inaugurate a weekly two-ship express service acrosss the Atlantic, a policy which could be implemented only by putting into service ships of great size and power. Finally there was, at a somewhat later stage in the proceedings, participation of government departments and the provision of government finance as instruments in the salvation of White Star and in the building of the new large Cunarders.

The exigencies of the time required bold and unprecedented action. Sir Percy Bates, who had succeeded Sir Thomas Royden, became Chairman of The Cunard Steam Ship Co. in 1930. He accepted both the responsibility and the leadership necessary for the advancement of business and a more efficient utilisation of resources. He was largely responsible for the conduct of the complicated series of negotiations with shipping companies, shipbuilders and government departments, though on all questions of policy he was ably supported by the shrewd advice of his brother, Mr F. A. Bates, the administrative efficiency of Cunard's General Manager, S. J. Lister, the board of directors and the technical staff of the

Company. As a result of his efforts The Cunard Steam Ship Co. was given a new spirit of business enterprise and a new direction in its history.

In order to understand the antecedents of these events we must go back to the mid 1920s. Towards the end of July 1925 Sir Frederick Lewis, Chairman of Furness Withy and Co. Ltd, made a suggestion to Sir Thomas Royden that Cunard and Furness Withy should jointly make an effort to acquire the vessels of the International Mercantile Marine sailing under the British flag.[1] Royden agreed and a meeting was arranged with Mr Franklin of The International Mercantile Marine Co. The meeting, however, did not take place as it had become evident that negotiations between Morgans of New York and another shipping firm for the sale of certain International Mercantile Marine Co. assets were underway.[2] It later became known that Harrimans were interested in purchasing the Morgan combine but that they would sell the foreign flag constituents, retaining only the American flag.[3] In this context Cunard was given the offer of purchasing the White Star Line. By July 1926, however, Royden had decided, after consultation with his fellow directors, that Cunard could not advantageously increase its stake in the North Atlantic trade at that time. He told Sir Frederick Lewis that they were not 'able to join in any deal having as its object the acquisition of the White Star Line'.[4] He would certainly not allow Cunard's interests to be played off against any third party.

Thereupon Sir Frederick Lewis continued the negotiations on behalf of Furness Withy and Co Ltd and agreed to buy the White Star interests held by the International Mercantile Marine Co, provided that the accounts, when examined, showed a return of 8 per cent.[5] When the figures failed to show anything like a return of 8 per cent Furness Withy refused to complete the sale and withdrew from the discusssions. The field was left open in November of that year for Lord Kylsant, Chairman of the Royal Mail Steam Packet Co., to negotiate the purchase from the International Mercantile Marine Co. of the whole of the issued capital of the Oceanic Steam Navigation Co. (White Star Line). The capital consisted of 5000 shares of £1000 each. The price agreed by Kylsant was £7 million, payment to be made as follows: £2 million on or before 1 February 1927; £1,250,000 on 30 June 1928; a like sum on 30 June 1929 and £2,500,000 on or before 31 December 1936.[6] The interest on the unpaid balance was calculated at the rate of 4 per cent per annum without deduction of British income tax. The agreement also provided that until the purchase was completed the shares should be deposited with trustees.[7]

The financial strength of Lord Kylsant's Royal Mail group was not sufficient to underwrite the deal. Accordingly, a new company was created (White Star Line Ltd.) and registered as a public company on 12 January 1927 with a nominal capital of £9 million. The capital was divided into £5 million 6½ per cent cumulative preference shares of £1 each and £4 million ordinary shares of £1 each.[8] The ordinary shares were held by the Royal Mail group of companies, subscribed for as follows:

	£
Royal Mail	995 993
plus directors' qualification and subscribers to memorandum of association	4 007
Union Castle	1 000 000
Pacific Steam Navigation Co.	500 000
H. & W. Nelson Ltd	500 000
Elder Dempster	1 000 000[9]

By a subsequent transfer, Royal Mail acquired 501,100 shares. The preference shares were guaranteed as to capital and dividend by Royal Mail and were issued to the public by or through the British, Foreign and Colonial Corporation Ltd.[10] Out of the proceeds of this public issue White Star Line paid the Royal Mail Steam Packet Co. £4,650,000 on account of the purchase price of the Oceanic shares, leaving the balance of £2,350,000 payable on or before 31 December 1936.[11]

Both Royal Mail and White Star Line Ltd duly met the liabilities in respect of interest on the outstanding instalments of principal until 31 December 1930. In December 1929, however, Lord Kylsant had applied to the Trades Facilities Act Advisory Committee for extension of maturity dates of certain loans granted to companies within the Royal Mail group.[12] As the interests of the companies in the Royal Mail group were so interlocked, the committee decided that an independent report on the position should be prepared by Sir William McLintock. By December 1931, however, the financial position of White Star Line Ltd was such that it was unable to meet the interest payment accruing for the year, a sum amounting to £94,000.[13] The Royal Mail Steam Packet Co.

was also short of funds and not able to make the payment of a like amount to the International Mercantile Marine.[14] This default proved to be a further and, perhaps, final aggravation of Lord Kylsant's enmeshing financial problems. Again, it is not relevant for us to examine the multiplicity of causes which eventually led to Kylsant's downfall and the attendant chaos resulting from the Royal Mail crash. We are concerned only with the effect of these events on the fortunes of the White Star Line Ltd. It is sufficient to state that on 10 June 1930 a meeting of banking and financial interests involved in Royal Mail was held, at which it was agreed to extend the maturity dates of loans until 31 December 1931 on certain conditions, one of which was the creation of voting trustees.[15] Trustees appointed were the Rt Hon. Walter Runciman, M.P., Sir William McLintock (senior partner of Thomson, McLintock and Co.) and General A. Maxwell (managing partner of Glyn, Mills and Co.). By June 1932 the position of Royal Mail creditors had so deteriorated that the High Court approved a Scheme of Arrangement.[16] The first objective of this ruling was to create new shipping operating companies to which the ships of certain companies in the Kylsant organisation could be transferred. It was hoped that by such action shipping activities would be carried on by separate companies free from financial restriction.[17] The second objective was to consolidate into one ownership the vessels belonging to different companies in the group engaged in the same trade. Finally it was proposed that there would be a moratorium until 31 December 1934, for each company in the group.[18]

The effect of this arrangement on the somewhat desperate position in which the White Star Line Ltd found itself was not wholly satisfactory. A considerable balance of the purchase price due to the International Mercantile Marine was still outstanding and the guarantees accepted by Royal Mail on behalf of White Star were no longer operative. It will be remembered that the Royal Mail Steam Packet Co. had guaranteed the dividend on White Star Line Ltd's preference shares. This obligation had been honoured up to 1 July 1930, but under the new Scheme of Arrangement the payment of such dividend was to be satisfied by the issue of deferred creditors' certificates bearing interest at five per cent per annum.[19] Accordingly the holders of White Star preference shares ranked as unsecured creditors of the Royal Mail Steam Packet Co. in respect of deferred certificates amounting to nine half-yearly dividends from December 1930 to July 1934. This obligation assumed great significance under the new scheme, the provisions of which called for the liquidation of White Star Line Ltd by 8 April 1935.[20] In this liquidation the holders of White Star Line Ltd preference shares ranked as unsecured creditors in the terms of the guarantee to the extent of £5 million. The terms also provided that the International Mercantile Marine should rank as creditors of the company *pari passu* with the holders of deferred creditors' certificates for the balance of the purchase price of the Oceanic Company's shares and interest.[21]

On the best possible construction that can be made of these events, there is little doubt that the financial position of White Star Line Ltd, with regard to both assets and the covering of liabilities to shareholders, was highly precarious. Whatever may have been the most important items in the long list of causes leading to the Royal Mail crash one may, perhaps, accept the judgement of Sir William McLintock that failure was attributable primarily to the nature of the financial structure of the group of companies under Kylsant's management, among which the Royal Mail Steam Packet Co. was an important element.[22] He pointed out that while it owned a number of vessels and certain properties, its principal assets consisted of investments (namely ordinary shares) in a large number of subsidiary and associated companies. In most of these there were substantial loan obligations, the interest and discount charges on which were payable by the Royal Mail irrespective of earnings.[23] When acute and long periods of depression occurred the financial structure of the company proved incapable of surmounting the difficulties besetting it as a whole. Finally Sir William McLintock stated that, in his view, the principal cause contributing to the magnitude of the failure was the purchase in 1926 of the shares of the Oceanic Steam Navigation Co. Ltd for £7 million.[24] As events turned out, the disadvantage was reciprocal, for White Star Line Ltd no less than Royal Mail was brought to the verge of bankruptcy.

II WHITE STAR NEGOTIATIONS

We shall see that in certain areas of business activity during the 1920s Cunard and White Star had worked in close and harmonious relationship.[25] Fierce competitive rivalry had given way to a more sympathetic understanding of each other's struggle to maintain their respective positions on the North Atlantic in the face of adverse influences. When Sir William McLintock intimated to Sir Frederick Lewis (some time before 17 July 1930) that 'the right policy for the Voting Trustees to follow with regard to the Oceanic assets would be to sell them', there was an unexpressed implication that Cunard might, in some way, be involved in the purchase.[26] Sir Frederick had in mind a purchase by Furness Withy and Co. Ltd and an invitation to Cunard to co-operate with him in running the various services. He called on Sir Percy Bates who told him that Cunard's control of the passenger business was essential and they were ready to explore the possibility of making an agreement with him.[27] This was followed by an invitation from Walter Runciman to Sir Thomas Royden and Sir Percy Bates to meet him in London where he suggested there should be close co-operation between the White Star Line Ltd and Cunard in order to effect a more economical working of the North Atlantic traffic. Sir Percy Bates made it clear that Cunard was mainly interested in the acquisition of the passenger agency from whomsoever bought the White Star Line, but that if this failed they might consider buying the White Star Line themselves.[28] When Sir Percy Bates next met Sir Frederick Lewis he made it clear that Cunard was primarily interested in acquiring the passenger agency 'and it was for him to consider whether this would make a purchase of the Oceanic unattractive to him'.[29] Tentative consideration was also given to the possibility of an agreement between Furness Withy and Cunard for joint purchase.

The next step was the careful preparation of information relevant to the possibility of such a purchase. Sir Percy Bates cabled Sir Ashley Sparks in New York asking for precise specifications of pier accommodation in that port and Mr S. J. Lister prepared a memorandum setting forth immediate points for consideration.[30] In his opinion any agreement reached ought to give Cunard the entire passenger agency (i.e. control of passenger business) both on this side of the Atlantic and in the United States and Canada and elsewhere should any other office of the Company be engaged in the Atlantic trade; in the second place, policy relating to Conference matters should be in Cunard's hands as should also operational arrangements and the sailing of the ships.[31] Only by such measures could economies of scale be secured. The final point stressed the need for a long-term binding agreement and, if such were accepted, 'those who were going to work with us in the management would have to be on the spot with us, and that is in Liverpool'.[32]

These were but first thoughts, although in subsequent discussions with Lewis during July 1930 Bates made no further concessions. At the July meeting of the Cunard Board it emerged as common policy that Cunard preferred to help Lewis to buy White Star, provided they could have the complete passenger agency; that if this were not acceptable to Lewis, Cunard would enter the bidding to buy White Star's Atlantic interests but not the Australasian part of its business.[33] This particular decision was influenced by the views of the Commonwealth and Dominion (Port Line) directors, whose interests were involved in the Australasian route 'and preferred not to reduce the number of entities engaged in the trade'.[34] In fact, Sir Percy Bates was in process of formulating a clear and decisive course of action based on a shrewd appraisal of the strength and numbers of all the other likely competitors. He correctly judged that Sir Frederick Lewis, on behalf of Furness Withy and Co. Ltd, would withdraw from the bid to acquire White Star's Atlantic interests, and in further communications with Sir Ashley Sparks gave a fairly precise indication of the way in which events might develop. 'I have still to hear from Lewis definitely', he wrote on 28 July 1930, 'but I think that last Friday's indication will be sustained. If so, it means that the most recent competitor for White Star Atlantic has retired.'[35] He then outlined the possible course of development in future negotiations; that the International Mercantile Marine Co. might desire to repurchase White Star Line Ltd; that Canadian Pacific Railway might be induced to enter the bidding. 'These chances were always inherent in the situation', added Bates,' and the Cunard position from a purchase point of view would be improved by the retirement of Furness Withy. I.M.M. Co., owning the pier leases can afford to disregard this point, but any other purchaser must consider it . . . I shall hear from Lewis in the next day or so and it is on the nature of his reply that our action depends.'[36]

Sir Percy Bates was quite prepared to wait upon events, particularly as the complicated and hazardous nature of White Star Line's finances precluded a speedy decision. 'They owe I.M.M. Co. £2,300,000', added Bates, 'to the Commonwealth of Australia Government £1,500,000, the balance due for "Bay" boats, Sir

John Ellerman £400,000, (balance of Shaw Savill); they are owed £3 million by Royal Mail for uncalled capital and Royal Mail guarantee the preference dividend, but what is this worth?'[37] As a postscript, he concluded his lengthy summary with the prophetic judgement: 'At one time I thought we might have to choose between White Star and building a new ship. Today, I think we may have to face both together. If we have, we shall do so on more favourable conditions of price and, unless C.P.R. should prove a real competitor, we know that any purchaser, other than ourselves, still entails a smaller number of big ships than at one time seemed possible.'[38]

This letter from Sir Percy Bates to Sir Ashley Sparks has been quoted *in extenso* because both the content and terminology are indicative of Bates's forceful personality. It is also clear that at this early date a plan of action was in his mind for combining the White Star purchase and the eventual operation of the new Cunarder No. 534. A meeting was arranged on 30 July 1930, between Sir Percy Bates, S. J. Lister and Walter Runciman, Chairman of the voting trustees appointed to dispose of White Star (and other Royal Mail) assets.[39] In a memorandum on what transpired at this meeting, Bates began with the assumption that the meeting had been called primarily to discuss close working arrangements regarding economies and sailing schedules arising from closer relationship between Cunard and White Star Line, an extension of a policy which had existed between the two companies for some years but the topic was not pursued. Instead Runciman asked for a complete statement of current negotiations between Cunard and Furness Withy with respect to the Royal Mail–White Star situation.[40] Runciman, who was in the position of a vendor, stated that 'Sir Frederick Lewis must not think that White Star Line was something to be picked up without a fair and satisfactory price being paid for it; that White Star Line could very well go along, as in fact could the whole show which was, in a sense, perfectly sound . . . they were short of cash, a matter which could be easily overcome'.[41]

Sir Percy Bates, like his predecessor Lord Inverclyde in 1902, was not dissuaded from his own course of action by such shadowboxing. His answer to Runciman made it clear that, in his view, there were two alternatives. The first was to have an agency of whomsoever bought White Star Line, the second was to consider acquiring it himself.⁴² To this, Runciman added a third possibility, namely that White Star Line and Cunard should enter into an arrangement whereby certain economies of scale might be effected thus putting the two companies into a stronger position than that possible under separate direction.⁴³ Bates pointed out some of the more obvious objections to such a proposal, particularly as Cunard could not afford to have capital so tied up because they were contemplating building two big ships which would eventually form one complete Southampton mail service.⁴⁴ This disclosure was a shrewd psychological move as it gave Bates a degree of manoeuvre in his bid for the White Star passenger agency. He went so far as to suggest that if the agency were given to Cunard, the second ship might be left to the other contracting party.⁴⁵ In view of what happened later, this meeting was of significance in that both Bates and Runciman had dealt with each other in open and fair discussion and had established a *rapport*, which proved to be an important factor in their dealings with Sir Frederick Lewis and Sir William McLintock.

Sir Frederick Lewis, who was under the impression that he was acting as intermediary with the voting trustees on Cunard's behalf, strongly favoured the splitting of White Star Line's interests. Under his plan Furness Withy would acquire the Australasian rights (including part of Shaw Savill, then owned by White Star Line) and Cunard the original Oceanic Company's rights in the Atlantic trade.⁴⁶ This plan would be effected by a share operation. By 5 August 1930, however, Bates had taken a more precise decision to offer cash for White Star Line's Atlantic ships and goodwill, accepting the proferred assistance of Brown Bros in New York to provide the financial backing.⁴⁷ Writing to Sir Ashley Sparks, he suggested that this course might provide a better solution for the ills of Royal Mail 'with a large offer of cash to them, as opposed to Lewis's notion of cash from them. This would leave us clear of all the welter of financial tangle . . . with its possible consequence of legal actions between conflicting interests'.⁴⁸ Having arranged satisfactory terms with Brown Bros for a loan, and having obtained an unofficial intimation from Sir Charles Hipwood of the Board of Trade that government assistance might be forthcoming for the building of a large passenger liner, Bates agreed to meet Lewis on 27 August 1930 for the purpose of bringing the negotiations to a head.⁴⁹ It was not a harmonious meeting;

Bates informed Lewis that Cunard were no longer interested in acquiring shares in White Star with the ultimate objective of dividing the business interests of that company. Lewis replied that he had expected any offers from Cunard to the voting trustees would have been made through him. Bates did not agree and summed up the current situation in clear and precise terms.[50]

There were now two courses of possible action to be submitted to the voting Trustees; the first, favoured by Cunard, involving the purchase of ships, goodwill and flag for cash; the second, proposed by Furness Withy and Co. Ltd, the acquisition of White Star Line by a purchase of shares. If the first alternative was approved, Cunard would proceed with the negotiations, if the second scheme was accepted, Cunard would leave the field clear for Furness Withy.[51] Cunard would then have to consider whether the agency or other terms offered by Furness Withy might compensate Cunard for refraining from building a second large ship for themselves.[52]

The suggestion of £3 million cash for White Star Line's Atlantic interests was based on a series of calculations made by Mr F. A. Bates of the current assets and liabilities of White Star given certain preconditions of sale.[53] The figure also equalled the amount of unpaid capital held by Royal Mail constituents in White Star. The final offer by Cunard was made on 15 October 1930. This involved £3,250,000 to be made up of £1,655,000 liability for trades facilities loans on *Britannic* and *Laurentic*; £310,000 balance due on half *Majestic* and *Homeric*; and £1,285,000 in cash.[54] The offer was to cover twelve ships plus White Star flag and goodwill in the North Atlantic, the whole to be contingent on Cunard's expected ability to make some additional arrangements with the Government in respect of its shipbuilding programme. In the event neither the proposal put forward by Cunard nor that submitted by Furness Withy was acceptable to the voting trustees and, for a time, negotiations were suspended.[55]

Meanwhile the Royal Mail Steam Packet Co's financial position was going from bad to worse. By January 1931 it was evident that if action were taken by any of the creditors, secured or unsecured, their company's position would become desperate. Several meetings of creditors were held and eventually, as we have seen, a moratorium was agreed pending the preparation of a Scheme of Arrangement.[56] In June 1931 there was evidence that the Treasury were becoming impatient with the voting trustees at the delay in bringing negotiations to a conclusion, and new proposals were submitted both by Bates and Lewis at the instigation of Montagu Norman, Governor of the Bank of England.[57] In essence Cunard suggested the purchase of certain ships of the White Star fleet. It was suggested that the purchase should be made by an offer of Cunard ordinary shares at a share valuation based on an amalgamated balance sheet of Cunard and its subsidiary companies, in which Cunard Atlantic ships were to be valued on a basis comparative to the values placed on those of White Star Line's Atlantic ships.[58] This basis was designed to enable Cunard to take over White Star Line's ships on terms fair to the Cunard share and debenture stockholders while, at the same time, giving White Star Line's interests their fair share of any future earnings from ships under Cunard rationalisation. *Georgic*, a ship then being built for White Star, was not included in the offer as at that time only some £300,000 had been expended on her.[59] In fact, Cunard had in mind the suspension of her construction because the tonnage already existing on her proposed berth was considerably in excess of traffic requirements.[60]

As time went on, the difficulty of arranging a purchase of White Star interests, whether in the Atlantic or in the Australasian trade, became more complicated by the competing demands of various groups of creditors. These ranged from White Star bankers, Glyn Mills, whose Chairman, Sir Herbert Lawrence, was trustee for the mortgage debenture stock, to the Northern Ireland Government, who had advanced resources for the building of *Britannic* and *Georgic* in an endeavour to sustain employment in Harland and Wolff's yard.[61] On the sidelines were the Treasury and the Bank of England who, since the moratorium on Royal Mail affairs, were now faced with the prospect of having to make good guarantees on the building of certain ships.[62] Discussions dragged on until October when the Bank of England produced a scheme endeavouring to resolve differences. The most important clause in this scheme was that Cunard should purchase the White Star North Atlantic ships for £3,750,000, to be made up as follows: £100,000 cash; £400,000 Oceanic 5 per cent debenture stock; £3,250,000 ordinary income debenture stock 5 per cent non-cumulative redemption service of 6 per cent.[63] In addition Cunard should purchase *Georgic* for £1,350,000, this amount to include £225,000 trades facilities loans with insurance companies (5 per cent interest for 15 years), £670,000 Bank of Ireland loan for 13 years, interest ½ per cent under Irish Bank rate, minimum 5 per cent and the balance of £455,000 by Bills acceptable to Harland and Wolff.⁶⁴ The Cunard Board was not able to accept these proposals and authorised Sir Percy to make a counter offer which, in turn, was declined.⁶⁵

By the end of 1931 all negotiations had broken down; 'from beginning to end', wrote Sir Percy Bates, 'it has been a most trying negotiation accompanied as it has been throughout with half-threats as to what the Government would do to us if we were not prepared to pay more than we ought. The breakdown, I think, is due to the fact that at no time have we been negotiating either with or through anyone who had any acquaintance with the North Atlantic passenger trade.'⁶⁶ Rightly or wrongly, he also blamed one of the voting trustees, Sir William McLintock (who had the support of some Treasury officials) for the repeated obstacles to Cunard's proposals. There was undoubtedly some personal antipathy between Bates and McLintock; but in fairness to the latter, he was acting in what he judged to be the best interests of White Star creditors, while Bates was acting in what he considered to be the best interests of Cunard. 'The last two moves in the game were as follows', added Bates. 'The Bank of England, being unable to submit a combined proposal for all the ships, produced one in two halves: the first one comprised all the ships, except *Georgic*, and involved a little cash and a lot of income debenture stock on terms which were absolutely impossible for us to accept. Even if they had been possible, the terms for *Georgic* were absolutely impossible, involving as they did a mix-up of trades facilities money with the assumption of an overdraft at the Bank of Ireland and the completion of the ship by means of a discount of bills drawn on us by Harland and Wolff... The Ulster Government further required the acceptance of these terms on the *Georgic* as a condition of their allowing *Britannic* to go along with the other ships (of White Star) and said that if we did not accept their terms, it would be better business for them to make arrangements to run *Georgic* and *Britannic* themselves.'⁶⁷

Judging from the available correspondence between all the parties to the negotiations, this was a fair and objective statement of the case. The Bank of England then invited Cunard to make a combined offer 'on our own terms' leaving them to deal with the

No. 534 and the formation of Cunard White Star 203

allocation of that offer, between the different interests.⁶⁸ Cunard thereupon offered £2,500,000 of income debenture stock on their terms plus £500,000 cash, the whole being contingent on Cunard's ability to make arrangements to deal with the bills of No. 534 'which contingency', said Bates, 'we were fairly confident of being able to manage'.⁶⁹ This proposal was however in turn rejected and the discussions came to an end.

III NO. 534 AND THE GOVERNMENT: HOPES OF A TWO-SHIP EXPRESS SERVICE

At this juncture it is necessary, in the interests of clarity, to consider Cunard's shipbuilding policy, particularly in relation to the building of No. 534. In November 1928 a committee was set up to discuss the question of motive power for a new ship with a contemplated speed of 27½ knots.⁷⁰ The motive power under consideration involved 125,000 shaft horse power (or 137,500 with 10 per cent reserve). It was obvious that with this power no greater speed than 27½ knots could be achieved. Throughout the summer of 1929 views were being increasingly expressed that Cunard should build replacements for the ageing liners *Mauretania*, *Aquitania* and *Berengaria*.⁷¹ Economic conditions together with the general financial position of the Company were, at that time, propitious and future prospects seemed to be reasonably assured for the implementation of such a policy.

At a board meeting held on 16 October 1929, it was therefore proposed that, upon consideration of new tonnage required, the following three plans should be given consideration: firstly, build one new steamship as a replacement for *Mauretania* and run that ship at 25 knots until a second new ship could be built to replace either *Berengaria* or *Aquitania*: secondly, to build two new ships together to be put into operation when *Mauretania* was withdrawn from service; thirdly, to build one new ship to replace *Mauretania* and convert *Aquitania* for the purpose of providing a second unit.⁷² The board approved the third scheme and, in order to meet and overcome competition from German and French shipping lines, it was eventually decided that the new ship should be of revolutionary design and of great size, power and speed. Sir Aubrey Brocklebank, a Cunard director, was much concerned with the early specifications and design. A model was built and after innumerable tank tests, simulating 'every sort of weather she may expect to meet on the Atlantic', a ship of 1018 feet overall, with a beam of 118 feet and a gross tonnage of 73,000 (later amended to approximately 81,000) was decided upon.[73] On 21 May 1930 tenders for the new ship were submitted to the board and authorisation was given for the opening up of negotiations for the preparation of a definite contract, provided that assurances were received of adequate insurance cover for the ship during construction and in service, and subject to suitable dock accommodation being available at Southampton, Cherbourg and New York.[74]

The reason for the second precondition must be obvious. In the event, guarantees were received that a new dry dock at Southampton, capable of meeting the size and requirements of the new ship, would be ready by 1933. The reason for the first precondition, however, needs more explanation as it is bound up with the historical nature of our theme. Before 1914 a serious problem had arisen concerning the insurance of large passenger liners, the market being apprehensive of the risks involved in underwriting full cover. Cunard had therefore entered into a mutual insurance scheme with other lines, including both British and foreign competitors.[75] On the outbreak of war in 1914 the scheme had perforce to be cancelled. By 1930 the position had not changed in any material respect. 'After all', explained Sir Percy Bates, 'these large and costly ships are relatively few in number, and it is not to be wondered at if the marine insurance market should find itself unable to deal with these specialities.'[76] The building of No. 534 involved risks which could not be covered and, accordingly, the Company approached the Government with the proposal that it should absorb whatever insurance risks either in construction or in operation, the British market proved unable to take. The Government, through the Board of Trade, were sympathetic and gave the necessary assurances in November 1930, which later were confirmed by the passing of the Cunard Insurance Act in December of that year.[77] Having obtained these assurances the contract with John Brown and Co. was executed on 1 December 1930.

The building of a ship of such size, power and luxury accommodation presented formidable problems to designers, engineers, contractors and financiers. The technical details of the ship and of her ultimate performance have been dealt with in many publications.[78] All that need be said here is that she was to be driven by single-reduction geared turbines working on four propellers, the boilers being of the water-tube type and fired by oil fuel. Many alterations were made to the original specifications in course of planning; in July 1930, for example, it was decided to increase the designed power from 150,000 to 158,000 S.H.P and to adopt outward wing turning propellers.[79] We are, however, primarily concerned with the way in which resources were made available for construction and what was achieved in meeting and overcoming the many adverse influences inhibiting their flow and allocation. In a special sense finance was not difficult to arrange because Cunard was able to capitalise on the goodwill and credit of the Company itself. Even so, under prevailing conditions, this was something of an achievement at a time when, because of the doubtful financial operations of the Royal Mail group, shipping company balance sheets were being regarded with critical and suspicious interest.

During the 1920s Cunard had, despite some adverse trading years, managed to sustain general financial strength. Between 1919 and 1930 depreciation to the extent of £15,267,287 had been written off the Company's own ships and £16,133,902 off those of subsidiary companies.[80] In the same period some £6 million had been paid in income tax. As the result of a well-defined policy which was based on the assumption that a shipping company must earn sufficient depreciation to cover the fleet, fairly large reserves had been built up as cover. As payment for No. 534, therefore, Cunard proposed to make primary use of the annual allocations set aside for depreciation which were not available for distribution by way of dividend 'as their retention in the business is necessary owing to the fact that all ships are a wasting asset'.[81]

The first and most obvious prerequisite in financing No. 534 was that Cunard should continue to earn sufficient annual amounts to cover depreciation on the fleet as a whole. The second and no less important condition involved the mechanism of financial flow through the discount market and the ability to secure low discount rates. To sustain the building programme during the 1920s Cunard had recourse to the London bill market. The generally favourable nature of the discount operations in the post-war period had been of invaluable assistance to the Company; for example, the shipbuilding bills which Cunard had under discount on the market at any one time reached a maximum amount of £4,896,526 in 1922;[82]

all these bills were extinguished by 1928. During the years 1922–4, covering the peak period of the Company's bills in the market, the rates of discounting ranged from $4\frac{1}{8}$ per cent down to $2\frac{3}{8}$ per cent. At the beginning of 1930, Cunard had no bills on the market and when discount facilities were again sought in December, consequent upon the signing of the building contract for No. 534, the Company's discounting was done at $2\frac{5}{16}$ per cent.[83] On two fundamental points, therefore, namely the financial standing of Cunard and the favourable rate at which funds could be made available, there seemed to be grounds for optimism. There was every prospect that the Company would shortly be in possession of a ship capable of meeting and overcoming competition from any other shipping line on the North Atlantic.

By December 1931 the spirit of optimism had been dissipated. As already stated, Cunard's trading position during the current year (in common with practically every other shipping company in the world) had seriously deteriorated and earnings were not sufficient to cover depreciation.[84] This in turn affected the Company's standing in the market and it became virtually impossible to raise further funds. Work on No. 534 had to be suspended and, for a period of 27 months, the half-finished ship lay idle on the stocks. This action, coinciding as it did with mounting figures of unemployment, had widespread implications. It was not only a serious blow to Cunard's power of recuperation; it was also a direct threat to the Company's competitive strength particularly as the French line, Compagnie Générale Transatlantique, assisted by direct government subsidy, was laying down a ship comparable in size and power with No. 534. On Clydebank the immediate result of the stoppage had a multiplier effect in reducing employment over a wide range of skills and services. This applied particularly to certain supply areas such as Darlington where a great proportion of the working population depended upon subsidiary contracts. For the nation as a whole, the vast hull, towering idle in the stocks became symbolic of the desperate state of economic stagnation. As Sir Percy Bates explained on 6 April 1932, the irony of the situation was that the hull was far advanced and 'only five months is required to make her ready for launching'.[85] Had a little more cash been made available at the moment of crisis it is possible that the ship would have been finished on time. Sir Percy, however, did not express any opinion whether, in the prevailing economic conditions, the ship if finished on time could have earned a profit.

The next few months witnessed strenuous efforts on the part of management to secure financial assistance and a resumption of work. Questions were asked in Parliament, especially by Members who represented Clydeside constituencies, and on 15 February 1932 Sir Percy Bates wrote to the Prime Minister, the Rt Hon. J. Ramsay MacDonald, thanking him for his answer to Mr Kirkwood in the House on 2 February. 'In view of the altered conditions in the world since the Cunard Insurance Act was passed', he stated, 'we desire to ask for help of H.M. Government in the early resumption of work on No. 534, and I would ask you as head of the Government whether you would indicate your wishes as to the manner in which we should proceed.'[86] This request was in response to a statement by the Prime Minister that the Government had not been approached by Cunard and 'if they are approached the Government will, as stated on 11 December, give careful consideration to any proposal made, but the Government cannot undertake to give direct financial assistance in this case.'[87] Sir Percy's solution was that the Government should make funds available on terms similar to those which had been negotiated for the building of *Lusitania* and *Mauretania*. To his surprise, Sir Charles Hipwood of the Board of Trade replied that the Government distinguished sharply between No. 534 and the *Lusitania–Mauretania* case: '.... that while the Admiralty were seriously interested in those two ships as armed cruisers, they no longer had any interest of that character in "534" or any other new ship. The main Government interest in "534" was that of unemployment.'[88] Despite counter arguments put forward by Sir Percy Bates, the official Government attitude remained rigid and, on 1 March 1932, the Chancellor of the Exchequer made it quite clear that financial assistance would not be forthcoming, though he expressed the hope that 'your Company and the merchant marine as a whole may find, through a gradual improvement in home conditions, and in world conditions alike, a progressive reduction of present difficulties'.[89] This was poor consolation both for Cunard and for the many thousands of unemployed on Clydeside. It inhibited any further direct approach and drove Cunard management into protracted negotiations of an indirect character for the salvation of their ship and the revitalising of their resources.

So far, we have been concerned with the building of one large ship, No. 534. During the course of the various negotiations referred to above, the idea emerged of building a second large ship which, if built and put into service, would enable Cunard to establish a two-ship express weekly service across the Atlantic. It seems clear from evidence in the Cunard archives that, up to the early part of 1930, neither the technical staff nor the Cunard board had considered the possibility of such a service. As already stated, the prospect of converting *Aquitania* into a second unit had been considered in October 1929; but such a combination could not have sustained an express service and the proposal was dropped. When the Government announced in April 1930 the provision of insurance cover on the building and operation of No. 534, the terms also included similar provision for a second new ship.[90] This was the first notice of a two-ship service; it was followed in September of the same year by a circular to shareholders from Sir Percy Bates making known the board's proposal. Although Sir Percy Bates has been credited with this conception it is possible that the idea originated as a result of work undertaken by the technical staff: for on 8 April 1931 Sir Percy declared that the main business of the Company 'is, and always has been, the transport of passengers and mails across the Atlantic. Today the Company's express service is maintained by three ships and, up till recently, no less a number of ships could have performed it; but modern marine engineering and naval architecture have made it possible for an express weekly service to be carried out with two ships. Consequently, in the ordinary way of business the Cunard Co. was bound to adapt itself to the new conditions and, when ordering a new ship for the express service, to provide such a ship as would eventually require but a single sister to fulfil the requirements of the mail contract and the passenger schedule'.[91]

IV GROWING COMPETITION AND THE NEED FOR ACTION: THE GOVERNMENT AND THE TRIPARTITE AGREEMENT

During the summer months of 1932 Sir Percy Bates and his fellow directors were much concerned with many abortive attempts to further the Cunard White Star negotiations. They altered the emphasis in the argument by drawing the Government's attention to the growing threat of foreign competition, in particular from the subsidised ships of French, German and Canadian lines. They also argued that the longer Cunard and White Star affairs were unresolved, the more difficult it would be for these two companies to regain their former share of North Atlantic trade.[92] The Government recognised the force of this argument and on 31 October 1932 Lord Weir, a well-known industrialist, wrote to Sir Percy Bates stating that he had been asked by the Chancellor of the Exchequer and the President of the Board of Trade 'to conduct a confidential enquiry into the trading and financial position of the British shipping companies carrying on mail and passenger services on the North Atlantic, with special reference to the New York–European berth'.[93] He was further required to give particulars of the character of foreign competition experienced (e.g. in respect of subsidies paid for the construction and operation of ships) and to report his conclusions. He asked Bates to supply him with the Company's balance sheets together with a history of the negotiations and proposals made at different times for acquiring the White Star Line Ltd. He also requested a complete list of policy statements issued concerning No. 534.[94] A few days later it was announced that Lord Essendon (formerly Sir Frederick Lewis) had in pursuance of the Royal Mail scheme of arrangement agreed temporarily to accept the Chairmanship of White Star Line Ltd.[95] The implication of these events suggested that, at last, government opinion was becoming more amenable, that in fact there was a prospect of bridging the differences between the contending parties in return for some kind of government financial assistance.

Sir Percy Bates was not shown a copy of Lord Weir's report until 15 February 1933.[96] He saw at once that the recommendation provided a way out of the impasse and informed the Chancellor of the Exchequer that his Company fully accepted this report.[97] After considering a number of alternative proposals which might lead to a fair settlement, Lord Weir had stated that 'the simplest and most direct method would be for the Cunard Company to absorb the Oceanic Company as far as the North Atlantic service was concerned'.[98] If such a scheme were to be successfully negotiated, there were innumerable problems to be overcome. The main problem, which had always been a stumbling block to progress, was concerned with the terms which Cunard could arrange to secure outstanding claims from White Star creditors under the Royal Mail scheme of arrangement and the size of the annual burden which Cunard would be required to accept on behalf of these secured creditors. Lord Essendon, however, did not accept Lord Weir's recommendation that White Star should be absorbed and put forward a counter proposal for amalgamation.[99] The prospect of agreement seemed to be as far off as ever and it was eventually decided to ask Lord Weir to arbitrate between the opposing points of view. His note of mediation stated categorically that 'amalgamation does not seem a fair reflection of the position of the two companies and, due to this, amalgamation would be difficult to achieve'.[100] Furthermore after reviewing the course of negotiations Lord Weir was forced to conclude that 'absorption has been in the picture on both sides' particularly as the Bank of England, in its offer of 15 October 1931, had contemplated such a possibility.[101] Finally he expressed the belief that a new company, created by amalgamation, could not offer any better basis on which to arrive at agreement on relative valuation of assets than that provided under a scheme of absorption.[102]

The immediate effect of this attempted mediation was to heighten dissension between the contracting parties, Sir Percy Bates accepting the terms proposed, Lord Essendon rejecting them on behalf of White Star creditors. One most important result of Lord Weir's intervention, however, was communicated to Sir Percy Bates on 27 March 1933. Two days earlier Lord Weir had attended a meeting at the Treasury and had reported to the Chancellor of the Exchequer on the state of Cunard–White Star negotiations.[103] Though nothing of substance had emerged from this meeting, Lord Weir had seen the Chancellor privately 'and had definitely arranged with him that, in the event of the whole deal being consummated, the Government's financial provisions would include £1,500,000 beyond the sum required to complete No. 534'.[104] In other words, a direct inducement had now been made, the implications of which were not lost on Sir Percy Bates. 'I said', replied Sir Percy, 'we had already spent £1,700,000 and that I was hoping to be able to get the whole of that loose if required.'[105] Nevertheless the change of attitude on the part of the Government, undoubtedly stimulated by the proposals in Lord Weir's report, altered Cunard's bargaining position and encouraged a fresh examination of the liabilities to be assumed should absorption take place.

The current position of the Government (as distinct from private) creditors of White Star can be summarised as follows:

	£
Northern Ireland Government,	
First Mortgage on *Britannic* and *Georgic*	534 300
Second Mortgage on same ships	995 650
British Treasury,	
Third Loan for same ships	800 000
This made a total of	£2 329 950

Other outstanding liabilities were:	
Glyn Mills and Oceanic debentures	
In hands of public	473 700
Held by Glyns	725 000
Making a total of	1 198 700
LESS cash on account of debenture holders	100 000
Leaving a net total of	£1 098 700[106]

The security for these debentures consisted of all the vessels in the White Star fleet except *Britannic, Georgic* and *Majestic*, the latter ship being free though subject to a floating charge of the 4½ per cent debentures.[107] There was also a fourth charge on *Britannic* and *Georgic* and a first charge on Oceanic's half-shares of sundry Shaw Savill ships, always excepting four motor ships mortgaged to the Bank of England.[108] The extent to which the debentures relied on Atlantic ships was estimated at £898,000. White Star also had a loan of £500,000 from the Bank of England secured on 17,315 shares of £5 each in Shaw Savill (then valued at between £15 and £20 per share) plus a first mortgage on Oceanic's half-interest in the above-mentioned four motor ships.[109] Finally, Harland and Wolff were owed £107,000 secured by a long-range mortgage on *Britannic* and *Georgic* 'which is worth nothing but its nuisance value'.[110]

Against such a formidable burden of secured liability, it was difficult to accept the claim by Lord Essendon 'that the ships were doing well'.[111] Even during years of reasonable trading conditions they could scarcely have earned a profit; under conditions prevailing in 1932 and 1933, they must have returned sizeable losses. It appeared to Sir Percy Bates and his co-directors that, compared with Cunard's financial standing, White Star was a 'worthless' asset.[112] He was also surprised at the extent of the Government commitment in White Star. It seemed to him that the Government had built up a very strong negotiating position for the Oceanic Steam Navigation Company, a position which gave them an advantage in their negotiations with Cunard. In a characteristic if rather bitter outburst Sir Percy summed up his feelings: 'A crude statement of the situation would read something like this', he wrote, 'H.M. Government say to Cunard "arrange to absorb Oceanic which as an entity we think has no chance of survival, and we will help you on No. 534 and her sister". This is quite sound logic and sound policy; but H.M. Government in one form or another is the principal creditor of the Oceanic and first of all by lending it more money to lose and, later, by agreeing to a moratorium, has placed it in a negotiating position which, from the Cunard angle is impossible.'[113] This may or may not have been a just assessment of the facts, but it led Bates to the conclusion that Cunard should stand firm and not agree to resumption of work on No. 534 until 'H.M. Government are tired of backing the Oceanic Company'.[114] He also pointed out that if the Government continued to back Oceanic the company would not legally regain its British title until some £2,350,000 (the outstanding balance of Kylsant's purchase price) had been paid to the International Mercantile Marine.[115]

In this manner, the argument was tossed from one side to the other in an endeavour to extract the greatest possible advantage. The available evidence suggests that Sir Percy Bates was both a shrewd negotiator and a man of dogged resolution in the maintenance of principle. In his long struggle to safeguard the interests of Cunard he was supported by the no less forceful personality of his brother, Mr F. A. Bates, and the persistence of Sir Ashley Sparks in New York. By comparison Lord Essendon's efforts to secure a fair result for the interests which he represented were vacillating and not always based on a real appraisal of events. Hence agreement was protracted, but by 27 April 1933 a more hopeful sign of progress was manifest following a meeting between Lord Weir and the Chancellor of the Exchequer.[116] At this meeting though the principle of absorption was confirmed, a new proposal was introduced – that a company be created as a subsidiary of Cunard to which all ships should come freed (by government assistance) from mortgage burdens. Mr F. A. Bates, however, strongly opposed these suggestions and persuaded Lord Weir that 'any absorption scheme would be too big a gamble for the Cunard Company'.[117]

The idea that a separate company should be formed to take over the assets of Cunard and Oceanic Steam Navigation Co. was not a new one. It had been suggested in previous discussions that such a company could act either as a means of amalgamation or as an instrument for absorption, but neither side had regarded such a creation with enthusiasm. It now appeared however that provided the right kind of government support was forthcoming, a new company, would be an appropriate means for the merging rather than the absorption of assets. In reporting on the state of negotiations to the Cunard board on 14 June 1933, Sir Percy voiced Lord Weir's changing opinion that if progress were to be made, an agreed proposal on 'new company' lines would have to be submitted.[118] The board thereupon instructed him to continue discussions with Lord Weir and Lord Essendon on 'new company' lines with a ratio of 60 per cent to Cunard and 40 per cent to Oceanic Steam Navigation Co in the new company, including the provision of new capital in the same ratio.[119]

At last the basis for an eventual agreement had been laid. Between June and December 1933, continuous drafts were submitted and re-submitted, the details of which need no elaboration. It is sufficient to indicate that they were concerned with four main items: the title of the new company; the form of government financial assistance to be provided in order that the transfer of assets be freed from liability; the extent of the savings to be made through a rationalisation of operational facilities and the safeguarding of personnel as a result of the merger. The discussions relating to the capital structure of the new company and to the composition of its Board were also eventually agreed, supported by the necessary sanctions from the Oceanic Steam Navigation Co's creditors. Agreement was reached on 30 December 1933 between H.M. Government, The Cunard Steam Ship Co. Ltd and The Oceanic Steam Navigation Co. and it was formally executed on 17 January 1934.[120] Four years of protracted discussion had ended in the formation of Cunard White Star Ltd and a new chapter in maritime management had begun.

V THE LAUNCHING OF CUNARD WHITE STAR LTD: *Queen Mary* IN SERVICE: FINAL ANALYSIS

The agreement of 30 December 1933, signed by the contracting parties on 17 January 1934, needed further consequential and ratifying action before the new company, Cunard White Star Ltd, could be given legal sanction. Parliament had to pass legislation giving the necessary authority for the financial provisions of the agreement and a series of legal documents had to be completed incorporating the new company, transferring the appropriate assets of Cunard and White Star to it and setting out new Articles of Association. It was not until the middle of June that these formalities were completed.[121]

The incorporation of the new company was made possible by a series of commitments which may be conveniently summarised as follows: firstly, the new company was to take over the North Atlantic goodwill and flags of the Cunard and Oceanic companies, freed from all mortgages and charges; secondly, the North Atlantic fleets of both companies (including tenders or shares in tender companies) were to be transferred to Cunard White Star Ltd; thirdly, subject to agreement with Messrs John Brown and Co. Ltd, the remainder of the construction of No. 534 together with the ship when completed, should be taken over by the new company.[122] It was made clear to Cunard shareholders that the transfer of assets would be contingent upon the passing of legislation by Parliament which, in turn, would depend upon the consent of holders of Cunard 5 per cent debenture stock and of the secured creditors of the Oceanic Company. Furthermore there was implicit in the new structure a consideration relating to the revision and holding of mail contracts.[123]

The matters involving legislation as a prerequisite to the implementation of the agreement were concerned with the provision of resources by the Government. These considerations may be summarised as follows: firstly, advances from the Treasury to the Cunard Company of a sum not exceeding £1 million (ranking as to security after the Cunard 5 per cent debenture stock) bearing interest at ½ per cent under bank rate until 1 January 1940. Thereafter the advance should carry a rate of interest appropriate to loans guaranteed by H.M. Government, the whole to be repayable on or before 1975 at the Cunard Co's option. This advance was to be transferred by The Cunard Steam Ship Co. Ltd to Cunard White Star Ltd to cover the first third of the cost of completing No. 534. Secondly, advances by the Treasury to Cunard White Star Ltd of a sum not exceeding £1 million in respect of the second one-third of the cost of completing No. 534 on the same terms as those agreed for the first £1 million. These second advances were to be secured by debenture stock of Cunard White Star Ltd with a first specific mortgage on No. 534 when completed. Thirdly, advances by the Treasury to Cunard White Star Ltd of a sum not exceeding £1 million in respect of the final one-third of the cost of completing No. 534 secured by income debenture stock carrying interest at 3 per cent up to 31 December 1939 and thereafter at 5 per cent. This stock was to have rights in the participation of profits with a second mortgage on No. 534 when completed. No interest was payable when a profit was, in the opinion of the board of Cunard White Star Ltd, unavailable for distribution.[124]

Finally, a sum not exceeding £1,500,000 was to be made to Cunard White Star Ltd to provide working capital, the first £750,000 to be secured on terms similar to those under the second set of conditions as stated above and the remainder by 5 per cent income debenture stock under similar terms as to the payment of interest.[125] There was a further clause requiring legislative sanction authorising a future advance of £5 million to Cunard White Star Ltd to cover the cost of an additional new ship or ships on terms analagous to those applying to the advances of £2 million under the second and third conditions outlined above. In return for the transfer of assets to Cunard White Star Ltd, the Cunard and Oceanic companies were to receive shares in that company credited as fully paid up allotted as to 62 per cent of the initial nominal capital to the Cunard Company and 38 per cent to Oceanic. The board of the new company was to consist of ten persons, six representing Cunard and four representing Oceanic with the added proviso that all directors must be of British nationality.[126]

The implementation of the agreement followed a consequential pattern of events. It will be remembered that the transfer of unencumbered assets to the new company required the consent of Oceanic creditors and Cunard debenture shareholders. The necessary consents were given before the end of March. The North Atlantic Shipping Bill, giving effect to the provision of government assistance, passed its third reading in the Houe of Commons on 16 March.[127] Directors of the new company were nominated on 9 May and Cunard White Star Ltd was incorporated with a capital of £10 million credited as fully paid with a premium of £1 on each share. On 17 May a contract of sale of assets to Cunard White Star was sealed, although the formal transfer did not take place until 19 June; transfer of the benefits of the Cunard Insurance Act of 1930 were not implemented until 22 August.[128] Transfer of assets to Cunard White Star Ltd also included those of the Cunard American organisation (including assets at Quebec and Montreal) together with the pier leases at New York. Obligations under the mail contract were taken over by the new company and formal notice was given to the North Atlantic Conference that the Cunard Company had disposed of both its assets and its interests in the North Atlantic trade.[129] In other words, this chain of events cleared the way for Cunard White Star Ltd to begin operations as a legal entity though, in fact, the new company had taken on responsibility for the activities of the parent companies since 1 January. Full assumption of authority, however, did not take place until 1 September.[130] As a final seal to this endeavour, Messrs John Brown and Co. were given formal notice on 26 May to begin work once again on the hull of No. 534. On 26 September the great ship was launched by H.M. The Queen with the name *Queen Mary*.

What had the various participants gained from this merger of interests? In return for the transfer of North Atlantic assets to the new company, certain White Star creditors had received a 38 per cent interest in Cunard White Star Ltd, the secured creditors receiving by way of settlement 2,280,000 shares held by the Ministry of Finance in the Government of Northern Ireland and 1,520,000 shares to the trustees for the Oceanic debenture holders. In the prevailing state of uncertainty this exchange of liability for future security implemented by government assistance was satisfactory to White Star creditors. They were released from the legal and financial sanctions imposed on them as a result of the Royal Mail crash and were given some hope that the reorganised investments would earn a return in the new company. For Cunard, there was a different emphasis. In return for their participation they had received a 62 per cent interest. The holders of their 5 per cent mortgage debentures had been given adequate guarantee by a first charge on the dividends of the Commonwealth and Dominion Line ordinary and preference shares and the preference shares of T. and J. Brocklebank owned by Cunard. The new Cunard White Star Company was in essence a subsidiary of The Cunard Steam Ship Co. Ltd. Though Cunard White Star did not become a fully owned subsidiary until some time later, the two companies were nevertheless under the same control. The prestige which had been built up over ninety-four years, culminating in the mighty asset of *Queen Mary*, was thus maintained.

Looking back over the years of negotiation, it is a matter of conjecture whether Sir Percy Bates and his fellow directors could have foreseen the end result. The first attempt to acquire the North Atlantic assets of the Oceanic Steam Navigation Co. had failed, and the sale to Kylsant's Royal Mail had led to consequences which complicated the course of negotiations after 1931 when Oceanic assets again came up for sale. From the single idea of acquiring White Star Line's North Atlantic passenger agency, Cunard was led to the point where absorption seemed to be the only possible course of action. Had it wished to do so, the Government could have provided finance for either or both companies independently. It was the Government, rather than the circumstances of the time, who imposed the terms which ultimately resulted in the merger.

In a final analysis one is tempted to ask whether The Cunard Steam Ship Company obtained any real benefit from the outcome of this merger. The obvious and immediate consequence was the resumption of work on No. 534, some working capital and a loan for the prospective laying down and construction of a sister ship (*Queen Elizabeth*). What, however, were the effects on Cunard's trading position? There were some economies of scale in the amalgamation of offices and consequential reductions in the staff of both companies. The ten ships of White Star had no outstanding characteristics making them more competitive than the Cunard ships, particularly as they were to be used in a period when transatlantic passenger travel was slowly emerging from deep depression. In fact, their relative profitability can be judged from the dates on which they were withdrawn from service. *Britannic* and *Georgic* continued for a period after the Second World War. *Georgic*, after being patched up, had a limited life as a one-class ship partly on the North Atlantic carrying students and partly on the Australian run carrying emigrants. *Britannic* was converted into a comfortable intermediate-class liner, but was too slow (under 16 knots) for competitive working. Her diesel propulsion was uneconomic owing to the high cost of inter-voyage maintenance. As a consequence she was no match for the new post-war units on the North Atlantic. We shall consider the effects of the merger on Cunard's general position in a subsequent chapter. We have already made a fairly detailed analysis of the capital structure of the merger, but by 1947 Cunard had purchased the 38 per cent minority shareholding in Cunard White Star Ltd, mainly from the Government of Northern Ireland, the Treasury and the Oceanic Steam Navigation Realisation Co., the price of 40 shillings per share giving 'the retiring partners full value for the build up strength without inflation'.[131] Thus the effective life of the merger was thirteen years; in 1950 the fleet reverted to Cunard and Cunard White Star Ltd ceased trading.

8
North Atlantic Conferences 1921–39

I AGREEMENTS F.I., S.I., T.I.: FLUCTUATIONS IN MEMBERSHIP: MAINTENANCE OF SECURITY IN HOME PORTS

As we have seen, the various North Atlantic Conference Agreements between shipping companies in the nineteenth century were either bilateral or multilateral as circumstances dictated. The first Atlantic Conference so designated was formed in 1908 between most of the British, American and Continental lines engaged in the passenger trade. Agreements were reached on first and second class minimum passenger rates and conditions. At the same time a pooling arrangement was established for third class traffic. This conference, which had its headquarters in Jena, was dissolved on the outbreak of the First World War but was reconstituted in skeleton form during the war by a few of the members and had its office in Paris.

When the Conference was formally reconstituted in March 1921, several agreements were promulgated. These included one on first class rates (Agreement F.1.), one on second class and cabin (Agreement S.1.) and one on Continental third class traffic (Agreement T.1.). The signatories included the Anchor and Cunard lines together with the principal French, German and Dutch companies.[1] Scandinavian lines such as Norwegian America, Scandinavian American and Swedish American, were brought into the Conference. The Canadian Pacific together with other companies within the Morgan group also became members. Within the latter group White Star and the American Line completed a comprehensive list of North Atlantic shipping interests. As a means of sustaining effective control two separate points of administration were created; the main Conference office was located in Brussels; but for the regulation of matters relating to the operation of agreements in the United States and Canada, the lines maintained an office in New York, known as the Transatlantic Passenger Conference.

The reason for the establishment of a New York office was a direct consequence of the requirements under Section 15 of the United States Shipping Act 1916. Under this legislation all shipping companies engaged in trade with United States ports were obliged to file with the United States Maritime Commission a copy of any agreement entered into with any other carriers which fixed 'among other things, transportation rates or fares'.[2] The commission reserved the right to cancel discriminatory arrangements which, in its opinion, were likely to work to the detriment of the commerce of the United States. Thus approval by the commission secured for the parties to any Conference agreement immunity from action under the Anti-Trust Laws. To obtain ready access to the commission the New York office was created within the framework of United States law, and Conference members had to agree to a stabilisation of rates 'which for the carriers prevent needless dissipation of revenue and ensure an even flow of earnings, and for the shipper or passenger, a regular and dependable service at rates which are not subject to frequent or sudden change'.[3]

Between 1921 and 1939, the various Atlantic Conferences pursued a threefold objective: firstly, to maintain the membership of all the principal carriers. It should, however, be noted that the Conference was not closed but open to all passenger liner companies operating a minimum number of sailings (usually six) across the Atlantic. Secondly, to protect berthing rights to companies in their home ports; this objective was not given due insistence after 1926; and thirdly, to secure agreement on minimum rates in all classes. The Royal Mail Steam Packet Company, having entered the Atlantic trade joined the Conference in 1921 by signing the three agreements F.1, S.1 and T.1. In the same year the Cosulich line operating from Trieste, the United American lines (for which the Hamburg–Amerika line, having at that time no passenger ships of their own, acted as European representatives) and the United States Mail Steam Ship Co., all signed the three agreements.[4]

It would be tedious to enumerate the various changes in the pattern of membership during the following eighteen years. The most important entrants were Hamburg–Amerika in November 1921 and North German Lloyd in January 1922. The ships of these companies had been taken over by the Allies after the Armistice in 1918 and it was not until November 1921 that Hamburg–Amerika was able to run three ships carrying third class passengers and thereby be admitted to agreement T.1. In January 1922 North German Lloyd became a signatory to agreements S.1 and T.1. Early in 1926 United America lines gave notice that their ships were to be taken over and operated by the Hamburg–Amerika Line and that they would retire from the North Atlantic trade; in the same year the America Line informed the Conference that they had ceased operating a North Atlantic passenger service and accordingly terminated their membership. This withdrawal was followed in 1928 by the Royal Mail which also had ceased operating ships on the North Atlantic.[5] These fluctuations in membership, however, were not vital to the maintenance of the Conference structure as most of the companies concerned carried but a fraction of the aggregate passenger traffic. It was only when disagreement occurred among the principal competitors that the Conferences themselves were placed in jeopardy.

The question of maintaining security for Conference members in their home ports and safeguarding them from the establishment of competitive services by other lines was an important item on the 1921 conference agenda. Following the Armistice in 1918 Cunard established direct services for passenger and freight traffic from Antwerp to the United States and Canada. Subsequently the Compagnie Générale Transatlantique had founded the Compagnie Transatlantique Belge with services from Antwerp to New York. These innovations were considered to be contrary to the principles on which conferences were based. 'We desire to express the hope', the conference minute stated, 'that the Cunard line and the C.G.T. may, perhaps, reconsider their action and thus remove the cause for the dissension which, while it remains must be a menace to conference relationships.'[6]

A more serious cause of disagreement occurred in 1926 when Cunard proposed sending their ships in the Channel service to Havre. The contention of the French line, C.G.T., was that under the 1921 resolution all signatories to this minute bound themselves not to use in a regular service the home port of any other conference line. Cunard's reply was not conciliatory, contending that the statement attached to the minutes of the 1921 meeting was merely a record of the conditions upon which the lines making the statement agreed to join the Conference.[7] This could not, therefore, be regarded as an enunciation of policy which all other lines had formally accepted. The C.G.T. could not accept this interpretation and, after bringing the dispute to all the members, withheld collaboration by declining to participate in any Conference matter.[8] In the absence of the C.G.T.'s vote, unanimity of action was no longer possible and accordingly, the various activities of the Conference were virtually suspended. The C.G.T. did not attend the statutory meetings held in April and October 1926 and the minutes remained ineffective. The meeting due to be held in April 1927 was also cancelled.

The disagreement was eventually referred to arbitration. On 7 November 1927 Cunard suggested that in order to clear any misunderstanding they would give authority to their Conference representative, Herbert Evans, to meet any official of the C.G.T., the latter company agreeing to join in formal conversations.[9] It was further proposed that Sir George McLaren Brown (Canadian Pacific) could nominate a third delegate. Sir George appointed William Baird and also suggested that M. hr. Van de Graaf of Holland America should take part in the discussions.[10] The mediation was successful and on 26 November the C.G.T. informed all Conference members that they had been able to reach an amicable understanding with Cunard. 'We are, therefore, agreeable', they stated, ' . . . to withdraw all the reservations made by us at the Principals' meeting in London on 29 April 1926.'[11] Following this declaration the French company rejoined the Conference. This decision was perhaps prompted less by a desire to accept Cunard's entry to Havre, than from a more pressing need to accept a general raising of tourist third cabin rates. To effect such a revision of the tariff the French line found it more expedient to be within rather than outside the Conference. As a consequence Cunard ships continued to call at Havre.

II DISAGREEMENTS ON RATES: REBUILDING OF RATE SCHEDULES: CONVERSION OF SHIPS' CLASSES

We must now examine the working of the Conference agreements in relation to the classification of ships and the various schedules of rates applicable to the different classes. The 1921 agreement had classified first class rates in accordance with the age, speed and gross tonnage of particular ships. Thus *Aquitania, Berengaria* and *Olympic* were given the highest rate of £50 or $250. The lowest category in group 5 were given rates of £37 or $185. Provision was made for rates to be revised from time to time and for the admission of new ships to one or other of the classifications. After a year's experience of the working of the 1921 agreement it was decided that a general revision was required. In 1922 a grading committee was appointed to examine the entire structure of first class, cabin and second class rates.[12] The recommendations were accepted by a meeting of principals held in November 1922. Some thirteen groups were assessed, ranging from £56 10s. for ships such as *Aquitania* to £39 15s. for the slower and less well-appointed ships. A new classification was put into effect in 1928 embodying ten grades of ships with a range of first class rates from £55 for ships in group 1 to £36 10s for those in group 10. Also in January 1928 procedures were adopted enabling the conversion of a higher rated ship to a lower grade to be made, though the basic minimum rates for all ships in all the various classes were to be fixed in accordance with the previously adopted principle based on age, size and speed. No line was permitted to reduce rates by changing the designation of the accommodation in their ships unless six weeks previous notice had been given to the Conference.

It was one thing to work out principles designed to achieve equity; it was quite another thing to apply them in practise. Anomalies always existed, the principal difficulties stemming from the failure to find a formula which would take into account the characteristics of the ships to be graded. In practice a line would be prepared to accept a grading which it felt was equitable or might improve its competitive position. Conversely it would tend to reject a grading which it felt to be unfair or likely to worsen its competitive position. Negotiations would therefore continue until a compromise was reached. This would usually be followed by an uneasy truce until a line decided that its interests were becoming seriously prejudiced. At this point the usual course was to give notice that it would cease to observe agreements and leave the conference. The conference would, therefore, be faced with the alternative of outside opposition or of inducing the recalcitrant line to return virtually on its own terms. Conference decisions, however, had to be unanimous, with the result that protracted hard bargaining would ensue until a decision satisfactory to all lines was achieved; more often than not the result was another compromise. In November 1930 the Red Star and Holland–America lines put forward claims for a closer classification between the rates for their lower graded first class ships and those of the higher rated cabin ships. As a result it was agreed that all first class rates should be reduced, the higher grades by $2 50¢ and the lower by $5.[13]

As passenger traffic across the Atlantic continued to decline during the period 1931–4, a wide range of proposals was put forward for a more economical employment of resources. When the figures for 1931 had been compiled an alarming situation was revealed. First class carryings in both directions were 34,000 less than in the previous year; other classes were similarly affected. Cabin class, despite conversions and the introduction of new cabin tonnage, carried some 62,000 fewer passengers in 1931 than in 1930; second class was reduced by 34,000; tourist class by 67,000 and third class by 120,000.[14] This gave an aggregate reduction of 317,000, which at a conservative estimate based on current prices represented a fall of $40 million in earnings.[15]

In the hope of alleviating this situation efforts were made to introduce lower rates, but it proved impossible to secure unanimous agreement. The dissenting lines were apprehensive that a rate reduction would not stimulate a sufficiently large increase in carryings and that revenue would continue to fall. On 15 March 1932, however, the rate sub-committee, under instructions from the statutory meeting of October 1931, began deliberations in Folkestone to review the whole of the rating structure. At the same time the newly reconstructed United States Lines (not then a member of the Conference) declared its intention to reduce rates by 25 per cent for first class, cabin and tourist and 5 or 10 per cent on third class.[16] This decision so disrupted the sub-committee's work that they were unable to make suitable recommendations. The new owners of the United States Lines intimated that they would not join the Conference while the existing rates were in operation, and as a result the Conference was technically dissolved. New schedules of rates were nevertheless compiled based on those adopted by the United States lines, although Canadian Pacific took unilateral action in applying a 20 per cent reduction on eastbound third class rates – a reduction which other lines immediately adopted.[17] Thus, when the principals met on 14 April the lower rate levels were virtually a *fait accompli*.

After a lapse of a few weeks, the Atlantic Conference was re-established and machinery for the prevention of violating agreements was strengthened. The new Conference instructed a subcommittee to put in hand the rebuilding of the various rate schedules. After minor amendments the schedules were ratified on 10 May 1932. First class rates were reduced by 20 per cent and ranged from $208 to $124. Unfortunately however, these new rates were no palliative for the declining trend in passenger traffic. First class carryings were 25,000 less in 1932 than in 1931; cabin class 24,000 less and second class 24,000 less; tourist class and third class alone showed an increase, the former by 2000, the latter by 28,000.[18] In the following year, 1933, there was an overwhelming fall on the figures of 1932 of 175,000 for all classes. In the absence of any elasticity of demand, therefore, companies preferred to press for an upward revision of rates; in November 1932 the Conference increased first class, cabin and second class rates by 6 per cent, tourist by $5 50¢ and third class by $5 westbound and $7 50¢ eastbound.[19] As a further endeavour to bring falling revenues within distance of relatively high costs, the number of sailings by each line was limited. Furthermore, as a result of a more active collaboration between the French and German governments in international affairs, problems relating to shipping were discussed and referred to the various Conferences.[20] There was therefore some pressure to secure an international understanding, firstly to limit tonnage for each service by adapting it to the real needs of the traffic and, secondly, to reach an agreement regarding the main international services in order to restrict the number, speed and tonnage of ships to be constructed. As far as Cunard was concerned the intrusion by foreign governments was unwelcome, particularly as at the time the Company was building *Queen Mary* and was in the throes of negotiations concerning the merger with White Star. Other companies were also in some difficulty in meeting requests of this kind. In the end therefore the Atlantic Conference left to each line the task of effecting the economies which the traffic position demanded. The pruning of services was thus effected by individual action. Total round trips in 1930 amounted to 2125; in 1931 the number had been reduced to 1770; in 1932 to 1496; in 1933 to 1411 and in 1934 to 1280.[21] This latter figure was the lowest to be reached in any of the inter-war years.

Another expedient applied in an attempt to equate service to demand was the conversion of ships from first class to cabin, from first class to tourist and from cabin to tourist. This involved continuous consideration of the entry of new ships of superior type, the rate relationship between the classes and the differentials between ships of each class. It was nevertheless virtually impossible to obtain agreement on the acceptance of basic formulae for the rating of one designated cabin class ship against another. In general, however, cabin rates had been influenced by the same pressures and considerations as those affecting first and second class rates. Following the difference between Cunard and C.G.T., cabin rates were fixed in 1928 between a range of £32 10s or $157 50¢ to £28 or $135 with different rates for foreign ports.[22] These rates were revised on 11 November 1929 and in 1932 there was a general reduction (in line with those in other classes) of 20 per cent. There followed the previously mentioned rise of 6 per cent in November 1932 and on 1 January 1934 there was a further increase of 10 per cent. There were renewed efforts to reform the rating machinery and to establish a co-relation in the rates of the different classes, but although many meetings of the principals and the sub-committee were held for this purpose, it was not possible to satisfy the requirements of all lines.[23]

It was at this juncture that Cunard White Star introduced *Queen Mary* and claimed cabin class rating for her accommodation. She was assigned a cabin rate of $262, some $8 less than the first class rate then ruling. Thereupon the French liner *Normandie* which had been scheduled at the higher rate, applied for, and was given the same classification as *Queen Mary*.[24] From 24 February 1936 the designation 'cabin class' (which had hitherto applied to older categories of ships) was henceforth to apply to luxurious accommodation in the largest and fastest ships of all lines.[25] The classification of rates which had been subject to a 5 per cent increase in 1937 remained in being, apart from minor amendments, until the outbreak of the Second World War in 1939. These rates ranged from $287 for group 1 ships to $131 for ships under group 22, constituting a wide range of choice for the oceanic traveller.[26]

Perhaps some background information is necessary in order to explain the substitution of first class by cabin class classification. With the introduction of *Manhattan* and *Washington* on the North Atlantic in 1932, the absurdity of having both first and cabin class categories became apparent. A number of shipping lines, including Cunard, were opposed to this anomaly. In fact, as early as 1930 Holland–America had reiterated their previous request that cabin class should be eliminated. By the time Cunard took its decision, therefore, the United States lines had had over three years competitive advantage, having advertised and operated *Manhattan* as the largest and fastest cabin liner afloat. Both *Washington* and *Manhattan* had two competitive grading advantages. In the first place, they were rated as being 24,000 gross tons but on British tonnage measurement they were over 28,000 tons; in the second place they were also scheduled with a speed of twenty knots, but in service they were one-and-a-half knots faster. In getting rid of first class Cunard ensured that all ships were graded on the same basis.[27]

It would be tedious, in the context of this study, to trace the fluctuations in second class classifications and rates. In general they were affected by the various revisions for first and cabin class schedules in a complementary way. Furthermore the introduction of round-trip rates affected this class very much in the same manner as that for other classes. The most important impact on the rating structure during the 1920s and 1930s was made by the introduction of the category 'tourist class'.

III INTRODUCTION OF TOURIST CLASS AND DISAGREEMENTS ARISING

Tourist or tourist–third cabin class was introduced to replace some of the traffic lost to the lines by the restrictions imposed on immigration into the United States and Canada. The new classification was designed to cater for the 'non-quota' immigrant, consisting principally of relatives of citizens of the United States, returning emigrants and temporary visitors for business or pleasure.[28] In addition it was hoped that by this means accommodation surplus to the emigrant traffic could be brought into use. If this accommodation was not luxurious, the moderate cost was likely to be an inducement to the holiday traveller as well as to lower income groups such as students. Although there was no specific ruling, it was assumed that the space to be used for this new class would be taken from third class areas, altered and improved as the needs of the traffic dictated. The lines which introduced tourist classification thus made three classes on their cabin ships and four classes on their first class ships. They were under obligation to add $10 to the then established third class one-way rates and $15 to the third class round-trip rates.[29]

The inception of this class necessarily led to a reallocation of space on ships and to a redefinition of particular ships as they were taken into service. The difficulty of securing agreement between the lines concerning such classification was a frequent cause of protracted discussions and negotiation which, in some cases, threatened the existence of Conference decisions. This was particularly the case in the eleven-year struggle which the Canadian Pacific waged to sustain their competitive position. On 12 December 1927 it gave notice of withdrawal from all Conference agreements 'in view of the invidious position in which we find ourselves as a result of recent action of certain lines in advising changes in classes on some of their ships'.[30] The Conference sub-committee issued a revised scale of tourist–third cabin rates based not only on the age, size and speed of ships, but also on the type of accommodation which was then in use by tourist–third cabin passengers. The Canadian Pacific, however, would not take part in any discussion unless the various lines returned to the *status quo* existing before the creation of regular Atlantic services by cabin ships designated for the exclusive use of tourist–third cabin passengers. In particular they strongly objected to the conversion of the Cunard ships *Andania* and *Antonia* and the Anchor–Donaldson's *Athenia* and *Letitia* to such a category, especially as these ships formed part of the British companies' fleet operating from Liverpool and Glasgow to Canadian ports.[31]

Cunard offered conciliation to Canadian Pacific by suspending bookings on the ships concerned in the disagreement. 'Beyond this', stated Cunard, 'we are sorry we cannot go because, in our opinion, in principle there is no difference between the carriage of tourist–thirds in these ships and the carriage of the same class in the passenger accommodation of vessels of our competitors hitherto set aside for the use of second cabin or cabin passengers while, on the other hand, as far as we can learn there has not been any offer on the part of other lines to discontinue the booking of tourist –thirds for such accommodation or to revert to the *status quo* of 12 months ago.'[32] Although this controversy did not technically affect the operation of Continental agreements, the wider issues did concern the maintenance of cabin and first class agreements by virtue of the Canadian Pacific's withdrawal from all agreements. It had become a matter of urgency for this prospective disruption of conference harmony to be eliminated. This harmony was, in fact, once again secured on 5 January 1928 when the Cunard Line agreed to retain their four ships in the cabin agreement. The classification of tourist–third cabin ships from and to British ports and the rates which came into force on 16 January 1928, ranged from $109 to $100 with round-trip rates from $196 20¢ to $180.[33]

Despite this settlement Cunard continued to press for the admission of their 'A' ships to tourist–third cabin as top class, but the Canadian Pacific maintained strong oppostion to the proposal. The real point at issue was that if Cunard reclassified their cabin ships as tourist–third cabin, Canadian Pacific would have had to lower cabin rates on their new tonnage. As agreement seemed unlikely Cunard informed the Conference on 3 April 1929 that they had no option but to convert.[34] Canadian Pacific replied that such action would destroy the North Atlantic rate structure. White Star also expressed the view that if Cunard took effective action their Canadian ships would be affected no wit less than those of Canadian Pacific. On 13 June Canadian Pacific returned to the attack in a long statement delivered to the conference. Their main points of contention were that the Canadian route was a much more seasonal route than that to New York or Boston because their two main ports, Montreal and Quebec, were closed to traffic for $4\frac{1}{2}$ months each year. Furthermore as Canadian Pacific was the only transatlantic line which had no regular United States service, any action tending to reduce revenue taken by a Conference colleague vitally affected their interests.[35] The volume of traffic carried to the United States was about six times greater than that to Canada, therefore the incursion of tourist class ships into the Canadian trade would reduce revenue disproportionately to the disadvantage of Canadian services. 'The Canadian Pacific', they stated, 'is the largest carrier on the St Lawrence and we could not afford to have our position jeopardized by permitting four or six or ten or more ships to carry exclusively tourist third cabin at reduced rates while our three Empresses and four Duchesses maintained their existing first class or cabin rates.'[36] Cunard was sympathetically disposed to the special circumstances of Canadian Pacific's case and once again agreed to defer their proposed reclassification.[37]

The case of Canadian Pacific was related to its dependence on purely Canadian traffic, two-thirds of the total being carried by them. They had every justification in fearing that the increase in the number of ships carrying tourist–third cabin passengers and the efforts to establish this as the top class, would affect their carryings in first and cabin classes. Their fears were well founded, for out of 28 ships engaged in the Canadian trade about 15 had converted accommodation to carry tourist–third cabin. As Canadian Pacific had intimated the problem was not so acute in the New York trade, as on this route only some 30 ships out of 100 had been converted to tourist–third cabin. The Canadian Pacific Company were therefore correct in their assumption that they were competing at a disadvantage, a disadvantage which would worsen considerably if tourist–third cabin was accepted as a top class in the Canadian trade.[38]

Consideration of this problem brought no general solution until the Red Star Line made the decision to abolish cabin class on their two ships *Pennland* and *Regina* and to service them as tourist–third cabin and third class carriers on their Antwerp–New York route beginning 1 January 1930.[39] Here again the Canadian Pacific was caught in an unfavourable position as they were also interested in the Antwerp trade, and they threatened to reduce cabin rates as a means of meeting the new competition. In this they were supported by Holland–America, who warned the conference that if the action of Red Star were approved a general reduction of all rates must follow if the lines were to sustain their share of the traffic. In such an eventuality Cunard would also be induced to reclassify the 'A' ships in their Canadian service. 'We believe that there is one way of avoiding similar controversies in the future', concluded the statement by Holland–America, 'merely, to lay down the rule that no conversions of third class or cabin ships into carriers of tourist–third cabin and third class passengers exclusively shall be made until general agreement has been secured that such a conversion is justified *vis-à-vis* ships employed by other lines, and further to be conditional upon a rate being agreed for ships advertised as converted.'[40] Red Star Line was proposing to charge a rate of $124 50¢ for the same accommodation as that for which Holland–America was obliged to charge $177 50¢. This gave a competitive advantage of $53 on ships which were 1000 tons smaller and 1 knot slower than Holland–America ships.

Meanwhile Cunard, who had submitted proposals for relief in the cabin rates of their 'A' ships with the object of permitting them to keep *Athenia* and *Letitia* in the cabin schedule, stated that if the principle of conversion to tourist–third cabin as top class (so strenuously opposed for their ships) was to be granted to other conference lines, the whole reclassification of their 'A' class ships would require consideration. Pressure was applied to the Red Star Line to induce them to abandon their proposed action, but without avail.[41] Red Star insisted on the conversion of their ships, claiming the legal right to do so under the terms of the Conference agreement. After further abortive attempts at conciliation Red Star gave notice of their withdrawal from all conference agreements. To counter the threatened break-up of the Conference a statutory meeting decided on 31 October 1929 that a revision of the entire rate structure should be put in hand. This had the effect of keeping Red Star within conference membership, but did not alter their determination to convert *Pennland* and *Regina* (now re-named *Westernland*) to tourist–third cabin top class carriers. The whole matter was eventually referred to an appeal court consisting of three Conference members. The court ruled that the rate be $17 50¢ above the existing one-way tourist–third cabin rate, with an additional $2 50¢ for outside accommodation on the top passenger deck. This award was generally acceptable though many lines feared it might have future repercussions on rates as a whole. Nevertheless, the Conference agreements were saved and conversion of two modern cabin ships to tourist–third cabin was accomplished. As far as Cunard was concerned they had obtained some concession in the cabin rate for their 'A' ships, albeit that in response to the wishes of conference members they had been induced to postpone their application for a tourist–third cabin top class rate for these ships in the Canadian trade. It was further agreed that no conversion should be made from cabin to tourist–third cabin (or from first class to cabin) until October 1930. The schedule of rates for tourist–third cabin ranged from $120 from British ports (French ports $130) to $102 50¢ (French ports $115).[42]

Hope of a more stable relationship, however, did not materialise. Early in April 1930 Red Star Line announced conversion of *Minnetonka* and *Minnewaska* to tourist class. Holland–America and Canadian Pacific lodged objections and asked that arbitration procedure should become effective. In reply the meeting of principals proposed a lowering of all rates by approximately twenty per cent. Red Star insisted on arbitration but refused to accept the terms when the award was announced. After further mediation the conference was finally forced to accept Red Star ships as tourist carriers virtually on the terms originally proposed.⁴³ In this, and in other instances, one can only draw the conclusion that it was becoming impossible for principals to settle differences between Conference members and that arbitration was a last resort in securing conference solidarity. The appointment of Sir Norman Hill as sole arbitrator (consequent upon the rejection of the U.S. lines of arbitration affecting their cabin class ships) was a necessary step in a constant endeavour to regulate rival claims and maintain harmony. The effectiveness of his arbitration was shown in 1932 when the United States lines introduced their two ships *Manhattan* and *Washington*.

Early in April 1932 Cunard lodged notice (under Article 4 of Agreement T.1) of their intention to classify *Andania* and *Antonia* as tourist ships.⁴⁴ As might have been anticipated this was followed by notice of withdrawal from all conference agreements by Canadian Pacific. They threatened to lower all their rates (excluding *Empress of Britain*) in order to maintain differentials with Cunard ships. White Star also gave notice of intention to reclassify some of their cabin ships to the tourist designation. Though Canadian Pacific deferred their withdrawal from the conference pending a satisfactory solution of the cabin–tourist controversy, no lasting solution could find general acceptance. On 7 April 1933 Cunard circulated a letter to all Conference members stating: '... we have been studying the results of the work of the committee ... and must admit to being seriously disappointed at the lack of progress recorded. Rightly or wrongly we have the impression that the Lines' Representatives were severely handicapped by being compelled to work within very decided limits, and their inability to travel outside of these. We fully realise the many difficulties surrounding the question and in our letter of 6 January (A.C.21,950) we said 'we cannot agree to have the discussions left over until the Autumn of this year'. We should then find ourselves confronted with exactly the same position as in October last.'⁴⁵ Under the circumstances Cunard directors were not sanguine that a solution of the difficulties was likely and they therefore gave notice of withdrawal from agreement F.1. Matters were indecisive until December 1933, when new schedules for all classes were introduced and became generally acceptable, subject to Cunard's withdrawal of the application for their 'A' class ships. Under this agreement tourist rates (operative from 1 January 1934) ranged from $121 (group 1) to $102 (group 12).⁴⁶

But Canadian Pacific was still uncertain of its position. On 15 February it gave notice of its withdrawal from all agreements. It was the only defence they had 'against a disturbance of the relativity between cabin and tourist-class rates and the effect which such a disturbance would have upon their cabin ships'.[47] In this action they were once more joined by Holland–America, who announced their desire to be free from conference obligations. Holland–America were attempting to secure rates for *Veendam* and *Volendam*, comparable in all respects with reclassified rates on the United States lines *President Harding* and *President Roosevelt*. These manoeuvres were, however, in the nature of threat and counter-threat rather than of intention. The three lines withdrew their notices and all their ships remained within the cabin schedule.[48]

In the autumn of 1934 several lines embarked upon a new policy of attracting travellers who wished to visit either Europe or the United States for short periods by lowering fares in the tourist and third-class round-trip rates. This inducement applied during the period of the year when there was plenty of space in these classes. From October 1934 to April 1935 special excursion rates were in force. The price was fixed by taking one-and-a-third times the eastbound rate; tickets were available for fifteen days from the date of landing. Unfortunately, the inducement had little effect on the volume of traffic and the excursion rates were withdrawn on 1 May 1935. They were not reintroduced until 1938, with considerable modifications. To some extent this type of rate was rendered unnecessary, for tourists could travel on the largest and fastest ships in every kind of comfort. *Queen Mary* and *Normandie* operated the same level of tourist rates, and all other passenger ships had ranging classifications in this class. Despite this, however, the old controversy between Cunard and Canadian Pacific concerning the introduction of tourist services on the Canadian route remained open and intractable of solution.

In 1936 Cunard White Star once again gave notice of intention to classify their Canadian ships as tourist top class. Canadian Pacific's reaction was immediate and predictable. They were, however, then in a less favourable position than they had been in the early 1930s. Negotiations were continued into 1938 and in February of that year a memorandum of agreement was submitted to the conference for confirmation. Full operation of this agreement was to be postponed until the statutory meeting in

October 'on condition that the Conference would grant till then a reduction of $5 in the cabin rate of Anchor–Donaldson's *Athenia* and *Letitia*, Cunard's two White Star 'A' ships and the three Canadian Pacific "Mont" ships'.[49] This was accepted subject to its being applied only when these ships were engaged on the Canadian berth. Despite objections to these proposals from other lines agreement was finally secured at a meeting of principals on 31 October. Under this agreement the four Cunard White Star Anchor –Donaldson ships were to remain in the cabin schedule with reductions in their cabin rates. In addition, these ships and all others (excluding *Empress of Britain*) operating in Canadian waters were permitted to reduce tourist rates by $2 50¢ while the St Lawrence was ice-bound.

An eleven-year-old struggle was brought to an end, never to be revived.

IV SHARE OF TRAFFIC TO EACH LINE

What can be learnt from these efforts to maintain the Conference structure and secure a reasonable share of the traffic to each line? The short-term competitive advantage obviously depended on how successful individual lines were in obtaining the most favourable calassification of their ships, especially those newly introduced. At the same time there were international repercussions affecting rates such as those concerned with the relative movements of sterling, franc and dollar prices following Britain's withdrawal from the gold standard in 1931. These events are reflected in changes in the share of the North Atlantic trade and in the relative fluctuations in transportation of the various classes by each line.

The relative figures show that between 1921 and 1933 Cunard carried the largest number of passengers, and between 1924 and 1929 the Company's share of total trade was approximately one-fifth. White Star was the next largest carrier; excluding 1925 it followed a similar trend to that of Cunard. In the year following the Cunard White Star merger their joint share amounted to just under 27 per cent of the total. Canadian Pacific on the other hand showed a declining trend over the period, but from 1927 to 1930 their share was relatively stable; it declined in 1931, regaining stability once again between 1932 and 1936. This lack of elasticity underlines the many attempts by Canadian Pacific to resist the incursion of tourist–third ships into their trade. The outstanding feature of these aggregates is the progressive increase in the share of trade taken by the two German lines, Hamburg–Amerika and North German Lloyd. In particular, the latter company returned a fairly substantial increase during the depression years 1930–34, the evidence suggesting that in a falling market it was capturing traffic from the British lines. The French line, C.G.T., gradually increased its share of the trade, rising from seven per cent (1924–7) and, by an annual increase after 1933 to nearly 13 per cent in 1937. Of the other lines, the United States Lines had a decreasing share of approximately 1 per cent per annum between 1926 and 1932, but from 1933 to 1938 they regained the position which they had held in the mid 1920s.

If we analyse these relative figures in greater detail by looking at the annual carryings for individual classes, the picture assumes a sharper focus and a deeper perspective. Within the figures of total earnings, Cunard's first class bookings were annually in excess of 30,000 for the period 1921–9, but there was a sharply declining share after 1930, and by 1933 carryings for this class had fallen as low as 10,000. Thereafter the merged Cunard White Star figures show an increase to 20,000 in 1935; but after 1936 the first class classification was abolished. There was a generally declining trend in White Star's first class carryings after 1926. By contrast the two German lines increased their carryings during the 1920s and, during the first two years of depression, maintained relative levels by capturing a share of this trade from other lines. The French Line showed a similar rising trend until 1930. There was, however, a sharp fall to 10,000 in 1932 and no real recovery until 1935.

In the category of cabin class, the share of carryings by Cunard increased from 1921 to 1928, but thereafter there was a decline until the merger with White Star. After 1936 the advent of *Queen Mary* helped to increase carryings to a total of 48,900. White Star had a rather more erratic fluctuation than Cunard during the 1920s though there was a general rising trend until 1928, followed by a decline until 1934. The two German lines increased their hold on this traffic during the 1920s, but experienced a sharp decline between 1931 and 1936, followed by a recovery until 1938. The French line also improved its position until 1927. Unlike most of the other lines, however, this company's carryings fell in 1928 and 1929 but recovered in 1930. This was checked in 1931 and there was a declining trend until 1936 when there was a sharp rise. Apart from 1929 the figures for the Canadian Pacific show a general fall in this class of traffic until 1933 when carryings amounted only to approximately one-third of those for 1926. From 1934 to 1937 there was a gradual recovery to approximately 65 per cent of the 1926 level.

In the tourist class there was a substantial increase in Cunard's carryings between 1926 and 1930, when the total exceeded 42,000. Thereafter, until the merger with White Star, there was a progressive decline to 16,000. From 1934 to 1937 there was a rising trend to approximately 62,000. The figures for the two German lines show a rapid rate of increase to 1930 when total carryings reached 54,000. Although this figure was reduced to 31,000 in 1933, the rate of decline was not as great as that for other lines and, by 1937, they had gone far towards recovering the deficiency. One may generally conclude that the German companies were able to maintain their tourist class carryings at a higher level during years of depression than corresponding carryings by other lines. As in the case of first class services they held a strongly competitive position in tourist traffic and undoubtedly captured trade from other lines, especially in years of low activity. To a lesser extent the French line strengthened its position in the tourist trade during the depression, carryings more than doubling between 1931 and 1932 followed by a continuous annual rise to a peak of 31,000 by 1937. By contrast Canadian Pacific had reached a peak in 1930 of 32,000 and was so severely affected by the depression that carryings had only reached about 55 per cent of this peak figure by 1937.

The importance of the tourist class to the earning capacity of the North Atlantic passenger lines may be judged from the fact that total carryings in this class rose from 25·8 per cent of total traffic in 1930 and increased annually to 32·3 per cent in 1934 – an increase of one-quarter to about one-third of total traffic in the years of depression.[50] This percentage continued to be maintained during the 1930s and had slightly increased to 32·5 per cent by 1937. Cunard's share of tourist traffic in 1930 was 16·1 per cent and White Star's 11·5 per cent, making a total of 27·6 per cent. The share of the two German lines was just under 21 per cent and that of the C.G.T., 2·5 per cent. By 1935 Cunard White Star's share had fallen to 20·8 per cent while that of the two German lines had risen to 23·5 per cent and that of the C.G.T. to 11·3 per cent. This gives some indication of the magnitude of the swing in favour of the principal Continental lines during this period and something of the extent of the decline in the carryings of Cunard and White Star. This was especially serious for Cunard and accounts for repeated attempts by the Company to obtain classification of 'A' class ships as tourist carriers in the Canadian trade. This was an area in which the Company could make a profitable inroad and extend its carryings in this class.

Finally an examination of the carriage of third class passengers reveals a rather curious situation. Although actual carryings by Cunard fell after 1932 and were by 1933 about half the 1930 level, their share remained fairly stable falling by only 1 per cent between 1930 and 1933, whereas that of the two German lines increased from 21 per cent to 26·8 per cent during the same period.[51] Comparable percentages for C.G.T. were 5·9 and 5·5. In other words the German lines increased their share of the traffic albeit in a falling market. This fact is of relative significance if only by way of indicating the activity and resilience of the German lines in a period of depression compared with the effectiveness of Cunard. In competitive terms the implications inherent in the relative strengths of rival companies served only to underline that too rigid a rate structure in certain classes might give undue advantage to some companies and act adversely on the carrying capacity of others. In this particular instance there is an indication that, ship for ship and rate for rate, the German lines were offering a more attractive service than other companies engaged in the North Atlantic third class passenger trade.

The conclusions drawn from the foregoing analysis may be given a somewhat different gloss if a longer series of years is taken and if one takes account of the introduction of new tonnage. In 1926 C.G.T. put *Ile de France* into operation. She was about 43,000 tons with a speed of 23 knots. As a result, their first class carryings increased from 19,000 in 1926 to 24,000 in 1927 and 30,000 in 1928, falling to 23,000 in 1930.[52] Between 1926 and 1927 Hamburg–Amerika introduced *Hamburg* and *New York* (22,000 tons/19 knots) and their first class carryings increased from 8500 in 1926 to 12,800 in 1927 and 13,200 in 1928, falling to 11,500 in 1929 and 10,100 in 1930.[53] In 1928 and 1929 North German Lloyd brought *Bremen* and *Europa* into service, 51,600 tons and 49,700 tons respectively with speeds of $26\frac{1}{2}$ and $25\frac{1}{2}$ knots.

A sharp increase in first class passenger traffic followed the entry of these ships, rising from 7400 in 1928 to 25,900 in 1930, but falling to 22,500 by 1932.[54] The same pattern is discernible in the figures for all other classes and for new ships of other lines introduced at later dates.

In 1930 Canadian Pacific had *Empress of Britain* (42,300 tons /nearly 24 knots) in service. First class carryings increased from 5200 in 1930 to 6000 in 1931, an increase in a period of deepening depression when all other lines were losing business.[55] Following the rise in ocean traffic after 1934 the introduction of *Normandie* (83,400 tons/28¾ knots) in 1935 and *Queen Mary* (81,200 tons/29·11 knots) in 1936, the competitive balance was again changed. The French line's first class carryings increased from 9300 in 1934 to 13,000 in 1935 (22,000 if cabin class is included). When *Normandie* was reclassified as a cabin class ship in 1936, C.G.T.'s carryings were 27,000, rising to 33,900 in 1937, but falling to 22,900 in 1938.[56] Cunard White Star's combined carryings increased from 19,700 in 1935 to 52,700 in 1937, falling to 36,600 in 1938.[57] It is true that the German lines had some competitive advantage in the carriage of tourist class passengers through the operation of *Bremen* and *Europa*, but with the introduction of *Normandie* and *Queen Mary* this advantage was diminished. By extending the analysis from 1935 to 1937 the comparative positions were as follows: carriage of tourist passengers by the German lines rose from 40,000 in 1935 to 47,000 in 1937; those for Cunard White Star from 48,000 to 62,000 and those for the French Line from 19,000 to 31,000; so by 1937 the percentage share of total tourist traffic stood at about 22·0 for the German lines, 14·4 for C.G.T. and 28·9 for Cunard White Star. The advantage to the German lines, sustained by *Europa* and *Bremen*, was now being eroded by the competitive strength of *Normandie* and *Queen Mary*.

But by itself an analysis of the crude figures of passengers carried is insufficient to give an accurate picture of the changing pattern of competitive advantage. In the matter of ocean travel, one has to take account of inducements offered to prospective travellers by the type, speed and accommodation of the ships in service. This fact was well understood by operators of the various Conference agreements through the introduction of a wide range of classifications. The classifications, however, were not rigid, being subject to constant modification in accordance with the fluctuation in levels of demand. The inference is that within the terms of a Conference system competitive strength still lay with those companies using their capital to acquire the most up-to-date ships. In terms of a company's shipping policy this fact had special significance in periods of declining activity, such as that experienced by shipping companies between 1931 and 1933.

V THE OPERATION OF THE FREIGHT CONFERENCE

If we now turn to the freight market a rather less complicated situation presents itself. The Operation of the North Atlantic Freight Conference was perhaps less important to certain lines than that of the passenger agreements. Like the passenger Conferences the freight Conference followed a similar pattern of disagreement and harmony.

Atlantic freight conferences were international in character, having developed from a series of *ad hoc* agreements between national companies into a universally accepted practice. By the 1920s they had a well-developed organisation and a permanent secretariat. They provided services to and from Britain, Europe and the Baltic. Their agreements embodied a dual rate system, since the U.S. Shipping Act 1916 forbade a rebate of any sort. Although the Conferences sustained reasonably stable rates it did not mean that individual rates did not alter. It was often in a shipping company's interest to encourage the flow of traffic, and if a shipper could show cause for some revision of the rate for a particular commodity, it would usually be considered by the lines. Moreover, if any particular rate of freight was considered too high, there was always the possibility that a merchant could obtain the services of a non-conference vessel. If such practices persisted at cheaper rates the forces of competition would reduce Conference rates. In the Atlantic freight market there were marked differences between eastbound and westbound cargoes, the former reflecting Britain's need to import half her food and raw material requirements, the latter being governed by the U.K.'s need to export manufactured products. Consequently westbound rates tended to be higher than eastbound rates.

From 1 March 1924 it was agreed that eastbound freight rates be increased by amounts ranging from 10 to 40 per cent over past rates. According to Cunard estimates this gave the Company an average increase of about 15 per cent.[58] By July 1924, despite the efforts of Sir Ashley Sparks, Cunard's resident director in New York, the rates on some eastbound commodities had been reduced and there was every indication that a rate war might ensue.[59] Cunard was not in a particularly strong position to take effective measures. 'While eastbound rates are dealt with by the New York Conference', it was stated, 'certain of the lines with headquarters on this side are anxious that a meeting of Principals should take place in the hope that some expression of dissatisfaction at the reductions made be communicated to the other side.'[60] The issue was eventually settled amicably and by the end of the year proposals were again put forward for a general increase in Atlantic freight rates. In 1925, however, a short rate war broke out between American lines; indirectly this unsettled the freight market on certain routes under conference agreement. The International Mercantile Marine, for example, carried cargo between European ports and those on the Pacific coast, with transhipment at New York, for their American Pacific line. These cargoes were shipped at low through rates – a practice which, according to their rivals the United America line, infringed conference agreements. But protests were ignored and United America began quoting low rates on cargo between America and the United Kingdom with transhipment at Hamburg,[61] and once again regular Continental and United Kingdom rates were disturbed. The issue was settled, this time by arbitration, but the episode was illustrative of the precarious nature of Conference agreements during periods of intense competitive pressure.

Apart from skirmishes of relatively minor import freight agreements in general were concerned primarily with the maintenance of rates. In September 1926 eastbound rates were raised as a means of meeting increased operating expenses. These revisions were applicable in a general schedule made effective from 1 January 1927 when levels were raised within a range of 15 to 25 per cent.[62] Improvement in trading conditions between 1927 and 1929 tended to minimise the effects of disagreement; this was especially the case in 1928 when rates fell fairly sharply, but in general harmonious relations were maintained within the framework of higher earning capacity, and the strength of the Conference system in the freight market (considered particularly as an element in Cunard's earning capacity) tended to be marginal in application. During periods of fluctuation the agreements were subject to strain, whereas in years of relative prosperity they worked with degrees of success in the promotion of stable rates, which sustained relatively higher receipts to shipping companies.

In the Mediterranean freight market the conference was confined to cargo liners and to British companies operating from Middlesbrough, London, Liverpool and Glasgow. Cunard operated services to Gibralta, Malta, Morocco, Italy, Alexandria, Levant and the Black Sea ports. By the beginning of 1922 Cunard had resumed its services to Mediterranean ports, the Levant and the Black Sea. The ships in service, *Cypria, Pavia, Tyria* and *Phrygia*, were all built before the turn of the century and were operated by the American Levant line; they were replaced in 1928 by *Bosnia, Bothnia, Bantria* and *Bactria* – all coal-burning ships. Although built by the American Levant line, they were transferred the same year by bill of sale to Cunard, and in 1930 Cunard disposed of her interests to Stanley and John Thompson. The changeover of the Mediterranean ships to Cunard management proved to be a little more costly, but apart from the years of depression the Mediterranean ships were quoted as being able to earn more than their depreciation.[63] The Mediterranean trade was useful for Cunard in its own right, particularly as a feeder service. During the 1920s the trade was operated under a pooling agreement, brought into existence as a result of the loss of ships during the war and the need to open up trade routes with minimum tonnage before shipowners could replace their losses. This pooling agreement covered the whole of the United Kingdom and continued in existence until 1952.

Some indication of the working of Conference agreements in Cunard's earnings from the carriage of passengers and freight may be judged from Tables 8.1 and 8.2.

Table 8.1

Year	Class	Average receipts per passenger	
		Westbound	Eastbound
		£ s d	£ s d
1925	1st	66 9 1	68 2 1
	2nd	29 4 11	29 8 7
	3rd	15 14 4	16 10 10
1926	1st	64 9 4	70 10 5

Table 8.1 (continued)

Year	Class	Average receipts per passenger Westbound			Eastbound		
	2nd	29	13	1	29	18	3
	3rd	16	4	5	16	11	9
1927	1st	63	1	2	67	4	8
	2nd	28	19	7	29	9	1
	3rd	16	0	6	16	4	5
1928	1st	64	4	7	69	8	6
	2nd	30	6	9	30	13	2
	3rd	16	4	9	16	7	4
1929	1st	63	16	8	69	19	6
	2nd	29	16	0	30	16	0
	3rd	16	11	4	17	1	5
1930	1st	63	16	2	66	10	2
	2nd	28	6	6	28	16	4
	3rd	16	14	10	17	4	0
1931	1st	52	4	3	56	1	8
	2nd and cabin	29	5	6	30	1	7
	3rd class tourist	17	7	0	17	3	4
1932	1st	50	17	7	54	19	5
	cabin	28	2	11	29	4	11
	tourist	20	14	3	21	1	4
	3rd	14	2	0	14	15	0
1933	1st	50	9	10	50	13	7
	cabin	27	12	1	27	7	7
		19	16	8	20	7	7
		14	6	11	14	11	0

Table 8.2

Year	Average receipt per ton Westbound £ s d			Eastbound £ s d		
1925	2	3	10	1	12	0
1926	2	0	5	1	15	8
1927	2	5	2	1	17	10
1928	2	2	4	1	12	7
1929	2	0	6	1	13	7
1930	1	19	10	1	13	7

Table 8.2 (continued)

Year	Average receipt per ton					
	Westbound			Eastbound		
	£	s	d	£	s	d
1931	1	19	4	1	18	1
1932	1	19	3	2	0	6
1933	2	2	4	2	0	9

The figures represent average receipts by Cunard per passenger and per ton of cargo carried.[64] Admittedly these averages do not indicate the extent of fluctuation in the general level of activity, but they illustrate the impact of a rating structure in unit terms on the level of earnings. In the carriage of westbound first class passengers average earnings remained relatively stable between 1926 and 1930, while eastbound figures were £5–£6 higher. After 1930, however, average eastbound receipts remained higher than westbound, but because of downward rate revisions there was an overall decline of approximately 25 per cent by 1933. Second class receipts (eastbound–westbound) remained stable, as did those for third class until 1930. Because of the introduction of new categories in 1931 it is difficult to ascertain comparisons. For westbound cargoes receipts were not subject to undue fluctuation between 1925 and 1929. There was a fall in the average receipts after 1930, but it was insignificant in a period of severe depression, and in 1933 average receipts rose to the level for 1928. By comparison eastbound receipts showed a surprising resilience and increased annually (1928–33) from £1 12s 7d to £2 0s 9d.

While applicable only to Cunard's voyage revenue, these figures are indicative of Conference agreements which tried to iron out the effect of trade fluctuations despite short-lived intervals of rate cutting. In the absence of such agreements the average receipts would probably have been subject to wide degrees of fluctuation with an adverse trend, particularly after 1930.

VI ADVANTAGE OF CONFERENCE MEMBERSHIP: VALUE OF CABIN CLASS SCHEDULE: CO-OPERATION BETWEEN CUNARD AND WHITE STAR

Cunard's continuous efforts to maintain rates within the various conference structures were but complementary to all the other expedients adopted to make services profitable under conditions of intense fluctuation. Though the history of Conferences was punctuated by disagreement, by claim and counter claim, by threats of withdrawal and by apparent lack of decisive action on the part of the statutory bodies, the advantages of membership probably outweighed the disadvantages. Taking into account the size, speed and type of ship employed by Cunard in the 1920s and 1930s the impact of agreement on rates and classification was essential to management. In the absence of such agreements unrestricted competition might have led to the survival of the fittest but it would also have led to the bankruptcy and extinction of many well-known companies.

At this juncture, however, we are not concerned with hypothetical argument. One of the most important innovations was the designation of cabin and tourist class ships. In particular, cabin class was originally applied to those ships which had no first class accommodation. They were usually old ships which could not compete with the fast, crack liners and were only capable of providing varying categories of cabin space. Then came a new phase in this type of accommodation. New ships began to be entered under this classification and a climax was reached when the United States lines entered *Washington* and *Manhattan* as cabin class liners. Sir Percy Bates, on Cunard's behalf, vigorously opposed this move, refusing to accept the position until *Queen Mary* came into service.[65] Thereafter, the top class of all first class ships was classified as cabin. As for Cunard's 'A' class ships, the Company had received a satisfactory classification for their use as cabin ships on the New York route as early as 1928.

Another important feature of the various conference agreements lay in the growing co-operation between Cunard and White Star long before the merger proposals came to fruition. In the matter of first class schedule rates Cunard attempted to safeguard earnings in the 1920s by working a private arrangement with White Star, whereby first class schedule rates on express ships were sustained.[66] By 1925, however, these rates came within the control of the conference and the arrangement between Cunard and White Star was terminated. Nevertheless, this agreement proved to be of value in combating intransigence among conference lines, in particular in offsetting more stringent competition from express ships belonging to the United States lines such as *Leviathan* and from the French line's ships *Paris* and *France*. As time went on the support of the one company for the other became closer and acted as an antidote to conference disagreements. There was a joint passenger arrangement between Cunard and White Star from Hamburg and although this was terminated in March 1927 freight business continued under joint allocation.[67] Furthermore, when the new mail contract was negotiated in the same year, each company agreed to accept from the Government £100,000 per annum for maintaining the mail service.[68] In 1931, in face of severe competition from foreign express ships on the mail route from Southampton, the two companies agreed to pool mail earnings, bringing into effect a joint service on a 50/50 basis.[69]

In other fields of enterprise, particularly in those peripheral to strictly conference agreements, working co-operation was extended and strengthened. In October 1928, for example, an agreement was reached with the Canadian Northern Railway, under which Cunard and White Star were to increase the number of calls to Halifax by ships eastbound in return for a cash bonus and increased support for the carriage of emigrants westwards.[70] Finally, as a counter to the problems of increasing costs, both companies agreed in May 1929 to renew existing contracts for the maintenance of joint agencies on the Continent and in Scandinavia and to continue the agreed division of traffic.[71]

Apart from these safeguarding devices, one receives the impression that attempts by Cunard and other British lines in the various Atlantic conferences to maintain, classify and increase rates were met with frustrating and tedious opposition. This was partly the consequence of the nature of the Conference machinery itself which proved incapable of implementing decisions, and partly the unwillingness of certain lines to abide by agreements once they had been negotiated. The whole process of organising a workable rate structure was also subjected to criticism and attack from interests external to the Conferences. In 1924, for example, Cunard and other lines engaged on the Canadian route came under a 'singularly misleading attack in a report made to the Canadian Government from a gentleman stated to be their special Commissioner'.[72] The burden of complaint was that shipping lines were charging excessive rates on the carriage of both freight and passengers. A further charge was made that the shipping lines practised discrimination against Canada in favour of the United States. Though the criticism may have contained some truth, it was difficult to substantiate. Nevertheless, the Canadian Government regarded this allegation as serious and actually considered financing an opposition line of steamships by way of retaliation.[73]

Another action which had an indirect effect on the harmony of Conference relationships occurred in 1928. As a means of extending earning capacity, Cunard had put *Caronia* on a weekly winter service between New York and Havana. This was an open route not subject to Conference ruling though, in order to allay suspicion, Cunard had informed the American lines of their intention to begin such a service. It was also carefully explained that the growing passenger traffic between New York and Cuba justified an increase in transport facilities.[74] As a further measure of good faith Cunard offered to quote rates appreciably above those ruling for the other lines engaged on the route. To their surprise, however, a rate war developed against them. Notwithstanding this, Cunard were able to maintain their traffic schedules throughout the season at some thirty per cent above their competitors.[75] Alarmed by this apparently successful incursion, the United States Shipping Board loaned *President Roosevelt* to the Ward Line, one of the American companies trading regularly on the Cuba route; rates were reduced by twenty-five per cent.[76] Despite such opposition, however, Cunard continued to make regular sailings during January–March, and in 1930 added a second vessel, *Carmania*, to the service.[77] Although this episode was not within the compass of the Conference structure the course of events tended to heighten suspicion among some members, of Cunard's intention to work outside the range of generally accepted agreements.

In general one can perhaps conclude that the operation of the North Atlantic Conferences adequately supported the oft-repeated assertion that, in times of relative prosperity, agreements worked well but that, under conditions of adverse trade fluctuation, they were subject to strain and breakdown. In Cunard's case they were but one among a number of devices for maintaining a share of a volatile trade in a constant endeavour to keep the margin between costs and revenue as wide as possible.

9
Advent of War and Survival
1935—45

I CHANGES IN CAPITAL STRUCTURE

From 1935 the status of The Cunard Steam Ship Co. was mainly that of a holding company. It continued the operation and control of the Liverpool–Havre cargo trade as well as that between the United Kingdom and the Mediterranean. Sources of information about the Cunard organisation as a whole, therefore, henceforth become twofold, the annual reports being concerned first with the working of The Cunard Steam Ship Co. Ltd and secondly with that of Cunard White Star Ltd. As a consequence two sets of accounts were presented annually to the shareholders. One can thus distinguish between the fortunes of the Mediterranean services and the difficulty of maintaining profitable traffic across the North Atlantic. This dichotomy is given greater significance when one attempts to compare working capacities in the years of peace from 1935 to 1939 with those during the years of war from 1939 to 1945.

Before embarking upon an analysis of the operations of the two companies between 1935 and 1945 a brief survey must be made of changes in capital structure. By comparison with what had gone before they were of a relatively minor character, though there were considerable changes in the control over long-term funds and, after 1939, by the implementation of a determined policy to reduce indebtedness. By 1935 the provisions contained in the agreement of 30 December 1933 between The Cunard Steam Ship Co. Ltd, Oceanic Steam Navigation Co. and H.M. Treasury concerning the transfer of Cunard assets to Cunard White Star Ltd, had been complied with by the Company and all sums due under the agreement from Cunard White Star had been satisfactorily settled.[1] This had been effected by the issue to the Company of the prescribed number of shares in Cunard White Star Ltd or by cash payments.

In 1937, consequent upon good trading results by Cunard White Star Ltd, the share premium account of £10 million was extinguished.[2] The following figures show how this account was disposed of in the Company's books:

1934	Reduction in book values of certain assets	£774 461
	Losses incurred by parent companies to date of sale agreements (19 June 1934)	£956 189
1935 and		
1936	Net losses on sale of ships	£1 920 687
1937	Amount written off ships (except *Queen Mary*) including £2 466 410 depreciation to 31 December 1936	£6 348 633
		£10 000 000

The result of this 'clean-up' of the balance sheet facilitated the writing down of assets. Provided that an annual allocation out of earnings of £976,280 was made for depreciation in respect of the older ships and *Queen Mary*, the current balance sheet figures reached for these ships would be reduced to scrap values when the *Queen Mary* reached the age of twenty-five years and when each of all the other ships reached the age of twenty years.[3] Sir Percy Bates believed this to be an attainable target subject to the proviso that future annual shipbuilding replacements should equal approximately the depreciation figure.[4] Such a policy, he stated, would enable the Company to maintain its position on the North Atlantic.

In this process, the financial relationship between Cunard and the Anchor Line had to be resolved. It will be remembered that Cunard's association with the Anchor Line had begun in 1912 with the purchase of the ordinary capital of that company of a par value of £250,000 costing Cunard £425,000.[5] The preference capital, which Cunard did not acquire, had level voting rights with the ordinary capital. Consequently Cunard did not have full control over the financial or shipping policy of that company. In principle the purchase of the interest had been soundly based as both companies derived mutual benefit, even though it was not until 1915 that their American organisations had been merged into single offices. Since 1915 the partnership between Cunard and Anchor on the American side had worked harmoniously.

In other respects, however, the association with Anchor Line had not been so successful. Towards the end of 1918 Cunard and Anchor had entered into shipbuilding contracts somewhat beyond financial capacity.[6] As we have seen, The Cunard Steam Ship Co. managed to recover from temporary post-war embarrassments; but the Anchor Line was moved 'by a spirit of emulation which decried attempts to restrain it as attempts at suppression'.[7] It was in such circumstances, as Sir Percy Bates declared later, that the influence of the preference capital began to make itself felt, mainly in opposition to Cunard's advice. With an over-supply of tonnage on highly competitive routes, Anchor Line's financial position was adversely affected. In 1924 they attempted to arrange for a trades facilities loan for £1,600,000 against mortgages on certain of their ships. The trades facilities board, however, had asked for collateral security of £350,000. In the event the Cunard Company came to the rescue of the Anchor Line by purchasing 35,000 Anchor Ordinary shares at £10 each;[8] but this effort subsequently proved to be futile in the face of a rapid decline in the volume of Atlantic trade, even though the Anchor Line's proportion of that trade was maintained by strenuous efforts 'and some favouritism in New York'.[9]

The final phase of this unhappy situation began in 1930 when, as a result of no dividend having been paid for seven years, Cunard wrote down their investment in Anchor Line by fifty per cent.[10] Two years later a moratorium was declared, followed in 1935 by voluntary liquidation of the Anchor company. For Cunard this involved the writing-off of an investment worth £775,000.[11] The close association of the two companies on the American side was also broken with the prospect of an intensification of competition for business both in New York and Glasgow. In the process of winding up the old company, whereby assets were sold by the creditors to the new company, Anchor Line (1935) Ltd, Cunard would take no responsibility for, nor endorse the terms and estimates extracted from a new prospectus.[12] This attitude was maintained despite the fact that technically they could be described as vendors and creditors through the ownership of a £10,000 shipbuilding bill which had come into their hands. Some of the creditors, nevertheless, expressed surprise that Cunard were not prepared to put yet more money into the Anchor Line in view of the protection which had always been forthcoming.[13] It was against this background, therefore, that the new Anchor company intimated their desire to establish their own organisation to represent them in America. Thus ended a shipping association which, in general, had been of some mutual advantage but had not fulfilled Cunard's financial expectations.

The next measure of capital reorganisation was of a purely technical nature. With a view to simplifying (by the abolition of distinctive numbers of shares) certain difficulties arising from transfer registrations, the fully paid ordinary shares of The Cunard Steam Ship Co. were converted, in 1937, into ordinary stock.[14] This action did not in any way affect any benefits or privileges which the ordinary shareholders then possessed. For their part, their declared concern was that the payment of dividends in default since 1931 should be resumed as soon as possible.

There were two other changes which need to be mentioned before we can begin to analyse the operating factors governing control of the two companies over resources during 1935–45. In April 1940 The Cunard Steam Ship Co. Ltd received an offer from the liquidator of the Anchor Line Ltd of 850 ordinary shares in T. and J. Brocklebank Ltd at a price of £250 per share totalling £212,500.[15] In the following month the purchase of these shares was completed together with a further 150 shares outstanding, and Sir Percy Bates was able to report to the ordinary general meeting that 'the deal was arranged on terms which were considered fair to all parties and the Company (i.e. T. and J. Brocklebank) is now all our own'.[16] As we shall see, the earnings of T. and J. Brocklebank together with those of the Commonwealth and Dominion Line (established as the Port Line in 1935) sustained the income of The Cunard Steam Ship Co. through the payment of dividends during the difficult years of the 1930s. After 1939 they helped Cunard in the provision of funds for certain debt clearances. In other words, the association of these two companies with Cunard was of mutual benefit in both trading and financial terms.

The second development was concerned with the relationship between Cunard White Star Ltd and the Oceanic Steam Navigation Co. Ltd. In April 1939 the Oceanic Steam Navigation Realisation Co. Ltd was formed for the purpose of holding Oceanic

Advent of War and Survival 1935–45 251

Company's assets (principally shares in Cunard White Star Ltd) and realising them for the benefit of Oceanic creditors.[17] When realised the assets were to be distributed in certain defined proportions depending on whether they were to be made available to secured or to unsecured creditors. The Realisation Company was formed with a capital of £1,250,000 divided as follows: 300,000 A shares to be held by H.M. Treasury and Ministry of Finance, Northern Ireland (secured creditors); 850,000 B shares to unsecured creditors (for over £4 million); 100,000 C shares to International Mercantile Marine Co. (in respect of £2,350,000 owing to them on the sale of Oceanic Company's shares to Royal Mail in 1926).[18] At this time the formation of the Oceanic Realisation Company was, by itself, of no material interest to Cunard. It was not until 1947 (as we shall see later) that it became an effective instrument in enabling Cunard to purchase the 38 per cent minority interest in Cunard White Star Ltd.

In these various ways the general improvement in the financial situation of The Cunard Steam Ship Co., and the amelioration of conditions arising from the Cunard White Star merger together with the building of the two Queens, led to a spirit of cautious optimism that Cunard as a whole might emerge from the war years in a relatively strong position. Sir Percy Bates gave expression to this prospective view by stating in 1941, 'the time is approaching when it may be possible with some reason, to hope for an improvement in our individual fortunes as stockholders, which years of careful conservation both of trade and assets, have I think fully deserved'.[19] He added that he did not base this expectation on war revenues. 'For years before September 1939, we have had a condition of no-peace and a species of near war which produced a steadily increasing frost on international movement, commerce and trade. This condition, which was disastrous for shipping, has been ended and will not be revived by any peace we shall make.'[20]

II EFFORTS TO INCREASE REVENUE AND REDUCE COSTS: THE NEW *Mauretania* AND *Queen Elizabeth*: THE MEETING OF FINANCIAL OBLIGATIONS: PROBLEM OF REPLACING WAR LOSSES

Having effected these necessary changes on the capital side of the two companies' accounts, the directors were more currently exercised by the continuous problem of increasing revenue and of reducing costs. This was no whit less serious or difficult of solution than that which their predecessors had been forced to overcome in the 1880s and the 1920s. In principle, the methods adopted after 1935 to induce profitability from a better utilisation of resources were very little different from those employed on previous occasions. Determined efforts were made to retire old and uneconomic ships and to replace them with fast modern ones. Continuous experiments were in hand for the reduction of the principal operating cost, namely fuel consumption, and labour costs were decreased partly by the introduction of labour-saving devices on board ship and partly by more efficient servicing of the ships at dockside.[21] Finally, overheads were reduced by the amalgamation of Cunard and White Star offices in overseas ports.

In the matter of the disposal of ships, *Mauretania*, *Olympic* and *Doric* were sold in 1935 and *Homeric* and *Majestic* in 1936, the latter being the eighth large Cunard White Star ship to be retired from service since the merger, thereby completing a total of 244,000 gross tons sent to the breakers' yards;[22] *Berengaria* suffered the same fate in 1938. As part replacement for these depletions, the *Queen Elizabeth* was put under construction at John Brown's shipyard. For the financing of this ship an agreement (supplemental to the tripartite agreement of 30 December 1933) was signed on 15 February 1937 and was published as a Government White Paper.[23] This provided the necessary financial support and sanctions for the contract with the shipbuilders which had been sealed on 6 October 1936. *Queen Elizabeth* was launched on 27 September 1938 but was not delivered from the builders' yard until after war had broken out in September 1939. In fact, the Admiralty were apprehensive that so large a ship lying in the fitting-out basin on Clydebank would provide a target for enemy bombers.[24] It was therefore decided at a meeting held at the Treasury on 29 September 1939 that the ship should leave the Clyde not later than February 1940.[25] Accordingly, on 6 February 1940 the Company were requested (under the Defence Regulations 1939) that the ship should leave the British Isles. So secret were the details governing this ship's movements that the world heard with some astonishment that she had arrived in New York on 7 March. Thus the necessities of war had interrupted the Company's designed plan for a 2-ship weekly service across the Atlantic and it was not until peace was restored that the two Queens could work in collaboration. Meanwhile, as part of the

Advent of War and Survival 1935–45

pre-war shipbuilding programme, the second *Mauretania* had been launched from Cammell Laird's shipyard on 28 July 1938 and had made her maiden voyage to New York on 17 June 1939.[26]

As a result of this policy of retiring old and uneconomic ships and of replacing them with large, fast, new ones, the Company was able to anticipate an increasing earning capacity and a reduction in operating costs. It was, therefore, a misfortune that the outbreak of war in 1939 should have dislocated the normal working pattern of this fleet. Nevertheless one can obtain some indication of the benefits accruing in 1938 and 1939 by the operation of *Queen Mary* within the framework of conference agreements.[27] In other ways, also, the Company adopted specific methods of increasing revenue. As we have seen, round-trip excursion fares at rates cheaper than those which normally were charged for third class and tourist traffic were reintroduced for prescribed periods within the 1938 holiday season.[28] The round-trip fare was reduced from £33 19s to £27 for third class passengers. Reductions applied on all ships operated by Cunard White Star Ltd and, in the case of tourist passengers, the saving ranged from £12 10s on *Queen Mary* to £9 10s on the Canadian ships. A special 14-day holiday cruise to New York, including 2½ days sightseeing, was offered at the inclusive tourist rate of £50 15s – a reduction of £12 10s on current fares.[29] Another important factor stimulating earnings was the introduction of a winter cruising programme. This included a world cruise and other sailings to the Mediterranean and the West Indies. Though the cruises in 1938 were not as lucrative as those for 1937, this pattern of operations was continued until the outbreak of war involving reduced Atlantic sailings in the winter months and the diversion of ships to cruising. The effect of such a policy has already been analysed in the figures of third class and tourist passengers carried.[30] The resultant effect on the earning capacity of Cunard White Star was shown in a marked rise in operating receipts.

The financial position of both The Cunard Steam Ship Co. Ltd and Cunard White Star Ltd was vastly improved during the war years from 1939 to 1945. As we shall see later, there was an effective allocation of resources not only for depreciation, but also in the creation of accounts for prospective liabilities in the shape of income tax and excess profits tax. Above all, the increasing annual net balances provided funds for the clearance of accumulated liabilities such as back dividends to stockholders and mortgage debenture holders as well as the redemption of debentures and other sources of debt.

In this process, The Cunard Steam Ship Co. Ltd, by increasing its assets was able to alter the direction of policy related to the raising of funds and strengthen its control over the deployment of resources. Tables 9.1 and 9.2 give an overall picture of the income, expenditure and net annual balances of the two companies.[31]

After 1937 there is no doubt that the operation of *Queen Mary*

Table 9.1

THE CUNARD STEAM SHIP CO. LTD

Year	Total net operating receipts (£000)	Other costs including depreciation (£000)	Net balance (£000)
1935	378·3	352·8	25·5
1936	361·7	339·0	22·7
1937	355·4	330·9	24·5
1938	359·3	323·1	36·2
1939	387·6	324·2	63·4
1940	680·3	534·2	146·1
1941	1022·3	792·6	229·7
1942	1064·2	720·5	343·7
1943	1027·9	715·8	312·1
1944	1043·8	659·9	383·9
1945	1093·9	648·0	445·9

Table 9.2

CUNARD WHITE STAR LTD

Year	Total income (£000)	Total disbursements (£000)	Loss or profit (£000)
1935	5956·9	6018·7	61·8 (loss)
1936	6881·3	6334·7	546·6
1937	8222·0	8075·7	146·3
1938	6950·0	6488·1	461·9
1939	7586·9	7165·4	421·5
1940	5649·8	4365·7	1284·1
1941	2199·7	1248·8	950·9
1942	1834·2	1214·8	619·4
1943	1716·3	1057·1	659·2
1944	1562·0	1012·7	549·3
1945	1566·0	965·4	600·6

added substantially to Cunard's earning capacity. The year 1939 had shown an increase of £700,000 over the first three-quarters of 1938 (despite only eight months of normal trading). 'I think the time has come', stated Sir Percy Bates, 'for me to be more particular on the financial performance of *Queen Mary*. She is widely known as a masterpiece of British construction; it may not be equally appreciated that financially she has been very successful from the start, as the progress made in marine engineering has focused in *Queen Mary* a new economy in transportation across the Atlantic. Since 1922, when the full effect of the U.S. Immigration Quota Law first made itself felt, no steamer has ever made so much money in successive twelve months, as *Queen Mary* has done since being commissioned.'[32] The ship's performance was all the more remarkable as, down to the outbreak of war, she was confronted in her class by competition of the fiercest description. Despite the disturbed political situation, she actually improved her earnings during the first eight months of 1939 over the average of the two previous years.[33] In addition, as we have already stated, the new *Mauretania* had been put into service and the rest of the ships had, as a whole, increased their own contributions to the revenue. The trend of the traffic was naturally abnormal in this immediate pre-war period, eastbound passages showing a decline and westbound an increase during unusual times of the year; but the results, as can be seen from the figures, were solid and afforded good prospects for the year as a whole.[34]

The impact of war augmented the varying degrees of abnormality. *Queen Mary*, for example, was detained in New York and ship after ship of the Company's fleet was requisitioned for government service. Much of Cunard's organisation in Europe was cut off and much of what remained was clearly of little practical value in the altered circumstances. Nevertheless the substantial increase in the revenue of both companies during the war years enabled Cunard to effect necessary financial adjustments and pay off arrears of indebtedness.

In the first place funds were made available for the implementation of a regulated depreciation policy for Cunard White Star ships. The basis for such depreciation had been laid down in 1937 but in the following year it had not been possible to allocate the necessary funds for the amounts required.[35] After making provision for the 1939 depreciation, therefore, a further £976,280 had to be made available in order to wipe off the arrears for 1938. This amount was written-off with the aid of £685,039 carried over into 1939 from 1938 and the balance from the carry-over into 1940.[36] As a result the net figure which had stood at £421,498 was reduced to a carry-forward figure of £130,257.[37] Also, in accordance with the trust deeds, the relative amounts of £210,800 (representing depreciation on *Queen Mary*) were paid off for the two years 1938 and 1939.[38] The amounts were remitted to the Treasury in cash and were, with Treasury approval, invested in 2½ per cent War Bonds.[39] Thus all arrears due to the requirements of a regulated depreciation policy, were paid and henceforth (at least until the end of the war) all depreciation charges continued to be met annually.

In the second place the improved revenues of The Cunard Steam Ship Co. Ltd enabled an effective redemption of the Company's 5 per cent mortgage debenture stock. Some £3,683,615 was outstanding on this stock out of a total of £4 million issued in 1925. Under the terms of issue, the stock was redeemable at par on 1 February 1946 or on or after 1 February 1941. On 16 July 1941 the Cunard board decided on a plan of redemption to take place on 2 February 1942.[40] To finance this operation, Cunard's wholly-owned subsidiaries, Port Line Ltd and T. and J. Brocklebank Ltd, arranged to lend the parent company the major portion of the total required.[41] The money came partly from war risk insurance received for ships sunk and also from the sale of some of the investments representing the accumulation of reserves over more than a pre-war decade.[42] Of the total amount required, T. and J. Brocklebank lent Cunard £1 million at 2 per cent and Port Line £2 million (later increased to £2,300,000). These loan facilities at low rates were an undoubted source of strength to Cunard and reflected at least one attribute of the relationship between a parent and its associated companies. Sir Percy Bates was explicit on this point. 'It is most important', he said, 'that you should understand that our subsidiary companies (to use a legal phrase) are termed domestically "associates". We have, if we choose to exert it, absolute control of all of them, but we do not want the dead response of one cog-wheel being driven round by another. We want life, and life means volition, thought, enterprise, all on the scale and on the level of the subsidiary company.'[43]

In expanding this point of view Sir Percy made it clear that

Cunard did not have to inspire her subsidiaries. They had their own sources of inspiration and resources. 'Rather do we work to harmonise their aspirations', he added, 'and try to see that they lie within, rather than without, the ability of the parent company, the Cunard, to provide any ultimate financial backing which might be needed.'[44] In 1944 the strength of Cunard's financial position was such that provision could be made for repaying the Company's further indebtedness to the Government. The board therefore gave approval for the allocation of £100,000 towards the redemption of the outstanding £1 million second mortgage debenture stock as from 5 May 1945.[45]

Parallel with this effort on the part of the Cunard board to redeem indebtedness, there was an equally determined effort by Cunard White Star Ltd to similar relief. In 1941 the board decided to repay the whole of the Company's debenture debt amounting to £7,950,000.[46] Thus there was a double repayment of debt, i.e. by The Cunard Steam Ship Co. Ltd of 5 per cent mortgage debentures and by Cunard White Star Ltd of £7,950,000 debenture stock of various kinds. These repayments removed capital charges ahead of the Cunard preference and ordinary stockholders on a sum of £11,633,615.[47] It also resulted in approximately £6,600,000 being made available to the Treasury for immediate war expenditure. The breakdown of the various repayments included in the £7,950,000 was as follows:[48] first mortgage debenture stock (account *Queen Mary*) £1,750,000; income debenture stock class A (account *Queen Mary*) £1,750,000; income debenture stock class B (account *Queen Mary*) £200,000; first mortgage debenture stock (account *Queen Elizabeth*) £2,500,000; income debenture stock class C (account *Queen Elizabeth*) £2,500,000. The actual mechanism for the transfer of these funds (to be paid by 21 October 1941) was that on Cunard's instructions H.M. Treasury realised the securities deposited in the depreciation accounts for *Queen Mary* and *Queen Elizabeth*, and transferred the proceeds to the Treasury to the sum of £1,364,251 9s 11d.[49] Transfers were also made from Barclays Bank and Midland Bank to Martins Bank, Liverpool, so that a banker's draft could be produced by Martins Bank in exchange for Cunard's cheque in their favour for £6,585,748 10s 1d.[50]

In the general context of making funds available to the Treasury for the promotion of the war effort, a loan agreement dated 21 July 1941, was made between the Government and The Reconstruction

Finance Corporation. Under the terms of this agreement, certain British-owned securities in America were pledged as collateral. In Cunard's case this involved their holdings in Funch Edye Inc and in 25 Broadway Corporation, New York.[51] In short, apart from the massive deployment of resources in the form of ships for war operations, Cunard made a distinctive contribution to the war effort in a variety of ways in the form of cash.

The third and final benefit accruing from an expanding income resulting in increasing annual surplus was in the payment of arrears of dividends to stockholders. On 8 December 1941 the dividend arrears on the 5 per cent cumulative preference stock were paid relating to the years from 1 July 1931 to 30 June 1933,[52] and the balance for the period from 1 July 1933 to 31 December 1941 was paid on 30 March 1942.[53] In 1941 Cunard White Star Ltd paid a 'maiden' dividend of 5 per cent and in 1943 a dividend of 6 per cent was declared on the ordinary stock of The Cunard Steam Ship Co.[54] The latter event prompted Sir Percy Bates to remark that 'Cunard ordinary stock is a speculative affair. It has emerged from a period of 13 years, during which no ordinary dividend was paid.'[55] At that time there were 13,480 stockholder accounts, of which 10,168 did not exceed £300; 8642 stood at £200 or less and 5542 at £100 or less.[56] Thus, the large units of stock were held by rather less than 17 per cent of the total number of stockholders. 'If I thought it were any use advising that no one should hold any more stock than he could afford to lose', added Sir Percy, 'I would give that advice; but by nature man is a gambling animal.'[57]

In general, both Cunard Steam Ship Co. Ltd and Cunard White Star Ltd had, by a wise utilisation of expanding resources during the war years, freed themselves from a heavy debt burden, most of which had been carried over a period of twenty years. Stockholders had received their due reward after years of patient waiting and costs (both operating and capital) had either been substantially reduced or kept stable. On 3 April 1946 Sir Percy Bates summed up the financial result of five years of war. 'Of the shipping companies', he declared, 'it is only the parent company which has any fixed debts at all. Our main fixed debts viz. £300,000 on the mortgage of the Cunard's Liverpool building and £900,000 due to H.M. Government on the second mortgage of shares in our associated companies (i.e. second mortgage debenture stock) with the ready assistance of our bankers, we have refunded since the end of the year. The gross saving of interest on these two items in a full year will be £15,000.⁵⁸ The redemption of the First mortgage debenture stock having been completed, the trustees, Martins Bank Ltd, redeemed to Cunard all the securities charged in their favour. 'For the first time in 42 years', added Sir Percy, 'the Company has no security of any kind pledged in support of its borrowings.'⁵⁹ It was against such a background that the board of The Cunard Steam Ship Co. Ltd felt it fitting to mark the occasion by adding a centenary bonus of 2½ per cent to the final dividend of 5 per cent for 1944.⁶⁰ 'The interim dividend paid last May, the final dividend and the centenary bonus now recommended', explained the Chairman, 'have all been fairly earned out of the profits for the year.'

Within this generally favourable financial climate, however, there was a more serious omission. The exigencies of war prevented the laying down of new merchant ships and, accordingly, the allocation which would normally have been made for this purpose had either to be held in reserve or devoted to other purposes. In the case of Cunard White Star, adequate provision was made annually for the writing down of ships but no funds were expendable on new ships. In fact some of the liquid funds made available from war risk insurance for ships sunk, were diverted to debt redemption operations. The problem of replacement was continually under discussion and was referred to in the Cunard report for 1940. 'During the war', it was stated, 'the Company will not be allowed to build new ships for the North Atlantic passenger trade. At the proper time, a cautious survey of the post-war world must be made, before embarking upon shipbuilding, as nothing is so disastrous for any shipping company as to build ships, especially at high prices, which are other than carefully suited to their times.'⁶¹ To this extent the lessons learnt from Cunard's post-1918 experience had not been forgotten. It was understood that at the end of the war there would be a surplus of the ordinary type of cargo ship but there would be a shortage of specialised ships such as refrigeration and passenger liners. 'I think the time has arrived', said Sir Percy Bates, 'when the building yards should be opened to specialised ships capable of serving their own needs when the guns stop shooting.'⁶² By the end of 1944, however, restrictions were being eased and in the following year, as we shall see later, Cunard was able to embark upon a shipbuilding programme capable of making good the depletions caused by war.

All things considered, Cunard made a wise disposition of available resources during the war years. The revenue at the disposal of The Cunard Steam Ship Co. Ltd came principally from the dividends of associated companies plus whatever increments could be earned from the Mediterranean services. For Cunard White Star the income for internal allocation came from those sources not subject to Government requisition orders. All earnings on government account had been credited to the Government and no commission had been charged on the management of thirty-nine government ships.[63] In such circumstances, therefore, it was no mean achievement to have freed the Company from debt and to have increased revenue. When the final balances were cast profits were not overlarge in return for the magnitude of the service performed. Cunard's case, therefore, is but one among many confirming S. G. Sturmey's general view that 'it does not appear that the liner companies made exorbitant gains during the war.'[64]

III REQUISITION AND WAR SERVICE: *Queen Mary* AND *Curaçao*

Having dealt with some of the more pertinent facts relevant to the financial structure of the two companies, it now becomes necessary for us to examine the impact of war on the operational side of Cunard's business, particularly that concerned with the management of the fleet. As in the case of the First World War, much has been written about the war service of individual Cunard ships. We are, however, mainly concerned with the business aspects of requisition within the broader framework of Cunard's total commitment to the war effort.

On 24 August 1939 Cunard White Star was informed that the Government proposed to requisition *Ascania, Laurentic, Aurania* and *Alaunia*.[65] This was followed by further directions during the next few days and when war was declared on 3 September, *Scythia, Britannic, Laconia, Carinthia, Andania* and *Ausonia* were all under Admiralty orders. *Franconia* was taken over on 20 September and *Aquitania* on 21 November,[66] meanwhile *Queen Mary* was laid up at New York and the Company was instructed by the Admiralty not to sail her.[67] She was later joined by *Mauretania*. This ordering and requisitioning of ships involved the Company in a variety of problems which had to be solved expeditiously. Withdrawal of these ships from service, with consequent cancellation of voyages, meant that the Company's prearranged sailing schedule had to be altered. Cunard White Star's schedule listed 47 sailings but only 12 could be completed as 11 out of 18 ships had been requisitioned.[68] On the administrative side there were difficulties arising from the operation of government agreements, charter parties with their folios of clauses and conditions, new forms of accountancy and regulations governing crew and manning arrangements. The passenger and freight departments were faced with the task of ensuring that offices, agencies, prospective passengers and freight shippers were notified of cancelled sailings and advised regarding alternative plans.[69] The marine engineering, naval architect, furnishing and other technical departments were called upon to carry out government requirements and to ensure that ships were handed over in proper condition.[70]

By the end of September 1939 the organisation of Britain's shipping resources was advanced. A Ministry of Shipping had been established in which shipowners, representative of every type and classification of sea carrier, and with experience in the complexities of ocean transport, were called upon to give their services. At the end of October the Minister of Shipping set up an advisory council of well-known shipowners, representatives of officers' associations and trade union leaders to give guidance on problems arising from all sections of the shipping industry. Sir Percy Bates and Lord Essendon were among those invited to serve. In December a liner organisation committee was formed to assist the Ministry of Shipping in dealing with prospective programmes of supplies – particularly vital imports – to be carried by the regular shipping lines.[71] Sir Percy Bates was also appointed a member of this committee.

The conditions of service governing the requisition of ships were embodied in three standard charter parties, T.97A, T.98A and T.99A. Each was based upon the corresponding charter party used in the First World War, with subsequent supplemental amendments made to take account of changing commercial practice in the intervening years. Charter Party T.98A was a demise charter appropriate for use in those cases where it was found convenient to take over the ship on a 'bare boat' basis. The requisitioning authority assumed responsibility for the manning, upkeep and other functions and liabilities involved in ownership, including liability for war and marine risks.[72] This charter party was mainly used for vessels taken into naval commissioned service. Charter parties T.97A and T.99A left owners responsible for finding, paying and victualling the crew, providing the necessary stores, maintaining the ship in a thoroughly efficient state and insuring her against loss or damage by marine risk, while the requisitioning authority assumed responsibility for all fuel and dues as well as for war risk insurance.[73] T.97A was primarily for use in the case of passenger ships employed as troop transports or hospital ships. T.99A was applicable to vessels engaged in carrying military stores, as well as those in commercial service (e.g. carriage of cargoes on government account) subject always to modification by the provisions of the draft heads of arrangement of the Liner Requisition Scheme.[74] In general, the financial provisions covering ships under these various forms of requisition concerned rates of hire and compensation for ships lost.

The fixing of rates was undertaken with the object of giving fair cover to owners' costs, making adequate provision for depreciation and allowing a reasonable return on capital. Each of the standard charter parties contained a clause under which the charterer agreed to pay a higher monthly rate for the ship, to be calculated according to the provisions of a form incorporated in the charter.[75] In the case of liners, the allowance for depreciation and return on capital was worked out separately for each ship at the rate of 10 per cent per annum on the basis of value. This percentage allowed 5 per cent return on capital after providing 5 per cent for depreciation. To this allowance was added (in the case of liners serving under the requisition scheme or operating under T.97A or T.99A) the appropriate 'basic' rate. This increment mainly represented the average cost for the class of liner concerned for various items of expenditure falling on the owner under the charter party. The 'basic' rate for passenger liners above 5000 tons gross depended partly on speed and partly on the composition of the crew.[76]

There was, however, a distinction between the rates paid for British ships and those for neutral tonnage – higher rates being usually paid on the latter. The effect of this caused annoyance among British shipowners especially as the contingencies of war prevented them from operating in neutral trades.[77] The discrepancy in rates had been caused by a general belief at the outset of war that there would be no shipping shortage. In the light of subsequent events this double rating system proved to be a considerable embarrassment to the Government. In the first place it became difficult to persuade British shipowners when they had freedom of action, to trade on dangerous routes at relatively lower rates. In fact, the principles governing the hiring of ships were not settled until August 1940, though many of the main features were in operation before then.[78] In the second place, it was necessary to bring tramp shipping within the framework of regulation. The owners of these ships did not have the necessary shore organisations to deal with day to day cargo operations. Consequently most tramp ships had to be put under the control of liner companies, and owners in effect lost control of their ships. As we have seen, the rates paid were designed to cover main expenses of operation including depreciation and these were modified from time to time as the exigencies of the situation demanded. The higher rates paid for the employment of neutral ships continued, though as more and more maritime nations were drawn into the war the problem of differentiation became less acute.

War service by ships in Cunard's fleet needs no detailed elaboration here. Apart from *Queen Mary* and *Queen Elizabeth* (whose war records will be considered later) it must be obvious that the concentration of such maritime strength was of incalculable value not only at certain decisive stages in the conduct of the war, but also in the strategy of ultimate victory.

Aquitania, the oldest ship in the fleet to give service in two world wars, after having been released from requisition in December 1939 following a collision with *Samaria*, was again put under the Admiralty in February 1940.[79] On 9 March she sailed for Wellington, New Zealand, later serving in Australian and Indian waters for the remainder of that year as well as throughout 1941 and 1942. *Mauretania* sailed from New York to Sydney on 20 March 1940 where the work of fitting her out for transporting troops was completed.[80] She began her trooping career on 5 May sailing from Sydney to the Clyde with over 2000 troops. Throughout 1940–2 she operated between Australia, India and Africa, carrying troops and supplies to the Middle East during the critical years of the African campaign.[81] *Britannic* was requisitioned as a troopship in August 1939. Her subsequent duties took her to ports the world over and on several occasions she was commodore ship of convoys.[82] *Scythia* served throughout 1940–2 carrying troops to the Middle East via Cape Town. When at Algiers in November 1942, during the allied invasion of North Africa, she was struck by an aerial torpedo and remained for several weeks in use as a Royal Naval barracks.[83] *Samaria* was requisitioned on 24 February 1940 and on 12 December was transferred to charter party T.97A.[84] *Antonia* was taken over on 1 February 1940 and on 12 October was transferred to charter party T.97A.[85] This charter only lasted for a short time and on 10 November the ship was again transferred, this time to T.98A.[86] *Georgic* was requisitioned on 11 March 1940 and put under charter party T.97A on 19 April as a troopship.[87] She took part in the evacuation of Norway and was at St Nazaire in June. *Lancastria* was also at St Nazaire on 17 June when she was bombed and sunk; also in the same month, *Carinthia* and *Andania*, sailing as armed merchant cruisers, were torpedoed and sunk.[88] Two years later (September 1942) *Laconia* was sunk by enemy action while serving as a troop transport.[89] Of the Cunard White Star's fleet, which had consisted of 18 ships amounting to 434,689 gross tons at the outbreak of war, the majority had been drawn into war service by the middle of 1940. In this fact alone the merit of the Company's effort at a time when Britain stood alone against seemingly insuperable odds must be recognised.

It now becomes necessary to put the contribution of the two Queens within the context of Cunard's total war effort. When *Queen Mary* was requisitioned in 1940 she had been in service for nearly four years. During this period the ship and her whole equipment had been tested and maintained in a high state of efficiency and it was a comparatively easy task to adapt her accommodation to the needs of trooping. *Queen Elizabeth*, on the other hand, had left the builders' yard on 26 February 1940 an unfinished ship. The hull and engines had been completed, but much remained to be done to furnish accommodation and provide auxiliary equipment. As her service was urgently required it was decided that completion should be undertaken at New York.[90] The idea of converting her to an airplane carrier was seriously considered, but eventually she was prepared for war service as a troop carrier.[91] The work of fitting out this great ship (which in the interests of American neutrality was carried through as a commercial proposition) was effected so expeditiously that on 13 November 1940 she was able to leave New York on her long eastern voyage to Sydney. It was originally intended to adapt her accommodation for troop carrying there, but the Admiralty later decided, she

Advent of War and Survival 1935–45 265

should be dry-docked and fitted out for military passengers at Singapore.[92] This change of plan avoided the necessity of having to cut her masts in order to allow her free passage under Sydney Bridge to the fitting-out basin.

In the spring of 1941 *Queen Mary* and *Queen Elizabeth* left Sydney for Suez sailing together in convoy, *Queen Mary* making her sixth voyage as a transport and *Queen Elizabeth*, making what was, in effect, her first voyage as a passenger-carrying liner. Throughout the summer the two liners continued their trooping service without respite; by December they had carried over 80,000 troops, the majority of whom had reinforced our armies in the Middle East.[93] With the entry of Japan into the war at the end of 1941, the Queens began their long service as transports for U.S. troops. By early summer 1942 the North African campaign was going badly for the Allies; Rommel was striking for Suez and reinforcements for the Eighth Army were urgently needed. An armada of transports, *Queen Mary* and *Queen Elizabeth* included, sailed from U.K. ports in support of our threatened forces in Egypt. The Queens made the long voyage to Suez via Freetown and Simonstown, thence by way of Cape Town and Rio de Janeiro to New York to embark U.S. forces.[94] From December 1942 to April 1943 (when both ships returned to the Clyde) they had carried 105,000 troops and steamed 339,000 miles. Each voyage had been made possible only by efficient organisation and teamwork on the part of officers, crews and military staffs, no less than by the active co-operation of the steamship lines and their organisations ashore. To have undertaken successfully so vast a movement of personnel needed coordination between the sea transport staff of the Ministry of War Transport, the War Office, the Admiralty and the U.S. authorities on the one hand and the ships' companies on the other. This resulted in what might be described as an achievement in transportation without parallel in the history of trooping. The net result was that the two liners, *Queen Mary* and *Queen Elizabeth*, were so organised that they could jointly carry 15,000 men, feed and house them during the voyage, disembark them and within the space of a few days recommence the operation. Their potential was duly recognised by the German naval command. Highest honours and substantial financial rewards were promised to U-boat captains should they sink or disable the two ships.[95]

Finally, the most important (and possibly most monotonous)

part of the two ships' service began with carriage of troops across the Atlantic. As the theatre of war shifted to Europe, vast quantities of supplies and an increasing flow of men were needed for both the invasion and conquest of the European mainland. Extensive alterations were made to the interiors of the two Queens. A larger number of passengers could be accommodated for a voyage lasting a few days than for a voyage across the Pacific and Indian Oceans. On the Atlantic run the liners could be more closely packed with troops. Every available space on each ship was fitted with 'standees' – a canvas stretcher strung on poles and mounted on steel uprights.[96] By this expedient the average number of troops carried on each vessel per voyage between May and December 1943 was around 15,000. Even in the following winter months this figure never fell below 12,000 on *Queen Mary* and 13,000 on *Queen Elizabeth*.[97] In other words, for every voyage lasting less than a week a whole division of infantry could be taken into the battle zone by the two ships.

The effort so far described was chiefly effective because the large, fast ships were in operation throughout the greater part of the war years. It is true that Cunard White Star suffered serious losses, nine vessels in all, but they amounted to a relatively small part total tonnage and carrying capacity. The fact that *Queen Mary*, *Queen Elizabeth* and *Mauretania* constituted in terms of tonnage and space, about one-half of the Company's carrying strength, increased the necessity for precaution in maintaining them as operational units. This was achieved despite attempted sabotage by enemy agents and the determined efforts of German submarine commanders to sink them.

There was, however, one incident which needs to be mentioned as an illustration of the hazards of convoy operations. On 2 October 1942 *Queen Mary*, while carrying out a convoy manoeuvre, was in collision with *H.M.S. Curaçao*, one of her escort vessels. The cruiser was crossing in front of *Queen Mary* when the collision occurred and was sheered in half, sinking immediately with the loss of 338 lives.[98] Protracted litigation followed this accident, the Company's solicitors being instructed on 15 September 1943 to issue a writ against the captain of *Curaçao*.[99] On 20 October 1943 the Treasury solicitor began proceedings against the Company. There the matter rested until 11 June 1945 when the hearing was begun in the Admiralty Court, brought by the Admiralty against Cunard White Star Ltd, alleging negligent navigation on *Queen Mary*'s part.[100] In defence a counter-claim of negligence was made on behalf of Cunard against *Curaçao*'s captain. Judgement was given on 21 January 1947; *Queen Mary* was found free from blame and the plaintiff's (the Admiralty) case was dismissed with costs.[101] The Admiralty thereupon took the issue to the Appeal Court and on 30 July appeal was allowed attributing one-third of the blame to *Queen Mary* and two-thirds to *Curaçao*, costs to be awarded proportionately.[102] Leave to appeal to the House of Lords was given and on 8 February 1949 the Judges affirmed the decision of the Court of Appeal and ordered each side to pay its own costs.[103]

It is not possible adequately to summarise the Cunard Company's contribution to the overall war effort. Bare facts and figures can only mark the end result of long hard years of achievement. The constant threat of destruction, the duty of men in peril and the efficiency of organisation which kept great ships in wartime occupation, provide the real essence of the Company's record in war. The tangible result was that Cunard carried 9,223,181 tons of vitally needed cargo; nearly £58 million had been collected in freight; 39 government ships had been managed and, by debt redemption, just short of £8 million had been made available to the Treasury for immediate war use.[104] Up to 31 May 1945 the Company's own fleet had carried a grand total of 2,473,040 troops, of which 1,243,538 were carried in *Queen Mary* and *Queen Elizabeth*.[105] In the North Atlantic these two ships alone had transported 869,694 eastbound and 213,008 westbound.[106] Cunard White Star Ltd had entered the war owning 18 passenger ships of 434,689 gross tons; at the end of the European conflict in May 1945 there were nine ships in service (excluding *Georgic*) totalling 345,921 gross tons.[107] These were the bounds of commitment in the cause of survival and a democratic way of life. That Britain had so powerful an instrument to call upon in time of national emergency can, perhaps, be attributed to history. For more than 100 years, wisdom and business judgement had kept Cunard alive and, in so doing, had maintained the Company as a forceful and essential part of our mercantile marine. In this context, Cunard's assets became part of a hidden strength which ultimately enabled Britain and her allies to win the war.

IV CUNARD'S GROWING AWARENESS OF COMPETITION FROM AIR TRAVEL

It now becomes necessary to discuss a sphere of the Cunard Co.'s managerial policy which, on the face of it, is not particularly relevant to the context of this chapter; though in chronological terms it is contained within the period 1934–45. Apart from the ensuing dislocation of normal business operations caused by the waging of war, the necessity for maintaining vital lines of communication between Britain, the United States and Canada advanced the need for air services across the North Atlantic. The prospect of massive aircraft production and the crossing of oceans by air posed an obvious threat of a new and powerful competition to passenger liner companies in a post-war world. It is of interest to note, therefore, that Cunard's directors had taken anticipatory actions on air travel some years before 1939 and were involved in continuous negotiations about it throughout the years of war into the first few months of peace.

In order to understand the nature of Cunard's approach to the question of air travel, it is necessary to go back to 1934. In November of that year, Sir Percy Bates received a letter from Mr J. H. Woods of H.M. Treasury informing him of proposals to exploit inventions for the construction of sea-dromes.[108] These proposals had been made by an American company through the sponsorship of a certain Captain Lynch. It was asserted that with the establishment of sea-dromes at strategic points on North Atlantic sea coasts payable loads could be transported in quantity and at commercial rates across the Atlantic.[109] The Admiralty and the Air Ministry were impressed by the proposition in technical terms and the Treasury were concerned that Cunard White Star should have an opportunity of considering the scheme in relation to their known commitments and future policy. Mr Woods was particularly anxious to know what attitude Cunard White Star might adopt towards such a scheme. Sir Percy was non-commital in reply and after the Company's naval architect, Mr G. McL. Paterson, had pronounced upon the technical aspects of the proposals, the implied conclusion was that the installation of sea-dromes was not practicable.[110]

Other proposals originating from private companies eager to obtain a foothold in the prospective development of transatlantic air traffic followed in succeeding years. On 23 July 1935, for example, Mr Henry Tate forwarded to Sir Percy Bates plans for promotion of an air line using large seaplanes with diesel engines.[111] The proposed routes were to be via Gibraltar and West Africa to the Cape and South America. A second service was to be instituted via the Azores and Bermuda to New York. One essential part of this scheme was that it should operate in conjunction with existing shipping lines serving these routes, the shipping companies providing the booking and office facilities and other necessary harbour services. Concurrently, another project sponsored by the Ralph Glyn group had as its object the training of officers in the mercantile marine as air pilots, and for shipping companies to operate air services in much the same way as railways ran road services.[112]

For Cunard these embryonic (and, as it turned out, abortive) attempts to inaugurate trans-oceanic airlines had a twofold implication. In the first place, there was the possibility that an airline supported by government might secure mail contracts, thus sharpening the competition in one of Cunard's traditional and, in one sense, favoured spheres of activity. In the second place, it was essential that the Company should not only give evidence of an interest in the development of air traffic, but should take steps to associate its interests with an airline likely to attract some form of government support. It seemed obvious to Sir Percy Bates that Imperial Airways would eventually be given government backing and he kept in close touch with Sir Eric Geddes, Chairman of that Company.[113] On 21 November 1934 he informed Geddes of his Company's doubts about the sea-drome proposals and added that Cunard's general manager was on the point of signing an agency contract with Imperial Airways in New York.[114] '... It occurred to me', he continued, 'that possibly I might use the existence of this contract as a means for satisfying the Treasury that Cunard White Star Ltd would be in some sort of touch with transatlantic flying.'[115] The response was favourable. In a note to his managing director (6 December 1934) Sir Eric Geddes stated 'that as Imperial Airways had a close association with Cunard White Star Ltd in the United States, it would be suitable and helpful if Imperial Airways undertook to co-operate with them and to keep in touch with them on transatlantic matters.'[116] This was followed, four days later, by a letter from Sir Percy Bates to Mr Woods at the Treasury, informing him of the progress of events with the concluding remark: 'I think that you can rely on this Company being sufficiently in touch with transatlantic flying to enable us to become associated in this business should such association become desirable or practicable.'[117]

In July 1935 Sir Eric Geddes informed Sir Percy Bates that the Government had agreed to support Imperial Airways as a 'chosen instrument' for transatlantic services together with the two main Imperial trunk routes from the United Kingdom to West and South Africa and from the United Kingdom to Australia, New Zealand and the Far East.[118] 'Under these circumstances', he added, 'it does not seem likely that the Government would look with any particular favour on any new flotations for services proposed over routes for which the Government intends to use the medium of Imperial Airways with the subsidy and mail contracts. As well as the Government's official blessing bestowed upon Imperial Airways, there would not seem to be very much room at the present stage of development of aviation for other companies to operate on those routes.'[119] Sir Percy Bates was thus made aware of the future possibilities of allying Cunard with Imperial Airways, and he took immediate action. On 1 August 1935 he wrote to Sir Warren Fisher, Chairman of the Air Development Committee, saying that he was unable to reconcile the aspirations of Imperial Airways, Tate's group and the Ralph Glyn group and asked whether it would not be best for Cunard White Star to inform the Tate group that they would wait upon the recommendations of the Warren Fisher Committee before engaging further in matters concerning the air.[120] Sir Warren Fisher agreed that it was premature for Cunard White Star to enter into any negotiations with private groups or individuals concerning the relationship between ocean carriers and air communications and that 'he would get in touch with Sir Percy when the time seemed appropriate.'[121]

The prospects now seemed to be auspicious. Cunard White Star were to be kept abreast of official thinking on this matter with every hope of participation in either a financial or an agency interest in a government-backed airline. So it seemed at the time, and Sir Percy had probably every reason to believe that he had read the signs correctly and that Cunard White Star were in a favourable position to participate in this growth of a new system of communication.

By November 1935, however, it became apparent that such

Advent of War and Survival 1935–45

hopes were not destined to be fulfilled. Difficulties arose concerning the United Kingdom terminal for the transatlantic air service. A point in Ulster had been under consideration but the Eire Government had made it clear that if such a proposal were made effective they would offer facilities on the west coast of Ireland for competitive foreign air lines.[122] When Sir Percy Bates met Sir Eric Geddes on 8 November 1935, therefore, the latter had to make known the Government's change of plan. With some embarrassment he said that he felt he had 'let Cunard White Star down' explaining that the Government had been forced to abandon the original idea of having the British terminal located in Ulster. 'They felt it most desirable', he added, 'to prevent the establishment of a foreign service operating from the Free State [sic].'[123] During the negotiations the Irish Government 'had proved extremely awkward'. For some time they had held out for a participation equal to that of the British Government. This could not be admitted as both the British Government and Imperial Airways were determined that control should be vested in the hands of the latter company.[124] The provisional agreement which had been reached with the assistance of Mr Stanley Baldwin and Mr Neville Chamberlain envisaged the establishment of a new company in which Imperial Airways should hold 51 per cent, the remainder of the shares to be divided between Eire and Canada should the latter country wish to be involved. Should Canada not wish to do so the proportions were to be 60 per cent to Imperial Airways and 40 per cent to Eire.[125] Such proportions left no room for participation by any steamship company. Thus it was that British Airways came into being without financial assistance from Cunard despite the protracted negotiations to bring the Cunard Company into a government sponsored air scheme.

Despite a belated effort by Sir Percy Bates to enlist the support of Sir Warren Fisher on Cunard's behalf, a move which Sir Warren had, perforce, to turn down, nothing further could be done. Sir Warren Fisher, however, did suggest to Sir Percy Bates that if Cunard still needed 'to take an interest in flying', the best course would be to take an interest in Imperial Airways.[126] This suggestion offered some inducement, for although the new Company was to have exclusive landing and departure rights in Ireland for transatlantic services, Imperial Airways had the same rights in Newfoundland and Cunard held their North American agency.

Nevertheless on 13 November 1935 Sir Percy Bates wrote to Sir Eric Geddes '. . . the alternative idea of an interest in your present company with its world-wide extent, as I feared, did not appeal to my colleagues. They all thought that it was too much "off our beat". A better plan would be the agency for the new company on the other side of the Atlantic.'[127] In pursuit of this latter idea, he continued, 'I think this would provide the direct association between Atlantic air and sea which we all think is desirable and also tend to counterbalance any purely extraneous influence in the new company almost as well as a direct interest in it.' Nothing came of this idea and for a time Sir Percy found all progress barred because of political necessity. The net result was that Sir Percy and his fellow directors temporarily lost both initiative and interest in transatlantic air travel; so much so that when on 21 June 1937 they were approached by Panmore Gordon and Co. offering to sell shares in Imperial Airways, the approach was not received with any great enthusiasm.[128] This offer of shares had been made by Imperial Airways as a means of raising funds for the rebuilding of their fleet. The shares were offered on underwriting terms to Cunard White Star, Orient, P. and O. and Royal Mail shipping companies. The Cunard White Star board did not accept and in reply Sir Percy Bates underlined the Company's position by stating that he did not see what good 'shares in Imperial Airways could be to Cunard White Star' adding with some emphasis that 'they needed their money.'[129]

So ended the first phase of Cunard's endeavour to obtain an interest in prospective transatlantic air travel. The second phase began on 11 November 1938 with a statement from Sir Kingsley Wood, Secretary of State for Air. This statement concerned the Government's decision to bring in legislation to effect an association between Imperial Airways and British Airways.[130] A public corporation was to be set up to acquire the undertakings of the two companies. Thus was created the British Overseas Airways Corporation. Sir John Reith, first Chairman of B.O.A.C., on taking stock of the situation in March 1939 came to the conclusion that amid all the moves and counter moves preceding the formation of B.O.A.C. Cunard White Star might have received unfair treatment.[131] To a direct enquiry on this point Sir Percy Bates replied, 'For whatever happened, I think the Treasury, in the person of my good friend and former schoolfellow, Warren Fisher, were a good

Advent of War and Survival 1935–45 273

deal more responsible than Geddes. Warren, who took and, indeed, still takes, the liveliest interest in our affairs desired that this Company some way or other should be in this transatlantic flying business; and as Chairman of the Air Development Committee, was naturally in a position of some influence. That, in the end, he was obliged to approve an arrangement which excluded us, did not in the least affect my relations with him or with Geddes, in spite of the fact that the arrangement was worked without consulting us.'[132] So far, so good; but with hindsight, it is difficult to understand why so prescient a man as Sir Percy Bates should have concluded his remarks to Sir John Reith with the reiteration that he regarded transatlantic air service 'as supplemental to our shipping service, not as competitive'.

There the matter rested until 5 December 1941, when Sir Thomas Brocklebank prepared a memorandum on post-war aviation policy and the likely effect of this policy on Cunard White Star's position as a transatlantic carrier. Briefly, his view was that it would probably be the desire of the Government after the war had ended, to resuscitate some form of imperial air service. His idea was that two separate companies should be formed, one by the Government for letter and parcel mail and the other owned by shipping companies for the carriage of passengers. Under such an arrangement the steamship companies would book passengers on a commission basis for an operating company under the management of experts in aviation.[133] This scheme was freely discussed and on 16 January 1942 Lord Essendon wrote to Sir Percy Bates stating that a deputation from the general council of British shipping had met the Minister of War Transport on the preceding day and that, among other questions, aviation was discussed.[134] At a meeting of the British Liner Committee held earlier in the day, Lord Essendon, as Chairman, had suggested that representatives of interested shipping companies should meet to consider the means whereby passenger lines might protect their trade against the possibility of competition from airlines. In fact, a government committee was already sitting to consider civil aviation and Lord Essendon thought it was important that the views of the shipping industry should be put to the Government for consideration.[135] In this context and primarily because of their involvement in previous negotiations, the interests of Cunard White Star were outstanding. Sir Percy Bates was, however, not hopeful that any effective action could be taken without more precise information about the relative strength of their anticipated competition. He wrote to New York in an endeavour to obtain facts about the costs of American construction 'which I could apply to the U.S. Maritime Commission Report of 1937 (entitled) Aircraft and the Merchant Marine...' 'What I am concerned to see', he concluded, 'is whether the economic advantage, i.e. the ability to compete with the air on British shipbuilding costs, versus American 'planes (which we would see in the U.S. Maritime Commission Report of 1937) is still in existence today.'[136]

The U.S. Report, to which Sir Percy referred, was a thirty-five-page document analysing the comparative costs of flying boats and super liners of the *Queen Mary* type. Among a variety of conclusions the view was expressed in this report that 'it would appear, therefore, that these services (one day to Europe by airplane and $2\frac{1}{2}$ days by dirigible) may in the near future be operated at a cost and with a fare equal to, or possibly less than, that of a super liner.'[137] It seemed to be obvious that fast airplane services with ample capacity for a large part of the passenger, mail and express traffic would compete seriously with super liners. There was a distinct possibility that such liners might lose their appeal and their justification as sources of investment. Sir Percy Bates and his fellow directors were not convinced by this argument and at the ordinary general meeting on 29 April 1942 he stated, 'just as with ships, so the war will end on a rising curve of production. True, the bombers will not make very good passenger 'planes for the Atlantic, but the development of production will enable good passenger 'planes to be produced and probably fairly rapidly. There will also be many thousands of men accustomed to flying 'planes and to their navigation.' The inference was that competition from the air would be a serious factor and that Cunard would need to enter the new element in one way or another, 'even though given a fair field the sea can probably hold its own.' It was recognised, however, that such a situation might be changed radically if air traffic were to be subsidised.

On 13 February 1942 a deputation of shipowners waited upon the Minister of War Transport. A report of this meeting and a memorandum drawn up by Mr J. C. Geddes was submitted to the Cunard White Star Board on 18 March. Up to that time there had been little development in the matter of future air transport;

though on 6 March 1942, the New York Office had replied to Sir Percy Bates's enquiry that 'for the most part, experts who should be trusted maintained that they could not even guess at the probable costs of such 'plane services'.[138] The whole question was, in fact, obscured by the overshadowing of war conditions and difficulties inherent in the calculation of future levels of wages and prices. Other inhibiting factors included the uncertainty of securing priorities on vital materials for construction and that production was controlled in the interests of the war effort. There were, therefore, degrees of scepticism shown at the accuracy of the figures in the Maritime Commission's Report of 1937. As far as Cunard was concerned, there seemed to be little purpose in pursuing the somewhat intangible course of negotiation.

Nevertheless, on 22 June 1942 Sir Percy Bates wrote to Sir Richard Hopkins (recently appointed Permanent Secretary to the Treasury) stating '. . . we are giving quite a bit of thought to the air and I expect that when the Cunard White Star accounts are settled next month, an amount of some dimension may be reserved with at least one eye on the air element . . . Can you give me any guidance as to how our entry – our inevitable entry as I think – into this new element may best be made?'[139] Sir Richard referred Sir Percy to Sir Alan Barlow and a meeting was arranged by the latter on 10 July at the Treasury. Nothing of a concrete nature emerged from this interview.

The next move was made in January 1943 when Cunard White Star approached the Director General of Civil Aviation indicating an intention of establishing and operating air services for the transport of passengers and goods, the intention being naturally dependent on circumstances and upon the granting of a licence.[140] To this the Director General replied on 17 February 1943 stating that until he himself knew what conditions would be attached to civil flying in a post-war world, he was in no position to give advice. However, the matter was not allowed to rest. On 25 February 1943 Sir Percy Bates and Sir Thomas Brocklebank called on Lord Catto and Sir Wilfred Eady to discuss the question of the disposal of the Oceanic Steam Navigation Co.'s shares in Cunard White Star Ltd. It was suggested that the Treasury should offer a substantial line of Cunard White Star shares to Pan American Airways with the idea of a reciprocal proportion passed on to Cunard.[141] Nothing, however, came of this proposal apart from the obvious intimation that the Cunard board was still pressing for an interest in air traffic.

In fact this pressure was maintained. On 19 May 1943 a further letter was sent to the Director of Civil Aviation asking whether he could provide the Company with answers to specific questions prepared by the Cunard board in connection with any applications they might make to the U.S. Civil Aeronautics Board for permission to offer transatlantic services from the United States.[142] The reply to this request was not encouraging. It was stated that, in view of the existing agreements with the governments of the U.S.A., Canada, Eire and Newfoundland relating to the formation of an operating company for British Transatlantic Air Service, 'H.M. Government are not in a position to support an application by Cunard White Star Ltd to the U.S. Government for a permit to operate an air service across the Atlantic'.[143] The implications of such phraseology ought to have been clear but on 30 September 1943 Cunard White Star and other members of the Atlantic Conference met the chairman and officials of B.O.A.C. in London. The meeting was called to discuss problems likely to arise in the direction and promotion of transatlantic passenger traffic after the war. In this context the prospective development of air services was of major importance. The focal point of the discussion concerned the relationship of fares between air and surface travel. Though no definite conclusions could be reached, both sides were of the opinion that until Government policy was made explicit no agreement was possible. In the prevailing circumstances progress could only be achieved by close co-operation between the companies and B.O.A.C., and to this end further meetings were arranged.[144]

On 1 October 1943 a meeting of the general council of British shipping was held to examine the question of aviation and a document which had been prepared by the council was considered.[145] Its contents classified the interests of different groups on the council who had indicated that they would have future interests in air transportation. It was decided to leave each group to carry the matter forward in its own way. As a first step the Atlantic group was left to the Atlantic conference lines, and the meeting was told about the discussions which these lines had conducted with B.O.A.C. on the previous day. Thus any immediate development on air transport across the Atlantic would be the first concern of the conference and it was agreed that no further communication on the Atlantic situation would be sent from the general council to the Government. On 19 November 1943 a meeting of the British liner trades of the Atlantic conference was held in London to exchange views regarding recent developments in connection with North Atlantic air traffic and other matters. It was decided, however, to postpone further discussion until the next meeting of the conference when it was anticipated that more information would be available on the attitude of various governments to the question of civil aviation. Nothing more was done, however, until January 1944. On 19 January Lord Beaverbrook (then Lord Privy Seal) made a statement in the House of Lords to the effect that B.O.A.C. had no monopoly except that of a subsidy and that there was nothing in its charter to prevent shipping companies from launching airlines without subsidy.[146] Though there was no precise indication of future Government policy the implications of Lord Beaverbrook's pronouncement were that Government thinking was beginning to crystallise and that, in consequence, there might be a more favourable attitude towards the claims of certain shipping companies.

Accordingly, on 15 March 1944, it was reported to the Cunard board that an order had been received confirming alterations in the Company's memorandum of association permitting the operation of air services, the resolution designed to give effect to this having been passed at an Extraordinary General Meeting on 27 September 1943.[147] It had not been necessary to take such action on behalf of Cunard White Star Ltd because provision for the exercise of these rights had been made in 1934 when the Company's articles were agreed by the Treasury and the Cunard Company. Despite the fact that the Government had been unable or unwilling to make a clear statement of policy, there is evidence that the Cunard White Star board held the view that the Company would be given some limited interest in a future arrangement to operate transatlantic air services.[148] On 27 March 1944 Sir Percy Bates circulated his views on post-war air policy to the directors. In his own terminology these views constituted a 'provocative creed'. They included *inter alia* the following points: Cunard White Star would prefer a flying partner rather than a 'fly over its own signature'; 'the air' stated Sir Percy 'will make its own passenger traffic without any deduction from the sea. Quite likely the air passenger traffic will increase the sea traffic'; the production end of the aircraft industry was not technically in a position to provide suitable airplanes for direct flight; when it was possible to produce satisfactory airplanes for such a service 'the passenger traffic will be profitable, not needing subsidies'.[149] These views were reiterated in his statement to stockholders at the ordinary general meeting held on 25 April 1945.

It would be tedious in this present context to enter into a detailed account of the various discussions and frustrations which continued as ingredients of the negotiations during the latter part of 1944. It is sufficient to add that, on 16 February 1945, the Atlantic lines (Cunard White Star, Canadian Pacific Steamships and Anchor) had a meeting in London with Viscount Swinton, Minister of Civil Aviation.[150] At this meeting it was made clear that the Government had decided that B.O.A.C. should be the British 'chosen instrument' as far as U.S.A. and Canada were concerned, though Canada was to have its own company operating the Canadian route. Against this background it was stated that if the Atlantic shipping lines wished to participate they might do so by securing a limited interest in B.O.A.C.'s Atlantic service. At the suggestion of Lord Swinton the discussions were held with Lord Knollys, Chairman of B.O.A.C. and, in March 1945 Mr Lister, Cunard's general manager, entered into direct negotiation with him on behalf of Cunard White Star.[151] From these meetings the impression was gained that the likely share of the capital holding by steamship companies in B.O.A.C. would not be more than 25 per cent, and of this Cunard might be offered 5 to $7\frac{1}{2}$ per cent. Lord Knollys was informed that Cunard White Star would be prepared to conclude with B.O.A.C. details of an agency agreement for the booking of passengers. The whole plan as outlined by Lord Swinton was subsequently issued as a Government White Paper. This publication was in fact the highwater mark of tedious and often frustrating negotiations which had gone on for more than ten years.

In 1945 a Labour Government was returned to power with Mr Clement Attlee as Prime Minister. His Cabinet colleagues were pledged, among other far-reaching proposals, to a policy of nationalisation of essential productive and service industries. Among the latter was included Civil Aviation. On 19 September 1945, therefore, it was reported that the change in government had held up further discussions between the shipping companies and B.O.A.C. both in the United Kingdom and in America.[152] For two months a state of uncertainty about the Government's air policy obstructed all attempts to make a conclusive agreement, but in December, contrary to previous advices, the Government announced that air transport in the United Kingdom was to be operated as a public service and placed under national ownership and control. This policy precluded Cunard White Star from taking any shareholding interest in B.O.A.C.

This decision was a bitter disappointment to the Cunard directorate and in particular to Sir Percy Bates, who had for long struggled against odds to attain for Cunard a share in a potentially dangerous competitive element. In view of what later transpired perhaps one should leave the last word on this story to Sir Percy himself: 'I do not know whether the air has a mistrust of the sea or of itself', he said on 3 April 1946, 'but H.M. Government has decided that there shall be no financial link between the two. I think that the decision is open to criticism, but I do not wish to press the point . . . However, no decision by any Government or any collection of governments can alter the fact that air and sea are but two parts of one whole, namely, transport across the ocean; and it would be incredible to imagine that the line of demarcation can be drawn with a fine pointed nib.' He concluded (with an obvious trace of bitterness) 'after being invited to participate, shipping companies are now no longer wanted. Well, speaking for our group, I accept that decision, yet I still believe that the two methods of transportation are complementary rather than competitive.'[153]

V THE DEATH OF SIR PERCY BATES AND THE EFFECTIVENESS OF MANAGEMENT IN PEACE AND WAR

The years of peace and war from 1935 to 1945 were fraught with danger and with difficulty for the Cunard organisation as a whole. The various strengths and weaknesses in the Company's position have, as far as possible, been demonstrated. These years undoubtedly saw a peak of achievement by the Cunard Company and represent the culmination of the work of one of its most distinguished managers and chairmen. When Sir Percy Bates died on 16 October 1946 there was a coincidental break with previous ideas and traditional spheres of responsibility. There had, perforce, to be a redefinition of policy to cope with the emergent problems of a post-war world. Though the traditions of more than one hundred years of service were to continue during the remaining twenty-five years of the Company's existence as a parent firm, the ideas, once so basic to shipping, had to give way before the insistent pressures of new forms of competition. Such changes were in fact a prerequisite of survival.

How can one summarise the effectiveness of management during the years of peace and war? In the first place, evidence suggests that the decision to build *Queen Mary* and *Queen Elizabeth* was financially sound; for in the two years of operation before war broke out in 1939, *Queen Mary* was a profit-making ship. In the second place, this period was a time of trial in which the financial stability of the Company was at stake. In 1934 no one could make an accurate forecast of the financial consequences of the Cunard White Star merger; the more so perhaps, because it was not possible to judge the extent or direction of fluctuations in world trade. Nevertheless by 1939 there were signs that management had made effective decisions in the interests of a more profitable utilisation of resources. Old and uneconomic ships had been sold, new and more dynamic policies had been introduced to increase revenue, costs had been stabilised and a depreciation formula had been put into operation. In other words the Company had met and overcome many of the problems which the merger had thrown up. The second test came with the outbreak of war, and we have seen something of the great contribution which the Company made to the war effort. The years of peace were those in which the highest degrees of skill and efficiency were demanded in the overall operation of Cunard's interests; the years of war were those in which the Company was called upon to serve the interests of the nation as a whole. It is not easy to cast a final balance of the dislocating effects of six years of war. It is true that, in purely financial terms, Cunard and her subsidiaries had been given the opportunity of freeing themselves from an accumulated burden of debt; but the changes brought about by war had undermined the very foundations on which Cunard's former strength had been built. The Company, therefore, entered a post-war world beset with difficulties beyond the range of previous experience.

Among these difficulties was the obvious threat of competition from air transport. This had been foreseen by Sir Percy Bates as early as 1934. He did everything possible by means of negotiation to bring Cunard into the new element; that he subsequently failed

Advent of War and Survival 1935–45

was due to no lack of initiative on his part but to a change in government policy. He did not, however, grasp the full implications of potential competition from transatlantic air services, believing to the last that air travel and sea transport were complementary. His successors were therefore left to face and cope with a situation which, in competitive terms, virtually destroyed the concept of the ocean liner as Sir Percy Bates understood it.

One can only judge the ideas, the ability and the actions of a man against the background of the times in which he lived and worked. Of the many famous men whose probity and business instincts carried Cunard successfully through the first hundred years of its history, perhaps Charles MacIver was most closely akin to Sir Percy Bates in character, outlook and achievement. Both were stern disciplinarians, both aloof in demeanour and both had the strength of purpose to expand and use resources in the future interests of their Company. They were equally alive to the dangers of competition and were active in creating the means for its alleviation; MacIver by establishing the principles of the first steamship agreement, Bates in adding to the refinements of a conference system. The essence of their success stemmed from their belief in freedom of enterprise. In short, the long history of Cunard was activated by the guiding spirit of such men and the inspiration which others drew from their ideas no less than in the management of the ships which they controlled and the services which these ships provided.

10
Cunard and the North Atlantic 1946–73

I THE CHANGE-OVER FROM WAR TO PEACE

In purely historical terms this volume should end with the death of Sir Percy Bates in 1946. There was obviously a line of division between his administration of the Company's affairs and that pursued by his successors. There was also the need to make the Company an efficient instrument in the rapidly changing environment of a postwar world; for Cunard, as never before, had to re-establish normal peacetime operations under abnormal conditions and subject to influences beyond traditional forms of control. History, however, cannot be put into a chronological strait jacket. Even at the peak of Cunard's achievements during the war, the processes of change were such that the future course of the Company's history was in one sense a matter of predetermination. In the last twenty years of the Company's history as a parent firm, the relative decline in economic strength was beset by uncontrollable external pressures and overshadowed by the struggle to make passenger ships profitable in operation. For the first time in its history the Company was in a position of having to fight a losing battle in an endeavour to meet and overcome forces alien to the good management of shipping and its widespread interests. It is not easy to obtain a perspective of these events, partly because the magnitude of source material does not lend itself easily to concise terms of analysis and partly because the nearness of events involves personalities. It is proposed, therefore, to add this chapter as a postscript to a story which might properly have been ended in 1946, with the hope that sufficient information may be given in outline to account for the struggle after 1957 to keep Cunard alive.

The obvious necessity, once the war had ended, was to obtain the release of ships from government control and re-employ them as revenue earners in normal peacetime commercial service. As a

Cunard and the North Atlantic 1946–73

means to this end, the United Maritime Authority was constituted to provide the shipping required for the transport of military and civil cargoes for a period of six months after the end of the war and to arrange for the return of ships no longer required for this purpose back to the country of registration. The release of tonnage from control (except for a measure of direction through licences) began on 2 March 1946. *Queen Elizabeth* was released in March 1946, followed by *Mauretania* on 2 September and *Queen Mary* on 27 September. All other ships in the Cunard fleet were under registration during the remainder of that year.

As ships were made available for normal peacetime requirements, considerable expenditure was involved in their conditioning and re-equipment. A considerable proportion of such costs was borne by the Government, but the Company had to provide a margin which, in aggregate, was a heavy burden to cover. The estimated charges for the reconditioning of *Queen Elizabeth, Queen Mary, Mauretania* and *Britannic* were £7,600,000; of this sum, the Company had to bear £2,250,000 representing the amount required for improvements and work on the Company's account. In addition, it was estimated that about £25 million was required for new ships to replace those lost during the war by Cunard and associated companies. All this anticipated expenditure, apart from overhauls, services and the purchase of tonnage, meant that the total outlay on maintaining and renewing the various fleets of the group amounted to £31,500,000.

One of the most serious problems facing Cunard's directors after the war was that of sharply rising building costs. Mr F. A. Bates, who had succeeded his brother as chairman, emphasised the gravity of the situation in a forceful example. He took the case of a certain cargo liner of 10,500 tons dead weight, built in 1925 and still in service in 1948; this ship had cost £160,000. To replace that ship in 1948 would cost some £625,000, of which £100,000 would represent improved specification, necessarily included to meet increased competition. Similarly, in the case of a passenger ship, such as one of the Queens, the value of which for the purpose of insurance in 1948 stood at between £5 and £6 million, would require about £15 million for replacement. 'When the cost of replacing an old ship has become three and four times the original', stated Bates, 'something more than the statutory allowance for depreciation before taxation is required. This can only come from any profits the Company may be able to make. These, after taxation at 10s in the pound, may be quite insufficient to replace the fleet, however much might be ploughed back into reserves.'[1]

How then did Cunard attempt to meet this very difficult problem of replacement? In the immediate post-war period, the Company had endeavoured to meet new commitments by chartering and by purchasing tonnage. After 1946, however, it was possible to implement a longer-term building programme. This involved the building of three cargo liners *Asia*, *Arabia* and *Assyria*, all of some 8,700 tons gross equipped with ample refrigerated space and powered by double reduction geared turbines. This number of ships was later increased to five with the purchase from Silver Line Ltd of *Alsatia* (ex *Silverplane*) and *Andria* (ex *Silverbriar*). *Media* (1947) and her sister ship *Parthia* (1948) of some 13,300 tons gross were dual-purpose ships each having accommodation for 250 first class passengers and hold space for 7000 tons cargo. Finally, *Caronia*, of some 34,000 tons gross, a passenger ship of *Mauretania* class, was put into service in 1948. It was perhaps unfortunate that *Caronia*, being equipped mainly for cruising, had provision for first and cabin classes only. She had no cargo capacity and although equipped with a swimming pool and laundry her passenger accommodation was not air-conditioned. She was labour-intensive – needing a crew of 700 to look after 500 passengers! With hindsight it is possible to state that her life could have been prolonged had she been equipped to carry first class and tourist passengers.[2] Parallel with this building programme were those concerned with the supply of new tonnage to the associated companies; so that by 1948 the services of the Cunard group as a whole had been brought, in some respects, within measurable distance of recovery to pre-war schedules. As a further impetus to Cunard's growing strength the remainder of the passenger ships under requisition by the Government were released during the course of the year and brought into commercial employment. In round terms, the ships of the group had, in 1948, travelled over 4 million miles, and had carried 2,750,000 tons of cargo and over 300,000 passengers.

There was, however, another aspect in the replacement of tonnage and a return to normal commercial conditions. This concerned not only the quality of management but the ideas which such management formulated and required to be implemented. In a strict sense, the Chairman, during these years, assumed a dominant position and consequently must bear responsibility for all major decisions of policy. It was obvious that, with travel having been restricted during the war years, there would be a large pent-up demand for passages across the Atlantic. Those shipping companies capable of meeting such demands would undoubtedly reap rich rewards. Once this demand had been met, however, there would be a gradual return to normal competitive conditions embodying a wide range of choice to the intending traveller. In the immediate post-war world the bookings for British and European travellers had to be restricted to businessmen; it was from America that the bulk of the passengers came. This in itself posed a serious problem involving the construction of new ships. American travellers had now become accustomed to, and expected, refinements in accommodation. Whereas in pre-war days first class travel had combined good food and excellent service, in the post-war world emphasis was laid upon better toilet facilities (including bathrooms and showers attached to cabins) and air conditioning. The incorporation of such facilities would, henceforth, determine the success of a first-class passenger ship.

Apart from first class specification, however, there was urgent need to meet an anticipated demand for tourist travel, and this in turn required improvement in both accommodation and cuisine together with the ancilliary requirements of service. The problem thus posed involved the building of a ship which could cater for these varying types of demand and, at the same time, be economical in operation. Against this background of requirements Cunard was ill equipped to provide adequate services. While the Cunard board felt confident that they could secure a reasonable amount of the express traffic with their two Queens, and possibly some of the intermediate traffic with *Mauretania* and *Britannic*, they had to consider shipbuilding plans involving changes in design for the New York trade and Canada. They also had to consider how best they could retain their widespread cargo interests. Of the remaining passenger ships, *Aquitania* had been kept in operation longer than anticipated, and *Georgic*, still showing signs of war damage, was capable of carrying only students or emigrants. *Ascania* and the three 600-ft ships, *Scythia*, *Samaria* and *Franconia*, were all over twenty years old with but a limited life ahead of them. Cunard had, therefore, only four ships capable of catering for the demands of post-war passengers.

In 1945 Sir Percy Bates and the general manager had discussions in New York regarding the type of further passenger tonnage to be built for the Company's business. Following their report to the board, the opinion was generally expressed that, while Atlantic traffic must be the principal objective of the Company, it was unwise (unless building for the express service) to build ships which could not easily be cruised, as it was thought that cruising had not only become a permanent habit but would increase in the future. They accordingly decided that any new passenger ships should be smaller but not slower than *Mauretania* with the number of classes reduced to two and incorporating such special cruising features as were not incompatible with successful operation on the North Atlantic.

These were sound guide-lines for future shipbuilding policy. Unfortunately, however, Sir Percy Bates died in 1946 and, with the removal of his strong hand, shipbuilding policy became subject to less far-seeing considerations. The immediate result of the Board's previous decisions was the laying-down of *Caronia* which, as we have seen, was labour-intensive and consequently not particularly economical in operation. It was also unfortunate that only one pre-war Canadian ship, *Ascania*, was available for service. This route had to be supplemented by the 600-ft ships which proved to be quite unsuitable for the purpose as they had to be berthed at Quebec instead of Montreal. This restricted their competitiveness, particularly as their cargo space was largely unused. The board had, therefore, to decide how best to implement the Canadian service and consider whether the same building policy should apply to the Canadian as to the New York service. It is arguable that the decisions of the successive chairmen during the 1950s were at variance with the plans formulated by Sir Percy Bates. They were, at times, at variance with the expressed views of technical and administrative staffs and this may well have contributed to the difficulties facing the Company during the latter part of the 1950s.

With the launching of *Assyria* on 19 January 1950, the Company's immediate post-war shipbuilding programme was completed. Within the difficult circumstances of the time, the decisions taken may be said to have achieved only relative and limited degrees of success. The fleet had certainly been given some new ships, while old and uneconomic liners had been sold. In this latter category, *Aquitania*, after some thirty-five years of service, ended her career on the Canadian route and was withdrawn in 1949. Thus by 1951 the Company had carried out both a full-scale programme of renovation and new building which, in the short run, eased the pressure on the services from Liverpool and Southampton but was not easily adaptable to a widening scope of future demand. This was not all. The Port Line was equally active, adding thirteen new refrigerated ships of the latest type to their Australian and New Zealand services; while Brocklebanks added ten new ships to their fleet serving India, Pakistan and Ceylon. Set against the background of restriction and financial difficulty arising from the economic circumstances of the time, the injection of this new tonnage with such an order of magnitude was no mean achievement. It remained a matter of concern that a certain lack of foresight had governed the employment of scarce resources in the passenger ships.

During the years from 1946 to 1956 there were three principal factors inhibiting the outlay of resources on a long-term shipbuilding programme. The first, which has already been mentioned, was the high replacement cost, the second was the devaluation of sterling in 1949 and the third was a direct result of new tax procedures in the computation of depreciation allowances. The operation of these factors coupled with a rapid rise in service and handling charges undoubtedly led to a drain of capital resources despite relatively favourable trading conditions. As a result the Company had to put expedients into effect both to increase resources and to achieve economies at all levels within the organisation. So great were the pressures, however, that Cunard found it virtually impossible to maintain financial strength in face of a growing depletion of resources. For the first time in its history, therefore, the Company found itself in the grip of the law of diminishing returns.

The immediate effect of the devaluation of sterling in 1949 had made it necessary to revise sterling and other soft currency passenger rates, while it also increased materially the cost of dollar disbursements. The first class minimum fare on *Queen Elizabeth*, for example, was raised from £91 to £130 10s, cabin class was raised from £56 to £80 10s, and tourist class from £41 to £59. Freight rates were not increased. Furthermore the restriction imposed on the country's dollar purchases in the U.S.A. and Canada temporarily reduced the flow of eastbound cargoes. As a counterbalance to this, however, there was some improvement in the volume of cargoes westbound. There were, nevertheless, more fundamental effects of devaluation on Cunard's long-term economic expectations. The consequences and the ultimate fears for the future stability of the Company were recurrent themes in successive chairmen's reports from 1950 to 1956.

In his statement to stockholders on 23 May 1951 Mr F. A. Bates was explicit. 'It is clear', he said, 'that devaluation has introduced a new factor, which greatly affects the replacement future. The directors continue to make additional reserves to supplement the depreciation, but the tax computation has not yet been revised to meet the new replacement factors. The Company has to deal with the twin-ills of multiplied replacement costs and inflationary taxation alike nationally imposed.'[3] By way of qualification it is relevant to add that these views were those of the banker rather than the shipowner. They did not take into account the nature of Cunard's trade. In the first place seventy per cent of the Company's passenger business emanated from North America. Dollar disbursements were met out of earnings and the resultant dollar remittances provided a useful premium when converted to sterling. In the second place, dollar rates remained unchanged and continued to be competitive. Finally, the increase in sterling rates had a relatively less important effect since travel was largely restricted to businessmen and immigration. Furthermore devaluation had two beneficial effects; it led to an increase in the volume of westbound freights and provided an incentive for travel to Europe. The difference in emphasis between the Chairman's assessment of the situation and the facts may well explain certain obvious mistakes in the Company's shipbuilding programme after 1950.

It is against a somewhat confused background that a singular change in the Company's history took place on 31 December 1949. As from that date the whole of Cunard White Star's fleet was transferred to the parent Company with contingent liabilities. We shall endeavour to examine the reasons for this change in the following section of this chapter, it is necessary here only to mark the change and place that change within the context of increasing financial difficulty. By May 1951 the longer-term effects of devaluation were capable of more accurate measurement. In particular this was so in assessing the depletion of purchasing power of the reserves set aside over a period of more than twenty years to replace the older ships. 'It will be noted', added the Chairman, 'that on this occasion, the word "profit" becomes "surplus" in the relevant items of the accounts, thus expressing the present uncertainty in the replacement problem.'[4] The depreciation allowance of £2,512,776 was little better than a notional figure as it was based on the original (and consequently unrealistic) first cost. In fact this notional sum related to ships in Cunard's fleet whose replacement cost stood at an estimated £120 million. In short devaluation coupled with a heavy incidence of taxation (both income tax and profits tax) were consuming large sums in cash which the Company had to find from net voyage receipts. At the same time, the computations on which the tax figures were based had little or no regard to the current cost of renewing the ships, so that competitive strength was reduced to the detriment of future earning capacity. Thus, the argument which centred upon the discrepancy between historic and current costs in the assessment of profit for taxation purposes assumed, by implication, a threat to the future of shipping companies such as Cunard.

The essence of this threat was made clear in an analysis of figures for the five years from 1949 to 1953. Out of consolidated profits for Cunard and associated companies of £47,107,000, taxation commitments accounted for £19,125,000; dividends for £3,290,000; £12,815,000 for 'normal' depreciation and £11,877,000 placed to reserve to meet the extra cost of building.[5] These figures represented the outcome of the Cunard board's policy under conditions of acute pressure. It had only been possible to replace tonnage at as slow a rate as was consistent with the bare maintenance of the Company's trade and goodwill. In view of the fact that ships cost about four times as much as those built before the war, the apparent depletion of Cunard's resources had confined the board to setting aside an annual sum which, added to normal depreciation, allowed replacement at only twice the pre-war cost. This, in terms of safeguarding the future position of the Company, was less than adequate, but it was the utmost that could possibly be achieved within the existing limits defined by current levels of trade after paying taxation and allowing a reasonable return to stockholders. The result was that the continuous drain on the Company's resources forced the board unduly to delay the provision of new and economic tonnage.

II THE PHASING OUT OF CUNARD WHITE STAR LTD: INCREASE IN CUNARD COMPANY'S CAPITAL

The continuous need to increase the Company's command over resources in order to meet escalating liabilities led naturally to an intensive effort on the part of management to expand earning capacity. The success or failure of these endeavours will be considered later. A more direct method of augmenting resources was through an increase in the capital of Cunard and its associated companies. To become effective, however, such an operation involved the future relationship between the Cunard Steam Ship Co. Ltd and Cunard White Star Ltd. In the event, what was decided led not only to the virtual extinction of the Cunard White Star merger, but profoundly affected the future of the Cunard Steam Ship Co. Ltd.

It will be remembered that the Oceanic Steam Navigation Realisation Co. had been established to hold its proportion of the assets of Cunard White Star Ltd. A fruitful and smooth working partnership had developed within Cunard White Star Ltd between the Cunard Steam Ship Co. Ltd, the Ocean Steam Navigation Realisation Co. and certain interests of H.M. Treasury and the Government of Northern Ireland. In July 1947, however, this partnership had ended because the Realisation Co. wished to complete its work. Accordingly, an approach was made to The Cunard Steam Ship Co. Ltd to purchase the 38 per cent minority shareholding of Cunard White Star Ltd. This purchase was in fact made effective on 30 July 1947 and, as a result, the whole of Cunard White Star's capital came under the control of the Cunard Company.

When the approach was made Cunard had to be sure that, in purchasing, fair terms could be offered in order that the retirement of the Realisation Co. might take place in concord and continuing friendship. After considering all the issues, the Cunard directors laid down the principle that they would pay a price worked out on the book value of the assets in the Cunard White Star balance sheet on 31 December 1946. This amounted to a round figure of 40 s per share. At this price the retiring partners received full value for the built-up strength without inflation, while the Cunard Company retained all of what might be called the built-in strength which any parent company might need to meet future commitments. The whole transaction involved the payment of some £7,600,000 and Cunard's bankers provided unsecured loans for the total amount.

These loans, however, were reduced by the end of the year to £4,881,300, partly by payments from current resources and partly from monies received from Cunard White Star Ltd in payment for real estate assets originally acquired by the Cunard Company, primarily for the conduct of its business on both sides of the Atlantic. These assets consisted of the total share capital in 25 Broadway Corporation, New York, which owned the Cunard building there and the assignment of the freehold property of Cunard, Liverpool, and certain other properties near the docks. These assets realised over £3,200,000. It was carefully explained that at the time of the formation of Cunard White Star Ltd in 1934 this real estate would have been transferred to that company together with the ships, but for the fact that their inclusion in the deal at that time would have disturbed the agreed percentages of capital between the respective companies. The continued use of these properties by Cunard White Star Ltd was secured by tenancy agreements but, from a practical point of view, it was desirable that these buildings should be in the ownership of the operating company. Thus, when the Cunard Company purchased the minority shareholding, an opportunity was provided for effecting the change.

The precise details of the transfers of capital to the Cunard Steam Ship Co. Ltd were given in a minute of 1 August 1947. The Company received 2,279,998 shares from the Ministry of Finance for Northern Ireland, 1,274,216 shares from the Oceanic Steam Navigation Realisation Co. Ltd, and 245,784 shares from H.M. Treasury. As far as the long-standing involvement of the Northern Ireland Ministry of Finance in the financial structure of Cunard White Star Ltd was concerned (and to which reference has been made in Chapter 7) a satisfactory conclusion had been reached. The final position was that against total issues of £2,032,389 on behalf of the old Oceanic Steam Navigation Co. Ltd (trade facilities loans) the Northern Ireland exchequer had received a total of £2,660,563. Thus ended a long chapter of obligation and liability and a duty faithfully discharged. The Oceanic Steam Navigation Realisation Co. was wound up on 25 August 1947.

Following this reorganisation the Cunard Company endeavoured further to increase its command over additional resources by an augmentation of capital. On 28 April 1948 authority was given to increase the Company's capital by the creation of 6,400,000 additional ordinary shares of £1 each. In May it was resolved to offer

2,228,105 new ordinary shares in the proportion of two new shares for each complete £5 of ordinary stock held at 35 s per share, the premium of 15 s on each new share being credited (after the deduction of expenses) to the share premium account, which by 31 December stood at £1,566,000.[6] The total number of shares issued and converted to ordinary stock was 7,798,346. The proceeds of this new share issue were applied to the reduction of the unsecured bank loans which, as stated, were made to enable the Company to obtain the minority holding of Cunard White Star Ltd in 1947. As a result this particular liability was reduced from £4,881,300 to £600,000. The repayment of the final balance was made on 13 May 1949. Thus in financial terms the Cunard Steam Ship Co. Ltd had secured control of the total assets of Cunard White Star Ltd to the satisfaction of creditors and, it was hoped, to the ultimate benefit of the Company itself.

On the purely administrative side of the business the phasing out of Cunard White Star Ltd was not effected until 1949. On 21 December of that year the Chairman reported that a review had been made with the directors of Cunard White Star concerning arrangements under which the business of Cunard White Star Ltd was being carried on. In fact, the affairs of this company were being conducted under the same direction and under the same management as the Cunard Company. While there was continuing unity in the operation of ships, there was some duplication of work in the secretarial and accounting departments. This led to certain, albeit minor dis-economies which stood in need of reform – a task which could easily be put in hand, especially as Cunard White Star Ltd was now a wholly-owned subsidiary of The Cunard Steam Ship Co. Ltd. It was therefore proposed that a simplification of organisation could best be achieved by the Cunard Company reassuming direct operation of the business either in its own name or that of Cunard White Star. In the event it was resolved that the whole of the undertaking and assets of Cunard White Star Ltd should be purchased immediately, i.e. before the close of business on 31 December 1949, in consideration of payment by the Company of £10 million and the assumption by the Company of all the then present and contingent liabilities of Cunard White Star Ltd.[7] Added to this was the intention that the Cunard Company should continue the business of Cunard White Star Ltd under arrangements to be made by the General Manager with the approval of the Executive and Finance Committee and that the assets and liabilities so taken over should be included in the balance sheet as at 31 December 1949. In other words, the merger between Cunard and White Star had ceased to exist and henceforth the conduct of business was to be undertaken by The Cunard Steam Ship Co. Ltd in its own right.

III EFFECTS OF PENAL FISCAL LEGISLATION: PLANS FOR NEW QUEEN

The years from 1940 to 1955 were years of incipient boom for shipping companies. The direct threat from jet aircraft had not yet materialised but was still an ominous threat to future shipping operations. As Douglas Lobley has stated there had to be rethinking about the function of the passenger ship 'from a pattern of all-round service on a fixed route'.[8] The result was that a dual-purpose ship was developed for Cunard, not in the traditional sense of dual purpose between the carriage of passengers and cargo but in the newer sense of scheduled service during the spring and summer season and cruising during the winter months. Unfortunately, however, this policy could not be generally implemented. *Media, Parthia, Saxonia, Ivernia, Carinthia* and *Sylvania* were not capable of dual-purpose operation as they had no facilities for cruising. It was only after *Saxonia* and *Ivernia* had been reconditioned that they could be truly classified as dual-purpose carriers. After 1955, however, profitability of enterprise was bedevilled by a variety of pressures, both national and international. These included the never-ending problem of replacement against a background of rising costs and penal taxation. Far more serious, however, were the effects of bad labour relations culminating in strikes in shipbuilding yards and among seamen, dockworkers, tally clerks and boilermakers. There were also long periods of idleness among longshoremen in New York and 'go-slows' in Indian, Australian and New Zealand ports. In Europe and the Middle East there were, in 1957, incidents of war or near war which threatened conflict on a world-wide scale. The bright hopes which had characterised shipping operations in the early years of the decade disappeared in the face of heavy loss sustained through industrial action, political unrest and the growing threat of competition from the air. Nor did the events of the 1960s bring solace to the shipowners. If anything, things got worse, rising to a peak of intensity in the seamens' and dockworkers' strikes of 1966.

Against this unhappy background of disruption and unrest must be set the salient fact that in shipbuilding, no less than in other forms of manufacturing activity, rapid advances were made in technology, especially during the late 1950s. As applied to shipping, the result was that these advances led to a dispensation of the need for 'scheduled services' of ships. Thus it was that when ideas began to be formulated for the replacement of *Queen Mary* and later *Queen Elizabeth*, technological progress enabled shipbuilders and designers greatly to exceed what had been achieved in the 1920s and the late 1930s. What finally emerged as *Queen Elizabeth 2*, therefore, was completely different in concept and performance from the original Queens. In order to understand the implications of this one must set such development within the pattern of Cunard's operational needs and shipbuilding capabilities since 1954.

Unfortunately the consolidated accounts of The Cunard Steam Ship Co. Ltd and subsidiaries contain no information relating to the performance of individual members of the group. Accordingly one can only make an assessment on the basis of the financial standing of the group as a whole. Up to 1954, there is evidence that earning capacity was maintained at a reasonably high level, annual net balances being over £3 million. There was, therefore, every incentive to implement a building programme suitably modified to employ available resources. *Pavia* (1952), *Lycia* (1954) and *Phrygia* (1955), each of about 3,000 tons gross, were put into the Mediterranean service. In 1954 *Saxonia* (later renamed *Carmania*) was the first of four dual-purpose ships of about 21,000 tons gross to be added to the Canadian route. She was followed in 1955 by *Ivernia* (later renamed *Franconia*) and *Carinthia* and *Sylvania* in 1956 and 1957 respectively. Unfortunately this policy failed in its purpose. As events proved they were the wrong ships and the potential cargo and passenger traffic could not be realised with these units.

Though the cargo side of Cunard's business was considerable, the Chairman was at pains in 1957 to emphasise that the real weight of Cunard's interests lay in passenger services on the North Atlantic.[9] This was particularly so in catering for American holiday travellers to and from Europe. The new ships added somewhat to the prospects of the Company and, in anticipation of profitable employment of resources, the board planned to lay down the keel of a new ship in 1958, which when completed would replace *Britannic*. This fact in itself indicated some confusion in the minds of members of the shipbuilding committee. Neither the Liverpool service nor the *Britannic* were as important as the Southampton express service. *Queen Mary* was, at this date, twenty years old and ready for replacement. Subsequent developments led to the proposed construction of an express vessel known as Q.3. This ship was planned as an extension of the two Queens and was to be capable of carrying slightly more passengers at thirty knots on the Atlantic during the season, with winter cruising as a possible secondary function. This concept, however, was somewhat behind current thinking on the function of large ships now made possible by advances in technology. Added to this was the fact that after 1957, a year in which the Company lost £1 million in revenue because of the Hungarian and Middle Eastern crises, adequate funds could not be assured. The situation was given more precise definition by the Chairman of Cunard. 'Owing to the setback in our financial fortunes last year', he stated, 'which does not enable us to obtain the full cash relief under the investment allowance, the board has considered it prudent to postpone the reservation of the berth for this new ship.'[10] In other words the project for Q.3 had to be abandoned. This was the first intimation to the staff of Cunard that shipbuilding policy, at long last, was becoming more enlightened.

In passing it should perhaps be explained that the investment allowances, to which the Chairman referred, had been introduced by the Chancellor of the Exchequer as a palliative in the argument about depreciation allowances and replacement costs. Having been denied the means to make adequate provision for replacement during the years of plenty (so ran the argument) the Company's endeavours were frustrated by a lean period, which did not even permit the full use of the investment allowance granted by the Chancellor for the trading year 1957. These investment allowances had been introduced in the budget for 1953 at the rate of two shillings in the pound. In 1956 the allowances were increased to 40 per cent (i.e. eight shillings in the pound) but, as already stated, Cunard was not able to benefit from this concession as an aid to the building of a projected new Queen. The reason for the Company's inability to claim relief was clearly stated. In 1957 there had been a fall of over £2 million in the operating surplus.

This caused a decrease in liability for income tax of about £917,000. On the other hand, the assessment of profits tax was mainly attributable to the amount distributed in dividends, and the reduction in the relief under investment allowance from about £802,000 in 1956 to £248,600 was due to the fact that insufficient profits had been earned in 1957 to claim the full amount permitted. The balance of the unabsorbed allowance which at existing rates of taxation would have given relief of nearly £1 million had to be carried forward against the profits of future years.

In every respect 1957 marked another important turning point in Cunard's long history. Between 1950 and 1957 sea traffic across the Atlantic continued to increase but thereafter it began to decline. In that year the number of passengers crossing the North Atlantic by sea had amounted to one million; by 1965 the figure had fallen to 650,000. During this same period of eight years total crossings by air had risen from one million to four million. Whereas in 1957 the sea–air ratio had been 50 : 50, by 1965 it had become 14 : 86. In essence this was a problem with an order of magnitude almost entirely beyond the capacity of the Cunard Company to break down. The very nature of the problem posed a threat to Cunard's continued traditional role as the provider of scheduled passenger services; the means of solution involved changes in policy so radical in concept that Cunard would virtually cease to operate as Britain's premier passenger shipping line. In fairness to the Cunard staff, however, it should be stated that superintendents, heads of departments and some of the management were labouring under intense difficulty. They realised that with the units available and the time necessary to augment the express service, they would have to make the best use of resources at their disposal while considering new plans to meet the problem of a rapidly changing situation.

IV CUNARD'S PARTICIPATION IN TRANSATLANTIC AIR TRAVEL

As we have seen, the Cunard board had been aware of possible competition from air traffic since 1934. Under Sir Percy Bates's chairmanship efforts had been made, without success, to secure Cunard's interests in this new element, always with the assumption that sea and air traffic across the Atlantic would continue to be complementary. We have also seen how Sir Percy's efforts were rendered abortive. In 1959, however, the difficulties which had formerly beset Cunard's attempts to enter the transatlantic air service were removed by the acquisition of Eagle Airways Ltd and associated companies. These companies had been founded some eleven years previously, and Eagle, in particular, had developed an extensive network of scheduled services in Europe and were also operating a wide network of services in the western hemisphere. Among these services Eagle had obtained government approval for operation on the route from London to Nassau in the Bahamas and to provide for 'First, Economy and Coach Class passengers on that route' with effect from 1 October 1959.[11] In this extension the European pattern of scheduled services was linked with the route network across the Atlantic. With the acquisition of Eagle by Cunard it was hoped that the latter's offices in the United States (17), Canada (9) and Europe (23) would facilitate and augment Eagle's existing sales organisation. On the reverse side of the coin Cunard expected that by this means overheads would be reduced 'from the revenue which will accrue'.[12] At the same time Sir John Brocklebank, Chairman of Cunard, reiterated the belief that sea and air transport should rightly be regarded as complementary rather than competitive. By way of underlining this persistent belief it was stated that the Cunard group's unrivalled experience in the carriage of passengers and cargo would be of great value in the conduct of air services.[13]

Concurrently with these negotiations to acquire British Eagle, Cunard entered into discussions with B.O.A.C. and other transatlantic carriers to investigate the possibilities of air–sea cooperation whereby it would be possible for passengers to travel one way by sea and one way by air and qualify for the return ticket discount. This proposal was undoubtedly made with an eye to the prospective use of the Boeing 707 and the De Havilland Comet IV whose advent on the North Atlantic had made a measurable improvement in comfort, time and convenience to air passages. As a further extension of Cunard's interest in air transport, application was made in July 1960 to operate a North Atlantic cargo service, though it was not until 5 January 1962 that President Kennedy approved the final certification for this service. Meanwhile, difficulties had arisen concerning the establishment of Eagle's anticipated direct service to New York. On 6 December 1960 application had been made to the newly formed Air Licensing Board for permission to operate a North Atlantic passenger service. As a prerequisite to this application it had to be shown that suitable aircraft were available and that they could be supported by an efficient organisation. As evidence of good faith negotiations had been put in hand for the purchase of two Boeing aircraft, powered by Rolls-Royce Conway engines. On 21 June 1961 a licence to operate over the North Atlantic was granted.[14] B.O.A.C., however, decided to appeal against this decision and they were successful in having Eagle's licence revoked. 'It was a great disappointment', said Sir John Brocklebank, 'when this licence, the first granted under the new Civil Aviation (Licensing) Act 1960, was revoked by the Minister of Aviation on 21 November 1961. Considerable costs in the neighbourhood of £700,000 were incurred by way of procurement of the Boeing aircraft and the preparation for the operation of this service and the route development.'[15]

These costs placed a heavy burden on the trading figures for the year despite reasonable expansion on the mid-Atlantic service from London through Bermuda and Nassau to Miami; similarly, that from Bermuda to New York, despite intense competition, showed an increase in the number of passengers carried over figures for the previous year. The fact remained, however, that the revocation of the licence for direct route operation across the Atlantic from London to New York, had prevented the full implementation of the original concept of integrating the European and American networks of services. Alternative employment had to be found for the two new Boeing aircraft. The first Boeing was put on the mid-Atlantic route as it was considered that this service would provide 'a convenient source of travel for residents in the southern and western states of U.S.A., Mexico and South America'.[16] The second Boeing (which was not due for delivery until July) was to be put out for charter. Thus management had effected a partial solution of a problem which, had it been allowed to worsen, might have involved Cunard in heavy irrevocable financial loss.

The financial implications of taking Cunard into air transport were as yet, perhaps, not fully understood. Admittedly, the first year of Cunard–Eagle's operation coincided with adverse trading conditions for all aircraft companies; but the political as distinct from the economic difficulties, with which Cunard had to contend, did not augur well for the future. Expedients had to be adopted which did not always allow Cunard to make the best or the most efficient use of resources. Shortly after the inauguration of the mid-Atlantic air services, discussions with B.O.A.C. (which, as we have seen had been intermittent over a number of years) were brought to a conclusion. An agreement was reached, with effect from 24 June 1962, to form BOAC–Cunard Ltd, in which Cunard took up a 30 per cent interest. This involved Cunard in a capital outlay of £8,100,000 (subsequently increased to £8,400,000).[17] This new company acquired the two Boeing aircraft ordered by Cunard–Eagle and became responsible *inter alia* for the financial results of Cunard–Eagle's transatlantic and western hemisphere operations. Some £28 million out of an authorised £30 million for this company was quickly taken up and prospects seemed to be bright. 'While our hopes of being able to fly the North Atlantic independently have been frustrated by the licensing authorities', it was stated, 'our participation in BOAC –Cunard Ltd gives us a substantial interest in the London–New York route, provides the sea–air association, which has been our basic aspiration in our air plans, gives us an interest in a much wider spread of services than we could have hoped to achieve independently and minimises the impact of our aircraft having to be taken out of service for any particular reason.'[18] Accordingly there was some justification for the expression of satisfaction that the bringing together of the principal British carriers on the sea and in the air on the North Atlantic route at last provided a service urgently needed by the agent, the shipper and the travelling public. The one fly in the ointment was that this company had been called into being at a time when all aircraft companies were being subjected to increasing competition.

The setting up of BOAC–Cunard had no continuing policy interest in the services of Eagle Airways Ltd, apart from those across the Atlantic. An arrangement was therefore made with Mr Harold Bamberg in which he bought back control of that company with a sixty per cent share holding and changed its name to British Eagle International Air Lines Ltd.[19] At the time this transfer was negotiated Cunard gave Mr Bamberg an option to purchase the remaining 40 per cent of the shares at any time after February 1966. He exercised this right in December and bought the outstanding shares from Cunard for £72,000. This release was, in itself, not only a wise move, but was in line with the policy and philosophy of Cunard's new Chairman, Sir Basil Smallpeice. We shall endeavour to discuss the general implications underlying Sir Basil's conduct of Cunard's affairs in the final section of this chapter. For the moment we must continue with our examination of the last stages of Cunard's association with air transport before the Cunard Company was taken over by Trafalgar House Investments Ltd in 1971.

Though the operations of BOAC–Cunard Ltd were generally successful after 1962, and by 1965 were contributing some £504,000 in dividends to the revenue of the Cunard group, it had become obvious by 1966 that a very heavy capital programme would be required in the near future.[20] Such rapid technological advances had been made in both the size and performance of aircraft that heavy investment was required in order to maintain competitive strength. According to the forecasts then being made concerning the future of BOAC–Cunard Ltd, it would be necessary to invest in both 'Jumbo' jet aircraft, each with a current price of £8 million, and supersonic aircraft, at an unknown price. These facts, which could not be gainsaid, presented the Cunard board with a financial problem involving so many variables that it became necessary for a reappraisal of policy.

In his annual report to stockholders for 1966 Sir Basil Smallpeice made it clear that it would have been completely beyond Cunard's capacity to have tried to provide 30 per cent of the new capital required for BOAC–Cunard. What figures are available would tend to prove the correctness of this assertion. By 1965 it had already become obvious that Cunard's stake in air transport was likely to incur intolerable financial burdens which, when set within the context of the Cunard group's total commitments, might threaten the continued existence of The Cunard Steam Ship Co. itself. An analysis of relevant facts tended to support such a conclusion. In the period from 1960 to 1965 there had been a substantial increase in the number of jet aircraft crossing the Atlantic. During these same years Cunard's passenger ships had lost £14·1 million, while at the same time the Company had invested £8·4 million in BOAC–Cunard Ltd. The loss of £14·1 million was represented by £7·4 million for depreciation (mainly on the *Saxonia* class of ship) and the remainder on organisational costs; hence, the loss as a whole could be attributed to approximately 50 per cent on capital and 50 per cent on revenue account. Against the background of these liabilities The Cunard Steam Ship Co. itself had only been sustained by certain operational adjustments, by the sale of investments and property which realised £12·9 million and by tax recoveries of £11·8 million. Evidence also showed that despite the growth in air traffic, aircraft continued to fly half empty on average throughout the year. The corollary was that airlines would seek to fill this space by cutting fares or by reducing rates of various kinds. 'Each time there has been a major cut in air fares, there has been a further growth in air traffic which, even if it is newly-generated traffic, and not primarily a diversion from sea, in any event makes it more difficult for sea to compete with air simply as a means of transport across the Atlantic.'[21]

By the end of 1966 Cunard's cash resources, both real and anticipated, had been depleted in two ways. The seaman's strike in that year had drained away £4 million, and the postponement of the delivery date for the new Queen to November 1968 involved the prospective loss of seasonal revenue for that year from the forecast cash flow. Furthermore in view of the Cunard group's inescapable capital commitents the board had, therefore, no alternative but to realise the investment in BOAC–Cunard Ltd. Negotiations took place in August and September 1966 and resulted in the sale of that interest for £11½ million in cash. This, in Sir Basil's opinion, was a highly satisfactory figure 'seeing that it acknowledged and freed the whole of your Company's share in the accumulated profits of BOAC–Cunard Ltd which it would otherwise not have been possible to draw out'.[22]

So ended Cunard's long struggle, first to achieve and secondly to maintain an interest in air transport. Their persistent belief expressed by successive Cunard chairmen since the time of Sir Percy Bates had not been justified by the facts. In the end the scheduled service of the large jet air liners conquered the scheduled service of the passenger liner. This, however, is too facile an explanation of events. As we now know, the transatlantic air companies themselves were to experience increasing difficulties in operation and in the accumulation of adequate capital resources necessary for existence in a highly competitive market. In retrospect, therefore, it was probably a correct decision to have taken Cunard out of the air business. The capital realised by such action would, it was hoped, be put to more efficient use in the service of Cunard's traditional role, namely that of sea transport. To this end a new and more positive concept had to be devised concerning the function of the passenger ship in the jet air age.

V RATIONALISATION AND ENTRY INTO CONTAINER SERVICES: THE FINANCING OF THE NEW QUEEN: PASSENGER SHIPPING AND THE LEISURE INDUSTRY:

When Sir Basil Smallpeice became Chairman of Cunard in 1965, he and the board were faced with the difficult task of making the Company pay its way. This was no new situation for, as we have seen, there were many occasions in the long history of the Company when policies had to be evolved to meet and overcome adverse financial and trading conditions. In the past, however, the nature and scope of the problem to be solved had always been contained within the structure of the shipping industry itself. By 1965 the pressures were such that a solution could not be sought solely from that vast fund of knowledge represented by past experience in the management of ships. If Cunard were to continue to exist, a 'new' philosophy directing the allocation of resources was required together with a change in the Company's function as a provider of shipping services.

The keynote of this 'new' philosophy was struck in 1966. 'If we were to continue to regard our passenger ships as only transport vehicles for carrying people from one place to another', stated Sir Basil, 'then the outlook would indeed be grim.'[23] It was now clear that ships could no longer compete with aircraft in either speed or price; but if in terms of marketing concepts a passenger ship be no longer regarded as a means of transport, 'but even more as a floating resort in which people take a holiday and enjoy themselves (and incidentally get transportation thrown in) then the market outlook is completely changed'.[24] By so altering the function of the passenger liner, it was argued, the Company would no longer trade in a contracting market — that of surface transport of passengers in a jet air age, but rather in that of a growth industry, the leisure industry. 'This is an industry', explained Sir Basil, 'which is undergoing great expansion and in which our share will be limited only by the economics of ships and the prices we have to charge to make them profitable'.[25] In this context the new Queen would play a vital part as a revenue earner; in fact, it was anticipated that she would earn about one-third of total passenger ship revenues and this would contribute a major share of funds towards any future development of the Company. Apart from this, however, it was decided to put all existing ships on a 'break even' basis before the new Queen's delivery in 1968. Cunard was returning to the sea with a purpose and a new hope.

It is arguable whether this new policy could have been made effective had not great technological advances been made in ship construction and design since the mid 1950s. As already stated, the new Q.4 was entirely different from the two first Queens. In her evolvement designers were undoubtedly helped by the experience which had been gained from operating *Carmania* and *Franconia*. These two ships had been converted to dual-purpose carriers in 1963 and employed as new ships capable of use in the holiday cruising industry. The new Q.4 was designed as a 'resort hotel' capable of following the sun and included in her anticipated itineraries many ports that her deep-draughted predecessors were incapable of entering. Her size about 65,000 gross tons – made her one of the world's largest passenger liners; but this fact imposed little limitation on flexibility of operation. Her draught and dimensions would permit her to use the Panama Canal (and Suez before closure) with access to ports with a 'marketing' appeal. 'For all her size', as Douglas Lobley stated, 'a service speed has been achieved in a hull, little smaller in actual dimensions than the Queens, but offering superior accommodation and amenities to an equal number of passengers. Add to that one engine room instead of two, two propellers instead of four, a quarter of the engineering officers and half the fuel consumption (520 tons instead of 1100 tons) and Q.E.2 begins to reflect the claims made for her.'[26]

If any further commendation were needed of this ship's flexibility, one could point to the simple fact that, by running in parallel with the French Line's *France*, she was able to operate a weekly Atlantic service in the summer months when demand was at high peak and be maintained at full capacity during the winter months in luxury service. She was the first large British ship planned and designed to capture the cream of the North Atlantic trade in the season and the cream of the sun-seeking leisure class in the winter. In this respect she fulfilled all the criteria laid down in the revision of policy in 1961, and accentuated by Sir Basil Smallpeice in his enunciation of 1965.

When the tenders for this ship were received at the end of

November 1964, it was clear that the cost would considerably exceed the figure of £22 million, the estimate on which Cunard's financial arrangements had been based. Furthermore as the builders supplying the lowest prices and most favourable delivery dates were not prepared to tender on a fixed-price contract, the extent of the margin could have been appreciably increased. Some economies had, of necessity, to be effected. In addition the information provided by the builders in connection with their tenders demonstrated that performance in many technical fields was better than 'in our conservatism we had allowed for and here again we were able to obtain substantial financial benefits in first costs'.[27] Nevertheless, despite savings, the figure seemed too high and it became necessary to review the whole of the arrangements for financing this venture. This review and ensuing negotiations ultimately led to the placing of a contract for the ship, which was signed on 30 December 1964 with Messrs John Brown's of Clydebank. The contract price of £25,427,000 was still in excess of the cost which would have been considered reasonable. Cunard, however, counted on receiving substantial benefits from investment allowances to be utilised under the fiscal legislation then in force against the taxed profits of subsidiary companies which had been declared as dividends to the parent company in 1964. The Cunard board was therefore satisfied that the net cost of the ship, after taking into account these investment allowances, would fall within the limits which they had set themselves. The contract price, though not a fixed price, included an allowance for escalation and contingencies during the building period.

To enable these arrangements to be implemented and to secure the full investment allowance for 1964, the whole of the purchase price was paid on signing the contract. Facilities had therefore to be made available to obtain adequate cover for the implementation of this action. This cover was, in fact, underwritten by the Finance Corporation for Industry Ltd.[28] 'As you will be aware', explained the Chairman 'the Board of Trade have undertaken to provide a loan of £17.6 million on delivery of the ship, repayable over ten years, and concurrently with the arrangements concluded with F.C.I. a consortium of British clearing banks undertook to cover this part of the cost during building, their loan being repayable when the Government loan is received.'[29] In such terms the new Queen could be regarded as a commercial venture made possible by a government loan of £17·6 million and an initial tax allowance of £4 million; but by 1967 this interpretation had been overturned by besetting financial complications. Substantial escalation in the levels of nearly all costs had taken place since the signing of the contract in December 1964.[30] This posed the problem of obtaining further finance and, in September 1967, another agreement was negotiated with the Board of Trade for the provision of additional funds necessary for the completion of Q.4 and putting her into service.

This involved a new government loan of up to £24 million in place of the original £17·6 million. The new provision, however, was divided into two parts. The first part of the loan, amounting to £14 million (including £2 million for working capital) was made to a separate subsidiary company entitled Cunard Line Ltd (which had been created as a management company in 1962). This subsidiary owned the first *Queen Elizabeth*, *Carmania*, *Franconia* and in due course was to take over Q.4. As a further cover the arrangements provided that on the anticipated sale of the first *Queen Elizabeth*, £2 million of the proceeds of sale should be applied to the reduction of the working capital condition attached to this loan. The remainder, £12 million, was repayable in twelve years from the delivery of the ship in equal half-yearly instalments and was secured only on the assets Cunard Line Ltd with no right of recourse to the parent company, The Cunard Steam Ship Co. Ltd. The rate of interest on the loan to Cunard Line Ltd was 4½ per cent for the first three years, after the delivery of the ship, and thereafter at the Government lending rate or such other lower rate as might be agreed. The depreciation provisions were to be made out of the earnings of the new ship and should cover the loan redemption requirements.

The second part of the new arrangement was concerned with an unsecured loan of £10 million to the parent company. This loan was to be repayable within five years from first drawing and carried interest at the rate of 4½ per cent per annum throughout the whole period. An important aspect of the agreement between The Cunard Steam Ship Co. and the Board of Trade was that, as long as any part of it remained outstanding, the Company should not make any distribution to ordinary stockholders out of capital reserves or realised capital accretions. It was also provided that the Company should not pay any dividends to ordinary stockholders in excess of 5 per cent unless the amount of such excess was covered at least twice by the amount of trading profits for the year. It was, however, agreed that, if the Company should increase its dividend under such terms, there should be an entitlement to pay dividends at the same level in respect of any subsequent financial year, so long as the amount of the excess over 5 per cent was covered at least once by the trading profits for the year in question. Another feature of the agreement inhibited Cunard from engaging in any new trading ventures without the permission of the Board of Trade, as long as any amount of the second part of the loan remained outstanding. In other words, both the financial provisions and other injunctions imposed on the completion and bringing into service of Q.4 made fairly stringent obligations on Cunard's future freedom of action in the use of resources.[31]

The significance of events after 1965 cannot be understood unless due weight is given to the successive decisions taken since 1961 for the more profitable use of the Company's resources. These decisions resulted from a reappraisal of policy begun in October 1961. Under the active direction of Mr T. Laird, the General Manager, in consultation with a team of colleagues, administrative and other arrangements were made for the implementation of the Board's decisions. In general, the Company involved itself in a searching examination of the structure and composition of organisation, ship operating costs and passenger and cargo revenue. The enquiry into organisation led to the formation of the Cunard Line. The North Atlantic services were put under this Company from 1 August 1962. Through its operation, greater responsibility was given to senior executives of the Cunard Company, relieving the members of the Board from matters concerning the day-to-day management of the fleet. Within this framework, certain economies in the use of manpower and executive ability were achieved.

The action resulting from this reappraisal of policy can be summarised briefly. In the first place it led to a realisation and a more profitable use of certain Cunard assets. To this end the book value of the New York building was eliminated from the accounts for 1962 as a consequence of the sale by Cunard House Ltd of the shares formerly held in 25 Broadway Corporation. This latter property was valued and disposed of on a leaseback basis, the whole transaction making an increase in reserves of £3,157,000. In the second place it was concluded that, in the light of changing conditions, the Company was no longer justified in continuing to operate their older and less economic cargo ships. Such ships were not suitable for current trading patterns and, as a necessary measure of economy, five cargo liners were sold, the services in the meantime being undertaken by chartered tonnage pending the delivery of four new, smaller cargo liners. In the third place a more realistic attitude was taken in securing a higher rate of return on some of the Company's reserve investments. During 1963 the major part of the holdings in British Government securities were sold and a substantial portion of the proceeds was loaned to local authorities at a much higher rate of interest. In the fourth place, as a measure of diversification, an offer was made and accepted in 1964 for H. E. Moss and Company Tankers Ltd. This company, which henceforth became part of the Cunard group, owned three modern tankers each of approximately 19,000 tons d.w. 'which are gainfully employed and can be expected to contribute a profit to the group's operations for the coming year'.[32] In the fifth place an extension of control was sought over the handling side of the Company's business through incorporation with Cunard Stevedoring Ltd which began operations on 6 April 1964. This company undertook work in Liverpool as stevedores and master porters for vessels of the Cunard group, in addition to a limited amount of work carried out for other shipping companies. It was intended to expand the activities of this stevedoring company and 'when places for the allocation of berths in Liverpool to master porters are implemented, to apply for allocation of berths additional to those permanently appropriated to the parent company'.[33] By such means it was hoped that a new and profitable use might be opened for some part of Cunard's resources. Finally, a new company, Cunard Insurance Ltd, was created in 1963. The main object of this company was to carry a percentage of the overall marine insurance on the fleets of the group as a whole. 'It is emphasised', it was stated, 'that this is a new company but it is hoped that, in due course, a useful contribution will be made to the group profits.'[34]

This review and subsequent action resulted in a certain amount of streamlining throughout the organisation as a whole. A procedure was established where *pro rata* reductions in staff would link up with withdrawal of ships. 'This we did', stated the Chairman, 'with much regret but we have provided compensation on terms which we hope has minimised hardship.'[35] At the same time the freight and passenger sections were reorganised at head office with the integration of departments and the overhauling of the entire United Kingdom, Continental, American and Canadian organisations. Special attention was given to operating costs, the highest item of expenditure being that of crew costs. It was not possible to contain such expenditure in face of persistent and organised pressure for increasing levels of wage rates and accordingly, other forms of economy had to be instituted.

Among the more positive efforts to ensure economies was the introduction of mechanical aids. With the co-operation of the Company's auditors, Messrs Cooper Brothers, the pay-rolls of both sea and shore staffs were mechanised as well as ships' manifests, sailing lists, crew manifests and miscellaneous documents. At the same time printing facilities for the publicity and other departments were centralised in Liverpool and Southampton. By these means greater efficiency was achieved, fewer staff were required and accountancy procedures at head office were reformed. All major contracts, which were the responsibility of the management, were put under searching review and renewed at favourable discounts; all major items of expense were put under the supervision of head office and budgetary controls were instituted for the Company's managements in U.S.A., Canada and Europe. In an endeavour to lower operating costs on board ship, a department was set up to concentrate on a programme of work study. A team of cost experts travelled on board various ships over a period of years and their findings were such that many of the improvements which they suggested were incorporated into the working of *Queen Elizabeth 2*. The net result of these investigations led to reductions in catering staffs and to greater supervision of overtime costs, an item of importance on all passenger ships.

In other ways strenuous efforts were also made to reduce costs and increase revenue by a better management of the ships themselves. The two Queens normally had two dry-dock overhauls in the course of a year. The technical superintendent was persuaded, as an experiment, to omit the summer dry-docking, which normally took place in July. As a result the Company was able to secure the revenue of an additional voyage for each

Queen during the height of the season and eliminate the costs of one overhaul. The two Queens were also made more attractive and more comfortable in operation. In certain weather conditions they had always been subject to a heavy roll. As stabilisers had proved successful in *Media* and *Parthia* it was decided to fit them in the two Queens, an installation which had the effect of reducing the roll on these ships to within three degrees. In the matter of air conditioning it was not possible, because of the prohibitive cost, to equip the whole of these ships, but some limited air conditioning was fitted in *Queen Elizabeth* in the crew quarters and tourist sections. Improvements were also made to the cuisine and to the general entertainment on board ship.

Having improved the ships the next task was to sell the product. An all-out effort was therefore made to secure party business. This type of business could be made competitive with air travel if the better class tours could be extended over six weeks. Over such a time it was found that the cost of the ocean travel became roughly equivalent to the extra time spent in Europe by the air traveller. Through the Company's close association with agents in the United States, a fair amount of business was built up, particularly during the fringes of the summer season i.e. in the early spring and autumn, when it was possible to introduce excursion rates. In pursuit of more aggressive selling methods *Queen Elizabeth* was put on short cruises to Nassau and a 25-day cruise to the Mediterranean. *Queen Mary* was chartered for specific cruises to various large group organisations. Funds were made available for increasing the activity of outside sales organisations with the object of presenting the image of a holiday atmosphere on board. In other words, a great deal was done before 1965 to make the Company's services more attractive to the holiday traveller with the ultimate object of increasing revenue.

Nor was the cargo side of the Company's business forgotten. More regular voyage patterns were instituted limiting calls at outports. Old and uneconomic cargo ships were sold and, pending new tonnage, ships were chartered and put into profitable operation. When new tonnage, such as *Media* and *Parthia* became available, they proved to be immediately successful. As a result of all the above-mentioned efforts the Company's financial position became greatly improved. Though deficits continued they were reduced as the following figures show:

	1961	1962	1963	1964	1965
		(£ million)			
Passenger and freight revenue					
CUNARD LINE					
Passenger ships	24·3	22·2	22·6	23·8	24·0
Cargo ships	6·8	7·5	8·2	10·5	12·1
	31·1	29·7	30·8	34·3	36·1
Surplus (deficiency) before depreciation and taxation					
CUNARD LINE					
Passenger ships	−1·1	−1·9	−2·0	−1·6	−1·5
Cargo ships	−0·1	+0·1	+0·2	+1·3	+1·4
	−1·2	−1·8	−1·8	−0·3	−0·1

It is obvious that, all other things being equal, operation of the passenger ships responded less effectively to the measures taken than did that for the cargo ships. Nevertheless, by 1965 it had become evident that the Company, by virtue of the stringent appraisal of policy, had been brought back to a break-even point in financial terms.

Against the background of prevailing economic conditions (and remembering that Cunard was still involved in air transport) these endeavours during the years from 1961 to 1965 to increase revenue from various shipping activities were significant in more than a financial sense. That their relevance was obscured by worsening conditions after 1965, involving the Company in a grim struggle for existence, must not detract from the skill of the enterprise of management in making a radical attempt to overcome financial difficulties. Welfare benefits did accrue from this policy of retrenchment and more profitable use of resources. At least this was so to one section of Cunard's personnel, namely the pensioners. By 1965 it had become a matter of urgency to improve the pension arrangements for both sea and shore staffs. It had not been possible to make any provision for pensions out of profits since 1957, and by 1963 it had become obvious that during following years serious liabilities would be incurred if pensions were to be maintained at reasonable levels. Accordingly a sum of £1 million was transferred from a depreciation provision, which was no longer required, to enable the Company adequately to meet pension obligations. This at least was evidence if any were needed of responsibility being accepted and effectively discharged. After 1965, however, the power of the Company to meet and overcome obligations was sapped by increasingly adverse economic pressures over which there was little control. The seamen's strike of 1966, the successive dock strikes and go-slows which increased the turn-round time of ships and further devaluation of sterling all exacerbated existing difficulties. By 1970 despite the efforts of management the means of survival were no longer under Cunard's control.

In 1965 Cunard's passenger ships with a revenue of £24 million accounted for some 40 per cent of the shipping business, and the cargo liners, with a revenue of £36 million, for 60 per cent. Of the total passenger business the transatlantic services brought in 70 per cent of the revenue and cruising contributed 30 per cent. A more detailed examination of the figures, however, showed that in 1965 while the cargo ships in the Cunard, Port and Brocklebank lines earned profits of £1·6 million (together with other net income of £1·3 million), Cunard Line's passenger liners made a loss of £2·7 million. In referring to this situation Sir Basil Smallpeice posed what he considered to be the essence of the problem. 'The nub of your Company's financial problem at present, therefore, is this continuing loss on the Cunard Line's passenger ships. This situation is often attributed to the age of certain of our ships; but this is not so. In fact, the Queens, despite their age, have earned over the years, an enviable reputation for comfort and service which is standing up well against the competition from our rivals' newest ships. This loss-making situation applies to almost all passenger ships in service at present on the Atlantic and is due to the fact that, while the huge jet aircraft have substantially captured the purely transport market, passenger shipping has, generally speaking, not yet adapted itself in this sphere for survival in a jet air age.'[36] The implication was that if Cunard could stop the drain from the passenger side of the business and break even within two or three years (and subsequently do much better than that), the Company's profit and loss account could be transformed. In fairness to the previous management, however, one must emphasise that the financial problem mentioned by the Chairman had been brought to the point of control and that contingency plans were in operation for the future.

There was, however, a determination to keep the organisation of the Cunard Line abreast of rapidly changing conditions, to improve further the marketing and selling side of the business and to accentuate existing measures for cost and budgetry control. For this purpose a new management team was formed under Mr Philip Bates's leadership (including Lord Mancroft and Lady Tweedsmuir) to implement changes in policy. 'Were it not for this confidence', stated Sir Basil, 'which I and my colleagues on the group Board feel in the ability of our new team to pull Cunard Line round in a measurable period of time, we might well have to consider liquidation of the Company's passenger business and abandonment of the passenger ships.'[37]

The principles underlying the inception and implementation of future policy were designed to achieve maximisation in the use of resources. First and foremost, Cunard was a shipping company with a long and honourable tradition. Quite apart from national considerations, there was an obligation to both stockholders and staff to try to make shipping profitable. 'At the same time', ran the Chairman's argument, 'we accept that we cannot keep shipping going simply for prestige or out of sentiment.'[38] Accordingly managements of all subsidiary companies were required to aim at earning a 'proper' return on capital employed. Each major section of the Company was enjoined to become profitable on its own without subsidisation. 'Where we find that any existing asset cannot be made profitable, we shall dispose of it.'[39] In general the group board was not prepared to approve new projects involving capital expenditure, unless the return on the equity capital employed, after provision for whatever outside finance might be obtained, was of a reasonable percentage. Thus the whole emphasis of this new managerial policy throughout the group was now being placed on raising the rate of return.

The first phase of this policy involved the elimination of any section of the group's assets making a loss. In this context, the difficult decision had to be taken of retiring *Queen Mary* from service in 1967 and *Queen Elizabeth* in 1968. *Queen Mary* was sold to the City of Long Beach, California, for £1,240,000; *Queen Elizabeth*, after an abortive negotiation for her sale, was eventually disposed of in 1969 for future use as a floating university in Hong Kong harbour. Some £1·3 million of the purchase price was received before the massive hull and superstructure were totally destroyed by fire. (If Cunard needed the symbol of the phoenix to represent decline and rebirth, perhaps the sad fate of this once proud ship might be taken in lieu of such a device.) In 1968 *Carinthia* and *Sylvania* were sold for a total of £2,450,000; *Caronia* was taken out of service and sold a few months later. The essence of the argument for disposal was that all these ships had become uneconomic in operation and would cost too much to convert them to the requirements of modern cruising conditions. By 1969, therefore, Cunard Line Ltd had only three passenger ships, *Carmania*, *Franconia* and *Queen Elizabeth 2*. In scaling down the passenger fleet to this size, there were consequential economies arising from reductions in shore establishments and staff. Offices were closed in Paris, Le Havre and Dublin and there were reductions of personnel in London and Southampton. As a further extension of this process of realising assets and cutting costs, Cunard Building in Liverpool and the Port Line building in Sydney were sold for a total of £3·6 million. Thus by reducing shore organisations and bringing them into line with the scale of passenger operations, the Company rid itself of a burden 'of overhead inherited from the past'.[40] As a result of such changes the passenger side of Cunard's business, which in 1965 accounted for nearly half the Company's turnover and made a loss of about £3 million, was by 1968 contributing one-fifth of turnover 'and we hope, will lose us very little'.[41]

Apart from the three passenger ships the group owned about sixty cargo ships operating to the west coast of North America, to India and Pakistan and Australia and New Zealand. Before 1965 these cargo services contributed some 60 per cent of Cunard's annual operating revenue, but in 1966 the Port Line made a loss and there was a deficit on all cargo services of some £300,000 compared with a profit of £1·6 million in 1965. The disappearance of the Port Line's profits, however, called for a basic review of that company's operations. It was true that in common with other shipping companies bad results were brought about mainly by a reduction in outward cargoes and by the effects of a prolonged drought in Australia. Nevertheless, though Port Line had made profits over the preceding ten years the rate of return on capital employed had averaged less than 5 per cent. If improvements were to be made, it seemed logical that rationalisation would have to be put in hand, together with a fairly rapid expansion of container services. As a corrective to the above statements, however, it must not be forgotten that the Port Line had annual discussions with the governments of Australia and New Zealand concerning the level of freight rates. A high rate of profit would have led inevitably to a demand for a reduction in rates. Accordingly, every increase in rates had to be justified.

Cunard was already a member of the container consortium known as Associated Container Transportation Ltd.[42] This group consisted of Cunard, Ellerman and Port Line interested in the Australasian trades, and the Ben Line and T. and J. Harrison engaged in other trades. The prospect of Britain's entry to the Common Market made it likely that in such event, trade between the United Kingdom and Australia would decline in both directions. At the same time it was anticipated that the overseas trade of Australia and New Zealand would continue to expand and that the Port Line would be able, through its association with the Crusader Line, to secure such growth. This latter company had been formed in 1957 to carry refrigerated cargoes from New Zealand to Japan with extended services in the trade between Australia and the west coast ports of North America. The Port Line had a quarter interest in this company.

In order to avoid duplication of tonnage, therefore, a scheme for the rationalisation of services was put in hand and in 1968 Port Line sailing schedules were pooled with those of the Blue Star Line. On both the Atlantic and the Australian services active steps were taken to speed up the transformation to containers within the framework of the relevant container groups, Atlantic Container Lines Ltd and Associated Container Transportation Ltd. As a result co-ordination between the Port Line and Blue Star enabled further reductions to be made in personnel in the United Kingdom and in Australia. In addition the management of the Atlantic freight services was combined with that of the Brocklebank Line through the formation of a new organisation known as Cunard–Brocklebank. The Brocklebank company had been struggling for some years to maintain its position in the Indian and Pakistan trades. This line had not earned any return on capital employed since 1957. The inhibiting problems were deep rooted and stemmed from the growing insistence of both India and Pakistan to carry at least half of their trade in their own ships. The nature of the cargoes made it virtually impossible to introduce container services and so different remedies had to be applied to resuscitating Brocklebank's flagging fortunes. Despite the fact that half the Brocklebank fleet had been well written down, further attempts at rationalisation had to be considered. One means of alleviation presented itself in the operation of the Moss tankers which were under the direction of Brocklebank management. These tankers continued to make a steady profit and it was accordingly decided to build up and develop this unit. 'We, therefore, decided to add two more ships to the fleet and last April ordered two products-carriers of 22,500 tons each for operation on the spot market.'[43] Total capital involved was £3·3 million of which £2·6 million was found from external sources. With the gearing resulting from the buying of these ships, substantially on outside finance, it was anticipated that an increase in return on capital employed in this unit would take place from 1969 onwards.

As a result of these various measures there was, by 1968, something of a turn-round in the Cunard group's financial position and by 1969 further improvement indicated that future prospects seemed to be bright indeed. 'In view of the Company's record over the preceding eight years', stated Sir Basil Smallpeice in his report for 1969, 'it is gratifying to have made a profit of £3¼ million in 1969 on top of a profit of nearly £2¼ million in 1968.' Some part of this improvement was undoubtedly attributable to increasing receipts from passenger ships, especially those from the operation of *Queen Elizabeth 2*. The losses on these ships had been reduced (before adjustment of depreciation) from £3·5 million in 1967 to £1·4 million in 1968. In 1969 they returned a profit for the first time since 1960 of about £800,000. This, together with the profits accruing from the operation of the cargo ships (principally the Port Line ships), gave strength to the belief that Cunard had, at last, been put on a sound financial footing.[44] It should, perhaps, not be forgotten that in the apportionment of credit for this situation the efforts made between 1961 and 1965 were preparatory to, and in one sense basic to, a successful change of policy after that date. As a conclusion to this prolonged struggle, it is possible to make an assessment that by 1968, after writing down the fleets out of reserves, the total of ordinary stockholders capital and reserves was £36 million. By comparison the 1968 profit after tax and preference dividends gave a yield of 5·55 per cent. It was not a high rate of return when compared with other rates on capital employed in manufacturing industry; but the level was not very much out of line with the average returns from shipping as a whole.

It might be wise to end this history of Cunard at this point. The negotiations leading to the taking over of Cunard's passenger ships by Trafalgar House Investments Ltd form no part of our terms of reference. As a preliminary to these negotiations, however, one might add a postscript. In 1968, changes in the Company's Articles of Association included provision for the conversion of the Government share of £20 into the ordinary stock. This government share, as previously stated, was taken up in 1903 in order to secure to the Government certain special voting rights. The implication of the change in 1968 meant that the link between Cunard and the Government, so long of benefit to each side, had now been broken. In this sense, if in no other, the historic and traditional role of the Company in relation to the interests of the state had ceased to exist.

VI CUNARD AND TRAFALGAR HOUSE INVESTMENTS LTD

The acquisition of The Cunard Steam Ship Company Limited by Trafalgar House Investments Ltd in August 1971 was an event of significance in the history of shipping, not only on the North Atlantic but worldwide. To many observers, particularly those skilled in the traditional art of shipping management, the takeover presaged the extinction of the Company. Doubts were freely expressed whether an organisation with so wide a range of interests as Trafalgar House could operate shipping services profitably, especially as it was feared that the management of ships would henceforth be subsidiary to the overriding claims of other major interests within the Trafalgar House organisation. From the point of view of the historian a period of three years of management is much too short a time to attempt a precise judgement of a new direction and a new policy, but certain facts relating to Cunard's more recent history need to be stated, if only as a final postscript to the past and as an augury for the future.

Trafalgar House Investments Ltd controls some 260 subsidiary companies engaged in a wide variety of activities including property and investment, contracting, civil engineering, mining and specialist undertakings, housebuilding, hotel ownership and management, industrial and general activities. Following the acquisition of Cunard, shipping and package tour operations were added

Cunard and the North Atlantic 1946–73   317

to this wide range of interests. Of the many problems consequent upon takeover facing the new directorate, the most important were concerned with finance. First, there was the need to make a realistic valuation of Cunard's assets and to incorporate these assets as far as possible in accordance with the financial policy of the Trafalgar House group as a whole. In the second place, it was necessary to make an assessment of the capabilities and the prospective profitability of the passenger side of Cunard's business. Finally there was an incentive to make an appraisal of, and reallocate the resources of Cunard-Brocklebank, Port Line and Moss Tankers so that new direction might be given to the development of bulk cargo and container services and oil products.

In August 1971 Cunard was taken over at a cost of £26 million and acquired assets of £43 million. Trafalgar House took the precaution of commissioning an independent revaluation of the fleet and as a result these assets were written down by £4 million net. Though conducted against the background of strikes and international currency adjustments, the reorganisation of Cunard within the Trafalgar House group took place with speed and efficiency. The shipping division was organised under a separate Board with the Chairman appointed from the main Trafalgar House Board. By the end of September 1972 it was reported that the incorporation of the shipping division had been achieved with such satisfactory results that a decision had been taken to add to it the cognate interests of the hotel and leisure business. Cunard's selling organisation in New York had contributed much to the success of the passenger ships and it was envisaged that it would henceforth assist the hotel business in the U.K. and the Caribbean. In this new type of operation the passenger ships themselves would support the hotels through the operation of travel packages offering holidays which combined a period at sea and a stay at one of the hotels. Such integration involved long-term expectation of profit and required the investment of fairly substantial resources in the shipping side of the programme. Two new passenger ships, *Cunard Adventurer* and *Cunard Ambassador* (previously laid down under provision by the Cunard Board), were already in service. A further two new ships of larger size had been ordered by Trafalgar House at an approximate cost of £23 million and would be delivered for service in 1975. These new passenger ships will be named *Cunard Conquest* and *Cunard Countess*. In addition extensive alterations were made to *Queen Elizabeth 2*, improving catering and dining room facilities. The new arrangements enabled the Company to dispense with separate sittings for meals so that passengers could, henceforth, be served to suit their convenience 'as in a first-class hotel'.

To some extent this new investment and reallocation of resources in passenger ships had been made possible by an improvement in relations with the National Union of Seamen. A short time before takeover, the Cunard Board had decided to withdraw *Carmania* and *Franconia* from service because costs were outstripping revenue. Strenuous efforts, however, were made to keep one of these vessels in service. Discussions were held with the appropriate trade unions to see whether it would be possible to recommission one of the ships on a different manning basis, namely with officers, engineroom and deck crews drawn from existing staff but with an external organisation taking over the catering functions, principally kitchens and restaurants. Such an arrangement would have cut costs and would have maintained employment for a proportion of the disbanded crews. The offer, however, was declined by the unions and the two ships were sold. By the end of 1972, a better spirit of co-operation had been achieved. The principle of concessionaire crewing had been accepted and this, in turn, gave encouragement to the prospective employment of resources in the passenger trades. It was anticipated that, by such co-operation, the passenger liners might resume a role in 'what in world terms is a great growth market involving large sums of foreign exchange'.

The receipts from passenger shipping, however, accounted for considerably less than half of Cunard's revenue. The majority of shipping income was derived from the cargo services of Cunard and the associated companies of Port Line and Brocklebank Line, together with the consortia operations and the oil products carriers belonging to Cunard's subsidiary, Moss Tankers. To these services must now be added the ships of Offshore Marine (a subsidiary of Cunard), servicing oil rigs in various parts of the world. It will be remembered that in 1966 Cunard entered the container trade. This decision not only involved new concepts in ship design and management, but called for the investment of large resources in containers and ancillary equipment. In reality it meant the building of a new generation of vessels and, in order to get the economies of scale to meet this new investment, Cunard considered a consortium type of operation for the North Atlantic trade. The Company became a partner in Atlantic Container Lines Ltd (A.C.L.) with Dutch, French and Swedish interests. The roll-on/roll-off container ship offered an answer to rising costs in a labour-intensive industry as well as a better system of transportation. Trafalgar House has continued the policy, started by Cunard in 1966, of investing large blocks of capital in containerisation. With an increasing amount of capital at risk, the pressure has grown for an orderly system of tariffs and regulations within the framework of a North Atlantic Conference system. As a result, a degree of stability has been brought to this trade and, as stated in the Interim Report for 31 March 1974, the 'cargo consortia and cargo liner interests are flourishing'.

The Cunard interests are also represented by Port Line within a consortium known as Associated Container Transportation (A.C.T.). This group includes Ben Line, Blue Star Line, Ellermans and Harrison. Within the general framework of this group Port Line, together with Blue Star and Ellerman Lines, have formed A.C.T. (Australia) which operates container services between Europe and Australia and New Zealand, and also from the East Coast of North America and Canada to Australia and New Zealand in conjunction with the Australian National Line. Port Line and Blue Star Line also continue to operate a joint Blue–Port service consisting of nine Blue Star and nine Port Line conventional ships. In much the same way the scope of Cunard-Brocklebank's seven-ship Eastern service has been widened through the provision of a joint service with P. and O. In this latter connection, there has been considerable growth in trade with Red Sea ports. Cunard-Brocklebank also runs an independent service from the Bay of Bengal to the East Coast of North America and to Europe.

Against the background of worsening economic conditions both at home and abroad, the profitability of the hotel and shipping division of Trafalgar House could be sustained only by the strictest management in the elimination of unnecessary costs and by new investment in areas of potential growth. By September 1973 shore establishments had been reduced, bringing them into line with present-day requirements. The Sunair/Lunn-Poly package tour business operating at the lower end of the market was sold and some seventeen of the older cargo ships (including twelve Port Line ships) were taken out of service. By March 1974, despite the somewhat gloomy forecasts for passenger ships, the Chairman was able to report not only that cargo was flourishing but that 'several significant long-term fixtures have been made during the last few months for our oil products carriers and bulkers'.

Cunard's interest in the bulk trades was increased by the delivery of three new products carriers during 1973, and eight bulk carriers each of 27,000 tons d.w.t. (of which two were subsequently sold) were put into service from Spanish shipyards. In addition, since 1971, orders for eleven new supply ships for Offshore Marine were placed with British and Dutch shipyards and two 39,000 d.w.t. oil products carriers were ordered from Canada. At 30 September 1973, the Cunard fleet consisted of three passenger ships of 94,187 tons G.R.; five container ships of 101,930 tons G.R. including vessels partly owned; seven oil products carriers of 164,159 d.w.t.; seven bulk carriers of 186,515 d.w.t.; sixteen cargo liners of 181,168 tons G.R. and twenty-five supply vessels of 16,018 tons G.R. This made a total of sixty-three ships at 386,983 tons G.R. and 701,227 d.w.t. – a not inconsiderable tonnage to operate and manage.

To those who may have had some misgivings consequent upon the Cunard organisation passing into the hands of a group such as Trafalgar House, the subsequent development must have brought degrees of consolation. The passenger fleet has been maintained with not unprofitable results and new investment has been made for the prospective enlargement of activity. Cargo operations have been sustained with the delivery of a new container ship and bulk carriers and additional oil products carriers have been ordered for Cunard's subsidiary, Moss Tankers. Strict financial management has sought to eliminate waste and increase potential earning capacity. Cunard's new role may be judged by the supposition that in relative terms shipping interests are not declining. The Company's new position may be estimated by the strength of its contribution to the Trafalgar House organisation as a whole. The shipping and hotels division of Trafalgar House Investments Ltd accounts for some 37 per cent of the group's total turnover and 21 per cent of net pre-tax revenue before interest on funded debt. One may, perhaps, conclude that under a new guise the name Cunard will continue to prosper and to reflect past achievement in a rapidly changing maritime and commercial environment.

VII CONCLUSION

In a particular sense the North Atlantic has always been regarded by shipowners as a battleground. Apart from the natural hazards of ice, fog and turbulence, this expansive range of waters has presented a challenging problem to sea captains, ship designers, merchants and governments since the frail ships of Columbus crossed its many horizons. Control of sea lanes linking the Old World with the New became a source of conflict between nations, partly through motives of greed under the cover of economic necessity and partly as a source of power in the struggle for maritime supremacy. No less important in this interaction of human skill, courage and self-interest, was the continuous process of technological advancement which made possible the conquest of weather, sea and tide. The first phase in the advancement and application of knowledge was represented by the development from the simple Liverpool snows which transported negro slaves from West Africa to the West Indies, to the barques, brigantines and clippers whose holds were laden with rich cargoes of cotton, tobacco and sugar. The second phase saw the adoption of steam power with the transition from wooden-hulled paddle ships to iron-screw ships powered by the compound engine. Such vessels were to carry westward the first flood of what was to become a mass movement of emigrants from Europe to the United States and Canada. The next phase was but intermediate before the last, in which steel leviathans powered by turbines catered for all classes of passengers and reduced the time of crossing from one side of the Atlantic to the other to less than six days. Finally technological evolution reached an ascending peak with the production of such ships as *Bremen, Europa, Rex, Normandie, Ile de France* and the Cunard Company's mighty Queens, before their comparative competitive advantages were set aside by the destructive thrust of a new system of transport in the form of jet aircraft.

Behind this long history of human endeavour on the North Atlantic had stood men with ideas and initiative; men who were prepared to risk their own resources in support of their enterprise. That they were able to do so was in no small part the result of long years of labour in the painful accumulation of capital. Thomas and Jonathan Brocklebank, Thomas and James Harrison, John Moss, Thomas Bibby no less than William Inman, George and James Burns, Charles MacIver, Thomas Ismay and Samuel Cunard, all worked a long hard apprenticeship before they ultimately became established as successful shipowners in their own right. What they all had in common, apart from boundless energy, was zeal in the pursuance of a purpose, skill in the administration of their affairs and judgement in the profitable use of their capital. They were business men *par excellence*. Let it be remembered, however, that their success was derived from the free use of their talents in an unrestricted society. It was only at a later date that the companies which they founded became subject to various forms of state intervention and control by government legislation. It is precisely because such changes have taken place that the business historian is provided with his theme for investigation. Consequently under the terms of reference governing the production of this book (which were to write a business history of The Cunard Steam Ship Co. Ltd), the analysis of source material and the ensuing narrative have been fairly strictly confined. The purpose has been to see how those men responsible for the conduct of Cunard's affairs utilised the resources at their command; how effective they were in understanding and in overcoming successive problems in financial, economic or technological terms. In Cunard's case the very essence of business decision-taking became increasingly subjected to overriding considerations of national policy; partly because of the prestige of the Company itself as a national asset, and partly because of the power and capacity of the Company's ships which were always at the service of government in times of emergency.

What are the conclusions that can be drawn from this particular study of Cunard's long history? It must be obvious that, for this Company, the North Atlantic was indeed a battleground. Yet in saying this there emerges a series of paradoxes. In the very nature of the struggle which had continually to be waged, there was evolved a long series of controlled agreements which limited areas of conflict and worked in the interests of harmony. In the first years of the Company's history the threat from the Collins Line was real, and by implication foreshadowed future dangers. This threat, however, was relieved by passenger and freight agreements and by the operation of a pooling arrangement. The struggle with other British competitors in the emigrant trade, and later with American and German lines, was equally, albeit painfully, resolved. In technological terms, the paradox is perhaps greater. On the face of it one cannot readily understand why Cunard, the first company to run regular steamship services across the Atlantic, should have allowed rivals to sap their competitive strength by a prior use of iron-screw ships, compound (and ultimately triple) expansion engines. We have tried to give a logical explanation for this. Yet after 1900 the Cunard Company was not only abreast of all new developments but was often in a position to initiate them.

In the sphere of human endeavour, the paradox was of a different dimension. It sprang from the attitude of mind of the men who were responsible for Cunard's use of resources: Samuel Cunard, Charles MacIver, the Burns brothers, the Lords Inverclyde, Sir Alfred Booth, Sir Thomas Royden and Sir Percy Bates were, each in his own characteristic way, exponents of the art and benefits of private enterprise. They were all men of character, strong in their belief that capital should be allowed to seek its highest return in a free market. Yet most of them were in some measure responsible for the imposition of limitations to freedom of action; Charles MacIver by his unquestioned acceptance of government regulations in the carriage of mails; John Burns in allowing ships to be used in peacetime as naval auxiliaries; the second Lord Inverclyde in binding the Company more closely with government policy under the agreement of 1903; and Sir Percy Bates in seeking and obtaining government assistance for the building of the two Queens. It should, of course, be emphasised that, apart from monies received under the mail contracts and certain other operating subsidies, all financial aid received from the Government for the purpose of building new ships was in the form of loans, which had to be and were eventually repaid. Of all the men who controlled the Company, Samuel Cunard, the founder, was the exception. He was a diplomat of the highest expertise and integrity. He had the foresight of genius coupled with the gift of choosing men of ability as his associates; but having achieved his ambition of founding the Company he gradually shed the responsibility of its administration, exercising his undoubted authority only when he felt that he had something worthwhile to contribute.

The final paradox can be found in the attitude of government towards the Company after 1949. It is well understood that the action of governments must often be dictated by expediency and by the changing economic circumstances; but even in the age of the jet aircraft Britain's maritime power still remains a national asset. To have imposed penal fiscal legislation without the adequate means of alleviation during the 1950s, thereby allowing Cunard's vital resources to be drained away, is still incomprehensible in terms of the national interest. Had all the hard lessons of the past been forgotten? Did Cunard's contribution to the winning of two world wars carry no weight in consideration of future national security? Apparently not, yet in the long run governments can be seen to possess a conscience. At the very time when it appeared that shipping companies had been left defenceless against the indifference of the state, easements were made in investment allowances and the burden of taxation was lightened. Furthermore, in Cunard's case, active co-operation was forthcoming from the Board of Trade in the financing of *Queen Elizabeth 2*. For this the Labour Government must be given credit, even though such financial help in general came too late to secure the Company from the consequences of earlier legislation.

The business of founding, operating and successfully maintaining a complex organisation such as that which The Cunard Steam Ship Co. Ltd had to manage, comprehends much that was common to shipping companies as a whole. Cunard's distinctive contribution, however, had stemmed from the regularity and safety of its services which earned for the Company a justifiable reputation and prestige. These assets were in turn capitalised by successive governments in the interests of national policy. In this somewhat curious dichotomy Cunard's business operations were compounded of private enterprise and controlled government assistance. Thus freedom of action was always tempered by the limitation of implied sanction. If the turbulence and immensity of the North Atlantic had to be conquered, the history of Cunard shows that this could be done by skill, courage and initiative backed at times by the financial power of the state. Though such a relationship may have been the outcome of economic necessity and political expediency, it was symbolic of something deeper in the consciousness of public opinion; for, though Cunard now operates under new management, the character of historical precedent still persists as a powerful inducement for survival. Trafalgar House Investments Ltd have, then, an incentive to keep Cunard ships in active service; because in the minds and hearts of those who made those ships, in the pride of the captains and seamen who sailed them and in the confidence of the many millions who were carried in them, the name 'Cunard' is and always has been synonymous with much that is best in Britain's maritime tradition and dependence on the sea.

Appendix

Ships built for the Cunard Steam Ship Co. Ltd, 1840–1934

Year	Ship	Builders	Hull
1840	Britannia	R. Duncan & Co., Greenock	Wood
1840	Acadia	J. Wood, Port Glasgow	Wood
1840	Caledonia	C. Wood, Port Glasgow	Wood
1840	Columbia	R. Steele & Son, Greenock	Wood
1843	Hibernia	R. Steele & Son, Greenock	Wood
1845	Cambria	R. Steele & Son, Greenock	Wood
1848	America	R. Steele & Son, Greenock	Wood
1848	Canada	R. Steele & Son, Greenock	Wood
1848	Europa	John Wood, Port Glasgow	Wood
1848	Niagara	R. Steele & Son, Greenock	Wood
1850	Asia	R. Steele & Son, Greenock	Wood
1850	Africa	R. Steele & Son, Greenock	Wood
1851	British Queen	Denny Bros, Dumbarton	Iron
1852	Arabia	R. Steele & Son, Greenock	Wood
1852	Alps	Denny Bros, Dumbarton	Iron
1852	Andes	Denny Bros, Dumbarton	Iron
1853	Balbec	Denny Bros, Dumbarton	Iron
1853	Taurus	Denny Bros, Dumbarton	Iron
1853	Melita	Denny Bros, Dumbarton	Iron
1853	Teneriffe	Denny Bros, Dumbarton	Iron
1853	Karnak	Denny Bros, Dumbarton	Iron
1854	Emeu	R. Napier & Sons, Glasgow	Iron
1854	Jura	J. & G. Thomson, Glasgow	Iron
1855	Etna	Caird & Co., Greenock	Iron
1856	Persia	R. Napier & Sons, Glasgow	Iron
1856	Stromboli	J. & G. Thomson, Glasgow	Iron
1857	Australasian (later the Calabria) Re-engined 1879.	J. &. G. Thomson, Glasgow	Iron
1858	Palestine	R. Steele & Co., Greenock	Iron
1858	Damascus	Denny Bros, Dumbarton	Iron

Appendix

Dimensions in feet			Gross	Engine	Propulsion
Length	Breadth	Depth	Tonnage	Power	
				I.H.P.	
207	34·2	22·4	1154	740	Paddle
207	34·2	22·4	1154	740	Paddle
207	34·2	22·4	1154	740	Paddle
207	34·2	22·4	1154	740	Paddle
219	35·9	24·2	1422	1040	Paddle
219	35·9	24·2	1422	1040	Paddle
251	38	25·3	1825	1800	Paddle
251	38	25·7	1831	1900	Paddle
251	38·2	25·4	1834	1800	Paddle
251	38	25·3	1925	1800	Paddle
266·6	40	27·2	2226	2150	Paddle
266.6	40	27·2	2226	2150	Paddle
183	29	18·8	772	430	Single screw
285	40·8	27·7	2402	3000	Paddle
230·6	34	25	1275	900	Single screw
230·6	34	25	1275	900	Single screw
201·6	30·6	18	774	500	Single screw
202	30·6	24·6	1126	850	Single screw
232·6	30·2	19·9	1255	900	Single screw
202	30·6	24·6	1126	850	Single screw
202	30·6	24·6	1116	850	Single screw
257	36·1	28·9	1538	1100	Single screw
300	37	28·8	2241	1200	Single screw
296	37	28·8	2216	1200	Single screw
360	45	31·6	3300	3800	Paddle
196·6	28·6	19	734	—	Single screw
338	42·1	29·5	2902	3000	Single screw
245	34·2	25·6	1377	1200	Single screw
245	32	23·6	1214	1000	Single screw

Year	Ship	Builders	Hull
1858	Lebanon	J. & G. Thomson, Glasgow	Iron
1860	Olympus	J. &. G. Thomson, Glasgow	Iron
1860	Atlas	J. & G. Thomson, Glasgow	Iron
1860	Marathon	Napier, Glasgow	Iron
1860	Hecla	Napier, Glasgow	Iron
1861	Sidon	Denny Bros, Dumbarton	Iron
1861	Kedar	Denny Bros, Dumbarton	Iron
1861	Morocco	Denny Bros, Dumbarton	Iron
1862	Scotia	R. Napier & Sons, Glasgow	Iron
1862	China	R. Napier & Sons, Glasgow	Iron
1863	Corsica	J. & G. Thomson, Glasgow	Iron
1864	Cuba	Engined by Tod & Macgregor, Glasgow	Iron
1864	Aleppo	J. & G. Thomson, Glasgow	Iron
1865	Java	J. & G. Thomson, Glasgow	Iron
1865	Malta	J. & G. Thomson, Glasgow	Iron
1865	Tarifa	J. & G. Thomson, Glasgow	Iron
1865	Tripoli	J. & G. Thomson, Glasgow	Iron
1866	Palmyra	Caird & Co, Greenock	Iron
1867	Russia	J. & G. Thomson, Glasgow	Iron
1867	Siberia	J. & G. Thomson, Glasgow	Iron
1868	Samaria	J. & G. Thomson, Glasgow	Iron
1870	Abyssinia	J. & G. Thomson, Glasgow	Iron
1870	Algeria	J. & G. Thomson, Glasgow	Iron
1870	Batavia	Denny Bros, Dumbarton	Iron
1871	Parthia	Denny Bros, Dumbarton	Iron
1872	Trinidad	J. & G. Thomson, Glasgow	Iron
1872	Demerara	J. & G. Thomson, Glasgow	Iron
1873	Nantes	Blackwood & Gordon, Port Glasgow	Iron
1874	Brest	Blackwood & Gordon, Port Glasgow	Iron
1874	Saragossa	J. & G. Thomson, Glasgow	Iron
1874	Bothnia	J. & G. Thomson, Glasgow	Iron
1875	Cherbourg	J. & G. Thomson, Glasgow	Iron
1875	Scythia	J. & G. Thomson, Glasgow	Iron
1879	Gallia	J. & G. Thomson, Glasgow	Iron
1881	Servia	J. & G. Thomson, Glasgow	Steel
1881	Catalonia	J. & G. Thomson, Glasgow	Iron
1882	Pavonia	J. & G. Thomson, Glasgow	Iron
1882	Cephalonia	Laird Bros, Birkenhead	Iron
1883	Aurania	J. & G. Thomson, Glasgow	Steel
1884	Umbria	J. Elder & Co., Glasgow	Steel
1884	Etruria	J. Elder & Co., Glasgow	Steel
1884	Oregon	J. Elder & Co., Glasgow (Fairfield Shipbldg. & Engineering Co.)	Iron
1893	Campania	Fairfield Co., Glasgow	Steel

Appendix

Dimensions in Feet			Gross	Engine	
Length	Breadth	Depth	Tonnage	Power	Propulsion
243·6	31·6	25·6	1383	1200	Single screw
265	36	27·2	1794	1500	Single screw
265	36	25·7	1784	1500	Single screw
336	36·2	25·7	1790	1500	Single screw
338	36·4	25·6	1790	1500	Single screw
265	36	27·2	1853	960	Single screw
275·8	36·2	25·7	1876	960	Single screw
275·5	36·2	25·8	1855	960	Single screw
379	47·8	30·5	3871	5000	Paddle
323	40·3	29	2529	2250	Single screw
224·3	32·2	21	1134	900	Single screw
327	42·3	29	2669	2250	Single screw
292·5	38·2	26·2	2143	1255	Single screw
337·4	42·6	27·7	2697	2550	Single screw
290	39	26·6	2244	1360	Single screw
292·5	38·2	26·2	2146	1260	Single screw
280	38	27·5	2061	1200	Single screw
280	38	27·6	2044	1250	Single screw
358	42·6	28	2959	2800	Single screw
321	39	27·6	2498	1500	Single screw
320·6	39·5	27	2574	1530	Single screw
360	42	34	3376	2480	Single screw
363	42	35	3428	2480	Single screw
312	38	27·6	2553	1670	Single screw
360	40	35·2	3167	1890	Single screw
307·5	34·1	24·5	1899	900	Single screw
307·5	34·1	24·5	1904	900	Single screw
240	32	27·5	1473	650	Single screw
240	32	27·5	1473	650	Single screw
316·3	35·3	24·5	2166	950	Single screw
422·3	42·2	34·5	4535	3160	Single screw
251·2	32·4	26·5	1614	803	Single screw
420·8	42·2	34·6	4557	3115	Single screw
430·1	44·6	34·4	4809	5300	Single screw
515	52·1	37	7392	10 000	Single screw
429·6	43	33·8	4841	3200	Single screw
430·5	46·4	34·9	5588	4000	Single screw
430·6	46·5	34·5	5517	4000	Single screw
470	57·2	37·2	7268	9500	Single screw
501·6	57·2	38·2	8128	14 500	Single screw
501·6	57·2	38·2	8120	14 500	Single screw
500	54	37·9	7375	13 500	Single screw
601	65·2	37·8	12 950	30 000	Twin screws

Year	Ship	Builders	Hull
1893	Lucania	Fairfield Co., Glasgow	Steel
1895	Carinthia	London & Glasgow Shipbldg. Co., Glasgow	Steel
1895	Sylvania	London & Glasgow Shipbldg. Co., Glasgow	Steel
1897	Pavia	Workman Clark & Co., Belfast	Steel
1897	Tyria	Workman Clark & Co., Belfast	Steel
1898	Cypria	Workman Clark & Co., Belfast	Steel
1898	Ultonia	C. S. Swan & Hunter, Newcastle	Steel
1899	Veria	Armstrong Whitworth & Co., Newcastle	Steel
1900	Ivernia	C. S. Swan & Hunter, Newcastle	Steel
1900	Saxonia	J. Brown & Co., Glasgow	Steel
1903	Brescia	J. L. Thompson & Sons, Sunderland	Steel
1903	Carpathia	C. S. Swan & Hunter, Newcastle	Steel
1903	Pannonia	J. Brown & Co., Clydebank	Steel
1903	Slavonia	Sir J. Laing & Sons, Sunderland	Steel
1905	Caronia	J. Brown & Co., Clydebank	Steel
1905	Carmania	J. Brown & Co., Clydebank	Steel
1907	Lusitania	J. Brown & Co., Clydebank	Steel
1907	Mauretania	Swan Hunter & Wigham Richardson, Newcastle	Steel
1909	Phrygia (ex Oro)	Sir Raylton Dixon & Co., Middlesbrough	Steel
1909	Thracia (ex Orono)	Sir Raylton Dixon & Co., Middlesbrough	Steel
1909	Lycia (ex Oceano)	Sir Raylton Dixon & Co., Middlesbrough	Steel
1910	Franconia	Swan Hunter & Wigham Richardson, Newcastle	Steel
1910	Caria (ex Clematis)	Tyne Iron Shipbldg. Co., Newcastle	Steel
1911	Laconia	Swan Hunter & Wigham Richardson, Newcastle	Steel
1911	Ascania	Swan Hunter & Wigham Richardson, Newcastle	Steel
1911	Ausonia (ex Tortona)	Swan Hunter & Wigham Richardson, Newcastle	Steel
1911	Albania (ex Cairn Mona) (ex Consuelo)	Swan Hunter & Wigham Richardson, Newcastle	Steel

Appendix

| Dimensions in Feet | | | Gross | Engine | |
Length	Breadth	Depth	Tonnage	Power	Propulsion
				I.H.P.	
601	65·2	37·8	12 950	30 000	Twin screws
445	49	31·9	5598	4400	Twin screws
445	49	31·9	5598	4400	Twin screws
332·1	45·7	22·5	2945	1800	Single screw
332·1	45·7	22·5	2936	1800	Single screw
332·1	45·7	22·5	2936	1800	Single screw
500	57·4	33·9	10 402	4750	Twin screws
330·6	45·2	22·5	3200	1800	Single screw
582	64·9	37·8	14 066	10 000	Twin screws
580	64·2	38·4	14 280	10 000	Twin screws
330	45·2		3235	1800	Single screw
540	64·5	37·4	13 564	8000	Twin screws
486·5	59·3	33	9851	4500	Twin screws
510	59·5		10 605	4750	Twin screws
650	72·2	40·2	19 687	21 000	Twin screws
				S.H.P.	
					Triple screws
650·4	72·2	40	19 524	21 000	3 turbines
					4 screws
762·2	87·8	56·6	31 550	67 000	4 turbines
					4 screws
762·2	88	57·1	31 937	67 000	4 turbines
				I.H.P.	
340	47·1	15·4	3352	1600	Single screw
310	44·1	15·7	2891	1100	Single screw
308	43·3	14·8	2715	1150	Single screw
600·3	71·3	40·4	18 149	13 500	Twin screws
318	43	25·2	3034	1800	Single screw
600·3	71·3	40·4	18 099	13 500	Twin screws
466·6	56·1	29·4	9111	4600	Twin screws
450·6	54·2	29·2	7907	4400	Twin screws
461·5	52·1	38·7	7682	3100	Twin screws

Year	Ship	Builders	Hull
1913	Alaunia	Scotts Shipbldg. & Eng. Co., Greenock	Steel
1913	Andania	Scotts Shipbldg. & Eng. Co., Greenock	Steel
1914	Aquitania	John Brown & Co., Clydebank	Steel
1915	Vandalia (ex *Anglo Californian*) (Nitrate Producers Co.)	Short Bros., Sunderland	Steel
1915	Valeria (ex *Den of Avilie*) (Barrie Ship Co., Dundee)	Russell & Co., Port Glasgow	Steel
1915	Volodia (ex *Den of Ogil*) (Barrie Ship Co., Dundee)	Russell & Co., Port Glasgow	Steel
1915	Vinovia (ex *Anglo Bolivian*) (Nitrate Producers Co.)	Short Bros., Sunderland	Steel
1916	Royal George	Fairfield Co., Glasgow	Steel
1916	Aurania	Swan Hunter & Wigham Richardson, Newcastle	Steel
1916	Pavia (ex *Campanello*) (ex *Campania*) (ex *British Empire*)	Palmers Co., Newcastle	Steel
1916	Valacia (ex *Luceric*) (Bank Line, A. Weir & Co. (Sold out of Cunard service in 1931— (the last war addition retained)	Russell & Co., Port Glasgow	Steel
1916	Feltria (ex *Uranium*) (ex *Avoca*) (ex *Atlanta*) (ex *Avoca*) (ex *San Fernando*) (ex *Avoca*)	Wm. Denny & Bros, Dumbarton	Steel
1916	Folia (ex *Principello*) (ex *Principe de Piemonte*)	J. Laing & Sons, Dumbarton	Steel
1918	Virgilia	Russel & Co., Port Glasgow	Steel
1918	Vardulia (sold out of Cunard service in 1929)	Russell & Co., Port Glasgow	Steel
1918	Vasconia	Russell & Co., Port Glasgow	Steel
1918	Vellavia	Armstrong Whitworth & Co., Newcastle	Steel
1918	Vennonia	Caledon Shipbldg. & Eng. Co., Dundee	Steel
1918	Venusia	Harland & Wolff, Belfast	Steel
1918	Verentia	Harland & Wolff, Belfast	Steel

Appendix

| Dimensions in Feet | | | Gross | Engine | |
Length	Breadth	Depth	Tonnage	Power	Propulsion
520·3	64	34·3	13 405	7500	Twin screws
520·3	64	34·3	13 405	7500	Twin screws
868·7	97	49·7	45 646	56 000	4 screws
425	56·3	36·3	7333	3310	4 turbines Single screw
423·4	56	28·7	5865	3640	Single screw
423·5	56	28·7	5689	3600	Single screw
418·2	54·4	29·3	5503	2920	Single screw
525·8	60·2	27	11 146	14 500	Triple screws 3 turbines
520·5	65·3	42·6	13 936		Twin screws 4 turbines
470	56·8	32·1	9291		Twin screws
460	57	28·9	6526	3500	Single screw
420	48·2	30·6	5253	4680	Single screw
430	52·7	25	6704	3500	Single screw
423·3	56	28·7	5679	2700	Single screw
423·3	56	28·7	5691	3000	Single screw
423·3	56	28·7	5680	3000	Single screw
400·2	52·3	28·4	5272	2700	Single screw
400·6	52·2	28·6	5225	2700	Single screw
400·4	52·3	28·4	5222	2700	Single screw
400·4	52·3	28·4	5185	2700	Single screw

Year	Ship	Builders	Hull
1918	Verbania	R. Duncan & Co., Port Glasgow	Steel
1919	Scythia	Vickers Ltd., Barrow	Steel
1921	Berengaria	Vulcan Works, Hamburg	Steel
1921	Samaria	Cammell Laird & Co., Birkenhead	Steel
1921	Albania	Scotts Shipbldg. & Eng. Co., Greenock	Steel
1922	Laconia	Swan Hunter & Wig. Rich., Newcastle	Steel
1922	Tyrrhenia (name changed to Lancastria)	Wm. Beardmore & Co., Glasgow	Steel
1922	Andania	Hawthorn Leslie & Co., Newcastle	Steel
1922	Antonia	Vickers Ltd., Barrow	Steel
1922	Ausonia	Armstrong Whitworth & Co., Newcastle	Steel
1923	Franconia	John Brown & Co., Clydebank	Steel
1924	Aurania	Swan Hunter & Wig. Rich., Newcastle	Steel
1925	Carinthia	Vickers Ltd., Barrow	Steel
1925	Alaunia	John Brown & Co., Clydebank	Steel
1925	Ascania	Armstrong Whitworth & Co., Newcastle	Steel
1930	Bactria	J. L. Thompson & Sons, Sunderland	Steel
1930	Bantria	J. L. Thompson & Sons, Sunderland	Steel
1930	Bosnia	J. L. Thompson & Sons, Sunderland	Steel
1930	Bothnia	J. L. Thompson & Sons, Sunderland	Steel
1936	*Queen Mary	John Brown & Co., Clydebank	Steel

* Queen Mary was planned by The Cunard Steam Ship Co. Ltd. but before completion was transferred to Cunard White Star Ltd.

References to all ships built after 1934, either for Cunard White Star Ltd or for Cunard Line Ltd, may be found in the text; see especially Chapter 10.

Appendix 335

| Dimensions in Feet | | | Gross | Engine | |
Length	Breadth	Depth	Tonnage	Power	Propulsion
				I.H.P.	
405·3	53	27·4	5021	2700	Single screw
				S.H.P.	
600·7	73·8	40·7	19 503	12 500	Twin screws 6 Turbines
883·6	98·3	57·1	52 022	62 000	Quadruple screws 4 turbines
601·5	73·7	40·7	19 602	12 500	Twin screws 6 turbines
523·1	64	43·9	12 767	6800	Twin screws 4 turbines
601·3	73·7	40·6	19 680	12 500	Twin screws 6 turbines
552·8	70·4	38·8	16 243	12 500	Twin screws 6 turbines
520·2	65·3	39·2	13 950	8500	Twin screws 4 turbines
519·9	65·3	39·1	13 867	8500	Twin screws 4 turbines
520	65·3	39·1	13 912	8500	Twin screws 4 turbines
601·3	73·7	40·6	20 158	12 500	Twin screws 6 turbines
519·7	65·3	39·2	13 984	8500	Twin screws 4 turbines
600	73	40	20 277	13 500	Twin screws 4 turbines
519·6	65·2	39·2	14 030	8500	Twin screws 4 turbines
519	65·3	39	14 013	8500	Twin screws 4 turbines
				I.H.P.	
292·3	45	20·3	2402	1800	Single screw
292·3	45	20·3	2402	1800	Single screw
292·3	45	20·3	2402	1800	Single screw
292·3	45	20·3	2402	1800	Single screw
975·2	118·6	68·5	81 235	158 000	Quadruple screws 16 turbines

Notes

The following abbreviations are used throughout the notes: CP Cunard Papers; MIP, MacIver Papers; BM, Board Minutes of The Cunard Steam Ship Co. Ltd; WS, White Star Papers; VR, Verbatim Reports of the Ordinary Annual Meetings of The Cunard Steam Ship Co. Ltd; SLB, Secretaries' Letter Books of The Cunard Steam Ship Co. Ltd; CLB, Chairman's Letter Books of The Cunard Steam Ship Co. Ltd; DLB, Directors Letter Books of The Cunard Steam Ship Co. Ltd.

Chapter 1

1. There is a tradition that an early ancestor emigrated from Wales to Germany at the beginning of the seventeenth century, cited in F. C. Bowen, *A Century of Atlantic Travel* (1930); there is a range of historical evidence giving support to the belief that the origins of the Cunard family went back to Thones Kunders. He was a Quaker who established himself as a weaver and dyer in Krefeldt. Kunders emigrated to Pennsylvania in 1683 and settled in Germantown following his craft and administering a large land holding. His sixth child, Henry, was born in 1688 and, on 28 June 1710 married Catherine Streepers. Henry and his bride settled in Whitpain and, in turn, left a considerable estate to their seven sons. It was this second generation which took the name of either Konrad or Cunard. Samuel's second son, Abraham, was the father of Samuel Cunard. The details of this ancestry are set out in F. L. Babcock, *Spanning the Atlantic* (1931). Babcock quotes the work of Abraham Martin Payne and Archibald MacMechan as authority for his statements.
2. MIP, Memo by Charles MacIver on Cunard and MacIver families.
3. Ibid.; F. L. Babcock, op. cit. p. 10.
4. Howard Robinson, *Carrying British Mails Overseas* (1964), p. 124; Edwin Hodder, *Sir George Burns, Bart.* (1890), p. 193.
5. CP, H. Eaves, 'A History of The Cunard Steam Ship Co.'. Eaves's unpublished history runs to some 800 pages and is arranged as a year by year account of the activities of the Company. The preliminary section deals with the early life of Samuel Cunard and is drawn from material some time in the possession of the Company.

Notes

6. Evidence from Louise Manny, *Ships of the Miramachi*; also a pamphlet by the same author, *Ships of Kent County*, which contains a photograph of Joseph Cunard.

7. Ibid.; for further information about the activities of the Cunard brothers, reference should be made to the shipping registers for Halifax and New Brunswick in the Public Archives of Canada.

8. This is, perhaps, a notional figure based on a rough calculation of Cunard's many financial interests. It does not represent an accurate figure for Cunard's control of capital resources. A more precise definition of Cunard's shipping interests can be gained from the shipping records housed in St John's University, Newfoundland; see also A. MacMechan 'The Rise of Samuel Cunard', *The Dalhousie Review*, July 1929, pp. 202–10.

9. *Ships of the North Shore*, Occasional Paper No. 11 published by the now no longer existent Maritime Museum of Canada at Halifax.

10. From information kindly supplied by Mr Basil Greenhill, Director of the National Maritime Museum, Greenwich.

11. CP, Copy of circular issued by the Admiralty dated 1838. See Edwin Hodder, *Sir George Burns, Bart.* (1890), pp. 191–3, in which is stated that George Burns received an intimation of the Admiralty circular from Sir Edward Parry but decided, at that time, not to engage in the North Atlantic steamship routes.

12. Howard Robinson, op. cit. pp. 124, 131, from information derived from the Falmouth Letter Books.

13. Howard Robinson, op. cit., p. 131.

14. Ibid.

15. Ibid.

16. Howe was on board the sailing ship *Tyrian*. While becalmed she was overtaken by *Sirius* returning from her successful voyage to New York. While mails were being transferred to *Sirius*, Howe went aboard and received firsthand accounts of the steamship's performances.

17. CP, Circular issued by Admiralty, previously cited.

18. Ibid.

19. F. L. Babcock, op. cit., p. 38; Howard Robinson, op. cit. p. 132.

20. Howard Robinson, op. cit., p. 132.

21. P.O. records, reports to P.M.G., 11 March 1853.

22. Frances Ann Kemble, *Record of a Girlhood* (1878), I, p. 286.

23. There is some controversy about the ordering of these events, but the information from original sources, CP Contracts and CP Contracts of The British and North American Royal Mail Steam Packet Co. and relative deeds 1839–40, confirm the statement made in the text.

24. J. Napier, *The Life of Robert Napier* (1904), p. 135, quoting letter from Samuel Cunard to Robert Napier, 21 March, 1839.

25. Ibid., pp. 124–5, quoting letter from Samuel Cunard, 25 February, 1839.

26. Ibid.

27. These included three steam vessels for the Dundee Shipping Co., two for the Aberdeen and Leith Shipping Co., three for the Isle of Man Steam Packet Co., three for the Londonderry Steam Packet Co., three for the Belfast Co., Glasgow and three for the City of Glasgow Steam Packet Co.; J. Napier, op.

cit., pp. 126-7, quoting letter from Robert Napier to William Kidston and Sons, 28 February, 1839.

28. J. Napier, op. cit., p. 62. *Berenice* was a paddle steamer with double side-lever engines, having three copper boilers worked at low pressure and fitted with expansion valves.

29. So cited by F. L. Babcock, op. cit., p. 39, though this author also confirms specifications as laid down in CP, Contract between Samuel Cunard and Robert Napier 18 March 1839, in which it is stated that the ships should be 'equal in quality of hull and machinery to the steamer *Commodore* or the steamer *London*, both constructed by the said Robert Napier, and equal to the *City of Glasgow* steamer in the finishing of the cabins', see text below.

30. J. Napier, op. cit. pp. 101-2.

31. CP, Contract between Samuel Cunard and Robert Napier, 18 March 1839.

32. Ibid.

33. J. Napier, op. cit., p. 134, quoting letter from Robert Napier to James C. Melvill, 19 March 1839.

34. F. L. Babcock, op. cit., p. 42.

35. CP, Contracts and agreements of The British and North American R.M.S.P. Co. and other related documents, 1839-40.

36. CP, Contract between Samuel Cunard and Robert Napier, 18 March 1839.

37. CP, Ships' specifications. The original correspondence from Samuel Cunard specified a number of 70 to 80 passengers.

38. MIP, Instructions to ships' captains laid down by Charles MacIver, 1840-8.

39. MIP, Samuel Cunard to David MacIver 20 July 1839; F. L. Babcock, op. cit., p. 44; the theme is continued in letters from David MacIver to Samuel Cunard, CP, David MacIver to Samuel Cunard, 16 April 1841.

40. F. L. Babcock, op. cit., p. 45.

41. CP, Contract between Samuel Cunard and the Admiralty for the carriage of mails to Halifax and Boston, 4 May 1839.

42. F. L. Babcock, op. cit., p. 45.

43. Ibid.

44. CP, H. Eaves, op. cit., under Preliminary section.

45. CP, Contracts of The British and North American R.M.S.P. Co. and relative deeds, 1839-40.

46. Ibid.

47. Ibid.

48. CP, Contracts dated 5, 23, 25, 26 and 28 May 1840.

49. Ibid.

50. CP, Original Deeds of Co-Partnership, 4, 6, 7, 18 and 25 June and 23 July 1839, Clause 18.

51. CP, Agreements under dates 23, 24, 26 and 28 December 1840.

52. Ibid.

53. CP, Agreements under dates 30 September and 8 November 1841.

54. Edwin Hodder, op. cit., p. 145.

55. Edwin Hodder, op. cit., pp. 145, 149.
56. D. B. McNeill, *Irish Passenger Steamship Services* (1969), p. 19.
57. Ibid.
58. Ibid.
59. MIP, Papers relating to the history of the MacIver family compiled by Mrs Lois Rae, grand-daughter of Charles MacIver.
60. Ibid.; also Edwin Hodder, op. cit., p. 161; Messrs Thomson and MacConnell were the company's agents in Glasgow, David MacIver the agent in Liverpool and Robert Napier was a co-founder.
61. Edwin Hodder, op. cit., p. 161.
62. MIP, Papers relating to the history of the MacIver family; D. B. MacNeill, op. cit., pp. 25, 27.
63. Edwin Hodder, op. cit., p. 149. Up to 1841 the style of the firm was J. and G. Burns (J. Napier, op. cit., p. 129) but thereafter the shipping side of the business was conducted under the style G. and J. Burns.
64. F. L. Babcock, op. cit., p. 49.
65. *Britannia* was under the command of Captain Woodruff. The detailed instructions to Captain Woodruff are extant in CP though the original copy has some pages missing and parts are now illegible.
66. CP, H. Eaves, op. cit., under 1840; *Unicorn* was built by Robert Steele and Son at Greenock in 1836 for the Burns's service between Glasgow and Liverpool.
67. CP, Ships' specifications; *Britannia* was 1154 tons with engine power 740 I.H.P., *Hibernia* and *Cambria* were each of 1422 tons with engine power 1040 I.H.P.
68. CP, H. Eaves, op. cit., under 1844. This episode was made the subject of a well-known painting see Plate 5.
69. CP, H. Eaves, op. cit., under 1843; F. L. Babcock, op. cit., pp. 73–4.
70. CP, Report of general meeting of partners 25 January 1844; *Columbia* was insured with the firm of Bennett and Browne for £45,000. The amount charged against Company's underwriting account for short fall £4877 thus making up *Columbia's* original cost of £49,877.
71. CP, Papers relating to mail contracts 1845–51.
72. This service was consequent upon the negotiation of a new mail contract (CP, R. Burns to Captain Coffin, R.N., 15 December 1847). Under the terms of this new contract the Admiralty required a service leaving Liverpool every Saturday for New York and Boston alternately, calling at Holyhead if necessary; the Boston steamship was to call at Halifax and the New York steamship if required by the Lords Commissioners of the Admiralty. In payment for these augmented sailings the mail subvention was raised to £173,340 per annum.
73. MIP, Papers relating to the MacIver family; CP, H. Eaves, op. cit., under 1849.
74. Ibid.
75. MIP, Contract of Co-Partnership of The British and Foreign Steam Navigation Co., 1 May 1857.
76. CP, H. Eaves, op. cit., under 1854. *Jura* (2240 tons) left Liverpool for Constantinople on 22 October 1854. She made nine voyages, including one to

St Johns and carried 601 officers, 14,300 men, 634 women, 922 children and 2785 horses. *Etna* together with 12 other Cunard ships was also taken into war service.

77. MIP, Declaration concerning title Burns and MacIver, 11 and 12 February, 1853.
78. Ibid.
79. MIP, Agreement 1 October 1855, details of which are cited in Deed of Co-Partnership, 1 May 1857.
80. MIP, Deed of Co-Partnership, 1 May 1857.
81. Ibid.
82. Ibid.
83. MIP, Correspondence, Samuel Cunard to Charles MacIver, 9 May 1857; ibid., 1 January 1858. A growing scarcity of resources led to the Burns brothers declining to enter the Australian mail service which Samuel Cunard had proposed. Edwin Hodder, op. cit., pp. 264–5.
84. MIP, Memorandum of agreement between the partners of The British and Foreign S.N. Co., 24, 25, 26 February 1858, under which the Burns brothers sold their interest in this company.
85. MIP, Correspondence Samuel Cunard to Charles MacIver, 9 May 1857.
86. MIP, Correspondence George Burns to Charles MacIver, 3 September 1856.
87. MIP, Correspondence Charles MacIver to Samuel Cunard, 4 September 1856.
88. MIP, Correspondence Samuel Cunard to Charles MacIver, 9 November 1858, referring to MacIver's views in a previous letter.
89. MIP, Correspondence Samuel Cunard to Charles MacIver, 1 January 1858.
90. MIP, Correspondence Samuel Cunard to Charles MacIver, 1 August 1859, referring to MacIver's objections about the transfer of commissions.
91. MIP, Correspondence Samuel Cunard to Charles MacIver, 5 June 1858.
92. Ibid., 9 November 1858.
93. MIP, Agreements, Memorandum of Agreement between the partners of The British and Foreign S.N. Co., 24, 25, 26 February 1858, Clauses 1 and 2.
94. Ibid.
95. MIP, Agreements, Heads of Agreement by partners of The British and North American R.M.S.P. Co., concluded 1 November 1859.
96. Ibid., Clauses 2 and 3.
97. Ibid., Clause 4.
98. Ibid., Clauses 8 and 9.
99. Ibid., Clause 16.
100. Ibid., Clause 14.
101. MIP, Agreements, Memorandum of Agreement between the partners of The British and North American R.M.S.P. Co. and The British and Foreign S.N. Co., concluded 23 October 1867.
102. MIP, Agreements, Memorandum and Appendix relative to The British and Foreign S.N. Co., 30 September 1866.
103. Ibid.
104. Ibid.
105. Ibid.

106. MIP, Agreements, Memorandum of Agreement between the partners of The British and North American Steam Packet Co. and The British and Foreign S.N. Co., 22 July 1867.
107. Ibid.
108. Ibid.
109. MIP, Memorandum explanatory of the discontinuation of The British and North American R.M.S.P. Co. and of the formation of The British and North American S.P. Co. (September 1867).
110. Ibid.
111. Ibid.
112. Ibid.
113. MIP, Correspondence, Charles MacIver to David MacIver, 17 August 1874.
114. Ibid.
115. MIP, Agreements, 4 March 1880.
116. MIP, Correspondence David MacIver to A. Squarey, 21 July, 1874.
117. MIP, Correspondence A. Squarey to David MacIver, 6 February, 1874. 'It convinces me', wrote Squarey, 'that your views and those of your father as to the management of the Cunard concern are so essentially different that there is no alternative for you but to retire from taking any part in the business.'
118. MIP, Correspondence, A. Squarey to David MacIver 18, 19, 22, 23 July, 27 August, 11 September 1874.
119. MIP, Correspondence A. Squarey to David MacIver, 27 August 1875.
120. MIP, Correspondence A. Squarey to David MacIver, 28 September 1875.
121. MIP, Press notices *The Times*, 21 April 1883; *Liverpool Courier*, 23 April 1883.
122. MIP, Agreements, 21 May 1878.
123. MIP, Agreements, preamble 4 March 1880.
124. MIP, Agreements, 21 May 1878, Clause 3.
125. MIP, Agreements, 4 March 1880, Article 2.
126. MIP, Agreements, preamble 4 March 1880.
127. MIP, Agreements, 4 March 1880, Article 6.
128. Ibid.
129. Ibid., Article 7.
130. Ibid., 4 March 1880, schedule of share allocation.

Chapter 2
1. CP, Mail Contracts. By 1852 the various contracts, including the branch services, amounted to £188,040.
2. There is extensive literature on this subject. The essential facts are epitomised in H. J. Dyos and D. H. Aldcroft, *British Transport* (1969), pp. 239–42. Many additional sources are quoted in these footnotes.
3. Liverpool Record Office, documents relating to the Inman Line; A. J. Maginnis, *The Atlantic Ferry* (1900), pp. 67–8.
4. CP, Ships' specifications, see Appendix 5.
5. Ibid.

6. CP, H. Eaves, op. cit., under 1856 and 1862; J. Napier, *Life of Robert Napier* (1904), pp. 192, 195.
7. CP, Ships' specifications, see Appendix.
8. For the effects of this on Cunard see CP, H. Eaves, op. cit., 1854–1862; for the effect on the P. and O. see Boyd Cable, *A Hundred Years of the P. and O.* (1937), pp. 135–6; MIP, *A Letter to the Rt. Hon. Sir C. Wood, Bart., M.P., First Lord of the Admiralty, on the Mail Steam Ship Contract System* printed for the author in 1856. The author styled himself as the writer of the *Universal Steam Packet Guide of 1841*.
9. CP, H. Eaves, op. cit., under 1854.
10. Ibid.
11. MIP, Correspondence, Charles MacIver to John Burns, 12 April 1857.
12. E. C. Smith, *A Short History of Naval and Marine Engineering* (1938), p. 176.
13. CP, Shipbuilding memoranda, 1865–70; W. P. Strassman, *Risk and Technological Innovation* (1959), p. 211.
14. CP, Ships' specifications, Appendix.
15. R. Bastin, M. A. Thesis 'Cunard and the Liverpool Emigrant Trade 1860 to 1900', p. 120.
16. CP, Ships' specifications, Appendix.
17. CP, DLB, File No. 1, p. 350.
18. Ibid.
19. R. Bastin, op. cit., p. 120.
20. E. C. Smith, op. cit., p. 240.
21. CP, VR, Ordinary General Meeting 10 April 1884.
22. W. J. Oldham, *The Ismay Line* (1961), p. 44.
23. CP, CLB, File No. 3, A. P. Moorhouse to J. Burns, 21 March 1891.
24. *The Times*, 3 September 1892.
25. CP, DLB, Memo to D. Jardine 28 May 1894; CP, H. Eaves, op. cit., under 1893. *Campania* and *Lucania* had triple expansion engines, 12 double-ended and one single-ended boiler; on trials the engines developed 31,050 h.p. giving a speed of 23·18 knots. Each ship had accommodation for 526 First Class, 200 Second Class and 300 Third Class passengers.
26. Ibid.
27. Ibid.
28. PP. 1873, *Royal Commission on Unseaworthy Ships*, XXXVI (C.853), 325.
29. Report of the Select Committee on *The Halifax and Boston Mails* (1849), 1–5.
30. Ibid.
31. Howard Robinson, *Carrying British Mails Overseas* (1964), p. 138; CP, H. Eaves, op. cit., under 1846.
32. Ibid.
33. Ibid.
34. CP, H. Eaves, op. cit., under 1847; CP, Mail Contracts, J. Austin, 'Liverpool and the Atlantic Ferry' *Proceedings of the Inst. Mech. Engineers*, 26 June 1934.
35. CP, Mail contracts; this figure remained constant until 1867.
36. *Report of the Committee on Contract Packets* (1853), 20, 30, 77.
37. Howard Robinson, op. cit., p. 143.
38. Ibid.

Notes

39. Ibid., p. 144.
40. R. G. Albion, *The Rise of New York Port (1815–1860)* (1970), p. 32.
41. Ibid.
42. R. G. Albion, op. cit., pp. 323–5; A. J. Maginnis, *The Atlantic Ferry* (1900), p. 48. *Washington* (2000 tons) and *Hermann* (2200 tons) were wooden paddle steamships.
43. MIP, Correspondence, Samuel Cunard to Viscount Canning, 21 May 1853; also quoted Howard Robinson, op. cit., p. 140.
44. David B. Tyler, *Steam Conquers the Atlantic*, (1939); R. G. Albion, op. cit., pp. 325–30; CP, H. Eaves, op. cit., under 1850.
45. R. G. Albion, op. cit., pp. 325–6.
46. R. G. Albion, op. cit., pp. 325–6; see also J. Kennedy, *History of Steam Navigation* (1903), p. 99. This objective seemed to be capable of realisation when in 1852 the Collins line succeeded in carrying one third more passengers than Cunard between Liverpool and New York.
47. MIP, Agreements. The firm of Brown, Shipley and Co. acted as agents for the Collins line and were responsible for the conduct of freight agreements between that line and other shipping companies.
48. R. G. Albion, op. cit., p. 326; J. Austin, op. cit., p. 94. The ships were fitted with side-lever engines, balanced poppet valves and four vertical tubular boilers.
49. R. G. Albion, op. cit., p. 326.
50. MIP, Contracts. To be strictly accurate *Baltic* was 17 hours faster than *Africa* and in 1852 the Collins ships generally completed their voyages some 14 hours faster than the Cunard ships. Information supplied by Mr T. Laird.
51. MIP, Memo from Charles MacIver to his partners, 1 March 1850.
52. R. G. Albion, op. cit., p. 328.
53. CP, H. Eaves, op. cit., under 1856; *Persia* was delivered in 1856 and in her first year made the crossing from New York to Liverpool on four occasions in less than $9\frac{1}{2}$ days; A. J. Maginnis, op. cit., pp. 30, 32.
54. R. G. Albion, op. cit., p. 328.
55. Ibid.
56. The evidence for this is derived from the intense interest taken on both sides of the Atlantic in the passage times of the various ships.
57. R. G. Albion, op. cit., p. 328.
58. Ibid., p. 330.
59. Ibid., p. 328.
60. CP, H. Eaves, op. cit., under 1856; R. G. Albion, op. cit., pp. 328, 330.
61. R. G. Albion, op. cit., p. 330.
62. MIP, Correspondence, Samuel Cunard to Charles MacIver, 1 May 1847.
63. Ibid.
64. Ibid.
65. Ibid.
66. MIP, Articles of Agreement made between British and North American R.M.S.P. Co. and William Brown, Joseph Shipley and Francis Alexander Hamilton on behalf of The United States S.S. Co., signed 29 May 1850.

67. Ibid., Clause 7.
68. Ibid., Clauses 8 and 9.
69. Ibid., Clauses 2 and 3.
70. Ibid., Clause 2.
71. Ibid.
72. Ibid., Clause 4.
73. Ibid., Clause 10.
74. Ibid., Clause 13.
75. MIP, Memorandum of Agreement, 11 November 1856, 'the Agreement existing between the two companies, dated 24 February 1853, is and shall continue suspended and be considered void from 31 March 1855 (when the last settlement was made) until the new United States Mail steamer *Adriatic* takes her place on the line'.
76. Ibid.
77. CP, Shipping advertisements and rates 1856–7.
78. MIP, Correspondence, James Brown to Brown, Shipley and Co., 13 December 1853.
79. Ibid.
80. MIP, Correspondence, 2 July 1853.
81. MIP, Memo on distribution of earnings 1850–55.
82. Ibid.
83. Ibid.
84. Ibid.
85. Ibid.
86. Ibid.
87. Ibid.
88. Ibid.
89. MIP, *Captain's Memoranda*, 25 March 1848. These were general instructions drawn up by Charles MacIver and distributed to captains by D. and C. MacIver.
90. Ibid.
91. Ibid.
92. Ibid.
93. CP, Instructions to Captain Woodruff, 1840 and reiterated in instructions to all captains, 1848. MIP, 25 March 1848.
94. MIP, 25 March 1848.
95. F. L. Babcock, *Spanning the Atlantic*, (1931), pp. 84–5, 103, 121, 125–6; *Liverpool Journal of Commerce*, 4 April 1932, 11 May 1932, 18 May 1934, giving accounts of Captain Judkin's exploits during his successive commands of *Columbia*, *Persia* and *Asia*.
96. CP, H. Eaves, op. cit., under 1848; MIP, Charles MacIver's instructions to captains, 1848.
97. A. J. Maginnis, op. cit., p. 155.
98. SLB, File 2, T. A. Bellew to Thos Gray, Board of Trade, 21 December 1878, stating that the Company had followed safe routes for a period of 38 years.
99. These tracks were incorporated into the advertisements of the Company. On the outward voyage it was stated that the ships followed the safest tracks

crossing the Meridian of 50 at 43 Lat., or nothing to the north of 43. On the homeward passage crossing the Meridian of 50 at 42 Lat., or nothing to the north of 42.

100. SLB, loc. cit.
101. Ibid.
102. Ibid.
103. CP, File on North Atlantic track agreements. In 1891, the five Liverpool lines agreed to follow certain routes. Following the *Titanic* disaster, representatives from 14 nations met in London at an International Convention for the Safety of Life at Sea, 1913–14, at which the selection of the routes across the North Atlantic in both directions was left to the responsibility of the steamship companies; but the 'High Contracting Parties undertake to impose on these companies the obligation to give public notice of the regular routes which they propose their vessels should follow'; see also Minutes of meeting held at Brussels 27 March 1913; see also CP, S. J. Lister; CP, Correspondence 29 March 1913. This agreement, with minor changes, lasted until 1924 when the companies working for a North Atlantic track agreement adopted the North Atlantic lane routes designated A, B, C, D and G.
104. MIP, Instructions from Charles MacIver concerning food complaints under date quoted.
105. Ibid.
106. Ibid.
107. MIP, Correspondence, 23 November 1872.
108. Ibid.
109. Sir W. B. Forwood, *Reminiscences of a Liverpool Shipowner* (1920), p. 35.
110. Sir Rowland Hill and G. B. Hill, *Life of Rowland Hill* (1880), II, pp. 183, 211; 6th Report PMG (1860); 14th Report (1868), cited Howard Robinson, op. cit., p. 257.
111. Ibid.
112. *Report of the Select Committee on Mail Contracts* (1869) v, 55–6, 60.
113. Ibid.
114. MIP, *British and North American Mail Contracts and Relative Papers*, 1869; PMG to Lords Commissioners of the Treasury, 8 February 1866.
115. Ibid.
116. Ibid., 26 April 1866.
117. Ibid., John Burns to Frank Ives Scudamore, GPO, 9 February 1869.
118. Ibid., Mail contracts North German Lloyd, 3 December 1868 and Inman, 12 December 1868.
119. Ibid., Mail contracts, op. cit., PMG to Lords Commissioners of the Treasury, 24 October 1867.
120. Ibid., Mail contracts, op. cit., John Burns to Frank Ives Scudamore, GPO, 9 February 1869.
121. Ibid.
122. Ibid.
123. Ibid., Mail contracts, op. cit., loc. cit.
124. Ibid., Mail contracts, op. cit., John Burns to the Secretary, GPO, 31 August 1868.

125. Ibid., Mail contracts, op. cit., PMG to Lords Commissioners of the Treasury, 24 October 1867.

126. Ibid.

127. Ibid., Mail contract signed 11 December 1868, Clause 2.

128. Ibid., Mail contracts, Inman 12 December 1868, Clause 13; Cunard 11 December 1868, Clause 16.

129. Ibid., Mail contract, N.D.L. 3 December 1868, Clause 1.

130. Ibid., Mail contracts, op. cit., John Burns to F. I. Scudamore, GPO, 9 February 1869.

131. Ibid., 'I may add', said Burns, 'that equally with ourselves Mr Inman has the strongest objection to any further curtailment of the duration of the Contract.'

132. Ibid.

133. CP, H. Eaves, op. cit., under 1880.

134. CP, H. Eaves, op. cit., under 1880, quoting minutes of general meeting date as cited.

135. CP, H. Eaves, op. cit., under 1880, quoting report and accounts at 31 December 1879.

136. CP, Prospectus for 1880.

137. MIP, Agreements, 4 March 1880.

138. CP, Ships' specifications, Appendix.

Chapter 3

1. See among others A. J. Maginnis, *Atlantic Ferry* (1900); F. E. Hyde, *Liverpool and the Mersey* (1971); Charlotte Erickson, 'The Impact of Push and Pull', *Nordic Emigration*, Uppsala University Research Conference 1969, 34–6.

2. F. E. Hyde, op. cit., Chapter 6, Section I, pp. 95 *et seq.*

3. U.S. Treasury Dept., *Arrivals of Alien Passengers and Immigrants into the United States from 1820 to 1893* (1893). The complexity of U.S. immigration statistics is fully analysed in Brinley Thomas, *Migration and Economic Growth: A Study of Great Britain and the Atlantic Economy* (1973), pp. 42 *et seq.* The various fluctuations in the level of emigration to the United States given in the chapter are linked to the earning capacity of the various Liverpool shipping companies and do not, therefore, always coincide with the more exact determination of fluctuations derived by Brinley Thomas from his analysis. For a further analysis of the American economy see W. W. McCormick and C. M. Franks, 'A Self-Generating Model of Long-Swings for the American Economy 1860–1940', *The Journal of Economic History*, XXXI, No. 2, June 1971, 295–343.

4. The cutting of costs undoubtedly led to a reduction of fares and conditions on board among the reputable lines were better than in the days of the sailing ship, but it took a considerable time to improve degrees of comfort.

5. A point frequently made in the advertisements of the various Liverpool shipping lines.

6. The seasonal fluctuations were peculiar to shipping companies in that fewer services were run during the winter months than in the summer months; the long-term fluctuations were governed by a wide range of underlying economic factors the impact of which have been fully analysed by Brinley Thomas.

Notes

7. F. E. Hyde, op. cit., pp. 112–3; M. L. Hansen, *The Atlantic Migration* (1961), p. 291.

8. Compiled from official U.S. immigration statistics, Treasury Dept., op. cit., to 1895; Reports of Bureau of Immigration from 1895.

9. CP, Estimates compiled by A. P. Moorhouse.

10. R. Bastin, op. cit., p. 8, quoting from O. MacDonagh, *A Pattern of Government Growth 1800 to 1860* (1961), p. 28.

11. Though this statement refers to emigration through the port of Liverpool, the relative pattern is observable in the figures quoted by Brinley Thomas, op. cit., p. 60.

12. Brinley Thomas, op. cit., p. 59.

13. M. L. Hansen, op. cit., p. 292.

14. University Library, Uppsala, Records of Larsson Bros, Emigrant Agents; also Olaf Thorn, *Glimpses from the Activities of a Swedish Emigrant Agent. The Swedish Pioneer*, Vol. X, No. 1., (1959).

15. Olaf Thorn, op. cit., pp. 8–9.

16. *Report on Scandinavian Emigrants through Hull*, PP. (1882) LXII, 279.

17. Ibid.

18. R. Bastin, op. cit., p. 11, quoting *Report on Emigration and Immigration (Foreigners)* PP. (1889) X.

19. Brinley Thomas, op. cit., p. 157.

20. Annual *Statistical Tables relating to Emigration and Immigration from and into the United Kingdom* issued by the Board of Trade.

21. CP, Moorhouse Diary, passenger carryings and voyage times.

22. *Liverpool Journal of Commerce*, 29 January 1875.

23. CP, Reports of directors to be submitted to AGM, 22 March 1894 and 29 March 1895.

24. *Liverpool Journal of Commerce*, 29 October 1875.

25. M. A. Jones, *American Immigration* (1960), p. 187.

26. Ibid.

27. Ibid.

28. CP, Shipping advertisements giving details of voyages, fares and accommodation, 1860–80.

29. CP, Moorhouse Diary, 1884–6.

30. CP, Shipping advertisements of voyages, fares and accommodation 1890–1900; BM, No. 2, 1886–93, *passim*.

31. e.g. Bothnia (1874) 4555 tons; Umbria (1884) 7718 tons; Campania (1893) 12,950 tons.

32. PP, 1881 LXXXII; Report on Emigrant Accommodation in Steamships.

33. The passengers Amendment Act of 1863, 26 and 27 Vict. c.51, carried the regulation of 1855 many stages further.

34. It was laid down that 20 clear superficial feet were required per statute adult on lower passenger decks and 14 such feet on upper decks.

35. This was no innovation. Many of the Liverpool slave ships in the late eighteenth century had been required to carry a doctor.

36. R. Bastin, op. cit., p. 25.

37. PP, 1860 XIV (328), 34; *S. C. Report on Packet and Telegraph Contracts*.

38. *Minutes of Evidence taken before the S. C. on Mail Contracts 1868*; evidence by William Inman Q.1688 *et seq.*, 20 March 1869.
39. PP, 1870 LX, 361; see also BOT Reports and Returns concerning British Merchant Shipping.
40. *Minutes of the Liverpool Steam Ship Owners Association*, 21 October 1874.
41. CP, H. Eaves, op. cit., under 1863.
42. See Appendix.
43. For the effect on Cunard see CP., H. Eaves, op. cit., under 1876. The rate was 2s 4d per lb. for letters and 2d per lb for newspapers etc. In 1877 the rates were raised to 4s per lb for letters and 4d per lb for other matters.
44. CP, Passenger returns 1870–80.
45. See Chapter 4, page 96.
46. CP, H. Eaves, op. cit., under 1872 *et seq*; MIP, Correspondence 1874–1878, Charles MacIver makes frequent references to such transfers.
47. See Appendix; this was *Gallia* of 4809 tons.
48. CP, H. Eaves, op. cit., under 1876 *et seq*. The ships sold included *Cuba* and *Calabria* (1876); *Java* (1877); *Scotia* (1878) and *Russia* (1879).
49. CP, Accountants' report, 1 March 1880.
50. PP, (1873) XXXVI (C.853), 683; *Royal Commission on Unseaworthy Ships*.
51. Ibid.; 686.
52. Ibid.
53. See Chapter 5, Section I.
54. VR, OGM, 11 April 1883; questions raised by Dr Fitzpatrick.
55. See Chapter 5.
56. *Liverpool Journal of Commerce*, 28 April 1881.
57. VR, OGM, 27 April 1881; ibid., 10 April 1884.
58. Ibid., 10 April 1884; ibid., 10 April 1885; CP, Moorhouse Diary 1884–5.
59. Report of the directors and accounts, 10 April 1884; 10 April 1885.
60. VR, OGM, 27 March 1889; ibid., 11 April 1901.
61. See Chapter 5, Section IV.
62. Report of directors and accounts, 24 March 1893; 22 March 1894; 29 March 1895.
63. CP, data collected from voyage books, verbatim reports and chairmen and directors letter books, 1890–1900.
64. BM, 14 September 1898; 29 March 1899; CP, H. Eaves, op. cit., under 1900. *Ivernia* had accommodation for 257 First Class, 308 Second Class and 1366 Third Class passengers of which 944 were in rooms; *Saxonia*, 360 first class, 211 second class and 1198 third class passengers of which 426 were in rooms. *Ivernia* had first class smoking room, library etc. and dining room on the shelter deck amidships and similar accommodation for second class; *Saxonia* had a first class smoking room forward and drawing room aft with dining room forward of the engines on the shelter deck. They were also equippped to take a large tonnage of cargo.
65. Information from references quoted in previous note.
66. VR, OGM, 10 April 1902.
67. This was an impression rather than an actual statement of fact. It is true, however, that at certain periods Cunard's competitive strength was weakened

Notes 349

by the faster and better equipped ships of her competitors. In the long run Cunard survived whereas many of her competitors were forced into bankruptcy.

68. Witness the statements made by William Inman, T. H. Ismay and the many attempts to take over Cunard after 1899.
69. *Minutes of Evidence S.C. on Mail Contracts*, Q.1404, 20 March 1869.
70. R. G. Albion, *The Rise of New York Port (1815–1860)* (1970), p. 327.
71. Ibid., p. 328.
72. *Minutes of Evidence S.C. on Mail Contracts*, Q.1385, 20 March 1869.
73. R. Bastin, op. cit., p. 57, quoting PP (1882) LXII (135), 2–37.
74. Ibid.
75. This was made possible by the application of increasing technology in the construction of ships and by the constant desire of Cunard's directors to lower costs.
76. CP, Shipping advertisements and voyage returns; information supplied by Mr T. Laird.
77. John Forster, *The Life of Charles Dickens* (The People's Edition), pp. 132 *et seq.*, 593 *et seq*; see also *American Notes* for an account of Dickens's crossing on *Britannia* in 1842.
78. Liverpool Record Office, Inman Line Official Guide 1878, p. 19.
79. J. W. Burgess, *Reminiscences of an American Scholar* (1934), pp. 86–8.
80. Correspondence with agents 1885–95, *passim*.
81. Executive BM, 9 November 1897.
82. *Minutes of Evidence S.C. on Mail Contracts*, Q.1471, 20 March 1869.
83. This was voiced in many complaints received by Cunard directors.
84. e.g. *Teutonic* (1889) twin-screw, steel, 9860 gross tons, 17,500 I.H.P., could carry 586 first and 566 steerage passengers; *Campania* (1893) twin-screw, steel, 12,950 gross tons, 26,000 I.H.P., could carry 526 first, 200 second and 300 steerage passengers. *Teutonic* had a speed of 20.35 knots, *Campania* 21 knots.
85. *Philadelphia Record*, 9 August 1903, quoted by R. Bastin, op. cit., p. 60.
86. From information supplied by Mr T. Laird.
87. VR, OGM, 13 April 1905.
88. CP, H. Eaves, op. cit., under 1863. This agency lasted for three years.
89. Ibid., under 1866; A. J. Maginnis, op. cit., p. 81.
90. According to J. Kennedy, *A History of Steam Navigation* (1903), p. 107, the steerage carryings to New York were Guion 27,054 and Cunard 16,871.
91. Brinley Thomas, op. cit., pp. 117–8.
92. The effect of these control stations on Cunard's carryings is discussed by the chairman in VR, OGM, 7 April 1904.
93. R. Bastin, op. cit., p. 63.
94. CP, Directors' report and accounts for 1890–1911.
95. CP, Correspondence between Vernon Brown and Cunard Head Office in the 1890s indicates the strength of this link.
96. CP, Correspondence between Vernon Brown and D. Jardine, 1890–1900 with reference to the operation of specific ships.
97. Brinley Thomas, op. cit., pp. 93, 160.
98. Ibid., pp. 156–7.

99. For the effects on Cunard see VR, OGM, for years 1893–8.
100. See Chapter 5.
101. PP, 1846 (563) XV, 30; *S.C. on Halifax and Boston Mails 1846*.
102. Ibid., 24–5.
103. Ibid., 24–30; evidence given by Samuel Cunard.
104. Ibid., 31.
105. This was implied in John Burns's evidence before the *Select Committee on Mail Contracts*, 20 March 1869 and confirmed in subsequent annual accounts of the Company.
106. PP, (1862) XXI, 257, p. 2; *Returns of Transatlantic Mail Steamers for 1861*.
107. Figures compiled from W. S. Lindsay, *A History of Merchant Shipping* (1876) IV, 257 and J. Kennedy, op. cit., p. 107.
108. Estimates from reports of directors and accounts 1880–5.
109. *Liverpool Journal of Commerce*, 26 February 1875, quoting report of National Steamship Co., for 1874.
110. Ibid.
111. DLB, Correspondence from various directors June to September 1886; CP, Moorhouse Diary 1884–6, rates for specific ships.
112. Ibid.
113. CP, Voyage accounts 1887; *Fairplay*, 1 April 1887, 359.
114. Estimated from Moorhouse Diary and voyage accounts 1886.
115. Ibid.
116. Liverpool City Museum Shipping Records, plans of Cunard, White Star and Inman ships built during the 1880s.
117. CP, Monthly returns, comparative statement by Moorhouse 1885.
118. CP, compiled from Moorhouse Diary 1884–6.
119. CP, Moorhouse Diary, ships' returns 1884–6.
120. Ibid.
121. Ibid.
122. Ibid., as shown in the above tables.
123. Ibid., as shown in the above tables.
124. Ibid., as shown in the above tables.
125. See Chapter 4 for rates quoted in the 1890s.
126. CP, voyage returns for the 1890s.
127. *Shipping World*, 1 May 1895, p. 29.
128. Brinley Thomas, op. cit., p. 380.
129. Calculations derived from voyage returns and accounts 1880–1900.

Chapter 4

1. A. J. Maginnis, *The Atlantic Ferry* (1900), pp. 54–9; Sir W. B. Forwood, *Reminiscences of a Liverpool Shipowner*, (1920), pp. 38–9; CP, H. Eaves, op. cit., under 1860; see also Liverpool Record Office, documents relating to the Inman Line; F. C. Bowen, *A Century of Atlantic Travel* (1932), p. 105; *Liverpool Journal of Commerce*, 8 January 1875.
2. J. Kennedy, *A History of Steam Navigation* (1903), p. 107.
3. Further reference to these companies will be made from the National Line Records, Chairman's Reports; White Star Records contained within the

Cunard archives and Guion Line Records, Harold Cohen Library, University of Liverpool; see also W. J. Oldham, *The Ismay Line* (1961).

4. R. Bastin, 'Cunard and the Liverpool Emigrant Traffic 1860 to 1900', M. A. Thesis, University of Liverpool, 1971.

5. Ibid., p. 74.

6. For accounts of these shipowners see F. E. Hyde, *Blue Funnel* (1957); F. E. Hyde, *Shipping Enterprise and Management: Harrisons of Liverpool* (1966); Sheila Marriner and F. E. Hyde, *The Senior: John Samuel Swire 1825–98* (1967); P. N. Davies, *The Trade Makers: Elder Dempster in West Africa 1852–1972* (1973); A. H. John, *A Liverpool Merchant House* (1959).

7. W. J. Oldham, op. cit., p. 29.

8. Ibid.

9. Ibid., p. 36.

10. MIP, *British and North American Mail Contracts and Relative Papers 1869*, passim for fears expressed by John Burns to his partners on this point.

11. *Proceedings of the Select Committee on Mail Contracts 1869*, Minutes of Evidence James Robinson Q.727.

12. Ibid., Q.221.

13. Ibid., Q.1457.

14. There were Conference agreements in operation in the Brazilian trades in 1871 (F. E. Hyde, *Liverpool and the Mersey* (1971), pp. 109–10), and in the China river trades in 1872 (Sheila Marriner and F. E. Hyde, *The Senior* op. cit., pp. 61 et seq.).

15. *Proceedings of the Select Committee on Mail Contracts 1869*, Q.1458 ff.

16. PP, *Progress of British Merchant Shipping*, 1882 LXII, 22.

17. Ibid.

18. PP, *Passenger Conveyance to America*, 1870 LX (288).

19. Ibid.

20. See F. E. Hyde, *Liverpool and the Mersey* (1971) for evidence of declining trends in the port of Liverpool.

21. R. Bastin, op. cit., p. 80.

22. National S.S. Co., Report of AGM for 1874; *Liverpool Journal of Commerce*, 26 February 1875.

23. See below.

24. National S.S. Co., Report of AGM for 1874.

25. CP, H. Eaves, op. cit., under 1874; *Liverpool Weekly Courier*, 6 June 1874.

26. CP, H. Eaves, op. cit., under 1874. According to Eaves there was no real foundation in the suggestion that the Cunard Company was proposing to relinquish services to Boston.

27. CP, H. Eaves, op. cit., loc. cit.

28. Chairmen's reports to annual meetings of Cunard, Guion, National and White Star Lines, 1875–6.

29. MIP, Charles MacIver correspondence, September 1874.

30. R. Bastin, op. cit., p. 82.

31. Ibid.

32. *Liverpool Journal of Commerce*, 14 May 1875.

33. Ibid.

34. MIP, Charles MacIver correspondence, 1–10 June 1875.
35. Ibid.
36. Ibid.
37. Ibid., 31 December 1875.
38. Report of the National S.S. Co., cited *Liverpool Journal of Commerce*, 23 February 1877; quoted R. Bastin, op. cit., p. 83.
39. *Liverpool Journal of Commerce*, 12 April 1877.
40. CP, in Cunard's case *Cuba* and *Calabria* were sold in 1876, *Java* in 1877, *Scotia* in 1878, *Russia* in 1879 and *China* and *Siberia* in 1880.
41. PP, *Report on Accommodation and Treatment of Emigrants on Atlantic Steamships*, 1881, LXXXII (C.2995), p. 123.
42. Ibid.
43. F. E. Hyde, *Liverpool and the Mersey* (1971), pp. 56–7.
44. D. H. Aldcroft, *The Development of British Industry and Foreign Competition 1875–1914* (1968) under the chapter 'Mercantile Marine', p. 357.
45. D. H. Aldcroft, op. cit., p. 361.
46. R. Bastin, op. cit., p. 88; CP, Report OGM for 1886.
47. Quoted from D. H. Aldcroft, op. cit., p. 357.
48. D. H. Aldcroft, op. cit., loc. cit.
49. *House Report* No.342; 46 Congress 3 Session 1880–1.
50. W. Tute, *Atlantic Conquest* (1962), p. 110.
51. Ibid., see also CP, File relating to the Anchor Line dated 1913.
52. A. J. Maginnis, op. cit., p. 68.
53. W. Tute, op. cit., p. 96; R. Bastin, op. cit., p. 89.
54. *The Times*, 19 and 20 January 1903.
55. CP, Complaints file 1890–1900.
56. CP, WS, January 1889, Memo from Sir Wm Forwood to T. H. Ismay.
57. CP, Correspondence, J. Ellerman to Lord Inverclyde, 5 July 1898, 8 July 1898, 26 August 1899, 22 March 1900.
58. CP, *Report on the negotiations between The Cunard Co. and the Government*, prepared by the Company's solicitors for the use of the chairman and directors, (1905), 12.
59. Ibid., 14.
60. WS, Correspondence between T. H. Ismay, J. Burns and Clement Griscom, August 1891 to March 1892.
61. Ibid.
62. CP, DLB; June to September 1886; WS, Report of meeting between White Star, Cunard and Inman directors held 18 August 1891.
63. BM, 10 March 1884.
64. WS, Letter dated 16 February 1885 from N. Anderson of Chicago to R. J. Cortis, WS Superintendent, New York.
65. Ibid.
66. W. J. Oldham, op. cit., p. 89, quoting letter from T. H. Ismay to J. Burns, 3 February 1885.
67. CP, Schedules of Freight and passenger rates, 1885.
68. CP, DLB, Correspondence between J. Boumphrey and Vernon Brown, 1885.

69. CP, DLB, Vernon Brown to D. Jardine, 23 February 1888.
70. D. H. Aldcroft, op. cit., provides material from German archives in support of this statement.
71. BM, 8 July 1885; CP, H. Eaves, op. cit., under 1885.
72. CP, H. Eaves, op. cit., under 1885; H. J. Dyos and D. H. Aldcroft, *British Transport* (1969), p. 273.
73. D. H. Aldcroft, op. cit., loc. cit.
74. D. H. Aldcroft, op. cit., pp. 361–2.
75. Ibid.
76. BM, for 1886 and 1887, also SLB, A. P. Moorhouse to Mr Heath, 30 April 1887.
77. CP, Passenger and freight agreements, July to September 1885. In fact, the cut European rates rose to a normal level and steerage rates were fixed at a minimum of £5 except for emigrants travelling from Hamburg to New York in the smaller and slower steamers of the Carr Line, on which the rates were fixed at £4 10s.
78. CP, SLB, A. P. Moorhouse to Mr Heath, 30 April 1887. 'The Cunard Company', wrote Moorhouse, '... charges much higher rates than any other line ... but the owners of the fast ships will not be content to (sanction) this, or any other difference, or be bound by any absolute rate. They will fill their ships if they can.'
79. CP, Congressional Records, Minutes of Evidence of the U.S. Commission of Enquiry into the operation of Agreement AA, 1914, extracted by P. R. Sheridan, evidence of Mr Cauty 'from 1880–1888 various agreements were in existence, but from 1889 to 1895 was a very strenuous time in the North Atlantic trades. All agreements went by the board, and this period was one of keen competition between all the Atlantic lines. Each line did what they thought best, and rates were down to an absolutely unremunerative level'; see also H. J. Dyos and D. H. Aldcroft, op. cit., p. 273.
80. The particular type of agreement entered into between British shipping companies after 1869 embodied discriminatory rates but not pools.
81. CP, Freight and passenger agreements 1890–95; for the anticipated effect of the outbreak of cholera on Cunard's business see SLB, A. P. Moorhouse to Vernon H. Brown and Co., 27 September 1892.
82. D. H. Aldcroft, op. cit., p. 349.
83. Ibid.
84. CP, DLB, File No. 1, D. Jardine to Vernon Brown, 25 July 1894.
85. CP, DLB, File No. 1, D. Jardine to E. Taylor, 1895.
86. BM, 27 October 1896; *Shipping World*, 16 December 1896, 719; the minimum rates for the Winter season were fixed for twin-screw or fast steamers at £15 with a differential of £3 for *Germanic, Britannic, Aurania, Servia* and the Boston steamers of the Cunard Co.; for the Summer season the minimum rates were £20 with a differential of £5. The agreement was to operate from 1 December 1896 provided that British lines with slower ships could be brought in on satisfactory terms.
87. CP, Track agreements, summary of events leading to Mr Lister's report, 29 March 1913.

88. CP, VR, OGM, 12 April 1898; 29 March 1899; R. Bastin, op. cit., pp. 101-2.
89. CP, VR, OGM, 29 March 1899; CP, H. Eaves, op. cit., for 1903; BM, 16 April 1903.
90. CP, VR, OGM, 29 March 1899.
91. See below Chapter 5.
92. CP, Estimates from extant voyage books; from information supplied by Mr T. Laird; VR, Chairmen's reports for 1902, 1903 and 1912.
93. R. Bastin, op. cit., p. 102.
94. *Report of the Royal Commission on Shipping Rings*, 1909 (Cmd.4668) Vol. 1., XLVII, p. 19.
95. Compare the evidence from The Liverpool S.S. Conference with that for the Far Eastern, the West Indian and other Conferences.
96. *Liverpool Journal of Commerce*, 16 February 1889.
97. F. E. Hyde, *Liverpool and the Mersey*, op. cit., pp. 115 et seq.; also CP, SLB, John Burns to M.D.H.B., 23 November 1893; 13 December 1893; 8 February 1894.
98. BM, 15 October 1903.
99. CP, Minutes of Evidence of the U.S. Commission of Enquiry into the operation of Agreement AA, 1914; evidence of Mr S. J. Lister 'in the rate war of 1904 the Third Class rate from Europe to America dropped to seven dollars'.
100. BM, 11 June 1904.
101. CP, U.S. Commission, op. cit., loc. cit.
102. BM, 18 August 1904.
103. CP, Chairman's report to OGM and accounts for 1904; OGM, 13 April 1905.
104. BM, 31 August 1904.
105. Ibid.
106. Ibid.
107. Ibid.
108. Ibid.
109. Ibid.
110. Ibid.
111. BM, 17 November 1904, reporting meetings of Conference held 24-28 October; also 15 December 1904.
112. Chairman's report, OGM 19 April 1906.
113. BM, 16 March 1905.
114. BM, 13 April 1905.
115. Ibid.; Chairman's report OGM 13 April 1905.
116. BM, 7 December 1905; 20 December 1906; 17 January 1907; 21 February 1907; CP, H. Eaves, op. cit., under 1905.
117. See statements in Chairman's report, OGM 13 April 1905.
118. Ibid.
119. Ibid.; 'they [the Continental lines] under their agreement called upon the I.M.M. Co., or the Combine, to attack us also'.
120. Ibid.
121. Ibid.

Notes

122. CP, H. Eaves, op. cit., under 1907; report of directors, 23 April 1908.
123. CP, Report of the directors for 1908 to be submitted to OGM 22 April 1909.
124. CP, CLB, William Watson to V. H. Brown, 24 December 1907.
125. CP, VR, OGM, 23 April 1908.
126. Chairman's report for 1907; OGM, 23 April 1908.
127. CP, H. Eaves, op. cit., under 1908; CLB, William Watson to V. H. Brown, 7 February 1908.
128. CP, Reports of meetings leading to 1908 agreement on rates; particularly correspondence from William Watson; see William Watson to V. H. Brown, 7 February 1908.
129. Ibid.
130. CP, H. Eaves, op. cit., under 1908; correspondence and agreement 1908; report of directors submitted to AGM, 22 April 1909.
131. Ibid.
132. CP, C. & DLB, A. A. Booth to Charles P. Sumner, 14 January 1914.
133. Congressional Records, proceedings brought by the U.S. Government under the Sherman Anti-Trust Law against The Cunard S.S. Co. Ltd and their defendants; CP, extracts taken by P. R. Sheridan.
134. Ibid., evidence on the working of Agreement AA.
135. Ibid.
136. Ibid., submission by The Cunard S.S. Co. Ltd.
137. Ibid.
138. CP, Extracts from the proceedings and findings of the U.S. Supreme Court concerning the operation of Agreement AA.
139. Ibid.; referring to the effect of Agreement AA on Cunard's trading position S. J. Lister said 'we never slackened off the least bit; the work went on just as it had gone on before.'
140. Ibid.; evidence of Mr Cauty; P. R. Sheridan, op. cit., pp. 15–16.

Chapter 5
1. CP, VR, Chairman's report for 1880; OGM, 27 April 1881.
2. MIP, Agreements, 4 March 1880, Article 2.
3. Ibid., Article 7.
4. BM, 6 March 1883, letter from D. and C. MacIver and Burns and MacIver concerning their functions as agents of the Company; VR, OGM, 11 April 1883; *Fairplay*, 16 May 1884.
5. MIP, Correspondence, David MacIver to Charles MacIver 1874–5 as cited in Chapter 1.
6. CP, VR, Chairman's report OGM, 10 April 1884, 'not only will they I believe, be good paying property, but will be the means of placing the Cunard Co. in a paramount position on the Atlantic.'
7. *Fairplay*, 16 May 1884.
8. CP, Report of the directors to be submitted to the OGM, 27 April 1881; VR, for the same date.
9. BM, 6 March 1883.
10. *Fairplay*, 16 May 1884.

11. CP, SLB, D. and C. MacIver to T. A. Bellew, 28 March 1883.
12. Ibid.
13. *Liverpool Courier*, 25 August 1883.
14. Ibid.; also VR, 11 April 1883, reply of John Burns to question about the retirement of the MacIver brothers as agents.
15. MIP, High Court of Justice, Chancery Division, Statement of Claim by the Plaintiffs (The Cunard S.S. Co. Ltd) against Charles, senior, Charles, junior, Henry and William MacIver, paragraph 9, defence delivered 11 February 1884.
16. Ibid.
17. CP, SLB, T. A. Bellew to John Burns, 24 January, 26 January, 31 January, 2 and 3 February 1883; Bircham Co. to secretary, 9 July 1883.
18. MIP, High Court of Justice, Chancery Division, paragraph 10, Statement of Defence.
19. CP, SLB, Charles MacIver to Bateson, Bright and Warr, 6 July 1883.
20. CP, SLB, A. P. Moorhouse to John Burns, 3 September 1884, 9 September 1884, 23 September 1884, 26 September 1884, 2 October 1884.
21. MIP, Press cuttings *Liverpool Daily Post*, 13 January 1885.
22. Ibid.
23. *Liverpool Daily Post*, 20 March 1885.
24. CP, SLB, A. P. Moorhouse to Charles Burt (solicitor), 13 September 1892, citing agreement of 16 March 1885.
25. CP, VR, 11 April 1883, questions by Dr Fitzpatrick and others.
26. CP, VR, 27 April 1881, 27 April 1882.
27. Ibid.
28. Report of the directors to be submitted to OGM, 27 April 1881.
29. CP, Moorhouse Diary, accounts of ships in North Atlantic and Mediterranean fleets.
30. Report of the directors to be submitted to OGM, 10 April 1884.
31. Ibid.
32. Ibid.
33. CP, VR, Chairman's report OGM, 10 April 1885.
34. Report of directors to be submitted to OGM, 10 April 1885.
35. CP, H. Eaves, op. cit., under 1885.
36. Ibid.
37. Ibid., under 1886.
38. Ibid.
39. CP, Moorhouse Diary, analysis of costs for each ship in the fleet.
40. CP, analysis from reports and accounts 1880 to 1914.
41. The Company had favourable long-term contracts for coal with United States companies (BM, 29 June 1892) and for high-grade Welsh coal. Contracts with British firms usually carried discounts related to the amount ordered and contained clauses varying the price per ton with current levels of wages. After 1899 the price of coal rose sharply. See Chairman's statement OGM, 10 April 1902 in which he reviews coal prices over previous seven years.
42. CP, VR, OGM, 10 April 1884; 31 March 1886; report of directors to be

submitted to OGM, 31 March 1886; ibid., 28 March 1888; ibid., 27 March 1889; ibid., 27 March 1890.

43. Many references to coal contracts are given in BM, 1885 to 1900; for this particular reference see 29 June 1892.

44. Report of directors to be submitted to OGM, 10 April 1900.

45. Despite this rise in price Cunard managed to secure favourable contracts at 15s for South Wales coal and 12s 7½d. for North Wales coal; BM, 27 June 1901.

46. CP, VR, 10 April 1902.

47. BM, 11 December 1901.

48. BM, 15 October 1903; SLB, 18 March 1905 giving a resume of discussions leading to creation of Turbine Committee, 20 August 1903; CP, H. Eaves, op. cit., under 1903.

49. CP, H. Eaves, op. cit., under 1903–4, quoting reports to Turbine Committee.

50. BM, 25 February 1904; 24 March 1904.

51. CP, H. Eaves, op. cit., under 1907 and 1914.

52. CP, VR, OGM., 22 April 1909; Stuart Mountfield, *Western Gateway* (1965) pp. 52, 65–7.

53. CP, VR, 23 April 1908; 22 April 1909.

54. F. E. Hyde, *Liverpool and the Mersey*, op. cit., p. 115.

55. CP, SLB, John Burns to M.D.H.B., 23 November 1893; 13 December; 1893; 8 February 1894.

56. Ibid., 23 November 1893.

57. Ibid., 13 December 1893; the Dock Board disclaimed the view put forward by John Burns.

58. Ibid., 23 November 1893; 'the strange conclusion would follow', wrote Burns, 'that by the trustees of the port these large ships would be actually driven from it.'

59. CP, VR, 22 April 1909.

60. Stuart Mountfield, op. cit., p. 52; T. H. Ismay's efforts to persuade the Dock Board to do this dated back to 1890.

61. CP, VR, 6 April 1911.

62. Ibid.

63. Compiled from CP, accounts and related papers 1880–1914.

64. CP, VR, 11 April 1912.

65. CP, Accounts and related papers; report of the directors, 10 April 1885; VR, 27 March 1889.

66. CP, VR, 29 March 1888; 30 March 1892.

67. CP, VR, 11 April 1901.

68. Report of the directors, 26 March 1891.

69. CP, H. Eaves, op. cit., under 1895. *Sylvania* and *Carinthia* were built by the London and Glasgow Shipbuilding and Engineering Co. for the Boston and New York Cattle and Cargo trade. They were of 5598 tons gross, twin screws with triple-expansion engines.

70. Report of directors, 29 March 1899.

71. Ibid., *Ivernia* was of 14,278 tons gross, twin screws with quadruple-expansion engines; *Saxonia* was of 14,297 tons gross with same engine power.

72. CP, VR, 10 April 1902.
73. Ibid.
74. CP, VR, 13 April 1905; see questions put by Mr Mayberry.
75. CP, Report of the directors, 21 April 1910.
76. Ibid.
77. Ibid.
78. Ibid.
79. Ibid.
80. CP, VR, 21 April 1910.
81. CP, VR, 21 April 1910; 6 April 1911.
82. CP, VR, 6 April 1911; BM, 16 March 1911.
83. CP, *Report on the Negotiations in relation to the Agreement of the 30 July 1903, made between H.M. Government and the Company, prepared by the Company's Solicitors for the use of the Chairman and Directors*, 2 vols (1905); hereafter cited Cunard and the Government; I, 17.
84. CP, H. Eaves, op. cit., under 1902; *Cunard and the Govt*, I, 22 et seq.
85. CP, H. Eaves, op. cit., loc. cit.
86. CP, *Cunard and the Govt* I, 57–60, quoting Circular to Shareholders of the Hamburg–Amerika Line.
87. *Liverpool Daily Post*, 18 March 1902; CP, *Cunard and the Govt* I, 55.
88. *Hansard*, 7, 12 and 15 May 1902.
89. CP, *Cunard and the Govt*, I, 403, agreement quoted in full.
90. Ibid., I, p. 32, 3 March 1902. Messrs Watson and Smith, stockbrokers of Glasgow, called upon Messrs Penny and MacGeorge, stockbrokers acting for the trustees of the late Lord Inverclyde, to find out what price would be taken for a large block of Cunard shares.
91. Ibid., I, 22: Mr O'Hagan's many activities are recorded in his autobiography, *Leaves from my Life*, 2 vols (1929).
92. CP, *Cunard and the Govt*, II, 3–12. Letters 1 to 15, T. A. Bellew to Lord Inverclyde and D. Jardine, 11 May 1901 to 28 October 1901.
93. Ibid., I, 32, 3 March 1902.
94. Ibid., I, 34–5.
95. Ibid., I, 38; Sir Christopher Furness had a first interview with Lord Inverclyde on 12 April 1902.
96. Ibid., I, 33.
97. CP, Correspondence, Lord Inverclyde to Lord Selborne, 12 March 1902.
98. Ibid., Lord Selborne to Lord Inverclyde, 13 March 1902; Lord Inverclyde to Lord Selborne, 18 March 1902; CP, *Cunard and the Govt*, I, 35.
99. Ibid., Lord Inverclyde to Lord Selborne, 18 March 1902.
100. Ibid.
101. CP, Correspondence, Lord Selborne to Lord Inverclyde, 5 April 1902.
102. Ibid.
103. CP, Correspondence, Lord Inverclyde to Lord Selborne, 29 March 1902.
104. Ibid.
105. CP, VR, 10 April 1902.
106. CP, *Cunard and the Govt*, I, 38, 12 April 1902.
107. CP, in fact as early as 18 March, Messrs Penny and MacGeorge had inti-

mated that the First Lord Inverclyde's shares might be saleable at £20 per share. Messrs Penny and MacGeorge to Messrs Watson and Smith, 18 March 1902.

108. CLB, Lord Inverclyde to J. Bruce Ismay, 18 May 1905.
109. CP, Correspondence, Lord Selborne to Lord Inverclyde, 24 April 1902.
110. CP, *Cunard and the Govt*, I, 46, 5 May 1902.
111. CP, Memo by Lord Inverclyde and A. P. Moorhouse, 5 May 1902.
112. Ibid.
113. CP, Correspondence, Sir Christopher Furness to Lord Inverclyde, 22 March 1902; *Cunard and the Govt*, I, 38.
114. CP, Circular to shareholders, 31 May 1902; H. Eaves, op. cit., under 1903.
115. *Liverpool Daily Post*, 2 June 1902; based on rumours arising from Griscom's approach to Cunard.
116. WS, Correspondence as to sale of shares in O.S.N. Co. Ltd, 3 June 1902.
117. Ibid., 4 June 1902.
118. Ibid., 4 June 1902, J. Bruce Ismay to C. Dawkins or J. P. Morgan, junior.
119. Ibid., C. Dawkins to J. Bruce Ismay, 5 June 1902.
120. CP, *Cunard and the Govt*, I, 53; Lord Selborne to Lord Inverclyde, 10 May 1902.
121. Ibid., Lord Inverclyde to Lord Selborne, 12 May 1902.
122. CP, Memo by hand, Lord Inverclyde to Sir Christopher Furness, 16 May 1902.
123. CP, Sir Christopher Furness to Lord Inverclyde, 8 June 1902; W. B. Peat to Lord Inverclyde, 11 June 1902.
124. CP, *Cunard and the Govt*, I, 64.
125. Ibid., 68; Sir Christopher Furness to Lord Inverclyde, 1 July 1902.
126. Ibid., Sir C. Furness to Lord Inverclyde, 3 July 1902.
127. Ibid., 70.
128. Ibid., Lord Inverclyde to J. Chamberlain, 1 August 1902.
129. Ibid., .
130. CP, J. Chamberlain to Lord Inverclyde, 4 August 1902.
131. CP, G. W. Balfour to Lord Inverclyde, 7 August 1902.
132. CP, G. W. Balfour to Lord Inverclyde, 26 September 1902; WS, Cable dated 1 October 1902.
133. CP, Agreement under Treasury minute, 31 July 1903, Second Schedule, Clauses 2A and 2B.
134. Ibid., Part I, Clause 5, Section 5.
135. WS, Agreement between H.M. Govt and the Anglo-American Shipping Combination, Clause 1.
136. Ibid., Clause 6.
137. WS, Messrs J. S. Morgan to J. B. Ismay, 13 October 1902; J. B. Ismay to Mr J. P. Morgan, 21 October 1902; J. B. Ismay to Sir C. Dawkins, 28 October 1902; J. B. Ismay to Sir C. Dawkins, 7 November 1902; J. B. Ismay to Rt Hon W. J. Pirrie, 7 November 1902; J. B. Ismay to Sir C. Dawkins, 24 November 1902.
138. Glyn, Mills papers, books marked 'Advances, Engagements' 6 vols, 1890–1918, Series, B/3 11, 23 September 1903; 15 October 1903; B/3 12, 9

November 1904; 1 December 1907. An overdraft to the O.S.N. Co. was increased from £400,000 to £550,000 and extended under subsequent arrangements to 1907. This information was supplied by Mr P. Cotterell, Department of Economic History, The University, Leicester.

139. CP, Analysis from reports of directors and accounts, 1880–1914.
140. Ibid., 1907–14.
141. CP, Report of directors and accounts for OGM, 15 April 1915.
142. *RC. on Unseaworthy Ships, Final Report and Minutes of Evidence* (1874) Vol. 7; Evidence by John Burns, 24 April 1874, Q.14,985.
143. Ibid., Q.15,006.
144. Ibid., Q.15,009.
145. CP, BM, 9 January 1883.
146. CP, Report of chairman (Alfred Booth) to extraordinary general meeting, 10 April 1913.
147. Ibid.
148. CP, Analysis from reports of directors and accounts, 1880–1914.

Chapter 6
1. CP, BM, 17 September 1914 and related minutes.
2. See Cunard official publications; Archibald Hurd, *A Merchant Fleet at War* and *The Merchant Navy*, 3 vols (1921–9); F. L. Babcock, op. cit., Chapter 13.
3. CP, H. Eaves, op. cit., under 1914 *et seq.*
4. Ibid., quoting files on wartime activities of the fleet; BM, 17 September 1914.
5. Ibid., BM, 19 November 1914; CP, H. Eaves, op. cit., under 1917.
6. CP, H. Eaves, op. cit., under 1914 *et seq.*
7. BM, 17 September 1914; 20 May 1915; 21 October 1915, *et passim.*
8. CP, H. Eaves, op. cit., under 1914 *et seq.*; BM, 15 October 1914; 25 March 1915.
9. Ibid, BM, 15 October 1914; 19 November 1914; 17 December 1914; 25 March 1915; 16 February 1916.
10. As a merchant ship, *Lusitania* sailed according to schedule.
11. CP, VR, 10 April 1913.
12. CP, H. Eaves, op. cit., under '*Lusitania* Sinking'; VR, 10 April 1913; *Lusitania* experienced trouble with the blading in her low-pressure turbines and had to be withdrawn from service for repairs and replacement of blades.
13. See especially Colin Simpson, *Lusitania* (1972).
14. CP, File of documents quoted by H. Eaves, op. cit., under '*Lusitania* sinking'.
15. Ibid.; Colin Simpson, op. cit., p. 91.
16. CP, H. Eaves, op. cit., loc. cit.
17. Colin Simpson, op. cit., pp. 104–9.
18. CP, H. Eaves, op. cit., loc. cit.
19. According to the evidence which Eaves used, the ship was struck by two torpedoes, but this is discounted by Colin Simpson, op. cit., p. 149.
20. Colin Simpson, op. cit., p. 149.
21. CP, H. Eaves, op. cit., loc. cit.; these figures differ slightly from those

quoted by Simpson.
22. CP, VR, 30 April 1919.
23. Ibid.
24. Ibid.
25. Ibid.
26. Ibid.
27. Ibid.; BM, 17 October 1918.
28. Ibid.; 'very special credit', stated the Chairman, 'is due to Mr Mearns, who carried the chief burden of responsibility.' A. D. Mearns was General Manager but in February 1918 became a director; BM, 20 February 1918.
29. CP, VR, 30 April 1919; BM, 10 July 1918.
30. CP, VR, 30 April 1919; BM, 18 September 1918; letter to Controller of Aircraft Factories, dated 16 September, informing him that the Company desired to be relieved of the management of the factory.
31. Ibid.
32. The Heads of Agreement were dated 14 November 1911; BM, 2 November 1911; VR, 11 April 1912.
33. CP, H. Eaves, op. cit., under 1912.
34. Ibid.
35. Ibid., J. F. Gibson, *Brocklebanks 1770–1950* (1953) II, p. 13.
36. CP, H. Eaves, op. cit., review of Anchor Line.
37. CP, VR, General Meeting and Extraordinary General Meeting, 26 June 1916; OGM, 25 April 1917.
38. Report of directors, 25 April 1917.
39. H. Eaves, op. cit., under 1916.
40. CP, Circular to shareholders issued with notice convening General Meeting, 26 June 1916.
41. CP, H. Eaves, op. cit., under 1916.
42. CP, Report of directors, 25 April 1917.
43. CP, Report of directors, 30 April 1919; the author is indebted to Mr Eric Reford for information about this firm.
44. CP, Report of directors, 30 April 1919; J. F. Gibson, op. cit., II, p. 47.
45. Ibid., citing agreement of 6 March 1919.
46. J. F. Gibson, op. cit., II, p. 47; CP, H. Eaves, op. cit., under 1919.
47. As given in J. F. Gibson's history op. cit.
48. J. F. Gibson, op. cit., I, pp. 87–121.
49. Ibid., I, p. 140.
50. Ibid., II, pp. 9, 10.
51. Ibid., II, p. 20.
52. CP, VR, EGM, 19 December 1911.
53. Ibid.
54. Ibid.
55. Ibid.
56. CP, VR, EGM, 11 January 1912; BM, 18 January 1912.
57. CP, VR, General Meeting 10 January 1912.
58. CP, Accounts, General Balance Sheet, 31 December 1919.
59. Ibid., 31 December 1920.

60. CP, VR, 30 April 1919.
61. Ibid.
62. Ibid.
63. This bears more than favourable comparison with the activities of other shipping lines. See P. N. Davies, *The Trade Makers: Elder Dempster and West Africa* (1973). F. E. Hyde, *Shipping Enterprise and Management: Harrisons of Liverpool* (1966). For a general picture see S. G. Sturmey, *British Shipping and World Competition* (1962), Chapter 3.
64. CP, VR, Adjourned OGM, 23 July 1919.
65. CP, VR, OGM, 30 April 1919; these two ships were still engaged in the repatriation of troops.
66. Ibid.
67. Ibid.
68. CP, VR, OGM, 27 April 1921; S. G. Sturmey, op. cit., pp. 37 *et seq.*
69. Brinley Thomas, *Migration and Econmic Growth: A Study of Great Britain and the Atlantic Economy* (1973), p. 191; CP, H. Eaves, op. cit., under 1921; VR, OGM, 26 April 1922.
70. CP, W. H. Roper, *The Atlantic Conference 1921–1939*, p. 229; VR, 26 April 1922.
71. CP, VR, 16 April 1924.
72. Ibid.
73. Ibid.
74. CP, VR, 1 April 1925; this action was taken under powers conferred by the Finance Act of 1923.
75. CP, VR, 1 April 1925; Brinley Thomas, op. cit., p. 191.
76. CP, W. H. Roper, op. cit., p. 13.
77. Approval was given by the Cunard board on 13 April 1921; CP, H. Eaves, op. cit., under 1921; VR, 26 April 1922; report of directors, 26 April 1922; Further measures included the closing down of the engine works at Kirkdale; VR, 25 April 1923 and the taking over of the firm of Charles Howson and Co. to undertake repair work in Liverpool; BM, 20 September 1922. The shares of this latter firm were taken over in October 1922.
78. CP, H. Eaves, op. cit., under 1921; the interest R. and H. Green and Silley Weir Ltd, was obtained by exchanging the share capital of Samuel Hodge and Sons Ltd for a consideration of £25,000 which was satisfied by the issue to Cunard of 25,000 fully paid shares of £1 each in Green and Silley Weir Ltd.
79. This subsidiary company was formed on 1 January 1921; CP, H. Eaves, op. cit., under 1921.
80. BM, 8 March 1922.
81. CP, Report of directors, 17 April 1921; CP, H. Eaves, op. cit., under 1921.
82. Under an Order in Council issued in May 1922, the Canadian Government severely limited the movement of emigrants to Canada apart from bona fide agriculturalists going to Canada to farm.
83. CP, Report of directors, 27 April 1921; 26 April 1922; 25 April 1923; 16 April 1924; 7 April 1926.
84. CP, H. Eaves, op. cit., under 1922; report of directors, 25 April 1923.
85. CP, Reports of directors, loc. cit.

Notes 363

86. CP, Report of directors, 26 April 1922; VR, 26 April 1922.
87. BM, September 1919; letter from GPO stating that no objection is raised to the transfer of the Company's mail service from Liverpool to Southampton.
88. BM, October 1926; 23 March 1927.
89. See discussions relating to the building of these two ships in Chapter 7.
90. CP, VR, 25 April 1917.
91. Ibid.
92. Ibid.
93. See under Chapter 8.
94. Conference statistics compiled W. H. Roper, op. cit.
95. CP, VR, 4 April 1928; 3 April 1929; 9 April 1930; 8 April 1931; report of directors, 3 April 1929.
96. CP, Reports of directors, 3 April 1929; 9 April 1930.
97. CP, VR, 9 April 1930; voyage books 1928–30.
98. CP, Voyage books 1929–33.
99. CP, VR, 7 April 1926.
100. Ibid.
101. Ibid.
102. Ibid., BM, 15 December 1926.
103. CP, VR, 7 April 1926.
104. CP, VR, 3 April 1929; H. Eaves, op. cit., under 1928.
105. CP, VR, 9 April 1930; Brinley Thomas, op. cit., p. 191.
106. See Chapter 8, Section IV.
107. CP, VR, 4 April 1928.
108. CP, VR, 9 April 1930.
109. CP, Annual estimates of fleet costs 1925–9. These costs were extracted and summarised from the voyage books.
110. CP, VR, 7 April 1926.
111. CP, VR, 6 April 1927.
112. Ibid.
113. Ibid.
114. CP, VR, 4 April 1928.
115. Ibid.
116. CP, Annual estimates of fleet costs 1925–30.
117. Ibid.; see also Chairman's reports for years 1925–30.
118. CP, Annual estimates of fleet costs; summarised extracts from voyage books.
119. Among these expenses was included the provision of a lifeboat to R.N.L.I. This lifeboat operated from St Mary's in the Scilly Isles and was on station from 1930 to 1955. During this period she saved 104 lives. She then took up relief duties until 1969, saving 131 lives up to that time. From information kindly supplied by Mr Patrick Howarth, P.R.O. for R.N.L.I.
120. CP, VR, EGM, 17 October 1927 and 1 November 1927.
121. CP, Report of directors and accounts, 4 April 1928; EGM, 17 October 1927, confirmed 1 November 1927.
122. CP, Report of directors for 1928.
123. CP, VR, OGM, 4 April 1928.

124. CP, Report of directors, 4 April 1928.
125. CP, Report of directors, 22 April 1909; VR, OGM, 22 April 1909.
126. CP, Report of directors, 28 April 1920.
127. CP, H. Eaves, op. cit., under 1920.
128. CP, VR, OGM, 6 April 1927. (Chairman calculated saving of £80,000.)
129. CP, Report of directors, 7 April 1926.
130. CP, VR, OGM, 7 April 1926.
131. Ibid., 4 April 1928.
132. Ibid.
133. CP, Report of directors, 8 April 1931.
134. Ibid., BM, January 1931.
135. CP, VR, OGM, 8 April 1931.
136. Ibid.

Chapter 7
1. CP, Diary of events leading to formation of C.W.S. Ltd, 2.
2. Ibid., 3.
3. CP, Sir Thomas was approached by Mr Holden of Messrs Haes and Co., stockbrokers acting on behalf of Harrimans.
4. CP, Diary of Events, 3.
5. Ibid.
6. CP, Agreement between R.M.S.P. Co. and I.M.M. Co., 27 November 1926.
7. Ibid.
8. CP, Diary of events, 3.
9. Ibid., p. 4.
10. Ibid., p. 4.
11. Ibid., p. 4.
12. Ibid.; see also P. N. Davies and A. M. Bourn, 'Lord Kylsant and the Royal Mail', *Business History* XIV, No. 2, July 1972, 103–23.
13. CP, Diary of events, 4.
14. Ibid.
15. CP, A previous meeting was held on 19 May 1930 to elect a committee; see also P. N. Davies and A. M. Bourn, op. cit., loc. cit.
16. CP, Diary of events, 5; several preliminary schemes were prepared and the final scheme was completed and sanctioned by the High Court on 24 June 1932.
17. CP, Provisions of the Scheme of Arrangement; P. N. Davies and A. M. Bourn, op. cit., loc. cit.
18. Ibid.; the moratorium was agreed pending the preparation of the Scheme of Arrangement.
19. Ibid.
20. Ibid.; the petition to the High Court was presented on 26 March 1935 and on 8 April Mr Justice Bennett made an order for the compulsory winding-up of White Star Line Ltd; CP, H. Eaves, op. cit., under 1935.
21. CP, Diary of events, 5.
22. Ibid., 6.

23. Report by Sir William McLintock, extracts quoted CP, Diary of events, 6.
24. Ibid.
25. See Chapter 8, Section VI.
26. CP, Correspondence, Sir Frederick Lewis to Sir Percy Bates, 17 July 1930, advising Sir Percy that the voting trustees had confirmed the policy of sale and that he was arranging to pursue his investigations; Sir William McLintock informed Sir Frederick Lewis some time before this date.
27. CP, Note òf interview between Sir Frederick Lewis and Sir Percy Bates, July 1930.
28. CP, Note of interview between Sir Percy Bates, Sir Thomas Royden and Walter Runciman. Runciman's invitation was dated 24 July 1930.
29. CP, Diary of events, 8.
30. CP, Copies of cables, 17–20 July; memorandum by S. J. Lister under date July 1930.
31. CP, Memorandum by S. J. Lister.
32. Ibid.
33. CP, Correspondence, Sir Percy Bates to Sir Ashley Sparks, 28 July 1930; BM, July 1930.
34. Ibid.
35. Ibid.
36. Ibid.
37. Ibid.
38. Ibid.
39. CP, Memorandum by Sir Percy Bates of interview, 30 July 1930.
40. Ibid.
41. Ibid.
42. Ibid., BM, August 1930.
43. CP, Memorandum by Sir Percy Bates, 30 July 1930.
44. Ibid., CP, Correspondence, S. J. Lister to Sir Percy Bates, 30 July 1930; CP, Circular letter to shareholders, 24 September 1930.
45. CP, Correspondence, S. J. Lister to Sir Percy Bates, 30 July 1930, referring to Sir Percy's statements.
46. CP, Correspondence, Sir Percy Bates to Walter Runciman, 31 July 1930.
47. CP, Correspondence, Sir Ashley Sparks to Sir Percy Bates 28 July; Sir Percy Bates to Sir Ashley Sparks, 5 August 1930.
48. CP, Sir Percy Bates to Sir Ashley Sparks, 5 August 1930.
49. CP, Note by Sir Percy Bates on interview, 27 August 1930.
50. Ibid.
51. CP, Note on interview by Sir Percy Bates, 28 August 1930.
52. Ibid.
53. CP, Memoranda by F. A. Bates, 10 October 1930.
54. CP, Correspondence, Sir Percy Bates to Walter Runciman, 15 October 1930.
55. CP, Correspondence, Walter Runciman to Sir Percy Bates, 18 October 1930.
56. See above p. 194.

57. CP, Meeting of Sir Percy Bates and Sir Frederick Lewis with Mr Montagu Norman, 24 June 1931.
58. CP, Sir Percy Bates to Montagu Norman, 12 August 1931; circular to shareholders, 10 December 1931; CP, H. Eaves, op. cit., under 1931.
59. CP, Circular to shareholders, 10 December 1931.
60. Ibid.
61. BM, 15 July 1931; 16 September 1931; 18 November 1931; CP, Letter from Mr Mahon (Bank of England) to C.S.S. Co. Ltd, 15 October 1931; See also memorandum by F. A. Bates, 10 October 1930.
62. Ibid.
63. CP, Letter from Mr Mahon to C.S.S. Co. Ltd, 15 October 1931, enclosing draft Heads of Agreement.
64. Ibid., Clause 2.
65. CP, Sir Percy Bates to Mr Mahon, 21 October 1931; note of meeting between Mr Mahon, F. A. Bates and Sir Percy Bates, 22 October 1931; C.S.S. Co. Ltd to Mr Mahon, 26 October 1931; Mr Mahon to C.S.S. Co. Ltd, 27 October 1931; C.S.S. Co. Ltd to Mr Mahon, 28 October 1931; Mr Mahon to C.S.S. Co. Ltd, 30 October 1931.
66. CP, Sir Percy Bates to a director, 3 November 1931.
67. Ibid.
68. Ibid.
69. Ibid.
70. CP, H. Eaves, op. cit., under 1928; the members of the committee were Sir Aubrey Brocklebank, Bart, Chairman, Engineer Vice-Admiral R. W. Skelton, The Hon C. A. Parsons, Andrew Lainge, A. C. F. Henderson, G. McL. Paterson, Sir Thos Bell, Commander C. W. Craven, R.N., Andrew Hamilton, John Austin and J. Rennie, Secretary. This committee held meetings on 6 December 1928 and 11 January 1929 but no definite decisions were reached. Douglas Lobley in *The Cunarders* (1969), p. 46, states that *Queen Mary* 'the first ship on the drawing board, grew in sketch form during 1926'.
71. These views were finalised at a meeting of the Cunard board, BM, 16 October 1929.
72. Ibid.
73. CP, VR, OGM, 8 April 1931.
74. BM, 19 November 1930.
75. CP, H. Eaves, op. cit., under 1930.
76. CP, Circular to shareholders, 24 September 1930.
77. CP, VR, OGM, 8 April 1931.
78. D. Lobley, *The Cunarders*, op. cit., and other official Cunard publications.
79. BM, 16 July 1930.
80. CP, Annual reports and accounts 1919 to 1930; circular letter to shareholders, 27 January 1932.
81. CP, VR, OGM, 8 April 1931.
82. Circular letter to shareholders, 27 January 1932; in which the Chairman gives a brief history of shipbuilding finance for the Company's ships.
83. Ibid.
84. Ibid., 10 December 1931.

85. CP, VR, OGM., 6 April 1932.
86. CP, Diary of events, 35.
87. Ibid.
88. Ibid., 36; memo by Sir Percy Bates quoting letter from Sir Charles Hipwood, 18 February 1933.
89. CP, Chancellor of Exchequer to Sir Percy Bates, 1 March 1932.
90. BM, 19 November 1930; this was the first intimation of the implementation of a two-ship service with new ships. The financial resolution was passed in the House of Commons on 10 November.
91. CP, VR, OGM, 8 April 1931.
92. CP, Summary of information, Sir Percy Bates to Lord Weir, relating to period May to July 1932.
93. CP, Lord Weir to Sir Percy Bates, 31 October 1932.
94. Ibid.
95. CP, official announcement of Chairmanship O.S.N. Co., 3 November 1932.
96. CP, Diary of events, 40; Lord Weir submitted his report to the Chancellor of the Exchequer and the President of the Board of Trade on 21 December 1932.
97. CP, Diary of events, 40; Sir Percy Bates was authorised by the Cunard board to accept the terms of the report; BM, 16 February 1933.
98. CP, Lord Weir's report; Sir Percy Bates to Lord Essendon, 28 February 1933.
99. CP, Lord Essendon to Sir Percy Bates, 20 February 1933.
100. CP, Mediation note on the North Atlantic problem; Lord Weir to Sir Percy Bates, 14 March 1933.
101. Ibid.
102. Ibid.
103. CP, Diary of events, 49; report by Sir Percy Bates of meeting with Lord Weir at Eastwood on 25 March 1933.
104. Ibid.
105. CP, Diary of events, 49–50.
106. Ibid, 50.
107. Ibid.
108. Ibid.
109. Ibid.
110. Ibid.
111. CP, Diary of events, 16 March 1933; Lord Essendon to Lord Weir, 25 July 1933.
112. See file of correspondence, Sir Percy Bates to Lord Weir and F. A. Bates, March to September 1933, used by kind permission of Mr T. Laird. The Cunard directors had made a full assessment of the age, composition and competitive strength of the White Star fleet, they were doubtful whether the fleet as a whole, if incorporated into a new company, could cover depreciation charges.
113. CP, Statement by Sir Percy Bates submitted to Lord Weir, 25 March 1933.
114. Ibid.
115. Ibid.

116. CP, Diary of events, 54.
117. CP, F. A. Bates to Lord Weir, 10 June 1933; note of interview between Sir Percy Bates and Lord Weir, 12 June 1933.
118. BM, 14 June 1933.
119. Ibid.
120. CP, Tripartite agreement and related papers.
121. Hill, Dickinson Papers; agreements book, C.W.S. Ltd, 99, 109, 121, 151.
122. CP, VR, Summary of main provisions of agreement included in notice to shareholders, 10 March 1934.
123. Ibid.
124. Ibid.
125. Ibid.
126. Ibid.; also BM, 9 May 1934, CP, H. Eaves, op. cit., under 1934.
127. *Hansard*, temp. cit.; Secretary's MS; CP, H. Eaves, op. cit., under 1934.
128. Hill, Dickinson Papers; 100, 110; CP, H. Eaves, op. cit., under 1934.
129. CP, H. Eaves, op. cit., under 1934.
130. Report of C.W.S. directors to be submitted to first OGM, 9 August 1935.
131. Report of directors to OGM, 28 April 1948.

Chapter 8
1. BM, 16 March 1921; approving on 9 March agreements covering first, second and third class passenger business which were signed by various lines at a meeting of the Atlantic Conference held in Paris on 3 March.
2. U.S. Maritime Commission; U.S. Shipping Act 1916, Section 15.
3. CP, interpretation by the U.S. Maritime Commission of the U.S. Shipping Act 1916.
4. CP, W. H. Roper, *The Atlantic Conference 1921–1939*, privately circulated and used by permission of The Cunard S.S. Co. Ltd, p. 8.
5. CP, extracts from Conference minutes 1921–30.
6. CP, extracts from Conference minutes; statement by Red Star Line attached to the minutes of the March 1921 meeting.
7. CP, extracts from Conference minutes, April 1926.
8. CP, W. H. Roper, op. cit., p. 23.
9. CP, extracts from Conference minutes, 7 November 1927.
10. William Baird was a Conference representative for the Canadian Pacific.
11. CP, W. H. Roper, op. cit., p. 23.
12. CP, extracts from Conference minutes, 1–7 July 1922 and November 1922.
13. CP, W. H. Roper, op. cit., p. 34.
14. CP, Figures from Conference statistics 1921–1939.
15. CP, Statements by chairman on Conference agreements; W. H. Roper, op. cit., p. 37.
16. CP, extracts from Conference minutes, 15 March 1932; statement from Mr Tarleton Winchester, a representative of U.S. Lines.
17. CP, extracts from Conference minutes, 14 April 1932.
18. Ibid., 10 May 1932; Conference statistics 1921–1939.
19. CP, extracts from Conference minutes, 24–25 November 1932.

Notes 369

20. Letter from C.G.T. dated 29 January 1932 for submission to the April meeting of the Conference. The French Prime Minister and the German Chancellor had exchanged notes regarding economic collaboration. As a consequence of this a committee of French and German shipowners was established to discuss current problems confronting the shipping business.

21. CP, W. H. Roper, op. cit., p. 42.

22. Conference minutes, 5 and 6 January 1928.

23. Minutes of the meetings of the Conference, November 1934 to November 1935 *passim*.

24. BM, 19 February 1936; reporting on Conference decisions 29 January to 1 February at meetings held in London and 6–8 February at meetings held in Paris.

25. Conference meeting, 24 February 1936.

26. BM, 20 October 1937; giving rates to come into effect on 1 November; there was also an increase of 10 per cent for rates in the summer season, over the off season, instead of 5 per cent as hitherto. There were also adjustments made to the length of the season and to the rates for higher-valued cabin accommodation.

27. BM, 19 February 1936.

28. BM, 18 November 1925; VR, 7 April 1926.

29. BM, 18 November 1925; referring to decisions taken at Conference meeting 9 November 1925.

30. CP, extracts from Conference minutes, telegram from Sir George McLaren Brown, 12 December 1927.

31. Ibid., telegram dated 29 December 1927.

32. Ibid., letter from Cunard, 30 December 1927.

33. CP, extracts from Conference minutes temp. cit.

34. Ibid., statutory meeting October 1928.

35. Ibid., letter from Canadian Pacific, 13 June 1929.

36. Ibid.

37. Ibid., letter from Holland-America Line, 2 September 1929; BM, 20 November 1929.

38. Statutory meeting October 1928.

39. CP, W. H. Roper, op. cit. p. 147.

40. CP, extracts from Conference minutes; letter from Holland–America Line, 2 September 1929.

41. Ibid., minutes of Conference meetings, October 1929.

42. BM, 20 November 1929.

43. CP, extracts from Conference minutes; reports of meetings December 1933, giving effect to new rates as from 1 January 1934.

44. BM, 17 February 1932; CP, VR, 27 April 1932.

45. CP, extract from Conference minutes; letter from Cunard to all conference members, 7 April 1933.

46. CP, Rate classification for ships of Conference lines, 1 January 1934.

47. CP, W. H. Roper, op. cit., p. 167.

48. CP, Statutory meeting of Conference, 1 March 1934.

49. CP, W. H. Roper, op. cit., pp. 177–8; BM, 16 November 1938.

50. CP, Conference statistics 1921–1939, tourist carryings.
51. Ibid., third class carryings.
52. Ibid., first class carryings.
53. Ibid.
54. Ibid.
55. Ibid.
56. Ibid., first and cabin class carryings.
57. Ibid.
58. BM, 16 January 1924.
59. CP, C. & DLB, Sir Thos Royden to Sir Ashley Sparks, 27 May 1925.
60. Information kindly supplied by Mr T. Laird from chairman's correspondence March to December 1924.
61. Ibid.
62. BM, 17 November 1926.
63. CP, VR, OGM, 26 April 1938.
64. CP, Compiled from voyage books and Cunard book of averages.
65. From information supplied by Mr T. Laird; 'Shipping Conference System', *The Journal of Commerce and Shipping Telegraph Annual Review*, January 1946, 201.
66. CP, VR, OGM, 16 April 1924; although this refers to Post Office arrangements, agreement was also made to sustain passenger rates; see also BM, 17 December 1924.
67. BM, 23 March 1927.
68. BM, 19 October 1927.
69. BM, 17 September 1930.
70. BM, 17 October 1928.
71. BM, 15 May 1939.
72. CP, VR, OGM, 1 April 1925.
73. Ibid.
74. CP, VR, OGM, 3 April 1929.
75. Ibid., CP, H. Eaves, op. cit., under 1928.
76. BM, 16 January 1929.
77. Report of directors, 9 April 1930.

Chapter 9
1. CP, H. Eaves, op. cit., under 1935; report of directors submitted to OGM, 29 April 1936.
2. CP, VR, OGM, 26 April 1938.
3. Ibid.
4. Ibid.
5. CP, VR, OGM, 24 April 1935; résumé of association with Anchor Line made by the Chairman.
6. Ibid.
7. Ibid.
8. CP, VR, OGM, 1 April 1925.
9. CP, VR, OGM, 24 April 1935.
10. CP, VR, OGM, 8 April 1931.

Notes 371

11. CP, VR, OGM, 24 April 1935.
12. Ibid.
13. Ibid.
14. CP, Report of directors, C.S.S. Co. Ltd, 26 April 1938.
15. CP, VR, OGM, 23 April 1941; J. F. Gibson, op. cit., II, p. 47.
16. CP, VR, OGM, 23 April 1941; statement submitted by Sir Percy Bates to this meeting dated 9 April 1941.
17. BM, CWS, 14 June 1939.
18. CP, H. Eaves, op. cit., under 1939.
19. CP, VR, OGM, 23 April 1941; statement submitted by Sir Percy Bates to this meeting dated 9 April 1941.
20. Ibid.
21. CP, VR, OGM, 29 April 1936; ibid., 28 April 1937.
22. CP, H. Eaves, op. cit., under 1936.
23. CP, VR, OGM, 28 April 1937; H. Eaves, op. cit., under 1936.
24. BM, CWS, 20 March 1940.
25. BM, CWS, 18 October 1939; referring to meeting at the Treasury 29 September 1939.
26. CP, H. Eaves, op. cit., under 1938; report of directors to be submitted to CWS, OGM, 26 April 1938; ibid., 26 April 1939; BM, CWS, 16 November 1938.
27. CP, VR, OGM, 23 April 1931; statement submitted by Sir Percy Bates, 9 April 1941.
28. See Chapter 8; CP, H. Eaves, op. cit., under 1938.
29. CP, H. Eaves, op. cit., under 1938.
30. See Chapter 8, page 238.
31. CP, Annual accounts and statements 1935–45.
32. CP, VR, OGM, 23 April 1941; statement submitted by Sir Percy Bates dated 9 April 1941.
33. Ibid.
34. Ibid.
35. CP, VR, OGM, 26 April 1939.
36. CP, VR, OGM, 23 April 1941; statement submitted by Sir Percy Bates, 9 April 1941.
37. Ibid.
38. Ibid.
39. Ibid.
40. BM, CSS, 16 July 1941.
41. CP, VR, OGM, 8 October 1941; statement submitted by Sir Percy Bates, 24 September 1941.
42. Ibid.
43. CP, VR, OGM, 26 April 1944; statement submitted by Sir Percy Bates, 5 April 1944.
44. Ibid.
45. CP, VR, OGM, 25 April 1945; statement submitted by Sir Percy Bates, 4 April 1945.
46. BM, CWS, 17 September 1941.

47. CP, VR, OGM, 8 October 1941; statement submitted by Sir Percy Bates, 24 September 1941.
48. BM, CWS, 15 October 1941.
49. Ibid.
50. Ibid.
51. BM, CSS, 20 August 1941.
52. BM, CSS, 19 November 1941; report of directors submitted to OGM, 29 April 1942.
53. CP, Report of directors submitted to OGM, 29 April 1942.
54. CP, VR, OGM, 29 April 1942; statement submitted by Sir Percy Bates, 15 April 1942; CP, H. Eaves, op. cit., under 1943.
55. CP, VR, OGM, 28 April 1943; statement submitted by Sir Percy Bates, 14 April 1943.
56. Ibid.
57. Ibid.
58. CP, VR, OGM, 24 April 1946; statement submitted by Sir Percy Bates, 3 April 1946.
59. Ibid.
60. CP, Directors' report and accounts for year ending 31 December 1945.
61. CP, VR, OGM, 8 October 1941; statement submitted by Sir Percy Bates, 24 September 1941.
62. CP, VR, OGM, 26 April 1944; statement submitted by Sir Percy Bates, 5 April 1944.
63. CP, CWS, Statement and accounts, notes by Chairman, 11 July 1945.
64. S. G. Sturmey, *British Shipping and World Competition* (1962), p. 147.
65. CP, H. Eaves, op. cit., under 1939.
66. Ibid.
67. Ibid.
68. Ibid.
69. Ibid.
70. Ibid.
71. CP, Documents relating to voyage planning and the requisition of ships.
72. CP, Voyage planning; documents relating to charter party T.98A; liner requisition documents T.97A etc.
73. Ibid.
74. CP, Liner Requisition Scheme, draft Heads of Arrangement, 26 January 1940.
75. Ibid.; H. Eaves, op. cit., notes on requisition scheme under 1940.
76. *Journal of Commerce*, 7 August 1940.
77. S. G. Sturmey, op. cit., pp. 143–4.
78. Ibid., p. 144.
79. CP, Voyage planning, 27 February 1940 under T.97A.
80. Ibid., under T.97A.
81. CP, Voyage planning, under *Mauretania*.
82. CP, Voyage planning; *Britannic* was released on 14 November 1939 but was requisitioned on 7 February 1940 under T.97A (made effective on 23 August 1940).

Notes

83. CP, Voyage planning; she arrived in Algiers on 22 November and was struck by bombs on 23 November.
84. Ibid., under *Samaria*.
85. Ibid., under *Antonia*.
86. Ibid.
87. Ibid., under *Georgic*.
88. Ibid., under *Lancastria*; CP, H. Eaves, op. cit., under 1940.
89. CP, H. Eaves, op. cit., under 1942.
90. Ibid., under 1940.
91. It was estimated that her size would accommodate 270 'planes, but the suggestion was turned down by the Cunard board.
92. CP, Voyage planning; *Queen Elizabeth* arrived Singapore 13 December 1940 and left 11 February 1941.
93. Ibid., under *Queen Mary* and *Queen Elizabeth*.
94. Ibid.
95. CP, H. Eaves, op. cit., account of the wartime activities of the two Queens.
96. Ibid.
97. CP, Voyage planning, number of troops carried per voyage.
98. BM, CWS, 21 October 1942.
99. BM, CWS, 15 September 1943.
100. CP, H. Eaves, op. cit., under 1945.
101. Ibid.
102. Ibid.
103. Ibid.
104. CP, Notes by Chairman attached to CWS accounts, 11 July 1945.
105. Ibid.
106. Ibid.
107. Ibid.
108. CP, Cunard White Star and Transatlantic Air Services 1934–46 (hereafter cited TAS); this file contains correspondence and documents between Sir Percy Bates, certain air lines and government officials, relating to a series of negotiations concerning transatlantic air travel.
109. TAS, J. H. Woods to Sir Percy Bates, November 1934.
110. TAS, Report by G. McL. Paterson. 'In essentials', the Report concluded, 'the proposition was theoretically possible . . . if it were not for the fact that the U.S. Navy Department were said to be interested in this project he would be inclined to say that it had not got beyond the drawing office stage of development and was not likely to do so.'
111. TAS, Henry Tate to Sir Percy Bates, 23 July 1935.
112. TAS, Sir Percy Bates to Sir Warren Fisher, 1 August 1935.
113. TAS, Sir Eric Geddes to Sir Percy Bates quoting course of negotiations July/August 1935.
114. TAS, Sir Percy Bates to Sir Eric Geddes, 21 November 1934.
115. Ibid.
116. TAS, Memo by Sir Eric Geddes temp. cit.
117. TAS, Sir Percy Bates to J. H. Woods, 10 December 1934.

118. TAS, Sir Eric Geddes to Sir Percy Bates, July 1935.
119. Ibid.
120. TAS, Sir Percy Bates to Sir Warren Fisher, 1 August 1935.
121. TAS, Sir Warren Fisher to Sir Percy Bates, August 1935.
122. TAS, Report of meeting between Sir Percy Bates and Sir Eric Geddes, 8 November 1935.
123. Ibid.
124. Ibid.
125. Ibid.
126. TAS, note of telephone conversation between Sir Percy Bates and Sir Warren Fisher, 8 November 1935.
127. TAS, Sir Percy Bates to Sir Eric Geddes, 13 November 1935.
128. TAS, Report of meetings and discussions, 21 June 1937 *et seq.*
129. Ibid.
130. *Hansard*, 11 November 1938.
131. TAS, enquiry from Sir John Reith addressed to Sir Percy Bates, 7 March 1939.
132. TAS, Sir Percy Bates to Sir John Reith, 8 March 1939.
133. TAS, Statement of Sir Thomas Brocklebank's proposal, 5 December 1941.
134. TAS, Lord Essendon to Sir Percy Bates, 16 January 1942.
135. TAS, Liner committee, 15 January 1942; report of Lord Essendon's statement from the chair.
136. TAS, Report of Sir Percy Bates's reply to Lord Essendon.
137. Reports of U.S. Maritime Commission 1937, relevant documents quoted TAS, submission by Sir Percy Bates, January 1942.
138. TAS, reply of New York office to Sir Percy Bates's enquiry, 6 March 1942.
139. TAS, Sir Percy Bates to Sir Richard Hopkins, 22 June 1942.
140. TAS, under January 1943; BM, CWS, 20 January 1943.
141. TAS, Report of discussions at the Treasury, 25 February 1943.
142. BM, CWS, 19 May 1943.
143. Ibid.
144. BM, CSS and CWS, 20 October 1943; reporting on discussions in September meeting.
145. BM, CWS, 20 October 1943; also reported TAS.
146. BM, CWS, 16 February 1944; reporting on events 19 and 20 January 1944.
147. BM, CSS and CWS, 17 May 1944; see also BM, CSS, 23 August 1943; VR, EGM, 27 September 1943.
148. BM, CWS, 12 July 1944; reporting on communication received from the Foreign Office in response to CWS enquiry; BM, CWS, 17 May 1944.
149. TAS, Report of Sir Percy Bates's statement, 27 March 1944.
150. BM, CWS, 21 February 1945; also reported TAS.
151. BM, CWS, 21 March 1945; also reported TAS.
152. BM, CWS, 19 September 1945; also reported TAS.
153. CP, VR, OGM, 3 April 1946.

Chapter 10

1. CP, Statement by Chairman, Mr F. A. Bates, submitted to AGM, 18 May 1949.
2. *Caronia* was the same size as *Mauretania*. This latter ship had been designed as a combination passenger and cargo ship. She would have had a useful life had not war occurred, but in the post-war world her 400,000 cu. ft capacity for cargo was unused and her tourist accommodation was poor. She was, therefore, ill adapted to meeting the demands of a post-war world.
3. CP, Statement by Chairman signed on 18 April and submitted to AGM, 23 May 1951.
4. Ibid.
5. CP, Statement by Chairman signed on 14 April 1954 and submitted to AGM, 19 May 1954.
6. CP, Report of directors, 18 May 1949.
7. BM, CSS, 21 December 1949.
8. Douglas Lobley, *The Cunarders* (1969), p. 44.
9. CP, Statement by Chairman signed on 17 April 1957 and submitted to AGM, 22 May 1957.
10. CP, Statement by Chairman, Denis H. Bates, signed on 16 April 1958 and submitted to AGM, 21 May 1958.
11. CP, Statement by Chairman, Sir John Brocklebank, signed on 27 April 1960 and submitted to AGM, 1 June 1960.
12. Ibid.
13. Ibid.
14. CP, Report of directors, 23 May 1962.
15. Ibid.; in fact, Sir John Brocklebank, somewhat to the dismay of the Cunard board, presented the purchase of British Eagle as a *fait accompli*.
16. CP, Statement by Chairman submitted to AGM, 27 June 1962.
17. CP, Statement by Chairman submitted to AGM, 26 July 1963; report of directors, 24 July 1964.
18. CP, Report of directors submitted to AGM, 26 July 1963.
19. Ibid.
20. One advantage of Cunard's association with B.O.A.C. was in the addition of working capital which came to Cunard as its proportion of cash received for forward bookings and excess of receipts over disbursements. These amounts represented interest-free loans of some magnitude.
21. CP, Statement by Chairman, Sir Basil Smallpeice, submitted to AGM, 28 June 1966.
22. Ibid., 27 June 1967.
23. Ibid., 28 June 1966.
24. Ibid.
25. Ibid.
26. Douglas Lobley, op. cit., p. 51.
27. CP, Statement by Chairman, submitted to AGM, 25 June 1965.
28. The arrangements were in the hands of R. F. Taylor, R. L. Adam and T. Laird. A brief was prepared and R. F. Taylor and R. L. Adam saw the Inland Revenue and the Treasury who agreed to help. There followed discussions with

the Bank of England and the clearing banks and with F.C.I. The whole documentation was completed within a month, R. F. Taylor and R. L. Adam taking care of the negotiations in London and T. Laird superintending technical details in Liverpool. The signing of the documents took place at the Bank of England under the chairmanship of Sir Humphrey Mynors, Cunard being represented by Sir John Brocklebank, R. F. Taylor and T. Laird.

29. CP, Statement by Chairman submitted to AGM, 25 June 1965.

30. Apart from wages and materials, any changes in specifications for the ship were extremely costly.

31. CP, Report of directors, 25 June 1968.

32. Ibid., 25 June 1965.

33. Ibid.

34. Ibid.

35. CP, Statement by Chairman, submitted to AGM, 27 June 1962.

36. CP, Statement by Chairman, submitted to AGM, 28 June 1966.

37. Ibid.

38. Ibid., 27 June 1967.

39. Ibid.

40. Ibid., 25 June 1968.

41. Ibid.

42. Cunard had been interested in container traffic for many years. During the Chairmanships of F. A. Bates and Col. Denis Bates the Company had attempted to join O.C.L. but the P. and O. had objected to their admission. Under Sir John Brocklebank, however, the Company joined A.C.T.

43. CP, Statement by Chairman, submitted to AGM, 27 June 1967.

44. This may be an overstatement of the facts. The cargo fleet had been profitable from 1962 to 1965 but in the three years 1966 to 1968, they lost £800,000. In 1968, however, the Port Line made an unexpected profit of £4.6 million.

Index of Persons

Abell, Sir Westcott, xiii
Adam, R. L., xviii, 375
Albion, R. G., 36, 37, 73, 343, 349
Aldcroft, D. H., 99, 105, 341, 352, 353
Attlee, Clement, attitude towards civil aviation, 278
Austin, J., 342, 343

Babcock, F. L., xiii, 336, 338, 339, 344, 360
Baird, William, 368; appointed as mediator in discussions between Cunard and C.G.T., 222
Baldwin, Stanley, and transatlantic air services, 271
Balfour, G. W., member of Cabinet committee to discuss Cunard negotiations, 142, 145; speech at Cutler's Feast, 146; writes to Lord Inverclyde, 146, 359
Ballin, Albert, 99, 105, 106, 111, 112, 114, 115, 138; attacks Cunard's control of Scandinavian traffic, 105; suggests Cunard should join Continental Pool, 106; breakdown of negotiations, 106; pressure from German Emperor, 114; part in Conference of 1908, 115; quarrel between German lines, 115; alliance with I.M.M. Co., 138
Bamberg, Harold, 299
Bannerman, Alex., 13
Bannerman, Henry, 13, 21
Bannerman, John, 13, 21
Barlow, Sir Alan, 275
Barnaby, K. C., xiv
Barr, Captain, 160
Bastin, Robin, xix, 61, 62, 74, 342, 347, 349, 351, 352, 354
Bates, Denis H., 375, 376
Bates, F. A., 212, 365, 366, 367, 368, 375, 376; calculation of White Star assets, 200; opposes absorption scheme, 212; succeeds brother as Chairman, 283, 375; views on shipbuilding, 288
Bates, Sir Percy, 167, 198, 217, 256, 273, 286, 296, 301, 367, 371, 372, 373, 374; succeeds Sir Thomas Royden as Chairman, 191; negotiations with Sir Frederick Lewis over White Star, 196 ff., 365, 366; insurance on building No. 534, 204; cessation of building No. 534, 206; asks Government aid, 207; proposal of two-ship service, 208; Lord Weir's report, 209; negotiations following Lord Weir's report, 210–12, 213, 367, 368; opposes Cabin classification for U.S. lines, 244; views on depreciation, 248; difficulties with Anchor Line, 249, 250; views on financial management, 251; financial statement on *Queen Mary*, 255; statement on Cunard stock, 258; financial statement on war years, 258, 259; member of advisory council, Ministry of Shipping, 261; member of Liner Organisation Committee, 261; early interest in transatlantic air services, 268 ff.; contacts with Sir Eric Geddes, Chairman of Imperial Airways, 269; suggests agency for Imperial Airways, 270, 272; negotiations to obtain share in B.O.A.C., 278; failure of these negotiations, 279; death of, and effect on Cunard policy, 279
Bates, Philip, 312
Beaverbrook, Lord, 277
Beazley, James, 98
Bell, Sir Thomas, 366
Bellew, T. A., 47, 139, 344, 356, 358
Benstead, E. R., xiii
Bibby, Thomas, 17
Bonsor, N. R. P., xiii
Booth, Sir Alfred, 131, 163, 175, 355, 360; views on aircraft production at Aintree, 163; shipbuilding policy of, 175; statement on accounts, 169 ff.; statement on expansion of Cunard's interests, 169; views on post-war development, 166 ff.; statement on alteration in format of accounts, 176
Boumphrey, J., 352
Bourn, A. M., 364
Bowen, F. C., xiii, 336, 350

Brinnin, J. M., xiv
Brocklebank, Sir Aubrey, 366; specifications and design for new fast ship, 203
Brocklebank, Sir John, Chairman of Company, 297, 375, 376; views on air transport, 297; revocation of Air Licence, 298
Brocklebank, Sir Thomas, 275, 374; prepares memorandum on post-war aviation policy, 273
Brown, Sir George McLaren, 222, 369
Brown, James, 37, 42, 344
Brown, Stewart, 37
Brown, Vernon, 78, 349, 352, 354, 355
Brown, William, 343
Browne, James, 13
Brunel, I. K., 28
Buchanan, Thos, 13
Burgess, J. W., 349
Burns, George, 12–20, 340; early shipping interests, 9, 14; association with Napier, 9; meets Cunard and David MacIver, 9; agrees to join Cunard and MacIver, 10, 13; enters into partnership, 10; functions as agent of transatlantic company, 12; supports Charles MacIver in founding Mediterranean trade, 17; shares in co-partnership, 17; financial difficulties, 1857, 18, 19; retirement, 19; ship construction, 12, 45; contact with Government departments, 45; death of, 57
Burns, George Arbuthnot, Second Lord Inverclyde, 139 ff., 175, 358, 359; view on rate war with Morgan Combine, 112; statement on coal prices, 128; hears of formation of Morgan Combine, 139; negotiations with British Government, 140–6; proposals for combine of British lines, 143–5; meeting with Sir Ernest Cassel, 145; meeting with Joseph Chamberlain, 145; proposals and agreement of 1903, 145 ff.
Burns, James, 12–20; early shipping interests, 14–15; share in transatlantic company, 13; functions as agent, 20; becomes partner in Mediterranean trade, 17; financial difficulties, 18; retirement, 22
Burns, James Cleland, 45; assumes shares, 19–25
Burns, John, First Lord Inverclyde, chs 1–5 *passim*, 342, 350, 351, 352, 354, 356, 357; assumption of agency and stock, 19–25; ship construction and mail contract negotiations, 45; negotiations for renewal of mail contract, 52, 345, 346; difference of opinion with MacIvers on shipbuilding policy, 70; on safety of ships, 155; views on emigrant trade, 78; announces formation of Liverpool Conference, 93; enunciates policy as Chairman of Cunard S.S. Co. Ltd, 119; litigation against MacIvers, 122–3; purchases MacIver interests in Company, 70; correspondence with M.D.H.B. on berthing of Cunard ships, 129; on Cunard's insurance policy, 155, 156, 360; negotiations with White Star and Ellerman for amalgamation, 102; death of, 139; approaches to purchase his shares, 358
Burt, Charles, 356

Cable, Boyd, xiii
Campbell, Sir James, 13, 21
Campbell, William, 13
Canning, Viscount, 343
Cassel, Sir Ernest, 145; meeting with Sir Christopher Furness, Sir Alfred Jones and Lord Inverclyde, 145; part in negotiations for Government support of Cunard, 145
Catto, Lord, disposal of O.S.N.Co.'s shares, 275
Cauty, Mr, 353, 355
Chamberlain, Joseph, 359; part in negotiations for Government aid to Cunard, 142, 143, 145, 146
Chamberlain, Neville, 27'
Chambers, William, 75
Chapman, David, 13
Coffin, Captain, R. N., 339
Collins, Edward Knight, early activity as shipowner, 37; organises Collins Line, 37; competition with Cunard, 38; supported by mail subsidy, 38; loss of *Arctic* 38; loss of *Pacific*, 38; agreement between Collins and Cunard, 39–44; complains of under-cutting by Cunard, 42
Connal, William, 13
Conway, D. K. J., xviii
Craven, Cmdr C. W., 366
Cunard, Abraham, 4, 336; emigrates to Halifax, 1; marries Margaret Murphy, 1; A. Cunard and Son, 2
Cunard, Edward, 20, 36, 45; provision for inheritance of shares, 20; organises offices in Halifax, Boston and New York, 36; death of, 23
Cunard, Henry, 2
Cunard, Joseph, 2, 3, 337
Cunard, Samuel, chs 1–3 *passim*, 45, 337, 340, 343, 350; early life, 1–8; receives contract for carriage of mails to Newfoundland and Bermuda, 2; Samuel Cunard and Co., 3; association with brothers Joseph and Henry, 2, 3; purchases *White Oak*, 2; growth of business interests, 3; financial interest in *Royal William*, 3; growing interest in steamships, 3; visits England, 3; secures mail contract, 8; meets George Burns, David MacIver and Robert Napier, 6, 7, 9; foundation and financing of British and North American Royal Mail Steam Packet Co., 10, 11; returns to Halifax, 12, 15; supports Charles MacIver in

starting Mediterranean trade, 16, 17; enters co-partnership to establish British and Foreign S.N. Co., 17; acts as mediator, 19; shipbuilding policy, 29, 30; views on rate-cutting, 35; mail contracts, 35; views on early steamship competition, 37; control at Halifax and Boston, 45; safe routes, 47; proposed withdrawal of contract for Bahama mails, 50; death of, 57
Cunard, William, 20; provision for inheritance of shares, 20; assumes control of Edward's shares, 23; capital holding under Agreement of 1880, 24
Cunard, William Samuel, capital holding under Agreement of 1880, 25

Davies, P. N., 351, 362, 364
Dawkins, Sir Clinton, 359; views on proposed rival British combine to I.M.M.Co., 143, 144
Dickens, Charles, 75
Donaldson, James, 13
Dorling, Capt. Taprell, xiv
Downie, Alex., 13
Dyos, H.J., 341, 353

Eady, Sir Wilfred, disposal of O.S.N.Co. shares, 275
Eaves, Henry, xiv, xviii, 336, 338, 339, 342, 343, 344, 346, 348, 350, 351, 353, 354, 355, 356, 357, 358, 359, 360, 361–73
Ellerman, Sir John, 352; attempt to control Cunard, 102
Erickson, Charlotte, 346
Essendon, Lord, *see* Sir Frederick Lewis
Evans, Herbert, 222

Fisher, Sir Warren, 270, 273, 373, 374; Chairman of Air Development Committee, 270; advises Sir Percy Bates on air service, 271; recognition of help from, 272–3
Fitzpatrick, Dr, 348, 356
Fletcher, Alex., 13
Forster, John, 349
Forwood, Sir William B., xiii, 48, 75, 127, 345, 350, 352; appraisal of Charles MacIver's work, 48; advice to fellow directors, 75; negotiates coal contracts, 127
Franklin, Mr, 192
Furness, Sir Christopher, 358, 359; proposal to take over Cunard, 139, 142; proposal for British combine, 144; meets Sir Ernest Cassel, 145; further negotiations, 145

Geddes, Sir Eric, 373, 374; Chairman of Imperial Airways, 269, 270; contact with Sir Percy Bates, 269–70; agency with Cunard, 269; attitude towards Cunard, 271; on attitude of Government, 271; breakdown of negotiations with Cunard, 273
Geddes, J. C., 274
Gemmill, John, 14
Gibb, Elius, 13
Gibbs, Cmdr Vernon C. R., xiii
Gibson, J. F., 361, 371
Glasgow, Alex., 13
Glyn, Ralph, air group, 269, 270
Coulden, H. M., xvii
Graaf, M. hr. Van de, 222
Graves, Charles, xiv
Gray, Thos, 344
Greenhill, Basil, xix, 337
Griscom, Clement, 352, 359; persuaded by Cunard and White Star to make Antwerp a terminal, 102; approach to Cunard to enter Morgan Combine, 141

Hadfield, R. L., xiii
Hamilton, Andrew, 366
Hamilton, F. A., 43, 343
Hansen, M. L., 347
Harrison, James, 92
Heineken, Herr, 115
Henderson, A. C. F., 366
Hill, Sir Norman, 232
Hill, Rowland, 345
Hinshaw, Robert, 13
Hipwood, Sir Charles, 199; negotiations on No. 534, 207, 367
Hodder, Edwin, 336, 337, 338, 339, 340
Holt, Alfred, 31, 69, 92, 129
Hopkins, Sir Richard, 275, 374
Howarth, Patrick, xx, 363
Howe, Joseph, 337
Hughes, Tom, xiv
Hurd, Archibald, 360
Hyde, F. E., 346, 347, 351, 352, 354, 357, 362

Inman, William, chs 2–3 *passim*, 60–1, 349; on mail ships, 51; technological innovation, 59; on passenger regulation, 60, 66; enters emigrant trade, 59, 91; joins Liverpool Conference, 93; death of, 101
Ismay, J. Bruce, 141, 143, 359
Ismay, T. H., 59, 92, 349, 352, 357; negotiations with M.D.H.B., 92; offers support to Inman Line, 101; induces American Line to use Antwerp as terminal, 102; on profitability of Cunard ships, 104; rate-cutting, 104–5

Jardine, David, 342, 358; correspondence with Vernon Brown and Co., 78, 349, 353
John, A. H., 351
Jones, Sir A. L., 92; attempts to form British combine, 143, 145; access to Cabinet, 143; meeting with Sir Ernest Cassel, Lord Inverclyde and Sir Christopher Furness, 145; collapse of scheme, 145

Jones, Ivor, xviii
Jones, M. A., 347
Jordan, Humfrey, xiii
Judkins, Captain, 46, 344

Kemble, Fanny, 5, 337
Kennedy, J., 343, 349, 350
Kennedy, President John F., 297
Kerr, Alex., 13
Kerr, John James, 21
Kirkwood, Mr, 207
Knollys, Lord, 278
Kunders, Thones, 336
Kylsant, Lord, 192, 193, 194

Lainge, Andrew, 366
Laird, T., xviii, 306, 343, 349, 354, 367, 370, 375, 376
Lamport, William, 96
Landsdowne, Lord, 6
Lawrence, Sir Herbert, 201
Leach, Frank, xvii
Leckie-Ewing, William, 13
Leitch, Captain, 48
Lewis, Sir Frederick (Lord Essendon), 192, 196, 212, 213, 261, 273, 365, 366, 367, 374; suggests purchase of White Star, 192; negotiations following Royal Mail crash, 196 ff.; negotiations on acquisition of White Star's Atlantic interests, 197; negotiations with Sir Percy Bates, 196 ff.; becomes Chairman of White Star, 209; counter proposal to Lord Weir's report, 210; negotiations for new company, 212–13
Lindsay, W. S., xiii, 350
Lister, S. J., 191, 194, 345, 353, 354, 355; evidence to U.S. Congressional Committee, views on Conferences and competition, 117; prepares memorandum relating to proposed purchase of White Star, 196; takes part in negotiations with Runciman, 198, 365; arranges agency contract with Imperial Airways, 269; efforts to secure interest in B.O.A.C., 278
Lobley, Douglas, xiii, xix, 293, 303, 366, 375
Lohmann, Herr, 99
Lynch, Captain, 268

McAslan, Alex. (execs of), 13
McCall, James, 13
MacConnell, Archie, 13
MacDonagh, O., 347
MacDonald, Rt Hon. J. Ramsay, 207
MacIver, Charles, chs 1–5 passim, 120, 281, 340, 341, 342, 343, 344, 345, 348, 351, 352, 355, 356; family background, 14–15, 336; enlarges MacIver shipping operations, 15; agent for transatlantic company, 15; charters British Queen, 17; enters Mediterranean trade, 17; share of stock in British and Foreign S.N.Co., 17; controversy with Cunard over transfer of stock, 18–19; controversy on Burns brothers retirement, 18–19; assumption of stock and management, 19–20; new constitution of Mediterranean and Atlantic companies, 19–20; assesses capital value of companies, 22; family disagreements over retention of control and management, 23; position under incorporation and Agreement of 1880, 24; shipbuilding policy, 27, 69, 70; evidence before R.C. on Unseaworthy Ships, 69; views on competition with the Collins line, 38; agreement with Collins line, 39, 40; control at Liverpool, 45–9; instructions to Captains, 45; safe tracks, 47; directions on economy in ships, 48; part in mail contract negotiations, 50–1; protests on B.O.T. regulations, 66; answers complaints on service, 75; acts as mediator with National Line, 97; assertion of agency functions, 119–21; advances capital for new line of ships, 121; litigation with Cunard S.S. Co. Ltd., 123; death of, 57; assessment of his work, 281
MacIver, Charles (the younger), 25, 70, 119, 356; retention of interest in new company, 25; agent for new company, 24, 119; disagreement on shipbuilding policy, 120; resigns as managing agent, 121; proposal to form new company, 121; litigation with Cunard S.S. Co. Ltd, 122
MacIver, David (father of David and Charles), 14
MacIver, David, 14, 339; competition with Burns brothers, 9; meets Samuel Cunard, 9; agrees to join Cunard in transatlantic venture, 10; taken into partnership with Burns and Cunard, 11; organises Liverpool terminus, 12; becomes agent for New Clyde S.S. Co., 14; founds City of Glasgow S.P. Co., 14; joins Charles under title David MacIver and Co., 15
MacIver, David (son of Charles), 341, 355; provision for share in company, 20; difference of opinion with his father, 23–4; proposal to start new company to Bombay, 23; resigns from Cunard, 23; enters Parliament, 23
MacIver, Henry (son of Charles), 25, 70, 119, 356; retention of interest in new company, 25; agent for new company, 119; disagreement on shipbuilding policy, 120; resigns as managing agent, 121; proposal to form new company, 121; litigation with Cunard S.S. Co. Ltd, 122
MacIver, John (grandfather of David and Charles), 14
MacIver, John (son of Charles), provision for share in Company, 20

Index

MacIver, William (son of Charles), 121, 356; proposal for line of ships to Mediterranean, 121, 122; litigation with Cunard S.S. Co. Ltd, 122
McLintock, Sir William, 199, 202, 365; prepares report on Royal Mail, 193; becomes Voting Trustee, 194; views on Lord Kylsant's management, 195; intimates involvement of Cunard in White Star purchase, 196
MacMechan, Archibald, 336, 337
McNeill, D. B., 339
Maginnis, A. J., xiii, 341, 343, 344, 347, 349, 350, 352
Mahon, Mr, 366
Mancroft, Lord, 312
Manny, Louise, 337
Marriner, Sheila, 351
Martin, James, 13
Matthie, Hugh, 14
Maury, Lt M. F., 47
Maxwell, General A., 194
Mearns, A. D., 163, 361
Melvill, James, 338
Merry, James, Jr, 13
Moorhouse, A. P., 342, 347, 348, 350, 353, 356, 359
Morgan, J. P., 359; formation and working of Morgan Combine, 137–8; intentions of, 109–13, 141–3; acquisition of White Star Line, 147–8
Morison, Cmdr H. E., xx
Moss, John, 17
Mountfield, Stuart, 357
Murphy, Margaret, 1
Mynors, Sir Humphrey, 376

Napier, J., 337, 338, 339, 342
Napier, Robert 13, 30, 337, 338, 339; reputation as marine engineer, 6; views on transatlantic steamship service, 7; meets Samuel Cunard, 7; engages to build ships for Cunard, 7–9; association with G. and J. Burns, 9; becomes shareholder, 13
Norman, Montagu, 366
Normanby, Lord, 6, 201
Norton, Mrs, 5

O'Hagan, H. Osborne, 139, 358
Oldham, W. J., 342, 351, 352

Parsons, Hon. C. A., 366
Paterson, G. McL., 268, 366, 373
Payne, Abraham Martin, 336
Pearce, William, 120
Pearson, Justice, 122
Peat, W. B., 359
Perry, Commodore C., 37

Piper, W. H. P., xvii
Pirrie, Rt Hon. W. J., 143, 359

Rae, Lois, xvii
Reford, Eric, xx, 361
Reith, Sir John, 272, 374
Rennie, J., 366
Robinson, Howard, 336, 337, 342, 343, 345
Robinson, James, 351
Rodger, Robert, 13
Roper, W. H., 362, 368, 369
Royden, Sir Thomas, 179, 182, 191, 192, 196, 364, 365, 370; views on passenger trade, 179; oil contracts, 182; decides against purchase of White Star, 192; economical working of North Atlantic traffic, 196
Runciman, Rt Hon. Walter, M. P., 194, 196, 198, 199, 365

Scott, David, 13
Scudamore, F. I., 345, 346
Selborne, Lord, First Lord of Admiralty, 139, 140, 142, 144, 145, 358, 359; negotiations preceding 1903 Agreement, 140–5
Sheridan, Charles, 5
Sheridan, P. R., 353, 355
Shipley, Joseph, 343
Simpson, Colin, xiv, 360, 361
Skelton, Vice-Admiral R. W., 366
Smallpiece, Sir Basil, xvii; becomes Chairman of Cunard, 300, 375; views on Cunard's participation in B.O.A.C., 300; sale of B.O.A.C. interest, 301; new ideas on transatlantic travel, 302, 303; financial statement on passenger ships, 311; establishes management team, 312; views on profitability of assets, 311–12; financial report, 1969, 315
Smith, E. C., 342
Sparks, Sir Ashley, 212, 370; accommodation for ships at New York, 196; communications from Sir Percy Bates, 197, 198, 199, 365; Royal Mail reorganisation, 198–9, 212; eastbound freight rates, 240
Squarey, A., 23, 341
Stirling, William, 13
Strassman, W. P., 342
Streepers, Catherine, 336
Sturmey, S. G., 260, 362, 372
Sumner, Charles P., 355
Swinton, Viscount, 278
Swire, John, 105

Tate, Henry, 269, 270, 373
Taylor, R. F., 375, 376
Thomas, Brinley, 346, 347, 349, 350, 362, 363
Thorn, Olaf, 347
Turner, Captain W. T., 162
Tute, W., 352

Tweedsmuir, Lady, 312
Tyler, David B., xiii, 343

Wallace, Patrick, 7
Wallace, T., 93
Watson, William, 114, 355; Chairman of Cunard, 114; conversation with German Emperor on rates, 114
Weir, Lord, 367; asked to report on North Atlantic shipping service, 209; suggests absorption of White Star, 209; acts as mediator, 210; sees Chancellor of the Exchequer, 212; possible settlement on No. 534, 209–10; effects of Report, 210, 368; continues discussions on new company, 213
Whitworth, F. J., xvii
Wilding, Henry, 141
Williams, Kendrick, xviii
Winchester, Tarleton, 368
Wood, Sir C., 342
Wood, John, 6
Wood, Sir Kingsley, 272
Woodruff, Captain, 339, 344
Woods, J. H., 268, 269, 373
Wright, James, 13

MIX
Papier aus verantwortungsvollen Quellen
Paper from responsible sources
FSC® C105338

If you have any concerns about our products,
you can contact us on
ProductSafety@springernature.com

In case Publisher is established outside the EU,
the EU authorized representative is:
**Springer Nature Customer Service Center GmbH
Europaplatz 3, 69115 Heidelberg, Germany**

Printed by Libri Plureos GmbH
in Hamburg, Germany